MAHARISHI & ME

MAHARISHI & ME

SEEKING ENLIGHTENMENT
WITH THE BEATLES' GURU

SUSAN SHUMSKY

Skyhorse Publishing

Note for Readers: This book is based upon both the author's recollection of past events and historical research. Some characters, events, and quoted statements have been edited, composited, or fictionalized. Often cited quotations are shortened without using ellipses. Check original citations for full quotations. Nearly all names have been changed to protect people's privacy, except for public figures, authors, and Transcendental Meditation organization leaders. Maharishi founded many organizations. The author mostly uses the term "TM Movement" or "Movement." Maharishi referred to TM teachers by various titles. The author uses the term "Initiators" in most cases.

Skyhorse Publishing books may be purchased in bulk at special discounts for sales promotion, corporate gifts, fund-raising, or educational purposes. Special editions can also be created to specifications. For details, contact the Special Sales Department, Skyhorse Publishing, 307 West 36th Street, 11th Floor, New York, NY 10018 or info@skyhorsepublishing.com.

Skyhorse® and Skyhorse Publishing® are registered trademarks of Skyhorse Publishing, Inc.®, a Delaware corporation.

Visit our website at www.skyhorsepublishing.com.

Divine Revelation® is a registered service mark.

10 9 8 7 6 5 4 3 2 1

Library of Congress Cataloging-in-Publication Data is available on file.

Cover design by Rain Saukas
Cover photo credit ©Getty Images/Rolls Press/Popperfoto (Maharishi) and By Parlophone Music Sweden [CC BY 3.0 (http://creativecommons.org/licenses/by/3.0)], via Wikimedia Commons (Beatles)

ISBN: 978-1-5107-2268-2
Ebook ISBN 978-1-5107-2269-9

Printed in the United States of America

Arise, awaken, seek an illumined teacher and realize the Self. Like the sharp edge of a razor is that path, difficult to traverse and hard to tread. Thus say the wise.

—KATHA UPANISHAD 1:3:14

Praise for *Maharishi and Me*

"Susan Shumsky had a front-row seat at a spiritual revolution that profoundly affected all of us. She tells the tale with personal candor, a keen eye for pertinent detail, and a perspective seasoned by time and experience."

—Philip Goldberg, author, *American Veda: From Emerson and the Beatles to Yoga and Meditation, How Indian Spirituality Changed the West*

"Susan Shumsky's book *Maharishi & Me* is a powerful exploration of guru and discipleship. Her humor, insight, and the intimate feeling you receive about their relationship is extraordinary. A great read for anyone interested in learning."

—Lynn V. Andrews, bestselling author, *Medicine Woman* and *Jaguar Woman*

"So many emotions churned within me as I read *Maharishi & Me*. In her incredibly heartfelt book, Susan Shumsky gives us a glimpse into a world that few people have ever experienced. Her graphic descriptions portray her awakening consciousness that occurred under Maharishi's guidance and also evoke the tempest that swirled around this iconic guru. Fascinating reading from a great writer!"

—Denise Linn, bestselling author of *Sacred Space*

CONTENTS

PART V: THE BEATLES' GURU

PART VI: INEVITABLE AND INESCAPABLE

PART VII: RIDICULOUS TO SUBLIME

MY REAL BIRTH DAY

AUTUMN 1966

The search for total knowledge starts from the Self and finds fulfillment in coming back to the Self, finding that everything is the expression of the Self.
                                                                    —MAHARISHI MAHESH YOGI

Not everyone remembers their own birth. But I do. That's because my mother's womb was not my real birthplace. My true birth took place on a sunny, Indian summer day of 1966 in Oakland, California—long after the date on my birth certificate.

I'd already embraced the bohemian lifestyle propagated by Timothy Leary: "turn on, tune in, drop out," and by the message of Bob Dylan's song "The Times They Are A-Changin." I'd moved from Colorado to counterculture-central—the San Francisco Bay area. I'd enrolled in a school of hippie students and beatnik teachers—California College of Arts and Crafts.

We "flower children" were desperately seeking altered states of consciousness (whatever that meant—I was pretty hazy about it). But after a few trips down the rabbit hole with Owsley's sugar cubes, I suffered a case of astral possession so alarming, it even shocked head shrink Dr. Stein. He labeled my condition "full-blown psychotic episode," complete with audible hallucinations, earthbound spirit attachments, terrifying LSD flashbacks, and, apparently, the requisite dose of Thorazine.

Once I'd partially recovered my sanity, my pleasures included a daily stroll home from college. There I relished a lavishly multicolored potpourri of tropical flowers in riotous vibrant hues, eucalyptus, and grassy perfume, swelling with fragrant intensity. On this particular day in 1966, however, after wandering through the maze of multi-scented florae, I encountered a most unusual emanation—on the sidewalk outside my apartment.

A kindly stranger approached. Though his commanding presence seemed ageless, he looked about age twenty. Standing 5'10", with an oval face, shiny black hair, and smooth, lustrous, unblemished skin, his body appeared soft and undefined, neither thin nor fat. Nothing about him was hard, athletic, or muscle-bound. He whispered through the air with fluid movement, without the faintest resistance. His posture and demeanor radiated a certain grace, even a glow.

Obviously out of his element, he seemed neither art student nor hippie. There were no paisley prints, beads, bell-bottoms, vests, buckles, hats, boots, sandals, mustache, beard, or long hair. His forgettable attire, consisting of a white cotton button-down shirt, brown khaki trousers, and loafers, made what came afterward all the more remarkable.

He regarded me with kind, twinkling brown eyes. They emitted a certain inscrutable feeling, hard to pin down. I sensed zero sexual energy around him, and, to my surprise, none toward me. His awareness drew inward rather than radiating outward. My impression was he was a monk, though I'd never met one, so I had no frame of reference.

A mysterious force surrounded him—loving, sweet, powerful, yet tranquil. He possessed a kind of magnetism and vibrated great peace—not a familiar feeling to me. He appeared happy, carefree, and serene, without hang-ups, agendas, or needs—unlike anyone I'd ever met.

He called himself Bob, and I asked if he wanted lunch. He said yes and we went upstairs. This wasn't unusual. I often invited strangers in. As a hippie, I'd broken free from my conventional Jewish surgeon's daughter's background. My free-spirit attitude was let-live, live-free, and be-me.

I told Bob all I had to offer was canned spaghetti and meatballs. He answered, "I will have a cup of tea, but I don't take meat. I am vegetarian." The only vegetarian I'd ever met was our cleaning lady, a Seventh Day Adventist, during my childhood.

Bob and I drank tea at my tiny breakfast table in the corner of the combined living room/bedroom of my two-room apartment. After tea, we adjourned a few steps to the couch. In the free-love spirit of 1966, I contemplated behaving my usual flirtatious way, but his body language, entirely self-contained, acted as a kind of anti-flirt sex-repellant. Though I wanted to seduce him, something inside stopped me dead.

"What have you been doing to clean your house?" he asked out of the blue.

What an odd question, I thought. I glanced around my tiny living space, but noticed nothing out of place. I answered, "I've been busy at art school, so not much cleaning has gone on lately."

He said, "I am a yogi, and because I am a yogi, I have the time to spend all day polishing the things in my house." As he said this, he motioned with his hands, as though polishing an imaginary vase or candlestick with a cloth.

What a bizarre and baffling statement. I wondered, *What's a yoggee?* I didn't think my house was dirty.

"Do you go to college around here?" I asked.

"My school is in consciousness," he answered. "I live and teach the wisdom of the ages."

This guy's really far out, I thought. *But what in God's green earth is he talking about?*

"I go to California College of Arts and Crafts," I informed him.

"I am an artist, also. My canvas is the blank screen of the mind, from which all thought springs. On this screen I create the art and craft of immortal life," he answered. He continued for several more minutes, making obscure statements I didn't understand and have long since forgotten.

Just as I was trying to figure what to make of him, Bob suddenly declared, "I have to go now, but I stay with you. I will never leave you. I will be with you always." He walked out the door and down the hallway, never to appear again (in that form, anyway). His abrupt exit after no more than a cupful of tea sprinkled with a brief repartee of enigmatic expressions, left me stunned and bewildered.

I was entirely unaware this encounter with "Bob" was my real birth—the beginning of my new life as spiritual seeker and ultimately spiritual finder. A few days later I chanced upon the book *Autobiography of a Yogi* by Paramahansa Yogananda, where I read about an immortal Himalayan yogi named Babaji, who could appear anywhere to anyone at any time.

PART I
HIPPIENESS TO HAPPINESS

Water the root to enjoy the fruit.
—MAHARISHI MAHESH YOGI

1

LOSING THE SELF
TO FIND THE SELF

Disciples cannot take knowledge from a master until they raise their level of
consciousness so knowledge will flow to them.
—MAHARISHI MAHESH YOGI

Spinning in the eye of his hurricane was at once glorious, stirring, and electrifying, and
wholly devastating, maddening, and mortifying. Riding an emotional roller-coaster, I
ricocheted from heavenly delight to hellish desolation and back.

This extraordinary man, who moved me so intensely, came from India—a land
of mysteries. Until the mid–twentieth century, its vast spiritual treasures remained
largely hidden from the West. A significant change occurred when he left for America's
shores and made "meditation" a household word. His brush with celebrities placed
him in the spotlight. But his true legacy was Transcendental Meditation.

As a former disciple, I lived in his ashrams for twenty-two years and served on his
personal staff for six years. For extended periods, I enjoyed close proximity to the most
renowned guru of the twentieth century—Maharishi Mahesh Yogi.

Submission to a guru is an abhorrent idea in the West, where worldly achievements,
individual assertion, and winning define us. Eastern wisdom is considered inferior to
science. However, the venerable Indian tradition seeks loftier treasures. There the goal
is to trade up ego identification for realization of the higher self *(atman)*.

India is where disciples seek gurus to guide them toward spiritual enlightenment.
But the alchemical process rendering this transformation has largely been concealed.
Disciples seldom write about their "spiritual makeover," as frankly, it's incredibly

embarrassing. Gurus don't reveal their closely guarded methods. Otherwise the spell they cast on disciples would be broken.

Loyal devotees impart only highest reverence toward their gurus and paint romantic pictures. They extol their guru's God-like qualities or quote their bespoken pearls of wisdom. Rarely do they divulge anything other than how great the master was, what miracles transpired, and what marvelous experiences were had.

Practically no one discloses the fact that, for the disciple to achieve *moksha* (freedom from the karmic wheel), the ego must die. The raw truth is this: realizing who we really are (infinite being) rather than who we thought we were (limited self), means giving up ego. That's why higher consciousness is termed *egoless*. Ego death isn't romantic. It can be devastating and shattering.

Irina Tweedie, author of *Daughter of Fire,* said that to realize their higher self, disciples must undergo "self-annihilation"— "turned inside out, burned with the fire of love so that nothing shall remain but ashes and from the ashes will resurrect the new being, very unlike the previous one."[1]

Many authors willing to let us peek through ashram windows are disenchanted dropouts who label ashrams "cults" and gurus "cult leaders." Such exposés portray insulting, exacting bearded men severely rebuking and correcting disciples.

To our Western mind, gurus might appear angry or abusive. But at what point do tough-love tactics cross into "abuse"? How do gurus differ from coaches, athletic trainers, or drill instructors? Why is it okay for tough trainers to coach protégés, yet not okay for tough gurus to train disciples?

Just as coaches bring out the best in their charges, true spiritual masters elevate their students. In a unique relationship of unconditional love, disciples surrender to gurus, and gurus lift disciples to God-realization. This time-honored Eastern tradition, which transforms students into masters, has survived for millennia—because it works.

I wouldn't dare liken myself to revered saints who've achieved enlightenment at their gurus' hands. However, Maharishi's relationship with his students, which I witnessed over two decades, was similar to that of other disciples with their great masters.

Why do Westerners find gurus and cultish ashrams repugnant, considering our dominant religion began with a spiritual master and twelve devoted disciples? That master treated disciples with tough love in a way that might resemble Maharishi. The disciples responded as we did under Maharishi's guidance—with actions deemed timid, immature, clueless, and sometimes faithless.

Only a handful of six million who learned Transcendental Meditation (The TM Technique) spent any time whatsoever in Maharishi's presence. Out of those who witnessed his antics, few understood his motives. Many who got scorched by his fire still remain baffled. A good number consider themselves victims.

This memoir will raise the veil to uncover how Maharishi captivated me, transformed me, and then released me to find self-empowerment in my own spiritual pathway. As I morphed from a painfully shy teenage rebel to a disturbingly self-doubting but determined young seeker, then into a spiritually aware teacher, I found what I was seeking, but not as expected.

Ultimately, I discovered the divine presence within me. Even though I no longer have a guru in physical form, I enjoy an intimate relationship with the inner guru. Anyone can experience this divine source directly, without accepting dogma, and without middlemen, such as priests, pastors, psychics, astrologers, rabbis, or gurus. Once we let go of ego attachment, we become our own guru and miracle maker. The kingdom of heaven is within us.

<hr />

I feel Spirit has guided me always. A higher plan has been at work, threading my life with divine intervention. Some might say I live a "charmed life." Though my days have been peppered with challenges, multitudes of blessings continually fall into my lap. Even during crisis, the solution always appears—usually instantly. Generally I don't let anything, including myself, stand in my way. If I want to accomplish something, I just do it.

Luckily, I found a simple way to experience divine love directly, at will—anytime I ask. This has given me great solace. Once I made this connection, never was I alone again. The anguish of separation was gone. This mystical connection of love, light, grace, and wisdom is the pearl of great price, more precious than rubies or gold.

This book is a way of sharing a few glimpses into my spiritual journey, and hopefully will help you make your own spiritual connection. My life has been (and continues to be) lived in devotion, led by Spirit daily—even when I was younger and didn't know it. For my journey started under unlikely circumstances—a family of self-professed atheists and agnostics. But that's for another book.

The story that follows reveals how I found myself by losing myself in the most highly celebrated guru to ever visit the USA and mentor to the Beatles, Deepak Chopra, the Rolling Stones, Beach Boys, Clint Eastwood, David Lynch, George Lucas, and countless other celebrities.

So we begin at the beginning, with my first baby steps toward the divine. Often such steps don't seem divine—but we'll get there eventually. For the yellow brick road is curvy and rocky, with many pitfalls. And sometimes the Wizard of Oz isn't a wizard at all. Sometimes the wizard is our self, and the guru is simply the mirror.

2

INTO THE LAND OF OZ

1966 TO 1967

Like a river gushing fast down the hill, plunging into the ocean, the seeker, finding the ocean of life, just surrenders himself. The channel is made. It flows.

—MAHARISHI MAHESH YOGI

I came into this world soon after the first atomic bombs were launched, committing genocide on the Japanese and thereby ending World War II. I grew up during the Cold War, under the perceived threat of nuclear war and an epidemic of bomb-shelter-building madness. Every time an airplane flew overhead (which was often, since we lived near an Air Force Base), my four-year-old self quaked in terror that a nuclear bomb would drop.

So, like others of my generation, even as a child I was seeking a world at peace. Whenever I wished on a birthday cake, wishing well, or falling star, my only wish was "world peace."

My other deep desire was to know God. During quiet times at night, I would ask God questions, but received no answers. I assumed either God was too busy, or I wasn't worthy to get a reply.

I was wrong.

Later I discovered anyone can experience God's presence, hear God's voice, and see God's vision. But first I walked a long, winding pathway beginning in the San Francisco Bay Area in 1966. That was the start for many baby boomers. Even if they didn't participate directly, they were swept up in a spiritual revolution. For my story is the story of an entire generation of spiritual pioneers that changed the world.

The perfect cliché of hippiedom—that was me in 1966. A "flower child," I fully embraced the counterculture lifestyle. The hippie movement was our new religion, where we supposedly lived in peaceful communes, loved everyone, handed out flowers to strangers, experimented with all things forbidden, "did our own thing" (meaning whatever, whenever), and generally created an alternate universe in a parallel dimension.

We were all broken in some way, and like Humpty Dumpty, sought to put our shattered pieces back together. We bucked "the establishment" that betrayed us. We "stuck it to the man" that churned out nine-to-five robots living plastic lives in cookie-cutter suburbs. We abhorred violence, politics, and useless wars in overseas jungles. What we sought was world peace.

In 1967, kids came from all over America to join us. About a hundred thousand gathered in San Francisco's Haight-Ashbury district. Dressed in outrageous costumes, they arrived in VW Bugs and buses painted with psychedelic neon designs. They crashed on the street, in hippie pads, or in Golden Gate Park. Everyone was talking love and peace and getting high. Many were runaways or tourists, but they found togetherness and utopia, even for just one "Summer of Love."

Harvard Psilocybin Project leaders Timothy Leary and Richard Alpert (a.k.a. Ram Dass) acted as official tour guides to altered states through LSD. But my personal goal was not about drugs. I was seeking *nirvana*—whatever I imagined that to be. I read every book I could lay hands on about higher consciousness. I tried to "turn on, tune in," and achieve what Leary, Alpert, and others claimed to get with psychedelics.

Leary and Alpert introduced us to the *Tibetan Book of the Dead* in their work *The Psychedelic Experience*. I also read Huxley's *The Doors of Perception,* Bucke's *Cosmic Consciousness, Self-Actualization* by Maslow, *Dhammapada* by Buddha, *Tao Te Ching* by Lau Tzu, and D.T. Suzuki's books on Zen Buddhism. I wanted a "meditation guide," as Alan Watts mentioned in his books, such as *The Way of Zen.*

<hr />

LSD and my ensuing stark raving madness didn't help me a whole lot. Then I met Arnold Roland. An LSD drug veteran, he claimed to have reached nirvana. He was willing to be my acid trip meditation guide. He could get pure, clean acid ("White Lightning")—not cut with meth like what I'd taken before, which radically messed with my mind.

The big day arrived. *Finally,* I thought, *nirvana.* Arnold and I checked into a rustic cabin in the Big Sur woods—perfect for my death and rebirth à la *Tibetan Book of the Dead.* We walked onto a bluff overlooking the Pacific and sat in the tall grass. The indigo sea faded into turquoise near the shore, white foam crashing on jagged rocks below. Under the vast azure dome, it was sunny, warm, breezy, and bright—great weather for dying.

"Are you ready to drop the tabs?" Arnold asked.

"Ready as I'll ever be." The severity of my fear was somewhat assuaged by Arnold's reassuring manner. "I'm gonna leap before I look," I squeaked.

Arnold laughed. "That's a stone groove."

Arnold and I washed down the little white pills with orange juice. Anxiously I lay back in the grass and closed my eyes. He sat on the ground, staring at me.

Suddenly my eyes popped open. Arnold was lying in the grass next to me, asleep. *What happened?* I shook him. "Arnold, wake up."

He sat up, shaking his head and tossing the sleep (and drug) from his brain. "I crashed," he said.

I looked out over the ocean. The water was now violet, in rapid motion, particles of atoms swirling, dancing the dance of life. "The ocean is moving," I said.

"Outta sight—bitchin," Arnold said.

I'm hearing music, I thought. *Flutes in the bushes. Drums in that tree. Violins playing over there. Birds singing. People singing. Jazz playing.*

"There's music in the bushes," I exclaimed.

"It's not in the bushes."

"Yes it is. I hear it in the bushes and trees," I protested.

"No. It's blowing your mind—it's all in your mind, chick."

"But it sounds so real. What time is it?"

"It's 4:30," Arnold said.

"4:30? What happened?" I asked.

"What happened to you? You've been lying on the grass for the last four hours in ecstasy with a beatific smile on your face. Spaced-out. Totally gonzo," Arnold answered.

"Four hours? That's impossible," I exclaimed.

"Look at my watch. It's been *four hours.*"

"But I don't remember anything," I said in dismay.

"You've been meditating for four hours. Heavy, huh?"

"Far out. Groovy, man," I tried to convince myself.

The wind started up and the sun made long shadows. It wasn't so warm anymore. We stared at the ocean for another hour, bundled in blankets. Not much was said.

I've been ripped off, I thought. *Where's my nirvana? I wasn't even here for four hours. What's the use of tripping when I'm out cold?*

We packed up and returned to the cabin. Arnold built a fire, we ate the dinner I'd packed, and had sex (it *was* the free-love generation, remember).

<hr>

A couple months later I met the tall, thin, pipe-smoking Frederick Jensen at an art school beach party. We hit if off right away. I moved into his redwood Berkeley brown-shingle pad with beamed ceilings and whitewashed walls. He lived with his best friend Stuart Ross. Fred and I often went camping in his VW van—to Yosemite, Muir Woods, Big Sur, and Lake Tahoe.

But my main focus was scouring bookstores on Telegraph Avenue for every text I could find about Buddhism, Hinduism, and spiritual enlightenment. Since UC Berkeley had an Asian Studies department, I sought books that helped me understand my psychedelic experiences.

One night I said to Stuart, "I've been reading books by Alan Watts. He said we need a 'meditation guide.' Do you know where to find one?" (Yeah, in 1966, good luck looking up "meditation guide," "yoga," or anything remotely similar in the Yellow Pages telephone directory!)

Stuart asked, "Have you ever tried to meditate yourself?"

I said, "No, but I'm willing to give it a shot."

I lay down on my bed (clearly, I didn't even know meditation should be practiced in seated position). I relaxed and sort of prayed for a meditation.

Suddenly an electric shock jolted through me. A cord of energy started running through the midline of my body, from my toes all the way up to the top of my head, moving in an endless stream. I felt plugged into the electric socket of the universe. Cosmic life force flowed through me in a most ecstatic way.

I lay on the bed for about twenty minutes, grooving to that electric energy cord. I figured, *Well, I guess this is meditation.* Little did I know I'd just experienced my first meditation and *kundalini* awakening concurrently, without drugs. (*Kundalini,* considered difficult to attain, is a rare spiritual energy flowing upward through the body.)

After that, sometimes I smoked a joint, crossed-legged, with eyes closed, and pretended I was Buddha. Electric energy hummed through my body. I floated off into nothingness. Though enjoying these experiences, I longed to meditate properly. I wanted a meditation guide, a *real* meditation guide.

Fellow art student Christo Papageorgou's long black bushy hair, beard, and mustache resembled a wild, tangled scrubland. His long, ragged fingernails proved him a guitar-plucking musician. But his dry mouth, raw nerves, and glazed, reddish eyes marked him a pothead. Sometimes we got stoned together. But in autumn 1966, he took me to the Transcendental Meditation Center.

I entered what seemed a holy place. Fragrant flowers and faint reminiscence of incense wafted through the serene air. From a photo hanging on the wall, the guru smiled—or more accurately, beamed. He was an Indian with long black wavy hair, beard, moustache, brown skin, and white silk robes. Long strings of beads encircled his neck. Most striking was the spiritual emanation radiating from his large, sparkling, magnetic, ebony eyes. If God wanted to visit earth and look like someone, I imagined this was how He would look.

"His Holiness Maharishi Mahesh Yogi," Christo said, pointing to the photo.

Enraptured, I immediately fell in love with this Indian man. "Why didn't you bring me here sooner?" I complained to Christo.

"People get turned off when I tell them about meditation," Christo answered.

"But I've been begging you to help me find a meditation guide."

Nine months seemed forever. That's how long I would have to wait for the next Transcendental Meditation course. But my dream was finally coming true. I was getting a meditation guide, a *real* meditation guide.

∞∞∞∞∞∞∞∞∞∞∞∞∞∞∞∞∞∞∞

After what seemed like eternity, it was August 1967, the peak of the Summer of Love. At a UC Berkeley classroom, Jerry Jarvis, who'd learned TM in 1961 and was president of the Students International Meditation Society (SIMS), drew a diagram on a blackboard. It looked like a thought bubble in a cartoon—several circles in graduated sizes, one above the other, with a wavy line drawn across the top and straight line across the bottom.

Maharishi explaining bubble diagram.
BBC Photo Library Archives

"The mind is like an ocean. Thoughts are like bubbles, beginning here in transcendental Being," he explained, pointing to the line on the bottom. "Each thought rises through subtle awareness until it bursts on the gross surface level, where we perceive it consciously." He pointed to the wavy line on top.

"In TM we reverse the thinking process, taking the mind back to its original source—transcendental consciousness. Our vehicle is the mantra. We repeat the mantra consciously. Then it becomes more subtle and powerful as we float down to the source of thought, pure Being. Our conscious mind travels from the outer, manifest relative field, to the inner unmanifest absolute, where we transcend to pure consciousness—a state of inner peace and contentment, where mind is alert and body is quiet. Heart rate slows down, breathing becomes still, but mind remains awake. This is called restful alertness."

Jerry explained how TM differs from methods like hypnosis, concentration, and contemplation, which keep the mind on the surface and disallow it from going deep within, into the transcendental state of Being. Everything he said made a lot of sense.

Finally, the day arrived for my mysterious initiation into Transcendental Meditation—August 5, 1967. I'd panhandled on Telegraph Avenue to save up the bread ($35) for my initiation. *Now I'll learn real meditation,* I thought. *I'm gonna take the leap of faith. Leap before I look.*

I was told to bring fruit, flowers, and a new white handkerchief for a ceremony. A woman took my conglomeration and whispered, "Sit here and fill out this form."

After a while, the same woman handed me a woven straw basket holding the entire kit and caboodle, with my form perched on top. *Why did they cut the stems off my carnations?* I thought. *How do they decide what mantra to give me?*

Half an hour went by without a sound. *It's so quiet here. What's that scent? Flowers and incense, and something else.*

"Susan, it's time. Please remove your shoes and come upstairs."

The woman motioned me to enter a room where her husband, Jerry Jarvis, sat on a chair in stocking feet in front of an altar covered with a white sheet. Brass vessels held white rice, water, candle, incense, and other objects.

I thought he was Jewish. What's he doing in front of this altar?

Jerry, whose round face resembled the man in the moon, and who beamed at me with moonlike serenity, placed my basket on the altar.

"Sit here," he said, and motioned me to sit next to him. "Today you will receive a mantra or meaningless sound chosen especially for you. After we learn our mantra, we keep it to ourself. Maharishi says, 'When we plant a seed, we don't dig it up to see if it's growing.'"

He looked at the form. "What's your age?" he asked.

"Nineteen," I answered.

"Have you taken any drugs in the last two weeks?"

"No. Not for a month."

"Do you have any questions?" he asked.

"Your presence is very big. Really far out, you know, powerful."

"When I teach, I'm in touch with him." Jerry pointed to a framed picture on the altar. "This meditation came from him—Swami Brahmananda Saraswati, Shankaracharya of North India, Maharishi's master."

"Is he still alive?"

"He attained his final *samadhi* in 1953. Are you ready?"

"Ready as I'll ever be."

"Now I'll begin and you'll witness a ceremony in gratitude to the tradition of masters who have given us this wisdom of integration of life."

Jerry stood in front of the altar and motioned me to stand next to him. My heartbeat sped into overdrive. He picked up all the carnations from my basket and handed me one. Then, while chanting in some strange language, he dipped a carnation in water and shook it in the air. Water sprayed everywhere, including all over me.

What religion is this? I wondered.

Jerry continued chanting while holding my flowers between his palms in a kind of pseudo-Christian prayer. He placed white rice and items from my basket onto a brass tray and splashed more water about. He smeared something like mud onto my handkerchief, twirled an incense stick, and whirled a lit candle around. He ignited what smelled like a drug in a hospital and traced circles in the air. Black smoke rose up. He grabbed the flower I'd been holding and placed all the flowers on the altar.

Then he motioned me to get down.

What? He's down on his knees with head bowed and palms together, like a Catholic. I thought he was Jewish. Idol worship! And he wants me to get down too.

I dropped to my knees stiffly and gawked at him.

He suddenly looked up at me and said, *"Aing namah."* This abrupt motion and weird sound scared the hell out of me—like a 3-D sci-fi movie, where a creepy alien popped out from the screen, speaking ET-tongue. My head jerked back. Then, after calming a bit, I asked myself, *Is this the word?*

"Aing namah, Aing namah, Aing namah, Aing namah, Aing namah," Jerry repeated. He motioned for me to repeat the mantra. I tried. *I'm getting tongue-tied.* He repeated it. Again I tried. *This isn't working. This is impossible.*

Finally I got it right. Jerry said to repeat it quieter and quieter. After a while, he instructed me to repeat it mentally.

He ushered me out and the woman put me in another room, where I tried hard to repeat the word. *Oh, my God, I can't remember it. What is that word? I'm a failure.* I was on the verge of tears when the woman returned. "Come with me."

Back to Jerry's room. He said, "What did you experience?"

"Nothing. I couldn't remember the word."

He repeated again, "Aing namah, Aing namah, Aing namah."

I repeated it.

Again to the other room for another half hour. But I forgot the word right away, and couldn't repeat it. Again I got shuffled back into Jerry's room.

"What did you experience?" Jerry asked.

"I don't know."

"Very good. Meditate like this tonight and tomorrow morning and then come to the meeting tomorrow night," he said.

"Okay."

I was too flustered and embarrassed to admit I'd forgotten the word again.

3

A NATURAL HIGH

1967 TO 1968

Man was not born to suffer. He was born to enjoy.
It is the natural tendency of the mind to seek a field of greater happiness.
The purpose of life is the expansion of happiness.
—MAHARISHI MAHESH YOGI

Back in my hippie pad, with walls painted psychedelic purple, green, and orange (to my landlord's horror), I sank into an overstuffed chair to try meditating again. *What was that word? "Hing yama." Was that it?*

The next night thirty people gathered in a classroom at UC Berkeley. Jerry Jarvis called each person next to him, one by one. When my turn came, he asked, "What is your mantra?" I whispered, "Hing yama." He corrected me.

Then Jerry led a group meditation: "Just sit and wait for a little while, about half a minute. Then start repeating your mantra. If you forget it and other thoughts come, don't try to hold on. Let it go. Then, when you remember again, just easily come back to the word. Remember, mental repetition is not clear pronunciation. It's a faint idea. Now let's begin."

The room went dead silent. I'd never been in a room full of people so quiet. I sat for a while, then started the mantra. After a few minutes I realized I wasn't thinking the word, but other thoughts. I went back to the word. The word changed. It became a vibrational energy in my head.

Suddenly I was in a deep place, somewhere I'd never been before. Down, down, down an elevator. Down to the bottom of a fathomless ocean. Out I stepped. It was perfectly calm. I let go of everything.

I sank into a placid pool of complete solitude, without a ripple, silent and motionless. Nowhere to go—only here. I immersed in emptiness and wholeness, both at once. Profound relaxation, contentment, and peace, deeper than ever imagined, emerged within me.

Time went by, but where was I? Did I fall asleep? No. I was still here with these people. But I went somewhere else. My body disappeared. It became nothing—light and transparent, like air. I was awake the whole time, but wasn't thinking anything.

Oh, yeah, I'm supposed to think the mantra. Repeat it again. The energy came back. *A vibration, not a word.*

Deep, deep, deep. My body barely breathed. Everything stopped. My mind became still. Deepest relaxation I'd ever felt. Body and surroundings disappeared. Drawn into bliss, I became limitless expansion. My "I" no longer associated with the body. "I" was vast, profound, wondrous, and free.

I was completion. I was the end of all seeking—expanded, perfect, and whole. A pool of immeasurable rapture welled up inside. Ecstatic euphoria. Nirvana. A humming, alive stillness washed over me.

Oneness.

Beyond words.

<hr>

After the meditation, Jerry said, "There are two aspects to life, the unmanifest absolute and the manifest relative field. The relative is the material plane of duality. Beyond the relative is an unmanifest field—absolute bliss consciousness, pure Being, which is transcendental in nature.

"Maharishi says TM is like dying a cloth. In India, cloth is dyed by dipping it into a vat of dye, then placing it in the sun to dry. Most of the color fades, but some sticks to the cloth. By repeating this process over and over, the dye becomes colorfast. This is how we attain Cosmic Consciousness. We meditate twenty minutes twice a day, then engage in dynamic action, and thereby integrate Being fully into our awareness. Maharishi says it's a five- to eight-year plan."

Five to eight years seemed like an incredibly short time, even for me at age nineteen. Cosmic Consciousness—permanent establishment of absolute transcendental Being 24/7/365, had been sought for generations from caves of India, monasteries of Tibet, to temples of Indonesia and Japan. Spiritual enlightenment, freedom from the wheel of birth and death, the end of reincarnation, and a state of eternal bliss—all realized in five to eight years? Really?

Charlie Lutes (Maharishi's right-hand man at that time) asked, "What's this business about Cosmic Consciousness in *five years,* Maharishi?"

"Ah Charlie, we have a confirmed meditator for five years," Maharishi replied. "New meditators will think, 'If I meditate five years, I'll be in Cosmic Consciousness.'"

Yes, it was a pitch, but we bought it. We longed to relieve our hopeless desperation. We craved the cessation of suffering and the end of the Vietnam War, Cold War, and war within our hearts that caused so much anguish. So we swallowed the whole enchilada plus dessert.

And yes, TM did work. It ended a good deal of pain. And we were changed. We were renewed. We weren't the Buddha yet. But twice a day for twenty minutes, we experienced something massively better than misery.

I thought I'd found the answer to everything—a way to experience what yogis call *samadhi,* Buddhists call *nirvana,* and Zen Buddhists call *satori.* My goal of spiritual enlightenment seemed within sight. During the following months, a new feeling of well-being, equilibrium, and continuity of inner contentment grew.

I raved incessantly about how meditation changed me, saved me. All I desired was to take meditation retreats, volunteer at the Center, become a Meditation Checker, go to India, and become a TM teacher (an "Initiator"). Fellow art students became impatient with my obsession with TM. But I was hooked—in what I believed to be a good way. At the time, I felt it was my best way.

◇◇◇◇◇◇◇◇◇◇◇◇◇◇◇◇◇◇

"Maharishi will be in Los Angeles this week. Wanna go?" a volunteer from Berkeley TM Center asked. We piled into two cars, a crew of sundry hippies, young, old, gay, straight. I was the youngest.

They informed me to say *"Jai Guru Dev"* (Hail to the holy teacher) when I see Maharishi. In this case *"Guru Dev,"* a common salutation in India, referred to Maharishi's guru, Brahmananda Saraswati, Shankaracharya of Jyotirmath, Himalayas, former religious leader of North India. When I learned TM, his picture sat on the altar.

We arrived in time for Maharishi's airport landing. About a hundred people made a double line with a central aisle to walk through. Nearly everyone held flowers— expensive flowers from flower shops. Nervously I clutched the scrappy, ripe wildflowers I'd picked along the road.

Then, like sunrays bursting at dawn, Maharishi appeared—a diminutive but muscular figure, about five feet tall, with large hands and thick fingers, wearing white robes, red beads strung in silver, and a shawl that looked like undyed cashmere. His long wavy hair and mustache were jet black. His beard had turned snowy. His ebony eyes sparkled with humor and wisdom.

Enveloped in a nimbus of splendor, he glided deliberately and gracefully through the corridor of followers. So small, yet powerful and majestic. His face radiated joy. His body shone with luster and grandeur. His feet—why, they were iridescent. And what strange sandals—polished foot-shaped wood with rust-colored rubber straps.

As Maharishi drew closer, my teeth clenched and jaw tightened with mixed emotions of excitement and a sort of terror. *What is making me afraid?* My hands turned cold and clammy as blood receded from my extremities. I gripped my wild-flowers tighter.

Blissful and childlike, he cooed, smiled, and giggled. Collecting flowers from both sides, he welcomed each devotee with warmth and exuberance.

Maharishi finally got to me. He stopped and looked me up, down, and back up again. His face became stern. He looked through me, not at me—as though he were scanning hidden corners of my mind. I felt naked.

What's he thinking? He seems to disapprove, I thought.

"Jai Guru Dev," Maharishi said in a high-pitched Indian accent. He snatched the wildflowers from my hands briskly, in what seemed a derisive gesture. He didn't smile. He smiled at everyone else, but not me.

"Jai Guru Dev," I finally managed to chirp, after he'd moved to the next person.

My nineteen-year-old mind started churning: *He doesn't like the way I look. My clunky handmade leather sandals held together with big ugly nails. My hairy legs and underarms. My secondhand rayon dress from the 1940s—dull gold printed with black patterns. No bra. Homemade glass bead necklace, disheveled hair, granny glasses. I must look like a ridiculous hippie to him.*

But he looks even more like a hippie. Carrying bunches of flowers, with long black hippie hair, white robes, long beads. He's wearing a skirt, not pants.

On the way to the lecture, my fellow travelers were busy talking about Maharishi. But I stared out the car window in silence.

At the auditorium, hundreds waited in a double line to greet Maharishi with flowers. He smiled at them all. *Why did he scowl at me at the airport?* I loathe to admit it, but I did sort of look like a scary Charles Manson Family reject.

<hr />

I'd read about disciples who first found (or more precisely returned to) their beloved masters (whom they've known for lifetimes). Nearly all described a heartfelt homecoming, love exchange, and immediate recognition.

My first encounter with Maharishi could not, by any stretch of imagination, compare with such wonders. However, guru first-encounters aren't always showers of rose petals and strains of violin strings. Sometimes they're violins strung with barbed wire.

Paramahansa Yogananda's first meeting with his guru Sri Yukteswar began as a love fest of hearts, daffodils, and butterflies. Within a few minutes, however, when Yukteswar told the youngster to return to his family in Calcutta, Yogananda obstinately refused. The mood then deteriorated rapidly into what Yogananda described as "controversial tension."

Yukteswar said in a stern voice, "The next time we meet, you will have to reawaken my interest: I won't accept you as a disciple easily. There must be complete surrender by obedience to my strict training."[2] Then the guru threw the boy into a tailspin with this zinger: "Do you think your relatives will laugh at you?"

Yogananda wondered "why the miraculous meeting had ended on an inharmonious note."[3] After this initial meeting, twenty-five years elapsed before Yukteswar again gave Yogananda any affirmation of love.

Considering the rebellious Yogananda's contentious meeting with his guru, I figured perhaps I was in good company. I speculated why Maharishi wasted no time administering harsh treatment. Was he resuming a long-standing relationship, picking up where he'd left off—as if I were already a close disciple? Or was he assuming a familial or fatherly role, where scolding was acceptable?

At the time, I didn't know Maharishi's scowl was just the first of many "tests" he would deliver over the next decade. This was the beginning (or perhaps continuation) of a unique relationship that would change me profoundly.

Many guru/disciple relationships start with a courtship. Irina Tweedie's guru, Radha Mohan Lal, said that at first the guru woos the student in order to get him/her to stay. But once the disciple loves the guru, then problems begin: "He will feel like crying 'Why does the Master not notice me, does not speak to me? Is he angry? Why is he here and I there?' and so on. Before this time comes one should run away quickly."[4]

Serampore, India: guru Sri Yukteswar, white haired and bearded on left; disciple Paramahansa Yogananda, dark haired on right.
Paul Fearn/Alamy Stock Photo

For me, running away wasn't an option. The moment I first laid eyes on Maharishi's photo at the TM center, that was it. I was all-in. I was never a guru dabbler, riddled with doubts, questioning whether this was a spiritual master or Mr. Ordinary Joe.

On his way to the stage, devotees handed Maharishi flowers or placed garlands around his neck. He emerged through walls of followers toward a dais bedecked as for a wedding, with formal floral arrangements in pastel tones festooned with ribbons and the whole *schmear.* Above a gold velour sofa, a large, elaborately carved picture frame held a painting of Maharishi's guru.

No one was smoking, which was rare for 1967. Maharishi said tobacco had a negative influence, so smoking wasn't allowed near him.

The crowd stood up at their seats and placed palms together, as though praying to Jesus. "Put your hands like this," someone said. "It's an Indian greeting." I assumed the prayer position like a dutiful Catholic.

Maharishi ascended the platform and, with palms together, bowed his head in reverence to Guru Dev's picture. He then turned to the audience and said, "Jai Guru Dev," smiling and shining, buried by massive colorful buds and garlands received from devotees.

"Jai Guru Dev," the crowd responded in unison.

Charlie Lutes, president of Maharishi's organization for adults, Spiritual Regeneration Movement (SRM), placed an animal hide over a white sheet covering the sofa. Maharishi sat on the hide, removing garlands and placing flower bundles onto a coffee table before him. His bare feet slipped out of his sandals. He crossed his legs, tucked his robes under them, and placed a pink rose in his lap. The sofa's immensity further emphasized his diminutive frame.

Maharishi surrounded by flowers.
Everett Collection/Newscom

After Maharishi took his seat, everyone sat down. His devotees always stood when he rose, and sat after he sat. Maharishi closed his eyes. The hall went dead silent. No one moved. Ten minutes passed. The only sounds were a few coughs. I peeked at him. He seemed to radiate and glow, exuding a powerful energy. He reminded me of the yogi who appeared at my apartment one year before, but looked nothing like him.

Maharishi picked up the rose from his lap. With a thick Indian accent, he spoke in a melodious tenor that flowed sweet and smooth as honey. In a gentle, soothing tone, more like song than speech, his words seemed to emanate from an ancient hall of wisdom where life was much simpler, or a place beyond time and space. It wasn't so much what he said, but the feeling it invoked, that echoed a faraway, other-dimensional land.

He began by saying that the natural tendency of the mind is to seek a field of greater and greater happiness: "Life isn't meant to be a struggle. Life is bliss. Man was not born to suffer. He was born to enjoy." He described the inexhaustible reservoir of energy and intelligence within, at the source of thought, which we can tap using the simple, natural, effortless Transcendental Meditation technique.

He spoke about going deep into the thinking process, into subtler and subtler states of thought and then eventually transcending thought. In that transcendental state, we experience pure being—absolute bliss consciousness.

Maharishi's voice flowed gently, sweetly, flute-like and ever enthusiastic. The end of many sentences was punctuated by a lyrical "hmm?" sound. As I listened, my mind became serene. My body became relaxed, humming with electric energy. Awestruck and entranced, I was immersed in his presence.

Maharishi continued to speak about the state of unmanifest being, which is reflected by our nervous system as "restful alertness," where the whole body settles down, heart rate slows, and breath becomes subtle and refined. At the same time, the mind becomes quiet and still as it experiences pure consciousness.

I closed my eyes and breathed deeply, as if imbibing his essence through the air. I bathed in his radiant energy. Every sensation was heightened. The room seemed to vibrate with increasing power, until the "I" that I thought was "me" got swallowed by the charged intensity of his atmosphere.

He continued: "In transcendental being, the self is not aware of anything else. It was aware of the thought, and now the thought has dropped off. The self remains all by itself. When I am awake in myself, this is self-realization. It is wise to know one's self first. And what we find is our existence is enormous, unbounded, eternal, bliss, infinite happiness, infinite energy, infinite intelligence. Look at the great possibility, hmm?"[5]

I was spellbound by words that rang true, by what seemed the only sane voice in a world gone mad, by the real promise of relief from suffering, and by an energy that transported me to another world—a rapturous wonderland. I was entirely captivated by the headiness of Maharishi's charismatic, magnetic aura, and his inscrutable air of mystery. His beguiling presence was at once impenetrably enigmatic and entirely irresistible.

Maharishi has all the answers, I thought. *Meditation is where it's at. I've got to put it out of my mind—the fact that he scowled at me and smiled at everyone else.*

In December 1967, Jerry Jarvis held a one-week TM retreat at Asilomar, down the California coast near Monterrey. On Friday night, during the first meeting, he said:

"This time is very precious. Now we must take advantage of this opportunity. We've been given this priceless knowledge, this ability to experience the fulfillment of Yoga Philosophy, the state of *turya*, which in Sanskrit means 'fourth state.' Until now, we've experienced three states of consciousness—waking, sleep, and dream states. The transcendental, fourth state of absolute bliss consciousness is our focus this weekend.

"Tonight we'll go to our rooms. Tomorrow we'll only come out twice—for lunch and dinner. The rest of the time we'll sit comfortably and meditate. Sit either in a chair, on your bed, or on the floor, however you are comfortable. Stick to the routine. Tomorrow night, when I see you next, we'll have a contest to see who has meditated the most hours."[6]

Surely he's kidding, I thought. *Meditate all day?*

Next morning I sat up in bed, propped pillows behind my back, and began. Hours went by. I thought, I went back to the mantra, thought, went back to the mantra, thought, back to the mantra. On and on and on. When I came out for lunch, I felt something I'd never felt before.

HAPPY. Really happy.

Back to my room. Meditating again. On and on and so forth. Until dinner.

I came out of meditation, stoned on my own energy. Joy welled up inside. My head felt bigger, as though stretched to stuff more consciousness inside. Feelings of buoyancy and vitality energized my body. Deep serenity and contentment saturated my mind.

The food never tasted so good. I never felt so great. I thought, *TM has got to be the key to the universe, the answer to all mysteries. The be-all, end-all of everything.*

That night at the meeting, Jerry asked, "How many hours did you meditate?"

Hands went up. "Twenty hours," one guy said.

People gasped.

"Sixteen hours," another said.

"Eighteen hours."

"Twenty-two hours."

More gasps.

I only meditated twelve hours. I guess I'm not doing that well. How could anyone meditate twenty-two hours? Didn't they sleep or eat?

The next day I did better. "Eighteen hours," I reported.

"Good," Jerry replied.

Good, he said. He thinks I did good.

⁓⁓⁓⁓⁓⁓⁓⁓⁓⁓⁓⁓⁓⁓

They served organic vegetarian food on the meditation retreat. Raised on Wonder Bread, white sugar, frozen vegetables, steak, potatoes, iceberg lettuce, and Crisco, I now discovered organic foods, macrobiotic cooking, brown rice, and colon cleansing.

I became a vegetarian. Reading Bernard Jenson's *Fasting Can Save Your Life,* I learned how disease begins in the colon, and embarked on a seven-day fast.

In keeping with my back-to-nature frenzy, I moved into an antiquated Brown Shingle duplex next to a stream in Oakland, with a wood-burning stove, outdoor john, antique furniture, beamed ceilings, bay windows, window seats, and French doors. I installed a mirror right over my bed and decorated the place with tapestries and lace hanging from ceiling and walls.

This became my love castle—and I became a love goddess. It seemed the more I meditated, the more I felt like gettin' my groove on. Maybe it was rebellion against "the establishment." I managed to get it on with as many men as I could possibly squeeze in—that is, into my busy schedule.

My philosophy was "free love." Commitment wasn't in my vocabulary. It was the "love generation," and I was a "love child."

4

FEELIN' GURU-VY

1967 TO 1969

The ocean is fulfilled, immovable, eternally content, but when someone wishes
to draw, it flows spontaneously. It all depends on how much the disciple draws.
—MAHARISHI MAHESH YOGI

My involvement with TM predated the involvement of rockstars. But my parents (and
the general public) were unimpressed until celebrities joined the bandwagon. Inexplicably, meaningless endorsements of the rich and famous endowed TM significant
gravitas.

In the 1960s, Southern California was abuzz with Eastern mysticism. Well-known
flutist Paul Horn, syndicated gossip columnist Cobina Wright, bestselling health food
author Gayelord Hauser, and later his lover, Hollywood icon Greta Garbo, all became
TM meditators. Doris Duke, flamboyant American Tobacco Company heiress, had
been a devotee of Yogananda and Kriya Yoga practitioner. After learning TM, she donated $100,000 to Maharishi, which financed building his Meditation Academy in
Rishikesh, India.

Efrem Zimbalist Jr., lead actor in the TV series *77 Sunset Strip* and *The FBI*, became deeply involved with TM. He was responsible for getting Maharishi on *The Steve Allen Show*. However, Maharishi's high-pitched voice, giggle, and long stringy hair
didn't play well.

Maharishi's popularity was rising in England, Canada, the European continent,
and South America, but in the USA, his following amounted to the Theosophy set.
However, that all changed when, in the mid-1960s, a host of rockstars and Hollywood
celebrities learned TM, including The Doors, the Beatles, Mick Jagger, and Marianne
Faithfull. Not far behind were the Beach Boys, Donovan Leitch, Grateful Dead, Mia
Farrow, Shirley MacLaine, and more.

September 1, 1967, Concertgebouw Amsterdam: Rolling Stones meet Maharishi after TM introductory lecture: l. to r.: Michael Cooper (photographer), Mick Jagger, a pregnant Marianne Faithfull, Al Vandenberg (photographer), Brian Jones.
Photo by Ben Merk (ANEFO)

Beatle George Harrison's wife Pattie Boyd noticed TM advertised in a classified ad in *The Times* of London. Pattie and her friend, fashion model Marie-Lise Volpeliere-Pierrot, were initiated in February 1967 at Caxton Hall.

Maharishi was scheduled to appear in London on August 24. His organizers planned an average hotel for the lecture. However, he insisted on the newly built, luxurious Park Lane Hilton, whose ballroom sat over a thousand people.

Pattie felt more alert and energetic with TM, and believed it changed her life. She inspired George, who then wanted his own mantra. Sculptor David Wynne showed George a picture of Maharishi's palm with its long lifeline and mentioned the upcoming lecture. George got tickets for Pattie, her sister Jenny Boyd, John Lennon, his wife Cynthia, Paul McCartney, his girlfriend Jane Asher, and Paul's brother Mike McGear. Yoko Ono also showed up—and afterward barged into John's limousine, wedged herself between John and Cynthia, and demanded a ride home. Ringo was at the hospital with wife Maureen, who'd given birth five days earlier.

August 24, 1967, London: Beatles attend Maharishi's lecture at Park Lane Hilton: l. to r.: Paul McCartney, Mike McGear (Paul's brother), John Lennon, Cynthia Lennon, Pattie Boyd, George Harrison, Jenny Boyd, Alexis Mardas. *Associated Newspapers /REX/Shutterstock*

After his lecture at the Hilton, Maharishi meets the Beatles backstage.
Mirrorpix/Newscom

John Lennon's hand-painted Rolls-Royce limousine.
© *KEYSTONE Pictures USA*

Pattie described Maharishi as "impressive," and herself as "spellbound." George said, "That's the first time anybody has talked about these things in a way I understand."[8] Some of the Beatles recognized Maharishi from Granada's *People and Places* TV program years earlier.

After the lecture, Vincent Snell, MD, orthopedic surgeon and the first Initiator in Great Britain, introduced the Beatles to Maharishi, whom they met for about an hour backstage. They expressed, "Even from an early age we have been seeking a highly spiritual experience. We tried drugs and that didn't work."[9] When George asked Maharishi about getting a mantra, he invited the band to attend a retreat in North Wales starting the next day, August 25. Attendees included the Beatles, Cynthia Lennon, Pattie Boyd, Jenny Boyd, Jane Asher, singer Cilla Black, so-called inventor Alexis Mardas, Mick Jagger, and his girlfriend, singer Marianne Faithfull.

August 25, 1967, Beatles on train to Bangor, North Wales: from front around circle, clockwise: George Harrison, Hunter Davies (biographer), Paul McCartney, Ringo Starr, John Lennon, Maharishi. *Trinity Mirror/Mirrorpix/Alamy Stock Photo*

Just as the train to Wales pulled away from London's Euston station, the Beatles boarded. Since John Lennon bolted ahead and ditched the luggage for Cynthia to handle, she got separated, left behind in tears on the platform. This seemed an apt metaphor for her state of mind, since Yoko Ono was quickly taking possession of John. Cynthia recalled, "I knew in my heart, as I watched the people I loved fading into the hazy distance, that the loneliness I felt on that station platform would become permanent before long."[10]

August 25, 1967: Beatles arrive in Bangor, North Wales: l. to r.: Brahmachari Devendra, John Lennon, Maharishi, Paul McCartney, Ringo Starr, George Harrison (carrying sitar). *Trinity Mirror/Mirrorpix/Alamy Stock Photo*

August 25, 1967, Bangor, North Wales: Beatles onstage with Maharishi:
l. to r.: Paul McCartney, John Lennon, Ringo Starr, George Harrison, Maharishi.
Daily Mail/REX/Shutterstock

After the train ride, three hundred course participants, including Cynthia Lennon and Jenny Boyd (who drove with road manager Neil Aspinall), stayed in dorms at University College in Bangor, sharing bunk beds and eating canteen food (or Chinese

eat-in). There Maharishi initiated the Beatles into TM.

Since drug abstinence was prerequisite to starting TM, the musicians stopped using drugs—for the first five minutes, anyway. Maharishi commented, "The interest of young minds in the use of drugs, even though misguided, indicates their genuine search for some form of spiritual experience."[11]

August 26, 1967, Bangor, North Wales:
Beatles follow Maharishi to the stage
carrying books autographed by the guru.
mptvimages.com

August 27, 1967: Beatles walk on campus at Normal College, Bangor.
Mirrorpix/Newscom

Beatles manager Brian Epstein was planning to attend the retreat, but an accidental drug overdose took his life on August 27 in London. Consequently, the Beatles stayed only for the weekend rather than ten days.

John Lennon told journalist Ray Coleman, "We want to learn the meditation thing properly so we can sell the whole idea to everyone. This is how we plan to use our power now. We want to set up an academy in London and use all the power we've got to get it moving. It strengthens understanding, makes people relaxed and it's much better than acid. This is the biggest thing in my life now and it's come at the time when I need it most. Brian has died only in body. His spirit will always be working with us."[12]

George Harrison said Maharishi was a great comfort to the Beatles when they lost Brian.[13] Yet Brian Epstein's relatives felt Maharishi acted callously by telling the Beatles that death isn't real, that Brian had gone on to his next stage of life, that they shouldn't be overwhelmed with grief, and whatever thoughts they have of Brian should be happy since those thoughts would travel to Brian—wherever he was.[14]

After the Beatles returned to London, George traveled around England with Initiator Vincent Snell for some time. When Maharishi first taught TM in England in 1959, he'd stayed with Vincent and Peggy Snell for seven weeks.

In autumn 1967, the Beatles continued to express enthusiasm about TM (and defend meditation to skeptical reporters) in multiple interviews, including *The Frost*

Report. John told *The Daily Sketch,* "We've never felt like this about anything else."[15] He even suggested to his co-Beatles, "If we went round the world preaching about Transcendental Meditation, we could turn on millions of people."[16] He wrote the song, "Across the Universe," an anthem to TM, which included the appellation "Jai Guru Deva."

Maharishi meets Beatles and their wives in London: l. to r.: Paul McCartney, Jane Asher on couch. Cynthia Lennon, Mike McGear, Ringo Starr, Maureen Starkey, George Harrison. John Lennon on floor. Vincent Snell, SRM leader of Britain, upper left corner. *Associated Newspapers/REX/Shutterstock*

Once the Beatles became public advocates, Maharishi found himself all over the press, and, over the next few years, his following exploded to millions. On September 8, 1967, Maharishi appeared in *Life Magazine,* posing with the Beatles at Bangor.[17] In a second *Life* article in November, "Invitation to Instant Bliss," Maharishi said, "It's so very simple. They keep telling me I must make it complicated so that people will think I'm saying something important."[18] A third *Life* article appeared in February 1968.[19]

September 26, 1967 marked Maharishi's first appearance on *The Tonight Show.* From the moment Maharishi appeared, carrying flowers, removing his sandals, and crossing his legs, Johnny Carson raised his eyebrows, rolled his eyes, and made snide faces. Still, the show resulted in thousands of eager students queuing around blocks to learn TM. In January 1968, just before Maharishi left for India with Mia Farrow, he returned to *The Tonight Show.* After that, mocking Maharishi became a recurrent theme of Carson's jokes.

Even so, Maharishi's popularity skyrocketed. *Time* magazine called him "Sooth-sayer for Everyman."[20] *The New York Times Magazine* declared him "Chief Guru of the Western World."[21] In *Newsweek* he was quoted: "Just as you water the roots of a tree, you have to water the mind through meditation."[22]

The February 6, 1968 cover article in *Look Magazine,* "The Non-Drug Turn-On Hits Campus: student meditators tune in to Maharishi," reported students learning TM at UC Berkeley, UCLA, Harvard, Yale, Wellesley, Northeastern, and U of Cincinnati.[23]

An article by Paul Horn in the same issue quoted Maharishi: "Meditation we don't do for the sake of meditation. We want some positive effects in life—something that will make a man more dynamic in his field of activity."[24] Paul Horn added, "Best of all, you can never have a 'bad trip' with meditation." [25]

◇◇◇◇◇◇◇◇◇◇◇◇◇◇◇◇◇◇◇◇◇◇◇◇◇◇◇◇◇◇◇◇

Before the Beatles ever appeared on Maharishi's radar, I was chomping at the bit to become an Initiator. TM Teacher Training Courses were offered during fall and winter—the only times Westerners could bear India's oppressive heat. In 1967, I applied for the next course, January 1968. However, at age nineteen, I was too young to qualify.

The Beatles spent a few weeks at that course in lockdown meditation mode. On the way to the ashram, George Harrison told a reporter, "A lot of people think we've gone off our heads. Well, they can think that—or anything they like. We've discovered a new way of living."[26]

After the Beatles arrived, the press couldn't get past the ashram gates. When reporters broke the lock and stormed the Beatles' quarters, Maharishi's *brahmacharyas* (celibate monk disciples) forcibly removed them. Then Maharishi enlisted a Gurkha to guard the gates round the clock. Security tightened and photographers were dislodged from the trees.

Starvation for news of the Beatles tantalized the public. Maharishi tried to quell journalistic passion with press conferences. Just outside the gates under the trees, rugs were laid on the ground for reporters. Maharishi turned these meetings into TM advertisements—not what reporters were assigned to cover. Requests to interview the Beatles ended in frustration: "They do not want publicity, fans or press. They want to be left alone to meditate."[27] "There's nothing to see inside the ashram except people meditating, which isn't very interesting."[28]

Most questions, i.e., about wealthy disciples, or the ashram's alleged luxury, or celebrities, or planned airstrip for a twin-engine Beechcraft, remained unanswered, as Maharishi responded with evasive rejoinders, punctuated by giggles. Ever patient and composed, he possessed an uncanny knack for boundless politeness, despite rude, vicious attacks.

Growing angrier daily, the press fabricated creative headlines: "Maharishi's con-gregation of actors, divorcees, and reformed drug addicts." "Wild orgies in ashram," "Beatles wife raped at ashram," "Cartons of whiskey delivered to Maharishi's guests at ashram."

Finally reporters had something to photograph when two helicopters, in their noise and fury, made a ruckus on the Ganges riverbank below the ashram—loaned by Bombay transportation magnate Kershi S. Cambata (one of Maharishi's followers), president of Cambata Aviation. Maharishi took a spin, John Lennon took another, and photos circulated worldwide.

When the new TM Initiators returned home, rumors spread—the Beatles had sev-ered their relationship with Maharishi due to inappropriate behavior with Mia Far-row. Soon after the Beatles' return, journalist Larry Kane asked them, "Is Maharishi on the level?"

John Lennon scoffed. "I don't know what level he's on. We had a nice holiday in India and came back rested to play businessman."[29]

On May 14, 1968, John said on *The Tonight Show,* "We believe in meditation, but not the Maharishi and his scene. But that's a personal mistake we made in public. Meditation is good and does what they say. It's like exercise or cleaning your teeth, you know. It works." [30]

In mid-June, Paul declared, "We made a mistake. We thought there was more to him than there was. He's human. We thought at first that he wasn't."[31]

John said, "I think we had a false impression of Maharishi . . . we were looking for it and we probably superimposed it on him. We were waiting for a guru, and along he came."[32]

Despite what the press portrayed as a vicious falling-out between the Beatles and Maharishi, their parting of ways didn't dent the exponential growth of his following. As for me, I was already hooked. So I didn't give one whit whether the Beatles liked, loved, hated, or were entirely indifferent toward Maharishi.

While the Beatles moved on, Maharishi's fame continued a meteoric rise. In the cover article of *The Saturday Evening Post,* May 4, 1968, he was quoted: "If one person in every thousand meditated, there would be peace for a thousand generations."[33] This key statement was Maharishi's essential purpose and message. His campaign was always to establish world peace through meditation. He often said, "For the forest to be green, every tree must be green. To attain world peace, each individual must be at peace." This always struck me as a most sensible idea.

From August 4 to 30, 1968, Maharishi taught a one-month Leadership Training Seminar to eight hundred meditators at Squaw Valley Ski Resort, Olympia, California. The seminar was like old-home month for hippies, a sort of ex-druggie family reunion.

What a motley bunch dragged up the ski slopes that summer! A gaggle of hips, beats, heads, straights, gays, dropouts, flower children, yippies, heavies, lovechildren, soul brothers and sisters, rockstars, groupies, all trying to get our shit together, looking for the ultimate contact high—*darshan* with the Beatles' guru. (Sanskrit for "sight," *darshan* refers to spiritual energy transmitted in a saint's presence.)

Maharishi, our ideal guide to inner space, was the ultimate hippie. He looked the part and fit right in with us misfits—long unkempt hair, love beads, white robes, funky sandals. Always laughing and doling out flowers, as though either holding or tripping, on a perpetual high, he did nothing but hang out, laugh, and groove to meditation.

1968, Squaw Valley: SIMS Leadership Training Course. Left of Maharishi seated on ground, Brahmachari Devendra. Right, Jerry and Debby Jarvis.

The Doors musicians Robby Krieger, guitarist, and John Densmore, drummer, made the scene. In 1965, fifteen people attended a lecture with Maharishi in Los Angeles at the home of Keith Wallace (later president of Maharishi International University). Krieger, Densmore, and Manzarek met there and formed The Doors, whose name was borrowed from William Blake: "If the doors of perception were cleansed, everything would appear to man as it is, infinite."[34] Maharishi's oft-quoted expression, "Take it easy, take it as it comes," became lyrics in their song recorded in 1966. John Densmore said, "There wouldn't be any Doors without Maharishi."[35]

Robby Krieger was shy, but with my braless mammilla peeking through my see-through lacey blouse, his shyness tended to dissipate. He invited me to his room and gave me a gigantic silver ring, set with an oval cabochon black star sapphire.

Jerry Jarvis, president of SIMS, along with wife Debby, totally flipped when they saw how I was dressed. With one look of alarm, they let me know it.

Lots of heavy hitters from LA joined in—rockstars, actors, producers, and directors. This guru attracted wealth like magnets attract metal. I was neither rich nor famous, but my Initiator Jerry Jarvis liked me. He arranged for me to do housekeeping at Maharishi's hidden cabin in the woods. I spoke with Maharishi privately and handed him an oil painting that took me all summer to paint—his portrait. It wasn't bad for a teenage amateur artist, but not exactly a Rembrandt. "I painted this. Do you want me to put it up on the mantelpiece?"

Maharishi looked at the painting and sort of crossed his eyes. "That depends on if they like it, hmm?" he replied.

What's that supposed to mean? Who are "they?" I wondered. It didn't cross my mind that this was Maharishi's polite way of saying the painting was crap.

I asked Jerry Jarvis, "Can I place the painting on the mantel?"

Jerry replied, "Why not? It's a good painting." A few days later I found the painting in the cabin's spare bedroom, stuffed in a closet.

Soon Jerry's wife, Debby Jarvis, banned me from doing housework in the cabin. A teenager with mousy-blond straight hair, named Mindy Leibowitz, replaced me. She was also granted the privilege of ironing Maharishi's clothing. Still, determined to get into his graces, I remained undaunted.

In the lecture hall, Maharishi sat on a deerskin placed over white silk fabric that covered his couch. The silk and deerskin purportedly shielded him from bad vibes. Above his couch, Guru Dev's painting reminded us of his cherished lineage, India's Shankaracharya Order, from which Maharishi claimed (controversially) that TM arose.

In his melodious voice, Maharishi addressed his swarm of dropouts: "In this Leadership Training Seminar, our goal is to gain efficiency in life, to learn to lead our fellow men in the art of living in happiness. The ultimate goal of life is absolute bliss consciousness. All else is secondary.

"We should contact and befriend the leader of cosmic life and tune into cosmic intelligence. Therefore, in order to be leaders, we must communicate with God, hmm?

We must get in touch with infinite bliss consciousness on all levels: intellectual, emotional, and environmental." [36]

My mind perked up when Maharishi said, "communicate with God." *That's what I always wanted. Can he teach me how?*

Maharishi continued, "A good leader makes his followers feel they don't have to undertake anything strenuous. We must show the world a pathless path. The goal is omnipresent and the path is within, hmm?" [37]

I hung onto Maharishi's every word. To my mind, he held life's greatest mysteries. He was going to transform the world. Intoxicated by his mystique, enraptured by his wisdom, I flew to Elysian Fields on wings of adoration.

Talking for hours with no break, Maharishi gestured animatedly with his muscular arms, large hands, and thick fingers. The rest of his body remained still, legs in pretzel position. He used a flower as a prop to illustrate fine points of Indian philosophy. Often he played with his beads. The audience barely moved. They seemed entranced, in rapt attention, hanging on every word, taking notes—or nodding off.

Sometimes Maharishi's scrawny Indian cook named Dunraj, wearing what resembled an oversized cotton diaper *(dhoti)* and long cotton shirt (*kurta),* walked onto the stage and offered Maharishi water in a sterling silver cup and white cloth napkin to wipe his beard.

Maharishi often opened the mike for questions.

"What to do about noises while we're meditating?" a man asked.

Maharishi answered, "Take a neutral attitude towards sounds."

"If you die before attaining enlightenment, what should you do?" an older woman asked.

"Feel the presence of God around you."

"Please describe where we go after death."

"The cause of rebirth is the unfulfilled state of life. The inner man, dweller in the body, is like a dweller in a house. When the house collapses, he collects all that is precious and runs out the door. Whatever is last idea at time of death decides the direction. If we remember a dear cat, we go to life of cat. Whatever has been dearest in life, what we cherish most. Physical machinery starts fading and what fades last will be deepest impression. In meditation we store more and more deeply the impression of transcendental consciousness. The impression becomes so clear that it becomes permanent and dominates all others."

"Do you believe in reincarnation?"

"I am opposed to it . . . One carnation is enough." Another time he declared, "Reincarnation is for the ignorant" (which means, after attaining enlightenment, we no longer incarnate).

"What is destiny or fate?"

"It's our own influence that we create for our surroundings to help or hinder us. This influence is created by our own thoughts, words, and actions."

"What is free will?"

"Well, you see, it is like this. Absolutely everything is fixed, and absolutely everything can be changed at any time."

"Why is there a population explosion?"

"If a man follows the natural course of evolution, he eventually evolves into a celestial being. Similarly, the lower species evolve into human species. Now man is jammed up because he's not evolving fast enough. The lower species continue to evolve, but man remains stuck on the human level and doesn't evolve to the higher celestial levels."[38]

<hr>

The seminar continued—lots of meditation, lots of lectures, lots of sex. It was always like that, but not Maharishi's fault. He emphasized how precious this time was and urged us not to "socialize"—his euphemism for sex. But his hippie followers possessed decided reluctance to keep their flies zipped. "Free love" was their chosen modus operandi.

"On this Seminar we must stay one-pointed. No distractions. No socializing," Maharishi said. "Now is the time for meditation, for you all to become leaders in the Students International Meditation Society."

Maharishi explained the "rounding" routine. One "round" consisted of yoga postures *(asanas)*, breathing exercises *(pranayama)*, meditation, then lie down ten minutes. Upon rising, we would sit up in bed and meditate five to ten minutes, then round until lunch, round again following the afternoon meeting until dinner, and lie down after lunch and dinner. After the evening meeting, we would go quickly to bed.

At that time, virtually no one practiced yoga or meditation in America. There were no yoga studios. We were yoga pioneers.

I followed the routine, just as Maharishi advised. I could follow orders if I liked them. And during that month, yes, I did remain celibate, unlike my roommate, whom I inadvertently walked in on one night, and noticed way too many extremities bouncing up and down on her bed.

Maharishi explained that during the course we might experience "unstressing," a.k.a. "unwinding." This meant going slightly nuts as we released trauma lodged in our nervous system. Because of our overly sensitive state of mind, meditating several hours daily, we were warned not to make any life-altering decisions during "long rounding." Maharishi said, "When the Ganges floods, it stirs up a lot of mud."[39]

Before leaving Squaw Valley, Maharishi interviewed those wanting to become Initiators. For some odd reason, these interviews transpired in the back seat of a car. Each interviewee took turns sitting next to him.

When my turn came, I said, "I'm the one who painted your portrait."

"Good, good," he said. "You want to teach meditation, hmm?"

"More than anything in the whole world." My sappy, starry eyes, and the swell of energy behind them, flashed so brightly that surely they must have blinded him.

Maharishi shuffled through my application form. "Then you will come to India to Teacher Training and then teach in Colorado."

"Colorado?" I balked. "I don't want to teach in Colorado. I live in California. I don't live in Colorado. I'm gonna teach in California."

He glowered, as if a disobedient child needed spanking. "You will teach in Colorado."

I didn't respond, but my mind rebelled vehemently. Going back to Squaresville, Colorado and my hypercritical, faultfinding parents was way below the bottom of my to-do list. Evidently, that's why Maharishi told me to do it.

Though all dreamy-eyed in fantasyland with hearts, lollipops, and rainbows about traveling to India, hanging out with Maharishi, and becoming an Initiator, I certainly didn't want to follow his highly inconvenient, annoying advice. Truth be told, I was childish and clueless. What I lacked in experience, I made up for with pigheadedness.

This was one of Maharishi's little "tests." Of course, at the time I didn't recognize it as a test. The guru never lets on what he's doing. He just sticks her with the barb and then watches her flail around like a bird caught in a net.

After the course, I returned to my quiet life in my back-to-nature home. Every bit of extra cash went toward taking meditation retreats, including a two-week course taught by Brahmachari Satyanand in summer 1969 in Squaw Valley.

Satyanand was a direct disciple of Maharishi's guru. After Guru Dev's death, he got married and went into business. When his wife died, he planned to move to Benares (now Varanasi) and wait for his own death. (Varanasi is deemed the holiest place to die.) But Maharishi laughed and called that a "stupid waste of time." He asked Satyanand to join him. Satyanand accepted.

I spent much of my free time volunteering at the TM Center on Channing Way in Berkeley (a two-story stucco building, previously a sorority house). As a Meditation Checker, I guided meditators step-by-step through the process. I also taught yoga

August 1969: TM Initiators at Squaw Valley. First row l. to r.: Colin Harrison, Nadine Lewy, Brahmachari Satyanand, Jerry Jarvis, Prudence Farrow. Second row l. to r.: Pearl Shipman, Telia Maher, Helen and Roland Olson (hosted Maharishi in Los Angeles), Debby Jarvis, Walter and Rae Koch, unknown. Back row l. to r.: Pete Ports, unknown, Paul Horn, Nini White, Robert Winquist, Tom Winquist, Al Bruns (Prudence Farrow's husband), Terry Gustafson (Jojo in Beatles song "Get Back").

asanas. One day Donovan, the singer-songwriter from Scotland, appeared out of nowhere to get checked. *Wow, I get to meet this cool rockstar*—or so I thought.

I checked Donovan's meditation, just like anyone else's. As I led him through the process, he had a deep experience of transcendence. When the session was over, I said, "I love your music. It's really groovy, especially 'Catch the Wind.' Are you enjoying your visit to California?"

"None of your business," Donovan snapped and bolted for the door.

Boy is he rude or what? I thought. *What a snob!*

I wondered whether I would act similarly if I were a rockstar. How exhausting to constantly get barraged by people you don't want to talk to! But was that an excuse? After all, I was an idealistic young woman, volunteering to perform a service of which even the great and mighty Donovan deigned to avail himself.

John Farrow
2013

meijer

815 S. Randall Rd.
Elgin, IL 60123 - #183
(847)717-6500   meijer.com

The Meijer Team appreciates your business
07/13/18
Your checkout was provided by Fastlane101

MEIJER SAVINGS
SPECIALS   1.76
SAVINGS TOTAL   1.76

SALE
GROCERY
*6661318106   SEAFOOD SNACKS
    4 @ 1.25
    was   6.76   now   5.00 N

TOTAL
            TOTAL TAX   .00
            TOTAL   5.00
PAYMENTS
  EBT FOOD   TENDER   5.00
XXXXXXXXXXXX9545   (S) BAL 3,169.12
  APPROVAL CODE 863093

            NUMBER OF ITEMS   4

  For additional savings and rewards visit
                mPerks.com
  For information on Meijer return policy
            visit meijer.com

[11m   NOW HIRING

        https://jobs.meijer.com

            A01830LNF1605JS

Tx:125 Op:552   Tm:101 St:183 12:55:46

meijer

6155 Kendall Rd
Elgin IL 60123 4133

the Meijer team appreciates your business
04/13/18
your receipt was provided by Fastlane 801

MEIJER SAVINGS
PECIALS   16
SAVINGS TOTAL   1. .70

AE
GROCERY
660131 3100   SEAFOOD SNACKS
1 @ 1.29
5.18   was   now   5.00 M

TOTAL

TOTAL TAX
TOTAL
PAYMENTS
EBT FOOD
XXXXXXXXXXX8143   TENDER
(S) BAL .0.39.12
APPROVAL CODE 660303

NUMBER OF ITEMS

For additional savings and rewards visit
mPerks.com
for information on Meijer return policy
visit meijer.com

NOW HIRING

Xx123   08353   S3183   12:

Handwritten annotations:

35 And Kaufman writing Partner Bob Zmuda

lung cancer

alopathie

Rod Stewart

Penn Lancaster

Despite many setbacks, over a couple years I managed to scrape up money for the TM Teacher Training Course. However, after applying and getting rejected from three courses in 1968 and 1969, I gave up on getting accepted—at least for the foreseeable future.

However, amazingly, in November 1969, I received a letter from SIMS National Headquarters, 1015 Gayley Avenue, Los Angeles:

"Your application has been accepted for the course in India which begins January 7 and will be completed April 7, 1970." Finally, fourth time's a charm! This was the first course younger applicants were permitted to attend. I was twenty-one and would turn twenty-two in India.

After my initial dance of glee, my mood changed drastically when I realized, since I expected it would be six more years before I would be accepted for the course, I'd already spent the money so painstakingly saved. But I did phone my parents. A couple days later my mother called back. "Susan, you've got some stock that we never told you about. Since it's your money, your father can't very well object, can he?"

I was glad to spend this money on what I believed was my most holy goal of becoming an Initiator. What's more, my mother agreed that traveling to India would be good for me. (Reality was, she was relieved I was no longer taking drugs, dressing like a wild hippie, screwing everything in sight, and all the other groovy things we did in the 1960s.)

It was December 1969. I was all set to go, with my course fee and plane ticket prepaid. I flew to New York to catch my flight to India.

I bundled up on a snowy day to take a pilgrimage to the hallowed halls of New York art museums. I'd always been an artist, and I believed works of art to be blessed acts, yielding sacred relics.

The Guggenheim was where I met him. Friendly and attractive, he invited me to walk around the museum. I enjoyed his company. He was highly knowledgeable about Klee and Kandinsky and other artists. After we ascended the spiral ramp and talked about the paintings, he asked if I wanted tea at the coffee shop. We had a bite to eat and continued our conversation. He seemed a completely rational individual. But at the end of our conversation, he said something so bizarre and shocking that I decided he must be out of his mind.

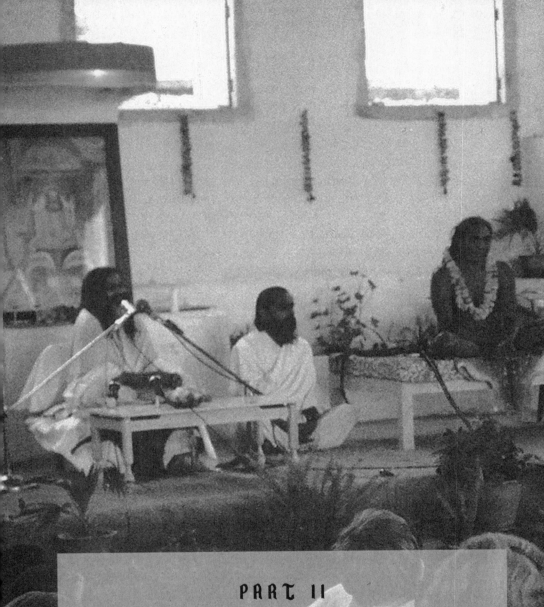

PART II

BLISSED-OUT

Cosmic consciousness, two hundred percent of life, means
fullness of inner silence and fullness of outer activity.
—MAHARISHI MAHESH YOGI

5

HOME TO INDIA

WINTER 1969 TO SPRING 1970

The life of a disciple is on the tender thread of love that connects his heart with the heart of the master. It is on the tender link of intelligence that connects his mind with the mind of the master.

—MAHARISHI MAHESH YOGI

The seemingly sane stranger at the Guggenheim turned to me and suddenly declared, out of nowhere, "Meeting you today is no accident. I was sent here to give you a message."

Sent here? I thought. *By whom?*

"This man you're going to study with in India is not as he appears to be," he continued. "You must cancel your trip now. Do not go to this ashram. You're not the first person I've told. I've warned others on their way to his ashram. I was sent to them also."

What? Is he nuts? I thought. His alarming message made my mind numb and mouth frozen. I couldn't utter a word.

He then stood up and walked out the door.

I was left in the coffee shop, stunned and paralyzed. *No. He must be out of his mind. This isn't really happening. He's just a lunatic. This can't possibly be real.*

I bolted upright and stumbled after him. I rushed out the door, calling for him in the icy dusk. *Where'd he go? No sign of him anywhere.* I walked back into the museum and collapsed on a bench.

Nothing will stop me. I'm getting on that plane tomorrow, no matter what. So, whether this divine visitation (I believe it was a visitation) was a warning or a test, I did board the plane, and I did arrive at my destination.

Mother India. Finally home. That was how it felt. Home, after a long absence, to a place so oddly familiar.

The pungent perfume of New Delhi: marigolds, turmeric, burning cow dung, jasmine, urine, mustard seed, melting candle wax, feces, coconut, saffron, sandalwood incense, coriander, hot *ghee,* cumin, boiling peanut oil, water buffalo milk, *beedies* (Indian cigarettes), fennel, and *paan* (spiced chewing tobacco) filled the air.

I welcomed India's clamoring symphony: Hindu women chanted mournful *bhajans* in high-pitched voices. Peddlers hawked their wares. Indian radios blared. Bicycle bells *ring ring rang*. Muezzins moaned in prayer. Rubber bulb horns *beep beep beeped* on motorized rickshaws. Taxi horns honked nonstop. Water buffalo hooves *clip clip clopped*. Temple bells chimed. Pundits intoned Sanskrit hymns. Animated voices spoke hundreds of dialects.

Taxicabs veered sharply, barely missing cows parked in the center of the road. Water buffaloes sauntered, swishing off flies with their tails. Motorized rickshaws madly zigzagged around traffic. Mercedes trucks, horns screeching, belched black soot. Bullock-drawn wagons plodded while black Indian-built Ambassador taxicabs followed at two miles per hour. Bicycle rickshaws trotted along, bells *ding ding dinging*. Buses *clank clanked* along, sagging from mountains of luggage precariously perched on roofs.

In the jungle-covered Himalayan foothills, Maharishi's Meditation Academy, Shankaracharya Nagar, was built on a 150-foot cliff on Manikoot hill, overlooking the Ganges from its eastern bank. Across the river downstream stood Rishikesh (*Hrishikesha*), a holy place of pilgrimage and haven of yogis, ascetics, devotees of God, and beggars. Hrishikesha is an appellation of Lord Vishnu, meaning "Lord of the Senses."

There were three possible ways to get to Maharishi's ashram in 1969: via a narrow auto bridge crossing the Ganges downstream at Haridwar, followed by a drive up a thirteen-mile, winding, potholed dirt road; or Lakshman Jhula Bridge, a narrow footbridge upstream, followed by a two-mile walk along the shore to a steep, rocky footpath; or a small ferryboat from the west bank.

Opting for automobile access, I rode from New Delhi on a nail-biting six-hour bumpy adventure of 150 miles, with the taxi driver weaving perilously to avoid every conceivable breed of vehicle and beast of burden, while leaning incessantly on his horn.

Finally, I arrived at the fourteen-acre Academy. In 1961 Maharishi leased the parcel for twenty years from Uttar Pradesh State forest department. In 1963 tobacco heiress Doris Duke "anonymously" financed building the ashram. When an Indian Swami asked for the same grant as Maharishi, Doris disavowed all association with Maharishi and TM.

The land was bordered by a dense, dusty, teak forest interspersed with evergreen rosewood *(sheesham)* and inhabited by langur monkeys, elephants, tigers, crows, peacocks, parrots, vultures, chipmunks, pythons, and cobras. Further north, jagged Himalayan peaks touched the sky.

A few huts comprised Shankaracharya Nagar, housing Maharishi's brahmacharyas and staff, post office, commissary, and laundry. Upstream to the north, the ashrams Gita Bhavan and Swarg Ashram were decorated with sculptures of Hindu deities and murals illustrating the Hindu scripture *Bhagavad Gita*. At the entryway to a fly-ridden hole-in-the-wall restaurant, Chotiwala, customers were greeted by a fat head-shaven teen wearing a topknot, dressed in fake sadhu garb and garish makeup. Across the river resided a small Shiva temple and Sivananda Ashram: Divine Life Forest Academy. Distant chanting and tinkling temple bells wafted across the river.

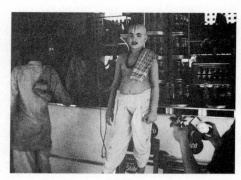

1970, Rishikesh: At Chotiwala Restaurant a teen in costume rings a bell with each customer's arrival.
Photo courtesy of Jared Stoltz

Under continual construction, Maharishi's ashram was a maze of gravel paths, streams, waterfalls, trees, flower gardens, and cement buildings painted in pastel colors. The place buzzed with scrawny men in dust-covered dhotis, and grimy turbans to absorb the sweat. Squeaky, rusty wheelbarrows filled with bricks or cement competed with animals crying in the jungle and the constant commotion of Hindi.

Potentate of his motley kingdom, Maharishi held court, sitting cross-legged on his deerskin draped over a chair, one knee propped on an armrest, scrutinizing every brick laid and nail hammered, yelling and gesticulating wildly, overseeing the entire circus—a mad contractor directing his crew of lunatics. Or so it seemed—especially with streams and waterfalls misengineered to flow against gravity and unlevel ponds filled halfway with cockeyed water.

That was how I got introduced to India.

∞∞∞∞∞∞∞∞∞∞∞∞∞∞∞∞∞∞∞

Maharishi lectured once or twice daily to his 108 students from thirty-five countries. The remaining time we spent in deep meditation. Every day I rose early, used an outdoor toilet and communal washbasin, took a cold or lukewarm outdoor shower, and "rounded" ten to fifteen hours, wrapped in blankets in my cold room.

We were housed in single-story, concrete, U-shaped barracks *(puris)*. A front porch, three steps up from the ground, lined the U. Its roof extended overhead, braced by slender pairs of pillars. A dirt path lined with whitewashed stones or bricks connected the puris.

My scantily furnished room, about eight by twelve feet, consisted of cinder block walls, cement floor, a wooden plank bed with a thin mattress, shelving, an unusable electric heater that blew fuses, a wooden table, a chair, and small filthy windows covered with cobwebs.

Monkeys bounced and made a racket on my roof daily. Peacocks screeched and displayed feathers. Crows cawed a deafening shriek. Skinny water buffaloes and mangy dogs snoozed in inconvenient spots. Centipedes, scorpions, spiders, and snakes invaded sleeping quarters and inhabited meditation caves.

Locals washed my laundry by beating it on rocks at the river. Clothes reappeared smelling like dirt, stretched out of shape, and filled with sand—but neatly pressed! A tailor sat on the ground, operating a hand-driven sewing machine by turning a wheel. I had no money for tailor-made clothing. I did, however, purchase three cotton saris.

Peter Russell from Great Britain (later a well-known spiritual author) directed the kitchen. Shaped like a trident, the leaky-roofed dining room had three wings—one for smokers, one for talkers, and another for silence, which Maharishi encouraged. I ate in the talking dining room, since keeping my mouth shut was never my strong suit.

Hot buffalo milk, hot tea with milk, and Ganges water (pumped up from the river) were distributed in stainless steel cups. Bland, overcooked vegetables devoid of spice (nothing like exotic delicacies served in Indian restaurants) were served on stainless steel trays. And reporters said Ringo couldn't handle "spicy food" at the ashram? That's a laugh!

1970 Rishikesh: Maharishi's lecture hall. *Photo courtesy of Jared Stoltz*

Lectures took place in a drafty, high-ceilinged hall with whitewashed cement walls, dirt floor covered with mats, a platform decorated with potted plants and flowers, high recessed windows where birds nested on the ledges and flew to and fro, and concrete "caves" in the basement, for cool meditations during hot weather.

Maharishi sat cross-legged on his deerskin and white-sheet-covered stuffed armchair on a raised dais before Guru Dev's picture. His microphone and flower vase rested on a white wooden coffee table. A handful of white-robed brahmacharyas (celibate disciples) assembled cross-legged on the platform.

1970: Rishikesh lecture hall. I am pictured with long hair in light-colored sari seated on floor near stage. On stage l. to r.: Jerry Jarvis, Maharishi, Brahmachari Satyanand, Brahmachari Devendra, unknown, unknown, Brahmachari Nand Kishore.
Photo courtesy of Jared Stoltz

From there, Maharishi imparted the wondrous esoteric knowledge I hungered for. I imbibed his wisdom as a calf laps up mother's milk. I sat cross-legged front and center, on a floormat between the four steps up to Maharishi's platform and a hundred chairs behind me in the hall. I stared at Maharishi like an awestruck, infatuated teenager, never averting my gaze. Drinking him in. Soaking him up. Wallowing in him.

Already enthralled with Maharishi, I became more so in this secluded, idyllic atmosphere of heavenly serenity. Just "being" was enough—with nothing to do and nowhere to go. Just "be." In love with Maharishi. In love with everything and everyone.

Quietly in love. I was stoned, mellow, in a perpetual orgasm. High on Maharishi, or high on consciousness, perhaps.

Meditating in this holy place, I drifted gently and placidly into a paradise of the mind—peaceful, deep, and euphoric. Cares vanished. Tranquility abounded. My body throbbed with blissful intensity. I meandered around pastoral surroundings, dazed and intoxicated. Fragrant flowers, lush foliage, exotic scenery, and charming creatures became all the more enchanting and ambrosial.

Generations of souls seeking spiritual enlightenment in austere caves along the Ganges pulsated in the roaring river and clamoring jungle. The mysterious echo of gurus and disciples reverberated throughout these holy lands for as long as India has existed.

Now I was part of it.

Thank you, beloved destiny, for guiding me here.

1970 Rishikesh: TM Teacher Training Course group photo.

Fellow student Susan Schmidt loved giving Maharishi flowers. Though it was winter, every night in the rose garden behind the lecture hall, she would find a rose to offer Maharishi. Often he would play with her roses during his lectures.

For several days Maharishi lectured about the absolute-unmanifest-being and the relative-manifest-duality. The big question was, "How does the absolute manifest?" Maharishi declared it was simply its inherent nature to manifest. Jim McFadden, who fancied himself a great intellect, debated with other students and became livid at Maharishi. He insisted, "It makes no sense. You can't say that."

1970 Rishikesh: group meditation. I am seated on the ground in second row, second from right, with curly hair in light-colored sari. Brahmachari Satyanand and Jerry Jarvis to right of Maharishi. Terry Gustafson, (Jojo in Beatles song "Get Back"), to left and above Maharishi. *Photo courtesy of Jared Stoltz*

Meanwhile, I watched Maharishi playing with Susan's rose. He said, "No. It's the relative and absolute, the manifest and unmanifest." Maharishi continued to drive home his point while plucking petals from the rose. With each petal he picked, the petals didn't fall into his lap. To my mind, they seemed to disappear.

With no petals left, Maharishi pointed to the stem and said, "You see, you see? The unmanifest. See? See? He cracked up with the most mischievous look on his face. As he continued pointing at the stem and saying "the unmanifest," he started laughing so hard, his whole body shook and he nearly fell off his chair.

At the end of his talk, Maharishi stood up. No rose petals fell from his dhoti. After the lecture, Susan Schmidt searched the dais. She found no petals on the floor, on his seat, or on the silk sheet covering his chair. The petals had simply vanished.

This was how Maharishi demonstrated the "manifest" and "unmanifest."

A great saint lived in a cave near Maharishi's ashram. Tat Wale Baba was born in about 1890, which would make him eighty years old, yet his body looked about thirty-five. He never cut his matted hair. He was a stern-looking character, hardened by renunciation and austere subsistence in forest life.

1969 Rishikesh: Tat Wale Baba in yoga posture at age eighty.

1969 Rishikesh: Tat Wale Baba lecturing at Maharishi's ashram. *www.gutenberg.org/Tat Wale Baba: Rishi of the Himalayas by Vincent J. Daczynski. Copyrighted; Free Use*

One sunny day a fellow student and I walked a couple of miles into the hills above Maharishi's ashram to visit Tat Wale Baba. All we found were Hindi-speaking men dressed in rags who said he wasn't there. Finally we got the message across—we wouldn't leave until we saw him.

We were invited into a cave, about twelve by fifteen feet, with a natural rock shelf he obviously used as a bed. Tat Wale Baba sat in a full lotus pose, his naked body ash smeared and his long hair in thick dreadlocks draped over his shoulders like snakes crawling onto the dirt floor. His copper-colored face emanated glorious radiance, the light that issues from a soul of profound brilliance, chiseled by asceticism, spiritual practices, and devotion to God.

"Come," he said. "You want food?"

I nodded. He muttered in Hindi to the men in rags. They brought chapattis, vegetables and rice served on banana leaves, and tea in stainless steel cups. We ate the simple repast the Indian way—with our fingers.

He invited us to meditate in two small caves about a hundred yards from his cave, down a steep hill. In a haven of infinite peace and comfort, Mother Earth enveloped me in deep silence—profoundly serene and intensely vibrant with spiritual grace and energy. My mind melted into a liquid sea, an ocean of unfathomable stillness, flooding every recess of my being.

I returned to Tat Wale Baba, who was seated outside on a rock. "Come and join me," he said. "Live in that cave and become my disciple."

I said, "I'm from Maharishi Mahesh Yogi ashram."

He got quiet for a long time, as if considering it. Then he finally said, "You are very much devoted to Maharishi."

There I am, far left, with long curly hair, looking at Maharishi. Jerry Jarvis is on the right, laughing.

I am in the far upper left corner, with long curly hair. Brahmachari Satyanand and Jerry Jarvis are to the right of Maharishi.

During the course, we celebrated the Hindu festivals Mahashivaratri (the night of the great Lord Shiva) with a candlelit ritual, and Holi (the spring festival) with a moonlight boat ride. Many students still clung to Western religion. But I was rapidly becoming a Hindu. Maybe I was a Hin-Jew, though the Jew part was vanishing.

We learned how to teach TM, give lectures, and chant the Sanskrit puja—an invocation ceremony performed whenever TM was taught, in gratitude to the "Holy Tradition," Guru Dev's lineage of masters. We were given rules regarding conservative dress code and behavior: For women, this meant modest dresses, and no trousers, jeans, or shorts. For men, this entailed suits and ties, but no beards or long hair. Maharishi was known for transforming tens of thousands of hippies into straight-laced, law-abiding TM representatives.

By the second week of April 1970, the course was officially over and nearly everyone had left the ashram. About fifteen people remained. Every night we assembled on Maharishi's bungalow roof and read passages from the *Vedas*.

One such night, electric bulbs strung on wires illumined the trees surrounding the cottage. From my vantage, the trees appeared tipped with gold. That night Maharishi drew an analogy between these trees and higher states of consciousness.

Jerry Jarvis, my Initiator and SIMS president, looked at me, speaking loudly enough for Maharishi to hear, "Some artist should paint a picture of this."

The next day I drew a rough colored-pencil sketch of dark trees illumined with golden light under a moonlit sky. I showed it to Maharishi.

He smiled and said, "Good, good. Explain."

2001: Maharishi's bungalow rooftop at his abandoned ashram in Rishikesh.

I pointed to the picture. "These trees represent states of consciousness. This tree represents Cosmic Consciousness. The second one is God Consciousness, and third is Unity."

Maharishi giggled and showed it to Brahmachari Satyanand. They laughed and spoke in Hindi. Maharishi gazed at me with sparkling ebony eyes. "Where are the people? All the people should be in the picture."

All the people on the roof that night? I thought. *There's no way! I can't do that!*

I started to say, "I don't think—"

Maharishi interrupted me. "Put all the people in the picture."

My mind couldn't wrap around such an unattainable task. Drawing all the people was entirely beyond my capabilities.

Another of Maharishi's tests. This one would continue for years.

<div style="text-align:center">~~~~~~~~~~~~~~~~~~~~~~</div>

Besides Maharishi and a few brahmacharyas, only six people remained during sweltering April. Maharishi sent us to visit the famous saint Anandamayi Ma (bliss-permeated mother). A chapter of Yogananda's book *Autobiography of a Yogi* was devoted to her.

Beside ourselves with joy, we six packed off in two taxis, bouncing along endless dirt roads, climbing into Himalayan foothills to Dehra Dun. Sitting cross-legged on a mat, we waited for darshan on the porch of the saint's house at sunset.

Anandamayi Ma finally appeared: simple, radiant, and blissful. Her ancient face, brilliant and lustrous, was carved with wisdom. She wore a plain white cotton sari with a yellow Turkish towel draped round her neck. She perched on a cotton mattress atop a wooden cot. Her husband sat down on a nearby chair. Blessings and divine grace poured from her. Visitors asked questions, which she answered in Hindi sprinkled with

Sanskrit. A German disciple informed the Blissful Mother we came from Maharishi Mahesh Yogi's ashram.

After an hour, the Blissful Mother turned to us and instructed us to convey the following message to Maharishi. She placed palms together above her forehead in *pranam* (bowing) gesture: *"Namah Narayana, Namah Narayana, Namah Narayana."* (I bow to the king of the universe.)

It wasn't until I got back to the taxicab that it hit me.

6

MELTING IN MAHARISHIVILLE

SPRING TO SUMMER 1970

It is a miraculous transformation of the personality, once one has raised one's level of breath to the level of breath of the master's heart and mind.

—Maharishi Mahesh Yogi

When I returned to the taxicab after visiting Anandamayi Ma, an enormous wave of bliss struck like lightning. Bliss was her name, and bliss was transmitted. Waves of ecstatic exhilaration filled me with a yet undiscovered depth of inner intoxication. My heart burst like sunrise, radiating joy. My body melted into a sea of flowing liquidity, peaceful and graceful. *Ananda*—bliss.

April was hot, 110 degrees of stifling jungle heat. Life was sluggish. Maharishi took us six devotees on an overnight junket to a British hill station in Mussoorie, with refreshing Himalayan breezes.

We stopped at an overlook to drink in the snowy, awe-inspiring peaks. Maharishi's gleaming dhoti fluttered in the breeze and shimmered in the sunrays. His hair flapped in the wind. I recalled *Lost Horizon* by James Hilton. Maharishi's majestic figure before the breathtaking Himalayas made me feel, *I'm in Shangri-la now. It's here, with him.*

In a Tibetan colony, hawkers sold silver jewelry, jackets, trinkets, sweaters, and boots. Smiling, rosy-cheeked Tibetans, with black straw-like hair and round brown faces leathered from harsh climate, donned colorful, embroidered cotton frocks embedded with little round mirrors.

Behind the Bamboo Curtain of Communist China, Tibet's borders were closed. Millions had been slaughtered, thousands of Buddhist monasteries destroyed. These refugees were fortunate to escape.

I felt wildly attracted to Lars, one of the six remaining in the ashram. We shared a
room overnight in Mussoorie, but nothing happened (if it had, I would have put up
no fight!). His long blond hair, thinning on top and arrow straight, fell over his right
eye and caressed his shoulders. His hazel eyes sparkled with an impish glint. Like many
on the course, he'd grown a full sandy beard and mustache. He wore lightweight white
cotton pants, a colorful long kurta shirt, and canvas sandals. His voice sing-sang with a
thick Dutch accent, and his ready, easy laugh snorted like a rebellious donkey.

Lars and I decided to take our own excursion—back to Anandamayi Ma. Just as we
arrived in Dehra Dun, the Holy Mother was boarding a taxicab. We followed her cab
along potholed dirt roads until she arrived at her new ashram, a picturesque, pristine
setting, brimming with evergreens, flowering trees, and waterways.

Anandamayi Ma: "bliss-permeated mother."
This photograph is reproduced courtesy of
Swami Nityananda

The Mother got out of her taxi and toured the property on foot, shouting orders
to construction workers. What impressed me was how much she reminded me of Maharishi, as if one and the same—constantly giggling at some cosmic joke, and that mischievous twinkle in her eyes, endlessly playing a trick on somebody.

One of her disciples told us, "You know, Ma never had a guru. She was always
God-intoxicated, even as a child. At an early age she began communicating with
spiritual beings. Those were her gurus. The guru dwells within us."

I asked him, "She contacts divine beings directly?"

"Yes, she's in God realization since very young," he replied.

I thought, *That's what I want, to hear the divine Voice.*

It was April 19, 1970. For us staying at the ashram, it was time to become Initiators. We younger course participants would become Student Initiators. We could teach people below age thirty.

Amidst a grove of trees at the edge of the bluff overlooking the Ganges, Maharishi's cottage comprised a small meeting room, tiny bedroom, bathroom, small kitchen, office, and porch above the kitchen. An outdoor staircase led directly onto the flat roof. Basement walls were tiled with Ganges rocks. In that "cave," Maharishi performed pujas.

Circa 2008, Rishikesh: Maharishi's abandoned bungalow, forty years after the Beatles visited. *Panoramio/by Achyut41*

In eager anticipation, I waited downstairs in the cave. Finally I was called into the next room and knelt clumsily on the carpet before Maharishi. He wrote a list of mantras for people under age thirty and handed it to me.

He placed his palm on top of my head. Closing my eyes, I transported into a serene, pulsating realm. Waves of deep silence flooded me with ecstasy. Bliss-struck, I opened my eyes and smiled at Maharishi, whose eyes penetrated mine, transferring a wave of rapture, vibrating spiritual energy.

I floated out of Maharishi's house, smiling, walking tall and confident. Overwhelmed by a profound upwelling of joy, my footfalls lightened. The trees, flowers, and people around me throbbed with joy. Everything around me seemed to say, "I love you."

On April 20, Maharishi was on his way to New Delhi for a few days, then to Bangalore for a TM Teacher Training course for Indians. Just as we six devotees were about to leave with him in taxicabs, I showed him my latest pencil drawing of shadowy people on the roof, Maharishi lying on a cot, and three trees in the background.

Maharishi said, "Good, good. But I need to see the people's faces. Where are their faces?"

Isn't he ever satisfied? How will I draw these faces? What I didn't understand was Maharishi had already begun working on me. As I was making new, improved versions of the picture, he was making new, improved versions of me.

Maharishi then turned to Satyanand, seated in the back seat of the taxi. "Get some paints and brushes, art supplies, whatever she needs, when we get to Delhi."

Enroute our taxicabs stopped at a restaurant. All rushed inside for lunch—all except me and Maharishi, whom I secretly observed from my taxicab. When food was brought to his car, he refused it. All he wanted was four servings of the strange concoction Indians called "Kwality Ice Cream."

Maharishi had the most dignified persona—never rushed, extremely staid, and sedate. However, I clandestinely observed him, crouched over, scarfing ice cream from paper cups with a wooden spoon, shoveling rapidly, vehemently, into his mouth. I chuckled at the incongruity of such childlike behavior from an otherwise perfectly self-controlled yogi.

Near sunset, the taxis stopped for one hour at a railroad crossing. Trains move at a turtle's pace in India, so I walked up to Maharishi's car and peered into the window.

Maharishi looked up and smiled. "Hmm?"

"Can I speak to you a moment?" I asked.

Maharishi turned to Satyanand, seated in the back seat. "Get out." Maharishi turned and looked at me. "Come, come. Sit."

I entered the back seat of Maharishi's taxi. "I can either leave India now, or I can come to Bangalore with you. Should I come to Bangalore?"

Maharishi responded with silence. He had a knack for ignoring questions, while assuming a person would make the right decision.

The gate at the railroad crossing lifted. "Drive on," Maharishi said. Satyanand, distraught, knocked on the car window. Maharishi motioned him to the next cab.

I was squeezed in the back seat of Maharishi's cab between a beautiful young woman, Vivian Dupont, and JP Srivastava—Maharishi's brother. The overweight JP occupied half the back seat, resting his head on my right shoulder, snoring. Vivian slept on my left shoulder. Fighting them off, I got no rest. Maharishi slept most of the trip. Though Vivian seemed self-absorbed, vain, and aloof, she was, mysteriously, greatly favored by Maharishi. Later I found out why.

A trip from Rishikesh to New Delhi should take six hours, but this took twelve. The taxicab kept overheating, breaking down every few miles. We reached New Delhi at 4:00 a.m. A strange juxtaposition—basking in Maharishi's darshan, sweating in 100-degree heat, and getting crushed by two passengers.

Satyanand took me to an art supply store to buy paints, brushes, and paper. *Now I have to put people's faces in the picture,* I thought. *How the heck will I do that?*

We six devotees flew with Maharishi from New Delhi to Bangalore (now Bengaluru) in South India—a city unsullied by the West, steeped in ancient traditions and spiritual vibrations. The weather was milder than Rishikesh, and a rainbow of tropical flowers bloomed.

What surprised me was the glaring absence of street beggars. Gorgeous young damsels abounded, decked in colorful shot-silk satin saris, hair braided perfectly, adorned with cascades of fragrant jasmine. An ambrosial sight and delightful scent!

We six assisted Maharishi as he taught TM Teacher Training to sixty Indian disciples. Maharishi kept us Westerners near him at all times, treating us like princes and princesses. His fountain of love, continually showering grace, never shut off. Whenever he saw me, he beckoned me to "Come, come" and sit near him.

Being loved by a God-infused master was unique. It was the first time I ever really felt loved. When he said, "Come, come," his words, like cotton candy, sweet, fragrant, and soft, melted even the most injured heart. The man I revered made me feel special. This was completely unfamiliar territory. I wanted more.

I lined up with the rest of the damaged to feed at Maharishi's exquisite love trough. His glance, his smile, his presence exuded torrents of love, sweeping every tinge of pain into wisps of nothingness, pappus fluff in the wind. All thoughts, negative, positive, or otherwise, disappeared when I was in his presence. Fears became insights. Heartache turned into joy. Insecurity became gratitude. I swam on waves of bliss in his rapturous ocean, vibrating in ecstasy.

A special Brahmin cook prepared meals for Maharishi and the six of us. We sat cross-legged on mats while delicate, delicious food and fabulous sweets were spooned onto our "plates" (sewn-together fig leaves). We chanted *"aam, aam!"* in unison to summon mangoes. We followed the Indian custom of right hand for eating and left hand for latrine activities.

Rama Rao was the first person to learn TM from Maharishi. In the group photograph on the next page, he's the dark-haired man in the back row, to the right of Guru Dev's picture. Mr. Rao invited us six to dinner. In India it's said, "Treat guests as God." So, traditionally, Indians don't eat until guests are fed. After our simple, delicious meal, prepared with so much love by Rao's wife, she presented gifts of saris to the women and dhotis to the men. I was gifted an orange cotton sari shot with black threads. I wore it for decades until it became threadbare.

May 1970: Group photo Bangalore Teacher Training course. I am seated cross-legged on ground, far right. *Photo courtesy of EGK & Son Photography, Bangalore, India*

Rama Rao reminisced about the early days. He was instrumental in helping Maharishi spread TM throughout Kerala in South India. In October 1955 a *yajna* (religious fire ceremony) took place in Cochin. He showed us the booklet *Beacon Light of the Himalayas,* which commemorated the event. It included transcripts, photographs, and a signed, handwritten message, "Maharishi's Message to Peaceless and Suffering":

"Oh ye of the peaceless and suffering humanity! My happiness desires to root out your suffering. Will you extend your arm and allow me to lift you up from the mire of misery and peacelessness? Come on, here is the call of peace and joy for you, come and enjoy the Blissful Grace and All Powerful Blessings of my Lord the Great Swami Brahmanand Saraswati, the Great among the greats of the Himalayas. I have found a treasure in the Dust of His Lotus Feet and now I invite you to share it with me and make yourself happy . . ."

In Bangalore we visited colorful Hindu temples where Maharishi lectured in Hindi. Pampered and spoiled, we six were always seated in the front row and honored as special guests—a few bratty young Westerners treated with utmost respect. But those truly deserving honor were the venerable founders of the TM Movement, like Rama Rao and Sri Venkatesham.

Late one night, Lars asked Maharishi, "Can you tell us about Guru Dev?"

Maharishi had a flair for the dramatic. His greatest oratory skill was his uncanny ability to elicit emotion from listeners. He paused and closed his eyes, as we waited with awed anticipation. Then he opened his eyes halfway, looking inside, rather than at us. Almost whispering, eyes downcast, he spoke slowly and quietly, with depth of feeling:

"All that I speak is but a reflection of his holy presence. He was living Brahman. I basked in the radiance of his presence. Such personalities as Guru Dev are born of the necessity of time."[42]

He explained that, even though all wisdom is in the Vedas, if humanity doesn't live it, it remains dormant and inaccessible. However, one man can revive it by embodying omnipresence, the fullness of wisdom. Then, from that one candle, many other candles get lit. Every generation then passes it on. "When thousands of people are living that, then this will be a world where angels will want to come. We want to leave a better world."[43]

In this way, Maharishi gave all credit to Guru Dev, in reverence. His vision was a world at peace, without suffering. He worked tirelessly daily toward fulfilling his "World Plan." He stated that the glamour of taking credit is dangerous, so we give homage to Guru Dev and to Cosmic Intelligence.

After our two-week trip to Bangalore, we returned to Rishikesh—to swelter in 115-degree heat. We stopped with Maharishi for a holy dip in the Ganges as we crossed from Haridwar. Women were required to be fully dressed in a sari or *shalwar kameez.* No swimsuits allowed.

While bathing in the Ganges, I flashed on past life memories as a *sanyasi,* bathing in the holy river. I was a man in a loincloth, thin and emaciated, smeared with ash, meditating in a cave near the riverbank. Then I was a Swami, bearded and long haired, wearing saffron robes. These memories were filled with great joy and few cares.

Back at Maharishi's ashram, everything moved slowly. It was so hot I couldn't think straight. Sitting up to meditate was difficult, even in the early morning, before the suffocating heat descended. Maharishi ordered us to stay in our rooms or his basement cave. No walking under the stifling sun allowed. No bathing in the Ganges, except early morning.

Curiously, out of us six, three shared the same name—Susan. Maharishi nicknamed each of us: Susan the Artist (Susan Shumsky), tall and uber-skinny blond with blue eyes; Susan the Singer (Susan Ballantine), tall, blond, porcelain-skinned, full-figured, with glasses and buck teeth; and Susan the Thinker (Susan Schmidt), short, stout, with short black curly hair. After this, Maharishi always called me Susan the Artist. A few weeks later, Maharishi changed Susan the Thinker's name to Susan the Great.

In June the summer heat yielded to monsoon. I was sitting with Maharishi in his bungalow. Suddenly a terrible wind erupted. His door flapped and clanked. The shutters banged. Rain began to pound in torrents.

Maharishi said excitedly, "Come, come." Up the stairs he ran. I followed him to the enclosed porch above the kitchen. He jumped about like a rabbit—atypical for his formal, dignified persona. He grabbed a mattress propped against the wall and dragged it to a window overlooking the garden. He said, "Come. Sit."

Sitting side by side on the mattress, we looked out over the ashram landscape. The trees were dancing and writhing violently, ripped by the wind. Rain poured a deluge. Mud splattered everywhere in an awesome display. We watched in silence for a long time.

Maharishi turned to me and said, "Such a terrible force in nature. What can man do? Just be a witness to it."

I didn't speak. A million volts of electricity bolted through my body. My mind became a pool of molten gold. I wanted to sit near Maharishi, gaze into his eyes, and drink in his vibe forever. My senses were awake and alive as never before. *To breathe the air that he's breathing*, I thought. *That's all that matters now.*

Maharishi leaned over and patted my head lightly. My eyes could no longer remain open. I sank into deep silence. The world disappeared. Nothing was left but a typhoon of bliss ripping through my body, cleansing and purifying every pore. Then I disappeared. Nothing remained but bliss. An ocean of ecstasy in waves of bliss.

Dumbstruck, melted into a tidal wave of nothingness, my eyes remained glued shut for an indeterminate time. What broke the spell was Susan the Great tromping loudly up the stairs, yelling, "Maharishi, Maharishi, where are you?" Soon afterward Vivian came upstairs to further spoil my beatific mood.

I struggled with yet another version of my painting of the trees and people on the roof. When I showed it to Maharishi, his comment: "I should be sitting up instead of lying down. And it should be bigger."

Though I was growing weary of restarting the painting repeatedly, I began a new version. One day, Maharishi asked me to bring it to his cave under his house. There he dictated a commentary, entitled "A Vision of Cosmic Consciousness, God Consciousness, and Unity Consciousness on a Moonlit Night with Maharishi."

I returned to my room, to complete a bigger painting. But when he saw this new version, his comment was, "I want to see who the people are. I want to be able to recognize them."

My heart sank again. *This is really beyond the pale. How can I possibly do this?* It seemed, no matter how many times I revised the painting, Maharishi would always ask for improvements. I didn't know his motive was to stretch my boundaries so I could express more potential as an artist, and ultimately, as a human being. Whenever he described his relationship with disciples, he equated himself to a carpenter, and his disciples to pieces of wood. He was whittling me into the real me.

The great female "hugging saint" who bestows grace upon thousands of devotees daily, Amritananda Mayi (Ammachi) said, "When the disciple approaches the Master, he is raw, rusty, primitive. The Master, the infinitely loving, divine alchemist, transforms the disciple into pure gold." [44]

I searched my memory, straining to paint a recognizable portrait of each person on the roof that night. I used the course group photograph as reference. For several portraits, I closed my eyes and attempted to visualize people's faces. I worked diligently, but didn't finish.

◦◦◦◦◦◦◦◦◦◦◦◦◦◦◦◦◦◦◦◦◦◦◦◦

Every new project animated and excited Maharishi. His eager enthusiasm for each moment and every person resembled a baby's thrills for daily new discoveries of life's wonders. One afternoon he called me to his cave and said, "This is the ashram we will build in Bhopal."

"Where's Bhopal?" I asked.

"Central India. A devotee donated some land to Maharishi," Susan the Great chimed in. Maharishi then showed me elaborate colorful drawings he'd made with felt-tipped marking pens.

"Can you make drawings of this ashram? This is how it should look." Maharishi described the ashram in detail and handed me his scribbled drawings and contour land maps.

Entirely overwhelmed, with zero knowledge about construction or architecture, I retreated to my room. Next day I returned to Maharishi's cave with felt-tipped-pen-drawn pictures that resembled his own amateurish scribbles. He raised his eyebrows in obvious wonder at my massive incompetence.

"The pictures should be line drawings, side view and top views," Maharishi said, "like this." He handed me some architectural renderings.

Maharishi had much more faith in me than I had in myself. Frustrated and distraught, I could foresee no pathway whereby my blatant absence of architectural training would deliver anything remotely approaching a positive result. Though I was a pretty good artist, there were definite limits conferred by a certain lack of education. Perhaps Maharishi saw something in me I couldn't see.

I handed the architectural renderings back to Maharishi, and said, sarcastically, "Maharishi, I'm an artist, not a landscape architect." Maharishi no longer called me to his cave, and he gave me no more assignments. This was just one of many tests I failed.

7

BEES TO HONEY

1970 TO 1972

The purpose of the relationship is to imbibe more and more of the master's heart, mind, and being into the disciple's being, just as the purpose of the gushing of the river towards the ocean is to own the whole of the ocean.

—MAHARISHI MAHESH YOGI

Willing to try any spiritual adventure with unbending resolve, I'd received the unheard-of blessing of staying with Maharishi and only five others for several months. That was the last opportunity a small group had close proximity to him for such extended time.

In June 1970, we six fortunate devotees waited in the New Delhi Airport to fly to the Italian Alps, where Maharishi would lead an Initiators-only course. For the past six months, we'd dwelt in a cocoon of pure love—far from the tense, all-businesslike West. So when Lufthansa pilots and stewardesses appeared in stiff uniforms and rigid, synthetic personae, the shock of reentry into callous Western civilization descended upon us. We could feel paradise slipping away.

At six thousand feet, Livigno ski resort was nestled in a valley of rolling hills encircled by alpine peaks. In this halcyon setting, our magic carpet ride of favoritism came to a screeching halt. We were just six out of hundreds of Initiators. We found ourselves demoted to a pension down the road, far from Maharishi's lodgings (except Vivian, that is).

For reasons unknown, I distanced myself from Maharishi and hung out with Lars, my Dutch crush. Was it because I felt ultimately undeserving of Maharishi's incessant, intense blast of divine love? Perhaps I subconsciously sought to revisit more familiar territory—pain, guilt, loneliness, unrequited love. Lars fit the bill for such dalliances with rejection.

At the end of the course, Maharishi asked me, "Coming to America with me?"

I replied, "No. I'm going to Holland. I want to do some sightseeing." Maharishi's eyes twinkled and he chortled in cynicism. I was busted. I could never hide anything from him.

As soon as I got to Amsterdam, I realized my blunder. Cool and distant, Lars spent little time with me. My only consolation was visiting the Rijksmuseum to see works of my favorite painter, Vermeer.

∞∞∞∞∞∞∞∞∞∞∞∞∞∞∞∞∞∞∞∞∞∞

After my Dutch misadventure, I joined Maharishi in August 1970 for his one-month course at Humboldt State University in Arcata, California. Opting for my silly Holland side trip didn't endear me to him. He revoked my insider-privilege welcome mat. Though Maharishi bubbled with love and laughed frequently, he was a strict, severe, exacting master with zero tolerance for less than 100 percent focus.

Fully determined to return to Maharishi's graces, I cooked him Indian sweets and sneaked into his house, to the chagrin of Jerry Jarvis's wife, Debby. Soon I was banned altogether. She didn't easily forgive see-through blouses worn in my former hippie incarnation.

I managed to worm my way into transcribing videotapes of the Humboldt course. Fortunately, in September Maharishi invited our group to meet him in Santa Barbara, where he was planning to build a meditation academy.

The property lay on a mountaintop with breathtaking views of the ocean. We drove up the steep road to explore it. Maharishi stepped out of the car and his dhoti flapped in the wind, clinging to his body. A gust whistled through the pines. His beads tangled in his hair, flying wildly in the gale. He shivered. "What a cold place" was his only comment.

It turned out the property was never used—no water for a well.

At the end of my visit, Maharishi said, "Come, come." I knelt on the floor as he reclined on a couch. (In India, disciples sit with eyes lower than their guru and never point their feet at him.) Those penetrating ebony eyes transmitted divine energy as he said, "Come to Estes Park. I'll be teaching Teacher Training Course. Come and teach meditation in Denver while I'm there. You can visit me whenever you like."

Apparently, Maharishi couldn't teach in Rishikesh anymore due to tax problems, and Estes Park would be his first course outside India.

I glowed with happiness.

∞∞∞∞∞∞∞∞∞∞∞∞∞∞∞∞∞∞∞∞∞∞

Upon arriving in Colorado in October, I discovered my parents had trashed all my possessions. But resentment didn't stop me from unceremoniously invading their home and using their good graces for my own purposes. I stayed with them, established a TM Center in Denver, and visited Maharishi in Estes Park often.

I offered an introductory lecture at a university. *The Denver Post* ran a story and three hundred people showed up. As I initiated the new students, my mind expanded and heart flowed with compassion. My forehead and crown buzzed with blissful energy. The presence of the Holy Tradition of masters became palpable. Guru Dev was the main ingredient in that spiritual mélange. The room sank deeper into silence and turned milky white. My mind expanded to dwell on many higher levels—all ecstatic.

By sunset, I finished leading twenty people into their first TM experience. I said to my fellow course Instructor, "If this is what it's like to initiate, then *bring on the people.* I could really get used to doing this!"

However much I loved initiating, with Estes Park nearby, the main thing on my mind was getting near Maharishi. To this end, each weekend I sped recklessly up treacherous, winding mountain roads at breakneck speed in my parents' big white Buick. I always brought homemade Indian sweets and a handmade rose garland to drape around Maharishi's neck.

In the hushed atmosphere of Maharishi's log cabin in the snow, he would meet Jerry Jarvis (head of SIMS), Charlie Lutes (head of SRM), another TM leader, or would be alone. His unfathomable love, grace, and deep silence permeated the small rustic dwelling, set amidst spruce and fir. In this still, silent landscape, I hovered in suspended time and space, intoxicated by the ambrosia of his charismatic presence.

If Maharishi was still in his bedroom when I arrived, I helped "Susan the Singer" clean the cabin or helped the cook Anthony Romano prepare lunch. Anthony was one of many I had introduced to TM.

During one visit, I lugged my latest version of the painting of rooftop and trees in Rishikesh. Maharishi said, "Good, good. I still can't recognize everyone's face. I want to be able to name each person."

I groaned inwardly. *Not again!* But I said nothing. I half smiled, half grimaced. By painting the picture over and over, I was doing what I couldn't possibly do, expanding my boundaries. But I realized Maharishi might never declare the painting "done."

Sufi guru Radha Mohan Lal told his disciple Irina Tweedie, "Whatever you do I will always tell you that *it is nothing* and you should do more! Otherwise how will you get rid of the shaitan of pride?"[45]

After three months in Estes Park, in December 1970 Maharishi left for Teacher Training Courses in Mallorca, Spain. I followed him in a mad dash to catch his plane. Sometimes I drove next to him and waved, speeding at eighty miles per hour. His comment when we arrived at Stapleton Airport: "Susan, you are really a good driver!" He smiled and gave me a rose.

I spent the next year in Denver, developing the TM Center. Jerry Jarvis promoted me to "Regional Coordinator" of Colorado, New Mexico, Arizona, Wyoming, and Utah. I traveled around the area, organizing and teaching meditation courses.

Maharishi returned to Humboldt in August 1971. But getting near him was difficult. The innocent days of India and Estes Park were over. A new group, the "International Staff," seemed very important. They appeared to have unlimited access to Maharishi. So I became absolutely determined to join the Staff.

At the end of the course, I approached Maharishi. "I want to travel with you to Austria and Spain, to take your courses in Europe. I've saved $2000."

"Where you got all that money, hmm?" he asked.

"I earned it teaching TM," I replied. Maharishi seemed incredibly surprised. I continued, "I want to take these courses, then stay and work on International Staff."

He asked, "What you will do?"

I replied, "Anything," gazing at him with entreating, starry eyes.

"Very good. Come and take the courses. Then work on Staff. Tell Debby to arrange your flight to Austria."

When I found Debby Jarvis, her eyes shot bullets at me. "I'll have to ask Maharishi about that," she scoffed.

Despite Debby's resistance, I was on the list for the plane to Austria via England. My greatest desire was to live in Maharishi's presence, so he was ever willing to say yes. It was up to me to make the most of this gift.

<hr>

In September 1971, we arrived in Kössen, Austria—quaint, clean, and pristine. Picture-postcard Tyrolean chalets with pitched roofs and slatted gables abounded. Wooden balconies lined with flower boxes spanned each building's entire frontage. The dark wood upper floors contrasted sharply with white plastered first floors, decorated with Gothic script and colorful insignias.

Kössen was like a scene from *The Sound of Music* movie set, where we might burst into song anytime and frolic about wildflowers on emerald rolling hills crowned by snowcapped mountains.

Maharishi assigned me to a pension closest to his chalet. Washing his clothing became my excuse to hang around him. I tried the industrial ironing machine in the basement. That was a mess. The silk came out stiff and starched. The way to successfully iron silk was to handwash it and iron while wet. Then it came out unwrinkled, shimmering, soft, and perfect.

Maharishi's dhoti (robes) consisted of two large pieces of silk. His were quite threadbare. New ones were immediately ordered from India. His loincloth comprised two strips of white silk. He tied one around his waist, the other around his crotch. His *lungi* (lower garment), about four meters of unsewn white silk, wrapped around his waist like a sarong. His *angavastram* (upper garment) draped about his shoulders like a shawl. Both of these tucked nicely into the waistband of his loincloth.

To maintain celibacy, a monk's loincloth holds his genitals in place. The penis is lifted up and testicles are pushed back while the loincloth is tied tightly around the crotch. This theoretically prevents night ejaculations and other unmentionable energy losses.

Maharishi's *shahtoosh* shawl, or "ring shawl," could be pulled through a finger ring due to its fine material. Yet the shawl kept Maharishi so warm, he never wore a coat. Touching this shawl was like caressing heaven or falling into a cloud. For one shawl (if you could get one, since they've been illegal since 1977) four to five Tibetan antelopes *(chiru* or *tsoe)* are slaughtered for their under-fleece, since they're wild and can't be sheared.

As I cleaned Maharishi's bathroom, I discovered exotic unidentifiable items. Years later I learned the weird, u-shaped, stainless steel thingamajig was a tongue scraper. And what about bronze cake makeup? It was to conceal his large white leukoderma spot on his right temple. He parted his hair on the left to hide it. Whenever the wind blew, he held his hair next to his temple on the right to prevent exposing the mark.

In 1975, when a skin-boy (nickname for personal secretaries who carried around Maharishi's deerskin and clock) from Canada named Edward requested that I buy bronze-colored makeup for "one of Maharishi's female guests," I replied, "I know exactly who the makeup is for. I used to have a job like yours, cleaning Maharishi's bathroom."

I wasn't sure which revelation Edward, dumbfounded and aghast, was more horrified about—that I knew Maharishi's secret, or that I'd ever had a job like his!

Back in Kössen, in addition to cleaning, I prepared Maharishi's meals with Mrs. Whitestone, an Initiator from Brighton, England. However, Maharishi's scrawny cook Dunraj soon showed up, and we were out of a job.

<hr />

Every day after Maharishi's lectures, I joined the small group gathered at his house. One day he said, "Susan, help Miriam edit the Symposium book."

The book consisted of excerpts from the summer 1971 International Symposium on the Science of Creative Intelligence at University of Massachusetts and Humboldt State College. The lineup of speakers included Buckminster Fuller and Nobel laureate chemist Melvin Calvin.

This project was the last thing I wanted to do. In my mind, Miriam Jacobs was a self-serving tyrant. Still, I did my assignment dutifully. I edited copy. She treated me like a speck of dirt.

Miriam waited outside Maharishi's door to read her book to him. She didn't invite me, but with sheer determination and *sitzplatz*, I got into the room by staying joined at her hip. Miriam started by reading a quote from Bucky Fuller: "Science, at its beginnings, starts with *a priori,* absolute mystery, within which there loom these beautiful behavior patterns of the physical universe where the reliabilities are eternal."[46]

At some point Miriam read the section I wrote.

Maharishi commented, "Very good. Very well written."

Miriam smiled. "Thank you."

It was the only section Maharishi praised. However, Miriam didn't bother to tell him *I* edited it. My wishful thinking believed he must know who wrote it. *He knows everything, doesn't he?* No, Maharishi didn't know everything. But he did know I had a facility for editing. Even I wasn't aware of that.

Which reminds me of *The TM Book* by Peter McWilliams and Denise Denniston, published in 1975. I happened to be in Maharishi's room when he first browsed through it. He looked at me directly and said, emphatically, "Such cartoon books you should never write." How did he know I would ever write any book? After all, I was "Susan the Artist." Now I've authored fourteen books.

<hr />

One afternoon I was visiting Maharishi's house. As usual, he was working on some project. Day and night he gave lectures or held court to staff and visitors, working incessantly without a moment's rest. He slept one to three hours. Then the merry-go-round/circus started again.

Once we got through Maharishi's door, it was bad form to leave before he dismissed us. Also, if we left, we ran the risk of not getting back in.

This time I had a problem. I was on my menstrual cycle. My periods were hideous. I bled profusely and had to change napkins often. My napkin was soaked through. There wasn't another. *My skirt might get stained,* I thought. *Maybe even the floor. If I leave, he'll think I'm rude. If I stay, I'll make a mess. Oh God, more blood!*

Suddenly Maharishi asked, "What is that smell?"

"What smell?" Maharishi's secretary asked. He sniffed.

I sniffed. *What smell?* I wondered.

Maharishi continued his work. He didn't pursue it. After about ten minutes he asked again, "What's that smell?"

"What smell are you talking about, Maharishi?" someone asked. Maharishi said nothing.

"I don't smell anything," another person said.

Maharishi's secretary said, "I'll open the window." A frigid wind swept through the room.

He continued working another fifteen minutes. Suddenly he asked, "What is that smell?" Then Maharishi turned to me, fixed his eyes on mine, and scowled with disdain. Why was he shooting daggers at me?

8

MAHARISHI MERRY-GO-ROUND

1971 TO 1972

A very tender, delicate field on which the disciple lives his life at the feet of his master. In its flexibility of tenderness, the link is absolutely stable, unshakable. On that firm basis, happenings come and go, but his mind is not on the happenings.

—MAHARISHI MAHESH YOGI

After Maharishi glared at me, I thought, *My God. Is he talking about my menstrual blood?* I sprang to my feet, barreled out of the room, and tore back to my pension, in horror that I'd tainted his refined, holy atmosphere with my repulsive, vile femaleness.

I examined my undergarments. *Yes, my napkin is soaked, but no blood is on my underwear, panty hose, or skirt. How could Maharishi smell the blood? Nobody else did.* If Maharishi could detect this from his couch, about fifteen feet from me, his sense of smell was mindboggling.

At the end of the course, Maharishi arranged an entourage to drive from Austria through the Alps to Italy, France, and Spain. Maharishi assigned everyone to a luxurious Mercedes—everyone, that is, except me, who was demoted to the back seat of a rusty blue Fiat with a German couple and their dog.

Driving through the Alps day after day, whenever Maharishi spied me in the back seat with the dog, he glared with contempt and broke into uproarious laughter. Though Maharishi's mangy dog Peter slept under his cot in Rishikesh, he publicly declared pets inferior creatures that drained our energy. So I was mortified. And though I kept pushing the damn thing away, she kept climbing on me, sleeping on my lap.

But what wasn't funny, the dog was in *heat*, bleeding all over the back seat and all over me. And Maharishi guffawed at me constantly, as if saying, "Your female offensiveness is so disgusting that you deserve this filthy car with this bitch bleeding all over you."

Was this punishment, or some mysterious poetic justice?

∞∞∞∞∞∞∞∞∞∞∞∞∞∞∞∞∞∞∞

Maharishi's passport disallowed entry into France, so he abandoned our caravan in favor of a plane. My task became driving a Mercedes to Spain. One passenger was Maharishi's chief graphic artist—Reginald Brooks, a tall, dark-haired, British, stunningly handsome, Peter Lawford lookalike, with distinctive features and square jaw. I was enchanted by his charming, cultured, refined nature.

We sped through French vineyards over country roads thickly canopied by sycamores said to be planted during Napoleon's reign, stopping at charming country inns to indulge in rich French delicacies. Then over the Pyrenees into Spain, where the landscape changed to white stucco houses and red tile roofs.

My crew and I put our vehicle on a barge and landed safely on the island of Mallorca. But one of the Mercedes headed for Mallorca didn't quite make it. The skin-boy driving it took a wrong turn, down some steps, and landed in the ocean. Kerplunk!

Maharishi would spend October 1971 to April 1972 at Hotel Samoa, Calas de Mallorca, amidst palm trees near the rugged, rocky Cala Antena coastline, dotted by hearty bushes and white sand beaches.

∞∞∞∞∞∞∞∞∞∞∞∞∞∞∞∞∞∞∞

Earlier that year, in April 1971, Maharishi's previous course in Mallorca had been the site of an international incident. A somber, uber-earnest devotee with thick eyeglasses and shaggy, overgrown mustache, Brendan Sutton was famous for hardly ever speaking or completing any sentence. Of course, he was assigned by Maharishi to man the course "Information Desk."

On April 23, 1971, John Lennon and Yoko Ono suddenly appeared at the desk to "collect" Yoko's seven-year-old daughter Kyoko Chan Cox. The child's father Anthony Cox and his wife Melinda Kendall were meditating on the course. Cox had custody of Kyoko, but a battle raged over visitation rights. [47]

Though John and Yoko wore dumb disguises, everyone recognized them immediately—including the Spanish hotel manager, whom we dubbed "Señor Bullfrog" (due to his constant croak of "Hola! Hola! Dígame! Dígame!" at peak pitch when answering the phone).

Needless to say, the Lennons got nothing out of Brendan. Señor Bullfrog called skin-boy Gregory to the desk to meet "Mr. and Mrs. Smith." When faced with John and Yoko, a gobsmacked, speechless Gregory was incapable of uttering a word.

Yet someone pointed the Lennons in the right direction, because they kidnapped Kyoko from daycare at 1:00 p.m. Cox reported the abduction to the Guardia Civil. By 5:00 p.m. John and Yoko were arrested in Palma at Hotel Melia Mallorca. By 8:00 p.m., Kyoko was returned to her father. The Lennons received a conditional discharge and flew to Paris.[48, 49]

When I first arrived in Mallorca that October, John and Yoko's dramas were furthest from my mind. I was focused solely on Maharishi. I felt I'd definitely *arrived*—in my farfetched, infantile fantasy, anyway. I enjoyed exclusive access to Maharishi's private floor, available only to International Staff. He gave me a job assigning rooms to Teacher Training Course participants. However, since I was paying my way, I asked if I could take the course. He answered, "Good, good. Begin rounding. And where is your sari? Saris you should wear every day."

"Even here in Spain?"

"Yes, every day," he responded.

From that moment on, I always wore a sari around Maharishi. First I slipped on my *choli* (sari blouse)—short-sleeved, skin-tight, cropped at the midriff. I stepped into a long cotton petticoat and knotted the drawstring. I wrapped the fabric, tucked it in, and pinned the pleats to my petticoat using two giant safety pins. If I didn't, all the material would unravel onto the floor—awkward! I was over 5'9" tall, and saris were designed for short Indian women who could tuck a foot of fabric into their petticoats. I squeezed bangles onto my wrists and slid my feet into delicate thonged sandals.

My simple cotton saris weren't expensive, but I took pride in how I wrapped them. Since I possessed zero self-esteem, at least I could be proud of something. Western women draped saris abominably—ankles showing, messy pleats, uneven hemline, draped too loose, clunky shoes, *pallu* (loose end) hanging too long. No Indian would be caught dead like that.

Once word got around that Maharishi told me to wear saris, a fashion trend developed. So I taught the Staff women proper sari-wrapping etiquette.

As I embarked on my stringent meditation program, I often heard Maharishi's laughter drifting down from his meeting room—right above my room. I wondered, *Should I have continued working rather than enter the rounding program? Did I make a mistake? What will happen after the course? Will Maharishi still let me join International Staff?*

One night in the lecture hall, Maharishi said, "This time is precious. No socializing. Focus only on one thing—experience of transcendent. Set up a section in dining room for silence." He told us our lifespan is measured in breaths. The contract for this body is limited to a specific number. If we breathe less, we live longer. "Don't waste energy. Be in silence as much as possible."

I went overboard, as per my typical trying-to-prove-I-mattered compulsions. Whenever I committed to something, I leapt before I looked—with both feet. So for four months I uttered no sound. I emerged from my room only for dinner and Maharishi's lectures. A badge pinned to my sari blouse announced, "IN SILENCE."

I ate lunch on my balcony—a little yogurt and fruit. From that vantage, a distant picturesque Mediterranean cove gleamed deep blue-green, sharply contrasting with the translucent sand and whitewashed houses. Sunlight danced like sparkling crystals on the water.

I loved meditation so much! I was on a perpetual high, in perfect equilibrium of mind and body (samadhi), deep, quiet, fathomless, at peace in the wholeness of being—more profound than ever imagined. Absorbed in silence, I abandoned all traces of the outer world, which blurred into faded obscurity. Nothing in that world was real. Like a cardboard cartoon cutout, it was empty, devoid of meaning. Maharishi was my world now. No longer did earthly pursuits hold any allure. Even if I wanted to go back (which I emphatically didn't), I couldn't. There was nothing to return to. That world was dead.

∞∞∞∞∞∞∞∞∞∞∞∞∞∞∞∞∞

Every day, as Maharishi headed toward the Mercedes to be chauffeured to Teacher Training Courses held at nearby hotels, I offered him a rose. Sometimes he gave me one. One day no car waited. Never fazed by anything, he said, "Fine, we'll walk there." So Maharishi, Gregory Ivanov, Keith Wallace, and I started walking toward his destination in Cala Millor—fifteen miles away.

Maharishi's skin-boy Gregory, said, "I better go find the car." He handed Maharishi's deerskin to Keith, a UCLA- and Harvard-trained neurophysiologist who conducted research on TM published in *Science, American Journal of Physiology,* and *Scientific American.*

After five minutes, Maharishi said to Keith, "Better go check on the car." So, with Maharishi's deerskin draped over my arm and my "IN SILENCE" badge pinned to my blouse, I strolled with him into the darkness. The only sound was our sandals crunching the gravel path.

Ten minutes later, Gregory and Keith picked us up. Off we drove to Hotel Karina, where several hundred students meditated ten to twelve hours per day for nine months.

In the lecture hall, Maharishi asked, "How many woke up early this morning?" Then, "How many looked out the window?" He chuckled and went on with his lecture. It turned out at breakfast several students had related seeing a disk-shaped UFO from their balconies, hovering over the ocean near a cliff. This UFO appeared to be sucking water out of the ocean and dumping it back again. When asked about it, Maharishi said, "It was a cosmic vacuum cleaner," and then dropped the subject.

Imagine thousands of people from every background and country meditating all day for months—a recipe for disaster. Maharishi assigned freak-out cases to two physicians, from the US and Germany, but the need became overwhelming. So he posted trusted disciples Carl Webb, Leonard Campbell, and Jim McFadden on psych-ward duty. Christening themselves the "Lunch-Wing Squad," they took turns dealing with meditation casualties, whom they dubbed "Lunch-Wings."

Ludwig was a small, intelligent, cultured German doctor who spoke perfect English. But when Carl and Leonard entered his room, the face of a demon glowered back at them. Ludwig sat shirtless with muscles so taut it appeared he could rip someone's head off. He hissed like a snake with eyeballs rolling around in his head. He was stabbing the air at lightning speed, right, left, right, left, while pointing index fingers like darts.

Ludwig's girlfriend Irma was sitting on the bed. Suddenly Ludwig jumped up, grabbed her head, and tried to crack it like an egg. Leonard and Carl tackled him and wrestled him away from her. Ludwig and Irma then sat on separate beds, and both began hissing, stabbing the air, and darting their index fingers.

Leonard didn't believe in demons and hadn't gotten the memo yet on *The Exorcist*. He was way out of his depth. So he ran to Maharishi's room and cried, "Ludwig seems possessed. I don't know what to do."

Maharishi told him, "Get Big Nurse." Leonard fetched Liz Collins, a British nurse of great height and girth.

Thundering like an elephant, Big Nurse barged into Ludwig's room clutching a large glass of water. Thrusting the glass at Ludwig, she bellowed, "Here, drink this." He shook his head and hissed. She repeated more forcefully. He continued hissing.

Then she grabbed Ludwig's neck and forced water down his throat. He had no choice. Either he would drink or drown. Big Nurse emptied the entire glass of water while he choked and coughed. When it was over, he lay back on his bed, entirely calm. Strangely, his girlfriend Irma stopped hissing also and settled down.

Fernando, an Initiator from Sacramento, was married with a young child. He moved his mistress Sophia into his home with his wife and child, and treated Sophia like a slave. But she was weak and allowed it. Sophia started seeing other men, which made Fernando insanely jealous. She told him to leave her alone, but he followed her to Mallorca.

While Sophia was attending Maharishi's lecture, Fernando broke into her room in Hotel Karina. Using a scissors, he cut out the crotches from all her underwear. He burned the crotches of the remainder of her clothing with a candle. Soon her room was on fire. The hotel personnel used fire extinguishers to quell the blaze. The hotel was evacuated and fire department summoned.

Later Carl and Leonard discovered, in the hotel basement, an altar with Guru Dev's picture garlanded with a string of crotches. Other crotches were strewn about the altar.

When Tod spoke, what came out was gibberish. When the Lunch-Wing Squad ordered him to return home, he struck a bargain. Tod would demonstrate his special superpowers for nine minutes to the entire assembly. Leonard promised to inform people, with no guarantee of attendance.

Tod claimed he could see in all directions at once and walk in every direction at once without ever tiring, using alleged wisdom from ancient Rome that he professed to have "cognized." The Lunch-Wing Squaders gathered for the demonstration.

The handsome, black, athletic, muscular Tod undressed and stood in the buff. He began looking forward, back, right, left, up, down, between his legs to the back, and every other direction and angle. Repeating this procedure more and more quickly, he whipped his body around so fast he could indeed see every direction. Tod's second demonstration was a kind of goosestep where he walked forward, back, side to side, so fast it appeared he was walking in all directions at once.

The Lunch-Wing Squad put him on a plane back to the USA and celebrated his departure.

Edwin's obsessive habit was "sewing" his head. Holding an imaginary needle and thread in his right hand, he pushed the needle through the bottom of his chin and pulled it out through various points on top of his head. He repeated the same motion with his left hand. This compulsive behavior continued incessantly.

Edwin was predisposed to wandering about the hotel buck naked. His Taoist revelation led him to rip a lamp off the wall in the hallway. He bent the brass arms of the candelabra until the "yin" and "yang" lights merged into oneness. As they merged, Edwin was electrocuted and fell backward against the door of an unsuspecting female meditator who screamed as his naked body flung backward into her room.

The Lunch-Wingers somehow managed to put Edwin on a plane. As the plane took off, they breathed a sigh of relief. However, unknown to them, Edwin wasn't on that plane. When the passenger next to him complained he was compulsively sewing his head, he was expelled and handed off to the Policia Municipal.

Edwin spoke no Spanish, so no one could figure out who he was. He was carted off to a psychiatric hospital and locked up for months, until someone finally deciphered his identity and contacted his parents, who came to collect him.

Marvin was a black guy who did pujas naked in the hotel hallway. He wandered about, yelling about being enlightened and God's messenger. Maharishi told the Lunch-Wing Squad to keep him calm until they could get him on a plane. Then he would be someone else's problem. At the airport the Lunch-Wingers warned him to keep his clothes on and make no loud speeches on the plane. They waited half an hour. When the plane didn't return, "Success," they thought. But over the Atlantic Ocean, Marvin charged the cockpit, screaming about his girlfriend and Maharishi. He was restrained. The Lunch-Wingers figured if they could get these maniacs to shut up for most of the flight's duration, the plane would arrive in New York and not return to Europe.

Joshua Kramer, highly paranoid draft dodger extraordinaire, on the FBI Wanted List, trembled at every border crossing. He was the most unlikely candidate to smuggle a suitcase from Spain to Switzerland with thousands of course participants' currency and checks to be deposited into the Swiss bank account. Naturally, he was Maharishi's man for the job. Joshua's jittery demeanor resulted in a complete strip search at a Spanish airport. His suitcase was confiscated and he went to jail.

Maharishi sent his trusted Brahmachari Devendra and international accountant Mary Connelly to negotiate Joshua's release. Days later, two skin-boys were dispatched to Madrid with a plain brown envelope in a briefcase. A limousine with Spanish flags on the bumper greeted them at the airport and whisked them downtown to a palatial government building.

The skin-boys entered a massive corral where Spanish horses had been trained long ago. They were served tea and cakes at a ginormous wooden table occupied by Devendra, Mary, and none other than General Francisco Franco, the Spanish military dictator, with his minions. All were bedizened in formal uniforms with gold and red sashes, gold medals, epaulets dripping with gold bullion fringe, and spun gold thickly embroidered on collars, lapels, and cuffs. After some small talk, Franco asked if they brought the "documents." The skin-boys didn't know what was inside the brown envelope until Franco's lackeys counted out the dough—$50,000 cash.

Joshua was returned to Mallorca, safe and sound, the following day.

After Joshua's bloody debacle, Maharishi assigned his trusted, dedicated skin-boy Gregory to smuggle course fees out of Spain. The first time Gregory withdrew cash from the bank at Palma de Mallorca, the stacks of pesetas wouldn't fit into a suitcase. They were delivered in a cafeteria cart. Within ten minutes everyone in Mallorca knew about it. So Gregory skulked to the far end of the island, sailed to Formentera, then flew from Ibiza to Geneva.

On subsequent trips, Gregory would fly to France or Italy before proceeding to Switzerland. He smuggled at least $500,000 per trip. When Gregory traveled, his only diversion was visiting museums. Unbelievably, since he always took the cash-stuffed suitcase with him, he would often check it at the entrance to the Louvre with a hat-check woman! Of course, she was unaware of its contents. After a while, with help from Maharishi's influential devotees, a limousine would meet Gregory at the airport in Geneva and bypass customs.

∞∞∞∞∞∞∞∞∞∞∞∞∞∞∞∞∞∞∞∞∞∞

Meanwhile, I was unaware of all these dramas. Deep meditation in silence had made me mellow to the point of stoned, barely functional, advancing toward cataleptic. I floated around the hotel in a bubble of blissful nothingness, nothing to think, nothing to do. Blithe and content, I wafted through my days like a helium balloon drifting happily in the breeze.

But now it was time to come out.

At lunch I came across Reginald, Maharishi's graphic artist.

"Hey, Susan. You're not wearing your badge. Are you out of silence?" Reginald asked in his British accent.

"Yep," I mumbled. It was difficult making my vocal chords vibrate.

"Well, what did you experience? It's been a long time, hasn't it? A couple of months?"

"Four," I whispered, barely audible.

"What did you say?" he asked.

"Four. Four months."

"Four months? Egads, time does fly, doesn't it?"

"Yep."

"Well how's your painting of the trees coming along? Have you been working on it?"

"Yeah," I rasped.

"I'd like to see it. Susan, you can speak now, you know. You're allowed to make whole sentences. Time to be congenial."

"Nothing . . ." I cleared my throat. "Nothing to say."

It was difficult to complete a sentence, let alone make small talk. Four months of silence taught me what comes out of our mouths is mostly trite drivel. We talk just to hear ourselves talk, or feed our egos. I concluded it's better to keep quiet unless there's something to say.

During silence I'd completed the painting of the rooftop and trees in Rishikesh. When I showed it to Reginald, he recognized all the people and said, "This is great, Susan. You must show it to Maharishi."

I had a crush on Reginald, but kept it secret. I felt such scandalous feelings were sinful when Maharishi advised us to be celibate. He'd said: "What is brahmacharya? If you keep on collecting and investing wealth, it gets collected. If you keep on spending it, money gets spent and never comes back. Then when hard times come, nothing is there. When you waste energy, nothing is left. Thinking is not powerful and practical. Your life is not brilliant. Your face becomes dull. Conserve energy and become powerful.[50]

Maharishi contended only a powerful nervous system and brain could stabilize unbounded consciousness. Celibacy maintains upward flow of life energy, channeling it into "the most delicate, useful, and precious product of life—*ojas*."[51] This divine radiance emanates from our skin, making our body lustrous and vibrant.

Ojas gets produced this way: Food becomes blood, which becomes marrow, which becomes semen (or rajas—female fluid), which becomes ojas.[52] This sweet oily substance appears on our face during long meditation. I experienced it firsthand. Bathing before meditation, not after, was recommended due to ojas production on the skin.

<hr />

A self-admitted sex addict, Donald Backster's sex drive interfered with his spiritual practice. In May 1975 he wrote the word "celibacy" on his application form for an advanced technique. He was nervous how Maharishi would respond, since "celibacy" wasn't a TM advanced technique.

When Maharishi read the form, he said to Donald, "Good. How long have you abstained?"

Donald replied, "Two years, but I need help."

Maharishi nodded, closed his eyes, and went deep into meditation. He surfaced about ten seconds later, and said, "It is good." Then he looked at Donald intensely. A hard bolt of energy hit Donald between his eyes. Stunned by the impact, a second bolt hit him again.

Donald noticed his seminal fluid rising upward. A sharp pain like an icepick pushed into his second chakra. It was painful and lasted about five seconds. The rising fluid transmuted into a dense vapor, which rose slowly and pleasurably up his spinal column through the central subtle energy conduit—*sushumna nadi*.

When the vapor reached his heart chakra, it paused and radiated from his chest in all directions with great splendor. The upward flow of dense vapor continued until it reached his forehead, where again it radiated brilliantly.

This was Donald's initiation into celibacy, by Maharishi's mere glance. The direction of Donald's energy changed permanently from flowing downward and outward into flowing upward.

<hr />

I cruised along, delighting in meditation and lectures with Maharishi. However, alas, my money ran out and entry badge expired. No one knew I was supposed to be on International Staff, so I was summarily banished from the lecture hall. After I found a bill shoved under my door, I panicked. In Maharishi's whirlwind, no procedure existed for getting a Staff badge. So I avoided both lecture hall and housing office.

I waited in the hallway outside Maharishi's room for weeks. His guards didn't know me. I used to be important—five months ago. Now I was nobody.

PART III

OPEN-EGO
SURGERY

No action can be performed successfully without a clear result in view.
The secret of success is conviction and persistence.
—Maharishi Mahesh Yogi

9

FROM BLISS TO BLITZKRIEG

1972

The influence of karma is unfathomable.
The man in Cosmic Consciousness automatically finds that without him striking a matchstick, all karma is burnt in the fire of knowledge.

—MAHARISHI MAHESH YOGI

It was February 1972 in Mallorca. I'd spent weeks of frustration trying to get into Maharishi's room, ignored by everyone. In the hotel lobby, as he headed toward his car, I held up my painting of trees in Rishikesh. He stopped and said, "Good, good. Who is there?" I named the people. In several cases he said, "Should be a better likeness." Maharishi was never done. He could always find something else to gripe about.

Several days later, nothing had changed. I was still waiting in the hallway outside his room to get in.

Finally Maharishi walked by, looked at me, and said, "Start on Holy Tradition." I had no idea what he was referring to, but I was thrilled.

Jerry Jarvis interpreted for me, "Maharishi wants a painting of all the masters of the Holy Tradition." I knew masters in the Shankaracharya lineage included Vasishtha, Veda Vyasa, Shankara, and others. I sang their names during puja whenever I taught TM. But I knew nothing about them, let alone their appearance. Jerry continued, "Maharishi gave this assignment to a British artist Frances Knight, but she's done nothing."

Realizing her project was assigned to another artist, Frances freaked—and dragged me to see Maharishi: "Do you want Susan to help me with this painting?"

"No," Maharishi replied with a mischievous twinkle in his eyes. "Each of you should do your own painting." He seemed to relish the idea of competing Holy Traditions.

With a felt-tipped pen, Maharishi drew several sketches of lines and ovals indicating the masters' placement in the painting. Ultimately he positioned ovals along a winding stream. I immediately understood his vision and drew a rough sketch. "Good. Very good," he said.

I asked Brahmachari Satyanand what the masters looked like. He helped me identify some masters in Indian magazines from Gita Press. I spent the rest of my time in Mallorca making Holy Tradition drawings.

∞∞∞∞∞∞∞∞∞∞∞∞∞∞∞∞∞∞∞∞

In April 1972, International Staff flew in two private planes from Mallorca to Maharishi's Teacher Training Course for two thousand meditators in the spa village Fiuggi Fonte, Italy. Our plane suddenly banked sharply as the planes nearly collided in midair!

I flew in Maharishi's plane because I happened to be in his room when he made seat assignments. Invariably, he only paid attention to what and who was directly in front of him. Nothing existed outside that room. No time existed outside that moment.

An enchanting, hilly, medieval village one hour southeast of Rome, Fiuggi is famed for oligomineral healing waters. My stark unheated room, with marble floors, shuttered windows, ultra-high ceilings, and shared bathroom, occupied the ground floor of a small pension on a steep, cobblestone pedestrian path. Course attendees stayed throughout the town, ate in fifteen dining rooms, and met Maharishi in an old movie theater.

Ascending innumerable ancient steps up narrow streets, I viewed medieval archways, colorful gardens, delightful fountains, and passels of Italian grandmothers clad head to toe in black.

The Italian countryside became inspiration for my Holy Tradition magnum opus. I spent heavenly days sketching the sun-laden trees and bushes, spellbound by smells and sights of the springtime burst of delicate young leaves and glorious flowers.

I created several Holy Tradition sketches and showed each to Maharishi. He told me to not show anyone my work. So, avoiding Frances like an infectious disease, I didn't answer the door when she knocked and yelled for twenty minutes.

Every time I worked on the sketch, I entered a timeless realm. The tangible grace of the masters filled and surrounded me with waves of spiritual substance. Electric love currents moved throughout my being.

After a few months, I completed a gigantic pencil sketch on butcher paper, over six feet tall. Maharishi praised it profusely and spent an hour making changes, while an increasingly large audience gathered to gawk.

Maharishi had sent an assistant to call for Frances, but she never showed. I was thrilled. Maharishi gave me license to awaken and express the true inner shameless, ruthless competitor hidden deep within me.

My Holy Tradition pencil sketch.

Slowly walking toward the dais, Maharishi greeted the ravenous masses in line, accepting flowers and beaming. One woman handed him a string of coral beads. "Will you bless these for me?"

He played with the beads, handed them back, and said, "All women should wear these."

Suddenly an epidemic of coral buying erupted. Deluged with coral to bless, Maharishi fondled beads and wore strands on his arms during every lecture. Afterward, people claimed their strands, from pale pink to blood red.

With my paltry stipend I bought a red coral bracelet (the color Maharishi wore) with a gold clasp. I tied a string to its ends. *Good*, I thought. *Now it's big enough for him to wear on his arm.* Maharishi arrived for his lecture. Several people approached the stage to hand him their beads.

I handed Maharishi my pathetic little coral bracelet—all I could afford. "Would you please bless these for me?" Maharishi glared at me, then the beads, like we were poison. He gingerly picked up the gold clasp with thumb and index finger, carefully avoiding the beads, as though the coral might infect him. Evading contact with my seemingly toxic skin, he then dropped the bracelet into my palm from some height with an expression of utter contempt.

I lowered my eyes and walked away in defeat. It seemed my coral beads hadn't been blessed. They'd been cursed. I figured he was chastising me for tying string on the beads. He didn't like manipulative behavior—at least not from me!

1972, Fiuggi Fonte, Italy: Maharishi teaches "Science of Creative Intelligence."
His scribbled notes cover his coffee table. *Associated Newspapers/REX/Shutterstock*

Maharishi's International Staff comprised a few dozen people, mostly from the USA, Europe, and India. They worked in video production, tape transcription, graphic arts, writing, printing, publishing, housing, housekeeping, food service, accounting, course leadership, and so forth.

German women, age thirty-something, ran the Finance Office. Hannah Hoffmeyer was in charge. She patrolled every penny, with each expenditure personally approved by Maharishi. Therefore Hannah spent much of her time in his room, waiting for authorizations. I thought she had one of the best jobs on Staff.

Hannah, about 5'3", always walked tall and confident. She had a square face, small chin, light blue eyes, and straight, dirty-blond, shoulder-length hair, which she habitually flicked away from her face. Her formal German accent, sober demeanor, and aura of precise efficiency turned me off—but I soon found out how kind and lovely she was.

"I haf some news for you," she said one day. "Maharishi said you are going to vork in Finance." This didn't sound like good news. *But it might be better than being shipped back to the USA on the next plane!*

Working full time on an adding machine was incompatible with working on the Holy Tradition painting. Soon I was out of the art business and into the business business. My job consisted of handling petty cash and other expenditures.

Since I was an exacting perfectionist, this job suited me. I took to it as a mole takes to dirt, digging deep into organizational mysteries. Suddenly, unexpectedly, my status rose on the International Staff scale. Our elitist club of three Germans and me were given highest rank, trusted by Maharishi unequivocally.

I sat in a tiny office with a door leading outdoors, dispensing pocket change to various Staff members and paying local vendors who dropped by. International Staff subsisted on a pitiful stipend. With $25 a month I paid for all personal needs. *It's a good thing I don't wear makeup*, I thought. *It's hard enough to keep stocked in sanitary napkins.*

Leonard Campbell was a tall, blond, attractive, California-beach-Kirk-Douglas lookalike with deeply chiseled features. An aspiring brahmacharya, his claim to fame was honesty. Maharishi trusted him unequivocally. When Maharishi entered Italy, Leonard opened a bank account in his own name. Then $50,000 was transferred from the Swiss account to his. Leonard drew out the cash, brought it to his hotel, and locked it in a safe in his room.

In Fiuggi, John Greenberg, who spoke Spanish but no Italian, accompanied Leonard to pick up the cash. Mr. Gionino, the bank president, tried to convey he wouldn't release it. Leonard insisted, but Gionino held his ground.

Leonard's voice rose, arms flailed about, and fingers pointed threateningly. He yelled, "Don't you understand? We're here to pour money into your little town's economy. Your hotel and food vendors won't get paid unless we get this money." (Leonard was one of those Americans who think if they speak louder, foreigners will magically understand them.)

Finally, Mr. Gionino shoved a magazine at Leonard and John with a photo of gangsters pointing machine guns. He conveyed if he released the cash, they would be mugged—or worse. He recommended they return on a random day without a briefcase.

Several days later Leonard entered the bank. Gionino didn't want employees to see anything, so he withdrew cash on the sly. He stuffed piles of lira into Leonard's socks, all up and down his trousers, underwear, and arms of his shirt. As though wrapped in a padded jacket, Leonard stole away from the bank and sneaked the cash into his safe.

Every day Hannah took operating money from the safe. At day's end, she brought the balance back. Leonard never let anyone other than Hannah enter his room. Rumor was he kept a pet snake in the safe. But it was a fake snake. Hannah was terrified of snakes, and Leonard thrust the thing at her one day. She overcame her fears, grabbed it forcefully near its head, and stared it down.

<hr />

At the end of Fiuggi Teacher Training Courses in August 1972, Hannah told me: "Maharishi's leaving for a few months to the States. He vants you to stay in Europe and replace me vile I'm gone. You vill be in charge of Finances for International Staff in Semmering, Austria, vere residence courses vill be taught by the German WYMS—Vorld Youth Meditation Society."

Whiney little fool, I grumbled, "But I'm *from* the States. I don't want to be here while he's there. I want to travel with Maharishi."

That day I would be made a Full Initiator, along with students on their TM Teacher Training Course in Fiuggi. Then I could teach TM to all age groups. After receiving the adult mantras, I hung around, waiting to talk with Maharishi privately.

"What your plans are, hmm?" Maharishi asked.

I paused, considering how to answer. *If I say I want to go to the States, he might dismiss me from Staff. If I say I want to stay in Europe, I won't get to travel with him. I don't know what to say. Got to say something. Here goes.*

"I want to do what you want me to do—what's best for me to do." The very moment those words left my lips, I thought, *Uh oh, I'm in big trouble.*

Maharishi paused for a long time. Then one of those mischievous twinkles sparked in his eyes.

"Then go to the States and initiate the people."

Oh My God! No! My mind screamed. My ears were hit with *the bomb*—unspeakable words everyone on International Staff dreaded, words that marked the abrupt halt to our glorious ride on Staff, words that meant *The End.*

No, I thought. *I refuse. I will not let this happen.*

In a panic, I protested, "But Maharishi, Hannah told me you wanted me to be in charge of finances in Austria. I want to stay on International Staff."

I'm so confused. What am I supposed to say?

Maharishi laughed at me. "Then go to Austria and then come to Spain. Come tonight and we'll talk."

Good. He wants to see me tonight, I thought. *I'll get this straightened out.*

When confronted with Maharishi's vastly intimidating presence, I would often become undone. Unfailingly, he would say the one thing that scrambled my brain so I couldn't think straight.

At dinner I found Hannah. "Maharishi told me to stay on Staff and work in Austria."

"But I thought you didn't vant the job. I already gave it to Joshua and Samuel Kramer," Hannah replied, annoyed.

"But that was supposed to be *my* job."

"I vill talk to Maharishi," Hannah said.

This is awful. I thought. *I shouldn't have complained. Now Hannah's given my job to those Jewish brothers from the USA.* Maharishi often spoke of the ideal master-disciple relationship. He glorified devotion and surrender. But I couldn't even follow simple instructions, for God's sake!

<hr/>

That night on the Fiuggi hilltop, I waited on the grass, leaning against the fence enclosing Maharishi's house. Others waited too: Reginald and Hannah, Joshua and Samuel Kramer, and about twenty more.

Maharishi's skin-boy Gregory appeared at the threshold three times, at 11:30, 12:00, and 12:30, and told everyone to leave. After each announcement, many people left, but I stayed. Finally, at 12:30, Gregory said, "Maharishi has just gone to bed. He says everyone must leave now. Come back tomorrow morning at 8:00."

The Kramer brothers looked at each other, got up, and headed toward a Mercedes. Reginald and Hannah got into the car. Everyone else followed suit, including me. They gave me a ride back to my *pension.*

I lay on my bed with mind churning. *Now I've really done it. Those Kramers will be in charge. Aarrgh! Guess I'll try in the morning.* I turned over and went to sleep.

Next morning at 8:00, I waited outside the gate again. The Kramers were there. "Hello, Susan," Joshua said. "Maharishi asked for you last night."

Last night? I thought. *When, last night? . . . Oh, those snakes. THEY GOT IN! As soon as they got rid of me, they went back up the hill. Now I am so screwed!*

As always, Maharishi only dealt with what confronted him that moment. If we didn't get in the room, we didn't get our assignment. Then we were done for, because Maharishi gave it to someone else.

So how did we get in the room? By lying, cheating, sneaking, stepping on people. By kissing-up to those in power. By staying awake until everyone left. By ignoring skinboys who ordered us to leave again and again. By returning after pretending to leave. In short, *any way* we could.

"When did you talk to Maharishi?" I asked Joshua and Samuel.

"We knew Maharishi wanted to see us, so we went back," Samuel said.

"Maharishi told me to come last night, too," I said. "But Gregory told us Maharishi went to bed."

"Well, you know Maharishi." Joshua laughed.

I guess I don't know him as well as I thought, I realized.

<hr />

Finally I got into the room, just before Maharishi left, along with several International Staff and WYMS guys, who were, to my mind, a pack of Nazi Schutzstaffel. They lived in their restricted conclave, guarded Maharishi as though he were the Führer, and treated everyone else as *Untermenschen.*

Maharishi said, "Susan, you will take the cashbox to Austria."

I asked, "Who will authorize the payments?" *That was my job. I was supposed to take over for Hannah.*

Maharishi ignored me. He continued talking about the Austria courses. "But who will sign the authorization slips for the payments?" I insisted.

Maharishi paused. Then he looked at Leonard Campbell. "You will. Leonard will authorize."

I could do nothing. I'd been shafted, with no one to blame but myself. Add this to your list of regrets, mistakes, and lost opportunities, Ms. Young and Foolish!

<hr />

Maharishi assigned Bud Neilson (his job was transcribing tapes) and me to travel to Austria by rail, with Grant and Claudine—leftover casualties who'd developed interesting problems during long rounding.

One of the walking wounded, Grant went into silence in Mallorca. Like me, he wore a badge "in silence." However, after the course, he was incapable of uttering a word. In Fiuggi, Maharishi often approached him and yelled at the top of his lungs, "speak, speak." No sound ever came.

The other mishap was Claudine, who couldn't stop dancing. It was the Jerk, Watusi, or Boogaloo. Her arms flapped and floundered while meditating, walking, or eating—in fact, anytime at all. Maharishi told her to sit very still. She did so for twenty seconds. Then her chair flew across the room as she exploded into dance. Maharishi laughed so hard that his beard nearly fell off, but it scared the crap out of her.

These two curiosities became our charges en route to Austria. Maharishi couldn't risk sending them home in their embarrassing condition. They would have to remain in Europe until normalcy returned. So as Bud and I sightsaw our way to Austria, we dragged these two oddities through the Assisi caves, St. Bernard monastery, Florence Uffizi museum, and Vienna canals.

Several such anomalies appeared on Maharishi's courses—involuntary movements, spasms, muscle contractions, facial distortions, and sounds. Maharishi called them "heavy unstressers," and placed them in a special room to meditate together. Since "unstressing released deep-seated traumas, Maharishi habitually described it as "something good is happening, hmm?"

Summer and autumn 1972 passed in a most peculiar place—Semmering, Austria, a Viennese Alps ski and spa town. Hotel Panhans, a regal, imposing, palatial structure about an hour's train ride southwest of Vienna, must have been grand in its heyday.

I realized every Jew on International Staff was there. Those in charge were German TM Teachers from WYMS (World Youth Meditation Society). I started to wonder, *Which German "Youth" is this? Welt Jugend, or Hitler Jugend?*

The first night, I heard horses and soldiers clattering. Soldiers laughed gruffly. Horses neighed. Bridles clanked. *Spooky.* I looked out the window. *Where can the sound be coming from?*

Next morning, after a fitful, sleepless night, I ventured downstairs to eat breakfast with Kristina (from the Finance Office), Joshua, Samuel, and Leonard. "I heard strange noises last night," I said.

"So did I," Kristina said.

"This place is creepy," Samuel agreed.

"I think I know why." Leonard said. "I talked to the hotel manager last night. During World War II, Himmler, Goering, and the SS occupied this building as a Nazi headquarters."

I gasped. "My God. You're kidding."

Leonard continued, "Nazi soldiers rode their horses right into the hotel and used the ballrooms as stables. Parts of the hotel have been abandoned for decades. After the Second World War, Semmering was occupied by Russia."

"You mean I was hearing poltergeists?" Samuel asked.

"It would appear that way," Leonard said.

"I got a real strange feeling, too. Visions of people being tortured in concentration camps all night long. I couldn't sleep," Kristina said.

Why did Maharishi send all Jewish International Staff to a hotel haunted by Nazis, previously SS headquarters, with Germans in charge? This was no accident.

A few days later, I ventured into the abandoned part of the hotel. A terrible feeling attacked the pit of my stomach as I walked through musty corridors. Turning a big brass handle, I opened a large, elegantly carved door. It creaked. I entered a huge ballroom, covered in dust. High ceilings were elaborately decorated with intricate murals and gold relief, thickly coated in dust. Elegant crystal chandeliers, dripping with dusty glass shards, sent chills down my back. A grand parquet floor, interrupted with elegant marquetry—

On my God, there's HAY on the floor! The SS stabled their horses here. Did the Russians use the ballroom to stable their horses? How long has this hay been here?

I turned around and fled the ballroom, never to return.

<hr />

Karl Werner, classical music composer and pretentious WYMS Führer, considered Americans lower class. The elite were required to dine formally. International Staff got shuffled with other hoi polloi to the ghetto dining room, deprived of nutrition and bullied like prisoners. Cabbage, white bread, and white potatoes in inadequate portions—that was dinner. Though of Irish origin, Leonard (a rare non-Jew among us) managed to convince Karl he was German. So he dined upstairs in the elegant WYMS banquet hall.

In horror I watched WYMS despots manhandle Reba Rabinowitz, head of Maharishi's tape library. They dragged her body, forcing her down the stairs, while she struggled to resist their demands: "You *vill* move into a new office. *Jawohl.* You *vill* cooperate."

"I'm not moving those tapes. I'll die first," Reba said.

Quite a reaction, I thought. *Whoa. Blitzkrieg of the Übermensch.*

<hr />

I received a letter by post (yes, back then we communicated that way) from the newly formed Maharishi International University (MIU) in California. "We are in the midst of going through the MIU Catalog with Maharishi here in Santa Barbara. Tonight we were discussing how growth of consciousness could be illustrated graphically. Maharishi recalled a painting you did in Rishikesh of trees against three different backgrounds. He could not have praised it more highly. Over and over he said what an exact representation of the different states of consciousness it is. He wants to have it made into posters."

This news sent waves of joy through my heart and tears to my eyes. *Maharishi remembers Susan the Artist!* Nothing ever came of it, however. Maharishi's plans were always brilliant and momentous. But rarely did anything materialize.

Meanwhile, privileged MIU professors, including Keith Wallace, David Orme-Johnson, Larry Domash, Albert Bruns (husband of "Dear Prudence" Farrow), John Farrow (Mia Farrow's brother), plus wives and kids, basked in Maharishi's darshan at Mike Love's 3.5-acre estate on a hillside overlooking the Pacific in Santa Barbara. Gardeners planted a homegrown veggie garden. Sama Veda pundits recorded the Vedas in a small pavilion on the property.

Maharishi named David Orme-Johnson Director of Research for all TM scientific studies. Though an overwhelming responsibility, David was up for the task. He and John Farrow compiled and edited the first book of TM research.

For me, stuck in Naziville, summer and fall passed in meditating, accounting, painting the Holy Tradition, picking wildflowers, and enjoying scenic views from Hotel Panhans. On International Staff we had time to sightsee in Europe. But my minuscule stipend usually prohibited such diversions. Still, one day I managed a train ticket to Vienna, strolled around the city, and visited the Spanish Riding School, home of Lipizzaner white stallions.

It was now November, and snow began to fall. Shivering, I wore long underwear under my sari and a wool sweater over it. WYMS refused to turn up the heat. Days and nights faded into each other. It was quiet—too quiet. Nearly all International Staff were gone. Maharishi had called them elsewhere.

1 0

A SACRIFICIAL LAMB

1972-1973

The happenings give the disciple the opportunity to be constantly in tune with the master, to come into his presence, be in his presence. Work is just a means to hang around him.

—MAHARISHI MAHESH YOGI

Just when I thought I was stuck in Nazi hell forever, in November 1972 Hannah phoned from Spain: "Maharishi asked me to call you. Do you vant to fly to La Antilla to vork in finan—"

"Yes. I'll get on the next plane," I interrupted. I packed my bags swiftly and off I flew with cashbox in hand, Holy Tradition painting, and all.

At the Teacher Training Courses in La Antilla, from November 1972 to May 1973, my job was keeping financial records for twenty-five hundred course participants. Many hadn't paid their full course fee. I worked day and night on this grueling project with no time to attend lectures. It was a nightmare.

I stayed in a small beach house and walked along the shore to my office. Fierce winds whipped waves into white foam clusters on ominous, wintry, blue-black Atlantic waters. Seagulls circled overhead. Dark clouds crowded the sky. At night the moon played hide-and-seek with the clouds, reflecting shimmering silvery light on inky water. Beautiful and dramatic, but frequently stormy with cold, furious wind—a far cry from the balmy Mediterranean.

One night everyone was out on a barge, howling at the moon I guess, since it was full. The buses already left for the dock. I was dragging toward my office, staring at the dirt path before me. Too much work. No boat ride for me.

Suddenly a Mercedes passed my solitary figure on the road. The car stopped. The window rolled down and Maharishi asked, "What you are doing, hmm?"

"Going to my office," I replied.

"No. Get in," Maharishi demanded. "You're going on the boat ride. Everyone must go." I hopped into the car. Traditionally, it's cosmically auspicious to be on the water with the guru on full moon nights.

The moment Maharishi stepped onto the boat, he was deluged with hundreds of devotees crowding and voracious eyes beseeching. By the time my car door opened, I was lost in the crowd. *No one noticed I rode with him.* The worst part was I actually *wanted* someone to notice. Had I somehow turned into a shallow status seeker?

I finally stepped onto the barge. It was cold. No—freezing. The stormy waves rocked the vessel to seasick proportions. The icy wind tore through my sweater, sari, long underwear, and socks. Maharishi, in his thin dhoti, shawl, bare feet, and sandals— he never wore socks and rarely got cold.

He tried to give a lecture, but roaring waves drowned out his voice. *What am I doing here? I've got so much work,* I thought. *No one can hear what he's saying.*

⋄∘⋄∘⋄∘⋄∘⋄∘⋄∘⋄∘⋄∘⋄∘⋄∘⋄∘⋄∘⋄

I was waiting outside Maharishi's bedroom at Hotel Fira. I don't know why, but I was alone. There were no attendants or devotees. Usually Johnny Gray was there (yes, future author of *Men Are from Mars, Women Are from Venus*). He was Maharishi's current skin-boy. But not this morning.

Suddenly Maharishi's bedroom door opened. He appeared at the threshold. His shimmering, white silk dhoti seemed to beam with innate radiance. A vehicle for his atmosphere of thick silence, his aura blazed in luminous transparency. His diaphanous feet glistened like two lotuses, emerging from a pond pristine and untouched.

But to my mind those lotus feet didn't appear to be walking. His effulgent corona seemed to float toward me, as if a graceful swan, incandescent and transcendent, materialized from his secret chambers, drifting in a soft, gliding movement in stillness.

He smiled mischievously and zapped a loving glance that infused me with a stream of divine blessing and blissful energy. What a gift of supreme compassion and grace, the unique spiritual vibration transference from master to disciple—*shakti-sanchara.* He opened his meeting room door and slipped inside, without a word or sound.

This was the kind of experience I lived for.

Johnny Gray showed up presently. Considering the behavior of other skin-boys, I think he was much too kind to qualify for the job. He ushered me into Maharishi's meeting room. We discussed course finances—who didn't have to pay, who had to pay, who should be sent home. My job was to convey messages and collect fees. Those in the "108 Program" paid their way to hang around Maharishi and pretended to work, but money didn't necessarily garner their acceptance in the program. In India 108 is a holy number. Indian rosaries (*malas*) have 108 beads for counting mantras.

This meeting made me feel important, which wasn't the point—or was it? What was the point? However important I felt, the next day I would feel the opposite. One day any miracle was achievable. The next day all hope was dashed. From majestic to rejected, elated to humiliated—with one glance, Maharishi brought out the best or worst in me.

∞∞∞∞∞∞∞∞∞∞∞∞∞∞∞∞∞∞∞∞∞

In the spring of 1973, Jerry Jarvis passed on a message from Maharishi that I had to communicate to the two thousand students in La Antilla and five hundred in nearby Punta Umbria.

I declared on the microphone, "Recently the value of the US dollar has dropped compared to the Spanish peso. Therefore the course fee will be raised. Each of you now owes another $50. Please pay as soon as possible. You will not become an Initiator until you pay this additional fee."

This announcement hit like a bomb. The crowd roared and shouted in anger. I was mobbed as I tried to leave the hall. Questions flew from every direction. Everyone assumed the fee increase was my idea. In their idealized concept of Maharishi, he couldn't possibly be behind it.

This incident endowed me an aura of severity. And if I didn't have enough headaches collecting course fees, now there was an additional bill for each participant. My workload had just doubled.

∞∞∞∞∞∞∞∞∞∞∞∞∞∞∞∞∞∞∞∞

It was the night before Maharishi would give final instructions and mantras to make thousands of Initiators. Sitting on the stage, he dispensed orders to International Staff. Catching my eye, he motioned to me.

"Go through each of your records," he said. "Calculate who's paid and hasn't paid their course fees. Staple a slip of colored paper to the lower left-hand corner of each record. Write in felt-tipped pen, either FULLY PAID or OWES $ and AMOUNT. Do that now, before tomorrow morning."

"Now?" I looked at my watch. I realized, *There are two thousand records. Two thousand!*

"Yes," Maharishi said. In his inimitable fashion, he shot me a piercing glance like an earthquake, shaking me to my core. My body exploded with energy. Flooded with Maharishi juice, enough to fill a swimming pool, I was nearly knocked over with bliss.

Now it was 1:00 a.m. I had to finish this impossible task by 8:00 a.m. So I asked for helpers. Maharishi recruited whoever happened to be in his line of sight. "Malcolm will help. And Susan the Singer—Susan will help you. Do it over there, in that corner of the lecture hall."

"Jai Guru Dev," I said, swimming off in a pool of bliss.

I brought all my records to the hall and began the project. Maharishi stayed for another half hour. The moment he left, Susan complained she was too tired. "Finish it in the morning," she said, and stood up to leave.

"But there *is no* morning. He's starting at 8:00!" I exclaimed. Susan ignored me. I couldn't blame her. She was in charge of the kitchen.

"I'm glad I'm not you," Malcolm said. "Got to go talk to Maharishi. Get someone else to help." Him I could blame. He was just being a "p" with a "rick."

I tried frantically to find helpers, but the moment Maharishi left, everyone was off to bed. Staying up all night doing arithmetic wasn't anyone's lollapalooza. *Typical. These lazy people can always be counted on to disappear the moment Maharishi stops babysitting them.*

I phoned Maharishi's skin-boy and told him my helpers had abandoned me. He informed me I would have to do it all myself. I returned to my office, desperate and frantic. I stayed up all night, painstakingly preparing each record for the looming onslaught of two thousand Initiators-to-be.

Finally I nearly finished—with just one hour to get back to my room, shower, change, and make it to the lecture hall with my stack of records. When I arrived, Maharishi called me over. "Everything is finished, hmm?"

"Not quite. I finished 1800 of the 2000 records," I replied. "I'll complete the other 200 today."

"Two thousand? What about the five hundred in Punta Umbria?" Maharishi barked.

"I didn't know you needed those today. I haven't started them yet," I said.

"No excuses," Maharishi yelled. Even though the so-called helpers left the entire task in my lap, I was the guilty party. "Where are the Punta Umbria records?" he snapped.

I said, "I'll get them from my office."

Maharishi said, "Tomorrow morning we go to Punta Umbria to make Initiators." He motioned to Hannah Hoffmeyer and Samuel Kramer and said, "Susan made a mess of all this. Sit behind her and watch her all day. Make sure she doesn't make any more mistakes."

So, as two thousand people shuffled by my table, one by one, I collected unpaid course fees and marked each slip FULLY PAID. Students took their folders up to the stage to hand to Maharishi, where he dispensed mantras. This gave me quite a reputation—Susan The Terrible. Yikes!

Amid this chaos, I attempted to add, subtract, mark, and staple the additional seven hundred records. Meanwhile, Hannah and Samuel sat right behind me like centurions. Much too exalted to stoop to my level, they didn't lift a finger to help.

That night I stayed up all night working again.

By the time Maharishi arrived in Punta Umbria, I'd finished my task, miraculously, with help from a kindly young Initiator, Theresa Olson, whose family had hosted Maharishi in Los Angeles during his first world tour in 1959.

A week later, I received a message to bring all my records to Maharishi's meeting room. Hannah Hoffmeyer and Thomas Martin, a wealthy young man from the USA, were there. He was in the "108 Program."

"Thomas," Maharishi said, "Susan's records are all a mess. Go through every one of them and check the math."

I was indignant, but said nothing. *My records are perfect. I double-check everything,* I thought. Insulted and outraged, I handed over my records.

A few days later, Thomas knocked on my office door and declared, "Your records have absolutely no mistakes that I can find."

"No surprise to me," I said. "Did you tell Maharishi?"

"Tried to. Every time, he changed the subject," Thomas replied.

"He often does that," I said. "He tells you to do something. Then when you've finished, he's no longer interested."

<hr />

June 1973—time for our next destination: Seelisberg, Switzerland, on Lake Lucerne. What a glorious place! So invigorating, with clean, rarified air and magnificent vistas. If heaven existed on earth, it was the Swiss Alps.

The most picturesque village on Lake Lucerne, Seelisberg stood on a spectacular precipice, twelve hundred feet above the bright cobalt lake. Stunning jagged peaks enchanted the eye for miles in every direction. Graceful swans and delightful boats glided to and fro. A charming red funicular railway carried passengers down to the dock at Treib, where steamboats ferried them around the lake. Serenity pervaded the air.

Legend says Switzerland was founded in 1291 at Rütli meadow, seated below Seelisberg. The oath of allegiance was purportedly sworn there by the original Swiss cantons, which banded together against the counts of Habsburg.

Seelisberg, Switzerland: Sönnenberg and Kulm hotels, connected by glassed-in walkway. *Ringier AG*

International Staff resided in two recently purchased hotels—Kulm and Sönnenberg, connected by a covered walkway above the road. Maharishi's lakeview room faced Fronalpstock across the lake, which bore resemblance to Mount Kailesh in the Himalayas—legendary home of Lord Shiva. Maharishi nicknamed it "Mount Shiva."

Maharishi on overlook in front of Sönnenberg with Mount Shiva in background.

Renovations began. Maharishi, chief contractor, directed builders personally, as per his typical micromanagement of everything. In a cream-covered ballroom on Sönnenberg's second floor, a semicircular amphitheater with seven rows of gold velvet throne-like chairs was constructed. White-pine curved desks with microphones were built into each row. Gold velvet drapery hung on the arched windows and as a backdrop for Maharishi's video production stage. Lavish flower arrangements and foliage surrounded his gold couch. Guru Dev's portrait sat above the couch. Maharishi's coffee table held a microphone, world globe, clock, blank drawing paper, colorful marking pens, and a bell. Flags of every nation surrounded the hall, which was carpeted in red.

If the US Capitol House Chamber and Buckingham Palace spawned a love child during the Indian Raj, it might have resembled this assembly hall (see photo on page 201).

Upon our arrival in Seelisberg, Maharishi said to me, "You've been working very hard. Now go to your room. Meditate and round." As usual, I took this to heart—and to the hilt. I holed up inside my room for eight weeks, spending all day rounding. A kindly man on Staff placed meals outside my door twice daily.

After two months, I received a note under my door. "Maharishi has been asking about you. He hasn't seen you for a long time."

The same night in the lecture hall, dressed in my sari, I showed my face. Maharishi shot me a disgruntled look. I approached and said, "I heard you asked about me."

Maharishi replied, "I told you to round, but not this kind of rounding." Apparently I wasn't supposed to disappear for eight weeks.

Three years previously, I'd taught a TM residence course in Abiquiú, New Mexico at Ghost Ranch, attended by fledgling meditators Rhoda and David Orme-Johnson. At that time, I predicted David would oversee all scientific research on TM. My prediction came true. David became chairman of Maharishi International University's (MIU) Psychology Department, and compiled five hundred studies for *Collected Papers,* a.k.a. *Scientific Research on Transcendental Meditation and TM-Sidhi Program.*

In 1973, David showed up in Seelisberg with an electroencephalograph (EEG) machine to measure brain waves. He theorized TM meditators would demonstrate brain wave coherence between right and left hemispheres.

David asked me to try his machine. He attached many electrodes to my head and I went into deep meditation. That evening at dinner David rushed toward me. "Come to my office tomorrow. I want to take more readings."

At the end of my third session, David said, "Take a look at your brain waves. Never seen anything like it. Maharishi's really impressed. Your brain waves are now famous."

"Wow. Really? Show me," I said.

"Look here, Susan. During each meditation your brain waves are perfect sine waves. That means perfect Alpha state."

At dinner Reginald stopped me as I was headed for tea. "There's the girl with the celebrity brain waves. Everyone's talking about them." I smiled at him.

That night I went to Maharishi's meeting room, hoping someone would mention my brain waves. David tried to discuss the EEG project, but Maharishi kept pointedly interrupting him mid sentence. I waited until everyone left.

"Maharishi, David measured my brain waves. Did you see?" I asked eagerly.

"It's not important." Maharishi scowled and waved me off in a dismissive gesture. I stumbled out of the room, tail between my legs.

Maharishi never let me keep a swelled head for even five seconds. He crushed every bud of ego aggrandizement before it blossomed into full-blown conceit. Other devotees, infinitely more smug than I, didn't appear to get such dismissive treatment. It seemed my great honor to enjoy the blue-ribbon prize for ego squashing.

It wasn't long before someone else's brain waves were more spectacular than mine, anyway—Theresa Olson.

∞∞∞∞∞∞∞∞∞∞∞∞∞∞∞∞∞∞

One night I went to see Maharishi after his evening meeting. After he said, "Go and rest" about five times, eventually everyone left—except me.

Maharishi asked, "Yes, what it is?"

I replied, "Maharishi, I've decided I never want to marry. I want to be celibate for the rest of my life and work for you."

"Hmm?" Maharishi asked. "The boys don't bother you?"

I said, "I don't see how they could." Just as these words rolled off my tongue, a forceful thought attacked my mind—*EXCEPT REGINALD*. It was such a loud, powerful thought that I surmised, *My God, Maharishi can certainly hear this thought. Eek!*

"What is your education?" Maharishi asked.

"I attended art school in California." *Why did he ask that?* I thought. *Doesn't he think I'm educated enough to make a decision?* So I asked, "Should I go back to college?"

Maharishi then paused for some time and considered it. "No," he said. "That is not necessary. You are a very good artist. We will talk about it again later. Come tomorrow 10:00. Now go and rest."

We never discussed my *brahmacharini* (female celibate disciple) aspirations again.

∞∞∞∞∞∞∞∞∞∞∞∞∞∞∞∞∞∞

When I noticed some Staff members' parents visiting Seelisberg, I asked Maharishi for permission to invite mine. He agreed. They would stay in the quaint Hotel Bellevue down the hill, by the railway's upper terminal. The last time I'd seen them was in Spain. We'd spent a few days sightseeing in Madrid and Toledo.

When I told Maharishi my parents would arrive tomorrow, he answered, "I will meet them privately."

Next morning, Maharishi called me to the Finance Office before I had a chance to see my parents. He chose that day of all days, of all months, of all years, to spend the entire day alone with us four Finance Department women. We met Maharishi from midday until late night, while he scrutinized every speck of minutia about every financial file ever created, and he made reams of notes about everything (I kept the entire pile of notes).

That night, just before leaving the Finance Office, Maharishi said, "Go and rest. Tomorrow I will meet you here again, 10:00."

I said, "Maharishi, my parents are in Seelisberg and they want to see me. Can I go sightseeing with them tomorrow?"

"Your parents are here?"

"Yes."

"Good. Then spend the day with them. Bring them to the hall at 8:00. Come here next day at 10:00 and I will meet you."

So I went sightseeing with my parents, boating on Lake Lucerne and visiting little villages around the lake. That night I introduced them to Maharishi in the lecture hall. He said to them, "Very good. Very good. I will meet you privately."

The next day we finance women met Maharishi again, from morning until late night. He never made it to the lecture hall, where my parents and a hundred other people were waiting. At the end of the night, he said, "Go and rest. I will be here at 10:00 tomorrow."

When Maharishi arrived at the Finance Office the following morning, I told him my parents were leaving the next morning.

He said, "I will meet with them privately today."

During the lunch break I phoned the Bellevue and invited my parents to the Sönnenberg to meet Maharishi. They waited in the hallway right outside the door all afternoon. Finally, our finance meeting ended that night, and I reminded Maharishi about my parents. He said to his skin-boy, "Call Susan's parents in."

He answered, "They were here earlier, but now they're gone."

Maharishi scowled at his skin-boy. "Why you didn't tell me they were here? I will meet them later."

I walked down the steep hill to the Bellevue. My parents were in nightclothes, getting ready for bed. "Why didn't you stay? Maharishi asked for you," I said.

"I *knew* we should have stayed. But your father wouldn't," Mother said.

"I'm not gonna wait around all day for that *shtunk*," Father said.

"He's not a *shtunk*. He's a saint," I said.

"We were in the lecture hall with him. We saw how everyone prays to him," he said.

"They're not praying. That's an Indian greeting, with palms together," I explained. "Why don't you get dressed and go see him?"

"For what?" he said. "We came to see *you*. You've been with *him* all the time."

"Can't we get dressed and go back up there? I want to meet him," Mother said.

"I don't," Father said.

"Then I'll come in the morning and we'll have breakfast," I said.

I trudged back up the hill, my mind screaming. *Why is my father so stubborn? They came all this way, for what? I wish they would just . . . Urrgh.*

The next morning, Maharishi came into the Finance Office to meet us four women.

He said, "Susan, where your parents are, hmm?"

"They left this morning for the States," I said. He didn't respond.

Once again Maharishi met us four women privately until late night. Just before he left, he said, "Go and rest. I will meet you 10:00 tomorrow morning. If I'm not here on time, then start without me."

For the past four days we four women had arrived on time at 10:00. Maharishi arrived one to two hours late every day. Because of his consistent tardiness, and his implication he'd be late again, we decided to arrive at 10:30. By that time Maharishi was in another room, meeting another group.

Maharishi's skin-boy told us, "Maharishi came to your office at exactly 10:00 sharp. When he found no one there, he went into another meeting."

He never returned to the Finance Office nor met our group privately again. It seemed the entire purpose of this marathon was to block me from seeing my parents. Did he think I was too dependent on them? Was his purpose to burn off my karma? Was it a test?

During the four-day confabulation, Maharishi's favorite disciple Jemima Pitman, a lovely woman from England whom he called "Ma," was present at times. At one point he said to her, referring to the meeting: "Now we have to go through this misery, but it is necessary."

I wonder why. Nothing came of it—except a pile of Maharishi's notes that I collected, which were never used.

<hr />

I wanted desperately to get closer to Maharishi. I felt I must stay with him and devote my life to TM. One night in Seelisberg I was waiting in line, as usual, to greet him after his evening meeting. He handed me a rose and said, "Come to my meeting room every morning at 9:00. Everyone who is in charge of something must come."

I was flabbergasted. I thought, *This is my dream come true.*

11

WHAM BAM, EGO SLAM

1973 TO 1974

One starts to think as the master thinks, act as his thoughts dictate. The process of attuning one's desire to the desire of the master takes one through all the culture that is necessary to live Infinity in every impulse.

—MAHARISHI MAHESH YOGI

I could hardly believe Maharishi said to come every morning! My fanciful twenty-five-year-old brain imagined this was my big opportunity. The next morning at 6:00 I dragged out of bed, showered, and did my TM program: asanas, pranayama, and meditation. I hated getting up early after Maharishi kept us up well past midnight.

At 8:55 I rushed downstairs to his meeting room. Ten people gathered, including Hannah, Reginald, Lars, Kristina, and Thomas. Maharishi said, "Come, come," when he saw me. "You and Kristina will be in charge of communications. You will read the mail to me every morning."

Wow, that's the job Maharishi had with Guru Dev! I thought.

The meeting lasted until 2:00 in the afternoon. Then Maharishi said, "Go and eat."

The following morning I rushed again and got myself to the meeting by 9:00. Kristina and I prepared the mail. Maharishi kept us until noon, but never asked about the mail. Lacking rest and meditation, I felt edgy the rest of the day. *But I must do this. This is the way to get close to Maharishi.*

The next morning I tried to wake up early, but got up at 8:00. *Oh no. I can't finish my TM program on time. I'll go late to the meeting.* When I showed up at 9:30, Kristina said, "I've already read the mail to him."

I wondered when these people had time to sleep, eat, and meditate. *How can I keep up this pace when we don't get to bed until 2:00 a.m.?*

The next day I slept until 8:00 again. At 9:30 I arrived. No one was in the meeting room. "The meeting's already over," Hannah told me. "You missed it."

What a bumbling fool and failure I am! I thought.

I couldn't handle staying up late, getting up early, waiting in Maharishi's intense madhouse, trying to read the mail, waiting again, trying again. Embarrassed and ashamed, I didn't return.

Oh God, this was a test and I failed, I thought. *How do these people do it?* Then it struck me. Maharishi often used to say, "When I was with Guru Dev, I didn't meditate much."

It's not important, Susan. You just missed your chance to do the job Maharishi did for Guru Dev. Add that to your list of wasted opportunities you'll regret for decades.

Strangely, as I write this, I now realize I loved and valued meditation more than hanging around Maharishi! I was nothing but an introvert. Let others get up at dawn and stay up half the night, competing for Maharishi's attention—for anyone's attention!

<hr>

Maharishi always made so many changes to my Holy Tradition painting that during my stay in Semmering, Austria, I decided to paint cutout figures and place them on a separate background. This way he could move them like puzzle pieces. So Maharishi spent two hours alone with me, moving them around my pencil-sketched background until he settled on their placement. After that I started a background with a stream, trees, flowers, and animals. I didn't get far. I was too busy in the Finance Office.

Though I knew virtually nothing about accounting, Maharishi called me to his meeting room and said, "Now you will choose which company will audit us."

Audit us? I thought. *Why?*

Hannah, Thomas, and I interviewed two Swiss accounting firms. I had no clue why I was meeting them, why anyone would audit us, or what criteria to use to evaluate them. After the meetings, Maharishi called us back in. "Which firm should we hire, Susan?"

Me? He's really asking me? The last person on earth he should ask? Is he serious?

I blurted out, "It seems to me, Price Waterhouse."

I didn't know which firm to hire. I'd never heard of the other firm. But I *had* heard of CPAs that appeared yearly on television, counting votes for the Academy Awards. If they were good enough for Hollywood, I guessed they were okay for Maharishi.

This was another test I probably flunked. I'll never know.

<hr>

In winter 1973, Maharishi called me to Hertenstein, a small hotel on a tiny Lake Lucerne peninsula. Its ferry dock was marked by a lovely white statue of Virgin Mary amidst flowering bushes. Mark Twain called Hertenstein peninsula "the most beautiful place on earth." Maharishi described it as "filled with very deep silence."

From November to December 1973, Maharishi sent me on a whirlwind rail tour of Switzerland. My assignment was to supervise the administrators managing Teacher Training Courses in Villars, Valbella, Engelberg, and Interlaken. Yet I knew nothing about these operations. Since I was the most improbable candidate to oversee these highly experienced administrators, I started to wonder what drug Maharishi had been smoking to exhibit such lapse in judgment! But seriously, maybe he had good reason, to be revealed. Finally it was—but not as expected. With Maharishi, rarely was anything as expected.

In December, when I arrived in Interlaken, I got a strange feeling to stay and help the Swiss woman in charge, Greta. She somehow convinced me to take her place, while she ended up in Hertenstein with Maharishi.

Victoria-Jungfrau was (still is) a grand, luxurious hotel. Antiques adorned many of its varied sleeping rooms. A splendid ballroom served as the meeting room. One beautifully appointed sitting room, about fifteen by thirty feet, was furnished with valuable antiques. The hotel manager demanded I lock it and post a notice, DO NOT ENTER.

Keeping this hotel in order was a big responsibility. Staff was a joke. Whenever I checked on so-called housekeepers, not once were they cleaning rooms. They were flopped on beds, meditating or listening to the radio. Soon I had a rebellion on my hands, since I had the gall to insist these lazy meditators (earning credit for a Teacher Training Course) arrive on time, get off their skinny butts, and get to work.

I tried to persuade course participants to sleep at night rather than play cards, party, and engage in sexual escapades. And filthy squatters decided to bring their entire flock from Germany to camp out and leave giant water spots across the elegant parquet floor of the hotel's largest sleeping room.

Eventually I gave up fighting all these losing battles, and the TM Movement had to pay thousands of dollars in damages.

One day I received a message from Maharishi: "Take all the Initiators on a rail tour to the top of the Jungfrau." So I arranged this unbelievably expensive excursion for hundreds of TM Initiators taking an advanced course. Early one morning, off we went.

The Jungfrau railway ran into and through tunnels in the Eiger and Mönch mountains, with two train stations right inside the Eiger. At those stations, passengers detrained to view spectacular scenery through panoramic windows carved into the rock face. As the train chugged along, passing out of the Eiger over the snowy landscape and upwards to the Jungfrau peak, something unusual happened.

The passengers were standing up, hanging out the windows on the east side of the railway cars, pointing toward the sun. Something looking like pale blue, pink, and gold angels encircled it. An exquisite, celestial exultation pervaded the air, as we ascended the mountain escorted by the spine-tingling sight of ethereal beings of light.

On the summit, the highest railway station in Europe, lay a magnificent glacier of immense magnitude, like God had spooned out a giant serving of vanilla ice cream and left a glistening indentation in the perfect, vast whiteness. Nothing existed but that pristine, seamless, snow-covered landscape and its utter stillness.

I took a deep breath, closed my eyes, and entered a realm beyond this physical plane, drinking my fill of the rarified air in that spiritually charged atmosphere. Subtle sensations and waves of serenity pulsated a heartbeat of mystic quietude in and around me.

The sun glistened like diamonds on the endless sea of whiteness. A gentle wind caressed my hair, stirring and intensifying the crisp, invigorating life-force energy that suffused this purest, high-altitude troposphere at the pinnacle of the world.

⋙⋘⋙⋘⋙⋘⋙⋘⋙⋘⋙⋘⋙⋘

"Maharishi wanted me to tell you that he will arrive in Interlaken next week, along with hundreds of people, to launch a Vedic Studies course. Maharishi says all the course participants will have to double up to accommodate the newcomers. Don't tell them yet," Maharishi's skin-boy Edward Tremblay told me over the phone.

This news left in its wake simultaneous explosions of elation and devastation. At first, Maharishi's arrival seemed thrilling. Then reality sank in. Though it appeared a marvelous turn of events, and I should have felt grateful, I felt terrified. *How will I handle this onslaught?*

Everything ran so smoothly in my neatly organized hotel. The idea of mass chaos overwhelmed me. A bomb was about to detonate in my pristine world. *No, I can't have a confusing jumbled mess. I've got to organize this massive barrage of humanity well in advance!*

As days rolled on, pressure closed in around me. My mind envisioned every kind of horror when hundreds invaded the Victoria-Jungfrau. *How will I match them with roommates? What if people complain?*

I felt I couldn't wait another second. In a panic, I grabbed the microphone and announced the great news. Maharishi would soon arrive to teach a special Vedic Science Course. "He'll be bringing many people with him. So you'll need to double up in your rooms. Please hand in slips of paper indicating who you want to double up with—"

"Double up in our rooms?" one man shouted in interruption.

"We refuse to double up," another chimed in.

"We paid for single rooms," someone else yelled.

The course leader, Kyle Robinson from New Zealand, shouted, "I'm with them." He descended from the platform and, with dramatic flourish, sat his derriere down in a front row seat. "I'm on their side. We refuse to double up."

Dumbfounded, I left the platform—to a chorus of hisses and boos.

I thought these Initiators would *delight* in news that the guru we idolized was coming. Instead, my ill-conceived disclosure ended in fiasco. I hadn't counted on their imbalanced mental state. Meditating ten hours a day had made them hypersensitive and unstable. No wonder Edward had warned me against giving advanced notice.

The Initiators didn't know Maharishi's hand was in any of it. But his hand plus his arm were in all of it. Overtly, he remained the highly exalted, all-benevolent maha-guru, untouched by base energies, while us pawns took the fall. He exuded divine fragrance of jasmine, while we on Staff reeked of fetid garbage.

Meanwhile, several hundred TM Initiators in Interlaken were in panic mode. There was no choice other than to phone Edward and confess: *mea culpa, mea culpa, mea maxima culpa.*

"I announced to the Initiators that Maharishi was coming and they would have to double up. They reacted very badly," I told Edward.

"Why'd you do that?" Edward asked. "Maharishi told you not to tell them yet."

"I'm sorry. I really messed up. I wanted to organize the move in advance. I thought it would be easier—"

"That was a big mistake," Edward interrupted. "I'll ask Maharishi and call you back later."

The next day I received a call from Edward: "Maharishi's very angry about your announcement. Tell them everyone can keep their own private room and Maharishi promises that absolutely none of his precious Initiators will have to double up."

Now all the puffed up Initiators with egos engorged to the stratosphere could sit on their assets, feeling validated in their sense of privileged entitlement. "Yeah, it was that bitchy Susan's idea to force us to double up!" And Kyle, the silly course leader with brainpower about equal to Elmer's Glue, could gloat profusely.

Then Maharishi asked me to find hundreds of hotel rooms in Interlaken for the massive incursion of humanity. It wasn't easy. I suffered for my misguided indiscretion. This was a major task, over which I lost major sleep. And following India's haggling tradition, Maharishi instructed me to "offer half" of any asking price. Not fun.

How much easier it would have been to follow Maharishi's initial instructions. The Initiators would have hated me, but they would have complied. Now they hated me and also lorded over me. Their derision was now justified.

The time came for Maharishi's arrival. I told some course participants to move out so I could set aside one wing for Maharishi and his special guests. But, after all that melodrama about doubling up, they begged to double up in Maharishi's hotel rather than take single rooms elsewhere. Still, some Staff and all new students had to stay in other hotels.

Debby Jarvis advised me Maharishi always preferred a small bedroom. I gave him a newly renovated corner room, carpeted in red. A large adjoining room, with blue carpet, served as his meeting room.

Old-time Initiators received preferential treatment—rooms nearest Maharishi and best lecture hall seats. Newer disciples found themselves further away. This was my little brainstorm, which I considered infinitely fair.

Strangely, I never considered asking Maharishi who should stay where. I was too shy. Instead I tried to anticipate what he wanted. Amazingly, I received few complaints. After all, who would dare complain when it was done so equitably (in my mind, at least)?

Time passed wonderfully in Interlaken. I enjoyed privileged access to Maharishi due to my position. But I rarely used that privilege. I did a needed service, and I did it invisibly.

Maharishi stayed for months.

One afternoon I happened to walk through the hallway from the dining hall to my office. To my utter horror, there was Maharishi! He'd parked his holy self on his holy deerskin on an antique needlepoint sofa in the locked, off-limits room. His skin-boy had found my hidden key.

The room was boiling over with masses of hungry eyes suffocating Maharishi. Hoards crammed mano a mano on priceless couches and chairs, making charts with marking pens on costly antique rugs, and leaving wet teacups and water glasses on precious furniture. The whole scene resembled a frat party in someone's basement family room.

Mortified, I marched up to Maharishi and whispered, "Maharishi, the hotel owner told me we're not allowed to use this room. It should be locked at all times. It's filled with priceless antiques."

Maharishi laughed at me, waved me off, and continued his meeting. In fact, he proceeded to meet there every day for weeks, damaging everything. The Movement ended up with a massive bill. The hotel manager blamed me, since I was warned to keep the room under lock and key.

One day Maharishi sent word through his skin-boy Edward: "Announce to the course participants as soon as possible that they must pay an additional $10 fee per night due to the course being extended for a few weeks."

Oh great, I thought. *Once again I'll be the scapegoat—the TM ogre.* I dreaded making another disagreeable announcement that would make everyone detest me even more.

That night, right after Maharishi's lecture, he was seated on the stage, answering questions privately. Jane Hopson, a well-known TM Teacher from Houston, Texas, was chatting with him. I figured this was a good time to make the announcement, since all were still gathered. No one ever left the hall before Maharishi.

About four hundred of his chief disciples were in attendance. Most were TM Initiators. The remainder were on Staff. I took this opportunity to grab a microphone.

At that same moment, Maharishi interrupted Jane. He said to her, "Shh, wait a minute. I want to hear what Susan is going to say." Maharishi snatched his microphone, which he'd previously pushed aside. He pulled it toward his mouth and assumed a stern expression.

Years later, Jane described this incident to me. At that time she was shocked by Maharishi's behavior. The thought ran through her mind: *"What is so important about Susan's announcement? It looks like he's getting ready to close in for the kill!*

After making some minor announcements, I hit the group with, "Everyone on the course will have to pay an additional $10 per night because the course has been extended." The crowd groaned. "This is the way you will make your payment. Please make your checks payable to—"

Maharishi interrupted and yelled loudly and sternly, "Stop this announcement now." Stunned and confused, I looked over at him. *Didn't he just ask me to make this announcement as soon as possible?*

Maharishi addressed the group, "Disregard this announcement. *None* of my precious Initiators will have to pay extra for their course fee. These people who hang around me, they are not in tune with me. They don't know my mind. Even my coming here was all confused. It was announced you would have to double up. No. My Initiators are very precious to me."

Maharishi's scathing words hit me like ten thousand daggers, ripping my chest open, stabbing my heart to shreds. Suddenly there was no Susan. There was only a pile of mangled tatters, torn to bits, stumbling off the stage in a daze, all eight hundred eyes in the audience glaring at me with loathing and disgust.

1 2

HEIGHTS OF HEAVENLY HELL

1974 TO 1975

The habit of quietly absorbing the shocks will be quite a great help to stabilize pure awareness. The technique is: Just feel not disturbed. The disturbing influence could be a blessing of Mother Nature to develop the habit to make best use out of every situation.

—MAHARISHI MAHESH YOGI

Beat by Maharishi's knockout punch, but not yet down for the count, I tried to make myself invisible as I lurched down the aisle toward the rear exit of the hall. Hundreds of mocking eyes glared, scorching me with condemnation.

My former best friends now greeted me with disdain. In a matter of moments, my life was in ruins. I was utterly disgraced before every TM leader.

As soon as I reached the hallway, out of sight of glowering eyes, I broke down, sobbing. Only one person came to my comfort—Debby Jarvis, the last person I would expect to show me any kindness. Debby had rebelled when I requested a plane ticket to Europe. She had banned me from Mrs. Whitestone's home in Brighton and from Maharishi's private meetings in Squaw Valley and Humboldt.

Debby is consoling me?

She hugged me and patted my back. "It's okay, Susan. You're going to be all right. He does this to everyone, you know. Don't take it personally."

"Why did he do that? Just this morning he told me to make that announcement," I cried.

Debby chuckled. "Why doesn't that surprise me? Humph. He set you up. Don't you see?"

"I don't understand," I said.

"No one escapes. We've all gotten busted, but in private—not in front of everyone. He must really love and respect you a lot."

"What? Are you crazy?"

"You must be strong enough to take it," Debby insisted.

~~~~~~~~~~~~~~~~~~~~~~~~~~~~

That night, I entered Maharishi's meeting room with great trepidation. He shot me a terrifying scowl. I tried to defend myself—always a mistake.

"Maharishi, this morning I got a message from Edward to make this announcement."

"Some people don't deserve to be guardians of this precious knowledge," he snapped.

"But what did I do?" I asked.

"My Initiators are very precious to me."

"But Maharishi, your secretary told—"

"Never, never speak about money while I'm in the room. You need to go and round. Greta will replace you. Now get out of my sight."

I gasped. Tangled and undone, I staggered from the room. Jolted by his brutal expulsion, my mind reeled at the imagined horror of dismissal on the next flight to the USA, never to see him again. My anticipated banishment from his sanctum sanctorum was unbearable.

Day after day I went about my tasks like a wooden doll. Stiff, rigid, vacant, I could barely talk or even think. It was hard to put sentences together. I averted people's callous looks, stared at the ground, and dragged around like a ghost, disoriented and bewildered. Time slowed down. I transported into a surreal alternate reality. Nothing seemed real.

Only Edward and Maharishi knew I was told to make that announcement. Everyone else thought I concocted the fee increase myself. I quickly discovered my real friends. Older, wiser disciples expressed compassion and hinted at their own humiliating Maharishi-ego-busts. Petty youngsters in the "108 Program" turned their backs and tittered as I walked by, arrogant contempt oozing from their brains. I became *persona non grata*—branded and banished.

It was demeaning beyond belief. I felt utterly crushed.

One week after this incident, I visited Maharishi's room, a big lump stuck in my throat. "Maharishi, you told me to go and round," I sobbed. "You said Greta would take my place. Where do you want me to go?"

"Greta? No. No need to go. Stay until we leave Interlaken," Maharishi said.

This didn't make me feel better. The claws of pain continued to rip my heart apart. Something inside cried out, desperate for relief, with none in sight. Little did I know, this ego bust was par for Maharishi's course.

⟨∞∞∞∞∞∞∞∞∞∞∞∞∞∞∞∞∞∞⟩

At lunch Harriet Fletcher and Leslie Marshall from Australia, two of Maharishi's closest disciples who worked in both the finance and housing offices, approached. "Can we sit here?" Leslie asked.

"If you don't mind being seen with the scourge of the earth," I said, staring at my plate like a corpse stares at nothing in particular. They laughed and said they wanted to talk about what had happened.

"What happened is my life is over," I said.

"Your life isn't over. Not by a long shot." Leslie laughed.

Harriet said, "During the years I've known Maharishi, he treats me alternatively like a queen and a worm. This time he treated you like the worm eaten by the worm. He set you up for the biggest ego slammer I've ever witnessed. For him to publicly humiliate you might be the most valuable experience you'll ever have."

"Yeah, if I'm a masochist. Sure," I said.

They laughed.

"Just look at it this way," Leslie said. "Not only do you get to find out who's real and who's phony. You also get to see how you think others perceive you. Maharishi is like a mirror. He reflects your feelings about yourself. You should be grateful. Maharishi knows you're strong enough to survive such a test."

Harriet agreed. "Few people get chastised by Maharishi in public. I've never seen him do it to a woman."

"Oh, great, I get the prize for 'only female made a fool in public,'" I said.

"No, Susan, you'll be remembered as one of those Maharishi loved most," Harriet said.

"Pshaw. That's *absurd*," I said.

"No, it's not," Harriet replied. "I've heard him praise you so many times. Sometimes he flatters us. Other times he degrades us. No disciple escapes the ego-stroking/ego-crushing seesaw. Everyone gets it eventually. Living with him is a shattering experience."

"You mean I'm not alone?" I asked.

"Not only aren't you alone. Welcome to the club. This has happened to *all* of us," Leslie said. "The new disciples have no clue. As Maharishi ripped you apart, they thought you actually did something wrong. But we knew it was a setup. We've seen it countless times. What these disciples don't know is *they are next*."

⟨∞∞∞∞∞∞∞∞∞∞∞∞∞∞∞∞∞∞⟩

An advanced course for male Initiators was meeting Maharishi in the lecture hall. Joshua Kramer got on the microphone and read a flowery poem. Then a puja began, but not for Guru Dev. It was for Maharishi! At the end, everyone ceremoniously bowed down!

Standing in the back of the hall, I was stunned to see hundreds of men on the floor, prostrating to Maharishi.

. . . What the heck? Something is seriously off!

Right after this incident, Maharishi flew off in a helicopter to visit another course in Switzerland. Dr. Lal, Indian Defense Minister under Mahatma Ghandi, was one of the passengers. While landing, the helicopter faltered and fell hard onto the ground. Maharishi considered this an omen that people bowing to him was a mistake.

At the end of our stay in Interlaken, as Staff prepared to pack up and leave Victoria-Jungfrau, Maharishi told me, in a derisive tone, it was time to "go and round." I figured, since I'd really screwed up, "rounding" was my punishment (pretty ironic, since I loved rounding).

As Harriet, Leslie, and I were riding in a Mercedes back to Hertenstein, they told me after the guys performed puja in the hall, Maharishi was furious. They'd never seen him so angry. During a conference call to all Initiators taking courses throughout Switzerland, he went on a forty-five-minute tirade, yelling, "TM is a science. TM is not a cult," over and over.

Whenever he could prevent it, Maharishi stopped devotees from the traditional Indian practice of prostrating at the guru's feet and other forms of adulation. Joshua, Samuel, and John, who arranged that puja ceremony to Maharishi, found themselves on the next plane home. They were blacklisted. I never saw any of them again.

<hr />

No one could ever predict Maharishi's actions. Soon after my birthday celebration in Hertenstein in 1974, he called me to his room. Despite the severe public reaming, I was astounded he still wanted me on Staff. He said, "Now go back to Interlaken and finish managing the courses there. Greta's coming back here."

"But I thought—" I began to say.

"Susan, the Initiators need you in Interlaken," he said.

I breathed a sigh of relief. *They need me.*

Once the Interlaken courses ended in March 1974, Maharishi called me back to Hertenstein. After a week he told me sternly, "Now go and round." It was like getting slapped around, then caressed, then slapped again—on and on and on. But this wasn't "punishment" or "reward." It was the guru burning off disciples' *sanskaras* (seeds of desire) and *vasanas* (deeply embedded habit patterns).

After my six weeks of exile, I found myself high in the Alps, amidst evergreens, where air was crisp and oxygen refined. With breathtaking views of Eiger, Mönch, and Jungfrau peaks, Mürren was one of the most silent places I'd ever visited. Maharishi held a Vedic Studies Course at the Palace Hotel. He called me to finish rounding there, so I could participate.

In that timeless place, where cars were banned, and the only ingress and egress by rail or cable car, Maharishi spoke of the pinnacle of Vedic Knowledge, *Vedanta,* meaning "end of the Veda"—the supreme knowledge, non-dual *Advaita* philosophy.

Maharishi began his course: "The study of the Veda is the study of knowledge. Knowledge leads to action, action to achievement, and achievement to fulfillment. Our purpose is life in fulfillment. We must have the total value of knowledge for the total value of fulfillment.

"Knowledge depends on experience. If experience is clear, knowledge is profound. The Veda on paper is only the signpost of knowledge. Real knowledge is structured in consciousness. As Guru Dev used to say, 'The knowledge that is in the book, remains in the book.' Veda is the blueprint of knowledge, to verify our experience.

"*Richo akshare parame vyoman yasmin deva adhi vishwe nishedhu, yastanna veda kim richa karishyati ya it tad vidus ta ime samasate.* The Vedic mantras are structured in the immortal, imperishable absolute pure consciousness, where all the devas [deities] reside. He whose awareness is not open to this field, what can the verses accomplish for him? He who knows pure consciousness is established in evenness, wholeness of life."[53]

After the course, Maharishi said to me, "Now work on high school." That meant making dozens of illustrations for a student course book: *Science of Creative Intelligence for Secondary Education,* based on Maharishi's recent brainstorm for making TM into a science—Science of Creative Intelligence (SCI).

High school! I thought. Well at least he didn't say the godawful, dreaded words no member of International Staff ever wanted to hear: "Go to the States and initiate the people." I hated the chaotic, crime-ridden streets of the United States. I never wanted to return. I loved the refined, orderly, heavenly air of Switzerland, within Maharishi's celestial circle and divine presence. I never wanted to leave.

Maharishi had purchased three gigantic Heidelberg offset printing presses that churned out Movement literature day and night (also handy when skin-boys needed to print license plates for the Mercedes!). Now I would be creating educational materials for Maharishi's publicity machine.

High school curriculum was an unmistakable step down the prestige ladder from my previous position. *Important people work on publications for adults, not high school,* I thought. It was May 1974, and I had to face the awful truth—I was no longer a key cog in Maharishi's wheel. I was locked out of the coterie of Finance Office elitism, and wasn't even working in Housing.

⁂

Soon everyone moved to Prätschli Hotel in Arosa, a few meters from the Aroser Weisshorn ski slopes. I awoke to melodies of Swiss alphorns and tinkling cowbells, tastes of Swiss pastries, fondue, and Toblerone marzipan, and views of velvet green mountainsides dotted with delicate wildflowers, mountains jutting in all directions, bright blue sky, fresh air, bleached clouds, and perfectly manicured alpine chalets lined with flower boxes. Heavenly!

Not long after our arrival, Maharishi called our high school curriculum group to the lecture hall. He informed us in a harsh tone, like a principal scolding delinquent students: "Now you will move to a hotel on the other side of Arosa. You must remain in your hotel at all times. You are not allowed to enter the Prätschli unless I invite you."

Our little band of artists and writers skulked away in shame. Deported to a remote ghetto, utterly demoralized and defeated, we wondered what transgression deserved such censure. Of course, the answer was "absolutely none." There was rarely known rhyme or reason for Maharishi's praise or penalty.

After my castigation via verbal lashing in Interlaken, I assumed this was my extended jail sentence. But for others in our group, I saw no need for their exile, unless they were just collateral damage—in the path of bullets aimed in my direction.

On August 10, 1974, I was surprised to get a phone call. "Maharishi wants to see you immediately at Hotel Prätschli. Bring your Holy Tradition painting and all the pictures of Gods and masters you've collected."

I was embarrassed about how little of the painting I'd completed since Maharishi's last viewing, one year previously. "Too bad it's not finished, hmm?" he said, clearly disappointed. *I wonder when he imagines I had time to work on it, 2:00 to 6:00 a.m.?*

Maharishi's crew videotaped what there was of my pieced-together painting. He drummed with his palm on his coffee table while composing catchy tunes in Hindi to nursery-rhyme tempos. Two American women played guitars and sang these songs. Someone showered rose petals over a large cutout photo of the King of Nepal mounted on a board. It all came together in a video, to be hand-delivered by TM Teachers to the King of Nepal for the Hindu holiday *Diwali.* This three-ring circus continued all day and into the night.

"Today is Krishna's birthday," Maharishi then exclaimed. He examined every picture of Lord Krishna I'd brought. With his felt-tipped pen, he placed check marks or numbers on them, and wrote little captions below them. Late that night, as Maharishi was leaving the lecture hall, he said to me, "I want the pictures of Lord Krishna put onto a video tape. Come again tomorrow 10:00."

After Maharishi left, I entreated the video department head, "Maharishi spent two hours going over these pictures of Lord Krishna. He said to put them onto a video tape."

"I won't do anything unless Maharishi tells me to do it directly," he retorted.

That was the last I ever heard of the Krishna pictures.

I rode back to my hotel, body buzzing with energy, ecstatically happy and vibrantly alive. It was never about the actions of the day, or their results. This and every other encounter with Maharishi were about the transmission of bliss consciousness—grace bestowed whether he commended, condemned, or otherwise.

※※※※※※※※※※※※※※

In August 1974 Maharishi was about to fly from Arosa to a course in Avoriaz, France. I was in his meeting room when his pilot Andrew Monroe warned, "We can't fly today. The forecast is dense fog all day."

"We will fly. Get your helicopter ready, hmm?" Maharishi insisted.

"But Maharishi, there's zero visibility. Helicopters are not like planes. I need to be able to see. It's against regulations to fly in the fog."

"We will fly. Go now and get ready."

"Okay," Andrew said. You just didn't argue with Maharishi.

About two hundred devotees gathered on the foggy mountaintop, waiting to send off Maharishi. He boarded the helicopter. By spinning his index finger in a circle, he motioned to Andrew to start the rotors. The crowd whispered, laughed, then gasped as the rotors spun, whipping into frenzy.

"The helicopter can't go! It's too foggy!" I yelled.

Andrew shook his head, indicating it was too dangerous. Maharishi then giggled. He lifted his hand, palm up, gesturing to Andrew to take off. The helicopter rose about fifty feet. But Andrew brought the helicopter right back down.

Maharishi spun his finger again to indicate to keep the motor running. Then he started to shake with laughter. The helicopter's rotors continued. The wind-beaten crowd moved back but continued watching intently. *What will happen next?*

Within five minutes the fog began lifting dramatically.

Andrew and Maharishi laughed, and the helicopter took off. By the time they reached cruising altitude, the fog cleared entirely. As the sun shone, the crowd cheered and clapped.

※※※※※※※※※※※※※※※※※

In November 1974, with the first sign of snow, Maharishi returned to Hotel Hertenstein on Lake Lucerne. Vedic Studies course participants stayed in his hotel. The only Staff assigned to his hotel were his dearest disciples, such as Jemima Pitman, and our high school curriculum group—rendering our formerly exiled group suddenly his most favored group (for no apparent reason). The remaining Staff shuffled off to Vitznau.

When Maharishi emerged from silence at midnight January 8, 1975, as he did every year, a handful of us close disciples met him. That year, his first words were memorable: "I see the dawn of *Sat Yuga*."

Baffled by his statement, I asked, "Maharishi, how can *Sat Yuga* come in the middle of *Kali Yuga?*"

Maharishi answered, "*Sat* is dawning, even in the midst of *Kali*."

The scriptures of India count immense cycles of creation, measured by lifespans of various deities. The shortest cycles (millions rather than trillions of years) are called *Yugas: Sat Yuga, Treta Yuga, Dwapara Yuga,* and *Kali Yuga. Sat Yuga* is the golden age—when peace, prosperity, and enlightenment abound. *Kali Yuga* is the age of darkest ignorance.

Though I never understood how Maharishi could declare *Sat Yuga* in the midst of *Kali Yuga*, he was one of many prophets who envisioned a coming New Age, Golden Age, or Age of Aquarius—including Satya Sai Baba, Bhaktivedanta Swami Prabhupada, and countless others. Sri Yukteswar's book, *The Holy Science,* made convincing arguments indicative of a planetary rise in consciousness.

On January 12, 1975, the International Staff, "108," and special guests celebrated Maharishi's birthday on the flagship *Gotthard,* the largest steamship on the lake. On that moonless night, flowers, flags, lights, banners, and scientific displays adorned the ship. Swiss alphorns were blown. Nobel laureate in physics, Dr. Brian Josephson, was an honored guest. However, few passengers realized the ship never sailed. It just sat at the dock, fogged in, with its engine running.

On this historic occasion ("historic" from the TM Movement's viewpoint, that is), Maharishi announced the dawning of a new age for humanity, based upon scientific verification of the benefits of TM: "When the number of people in the city practicing Transcendental Meditation reached 1 percent, the crime rate went down. If 1 percent of the people could change the tendencies of the people, then it's possible now to create a new world, free from problems, and eliminate suffering from society."[54]

Maharishi envisioned the elimination of darkness with the first ray of the rising sun, evidenced by hundreds of research studies on TM. These studies proved that TM enriches all areas of life. On the basis of this success, Maharishi declared: "Science has guided us to the dawn of a new age."[55] "Through the window of science we see the dawn of the Age of Enlightenment."[56]

This memorable occasion was immortalized in an eighty-page twelve-by-fifteen-inch coffee-table book printed on thick ivory paper with gobs of gold ink. Oh, how Maharishi loved gold ink!

On a glass-top boat ride that spring, Maharishi proposed a pamphlet based on his "Vacuum State Chart," equating consciousness with ten qualities of the vacuum state of physics: perfect orderliness, unmanifest nature, non-change, source of all change, unboundedness, home of all knowledge, home of all the laws of nature, field of all possibilities, self-perpetuating, and infinite correlation.

This pamphlet would quote world religious scriptures, TM experiences, government constitutions, world literature, great artists, scientists, and philosophers. I was inspired by this notion and decided to research it. Off I went to Zurich's public library to find quotations corresponding to these ten qualities.

A physics major at Allahabad University, Maharishi loved proving his theories and practices scientifically. To this end, he founded Maharishi European Research University (MERU) in Weggis, Switzerland in 1975 and invited scientists to draw analogies between ancient Vedic wisdom and modern science. I enjoyed these intellectual diversions. I could listen for hours to the most tedious research, which I somehow found highly entertaining.

Did I say I was a nerd? Uh . . . I would say so.

David Orme-Johnson, Larry Domash, and John Farrow (Mia Farrow's brother) amassed scientific studies validating TM's efficacy. Reginald assigned me to design a 128-page book with the rousing title: *Scientific Research on the Transcendental Meditation Programme.* After five dull months of slaving (with other artists I'd recruited) at the incredibly tedious task of layout and paste-up before the advent of computers, I finally sent word to Maharishi it was completed.

Maharishi replied, via his skin-boy, "Susan should give it to Reginald."

This made me incredibly furious. Maharishi wouldn't let me present my hard-earned work directly to him. Instead Reginald would get both the glory and the darshan. I made up my mind: *I'll never do another job for Reginald. Never again!*

In May 1975 Maharishi sent International Staff to Hotel Annapurna in Courchevel, French Alps, where he began an experimental program. A six-month advanced course for Initiators claimed to teach *siddhis* ("perfections")—supernormal powers expounded in *Yoga Sutras,* an ancient scripture written by the sage Patanjali.

Maharishi said everyone must take this "TM-Sidhi Course." If we couldn't afford it, we should go home and raise money. The Staff rapidly dwindled to practically zero. Old-timers like Jerry and Debby Jarvis attended the course. But we Staff were left out. Maharishi was busy in top-secret meetings or flying off to Biarritz, Zinal, and other locations where the new course was held.

Rumors spread and multiplied. "Today Maharishi taught them to disappear, and Jerry Jarvis became invisible." "They're learning how to manifest things." "Maharishi taught them supernormal strength." "They learned ESP." "Tonight they all levitated."

∞∞∞∞∞∞∞∞∞∞∞∞∞∞∞∞

Determined to work directly with Maharishi and avoid Reginald like the plague, I hung around Maharishi closely. Whatever he was interested in, I became interested in. Whatever he worked on, I worked on.

Maharishi's focus was his six-month course, renamed Age of Enlightenment Governor Training Course—AEGTC. He assigned me to make charts of the course schedule (though I hadn't taken the course) and graphics showing scientific findings of the course's extraordinary effects.

I edited and designed a pamphlet validating TM's effect on large populations—"The Maharishi Effect." It showed how practicing TM in groups reduces crime and violence.

I designed, illustrated, and printed a children's book slathered in gold ink within an impossible three-day deadline. It even included music notation of a song composed by Maharishi. His only comment: "Why aren't the illustrations in color?"

Really? In three days?

I designed a currency note called a "Maha" (a new monetary system conceived by Maharishi, which later morphed into the "Raam" currency now used by the Movement), and happily engaged in dozens of other graphic design projects.

∞∞∞∞∞∞∞∞∞∞∞∞∞∞∞∞

In November 1975, Maharishi was about to take a trip to the USA for two weeks, to visit the new Maharishi International University (MIU) campus in Fairfield, Iowa and a facility in the Catskills. Though disenchanted with the States, I wanted to travel with Maharishi for a brief visit to see my parents. For five years I hadn't set foot in America.

I was incredibly nervous about asking Maharishi's permission. I thought for sure I would hear, "Go to the States and initiate the people." It seemed particularly risky to ask at that time, when he was sending Staff home right and left. As I considered broaching the subject with Maharishi, I became increasingly anxious.

PART IV

MAHARISHI'S SPELL

People are influenced by what we are,
what we radiate. This has greater appeal than what we say.
—Maharishi Mahesh Yogi

EYE OF THE HURRICANE

The ideal relationship, in my mind, was that one has to be for him and that's all. It's the delicate, tender, inner thread of life that breathes wisdom into the life of a disciple.

—MAHARISHI MAHESH YOGI

The life of a spiritual master is not about the events. It's about his effect upon hearts of those he touched. Maharishi not only affected me profoundly. His influence was felt worldwide. He transformed a generation and lifted the consciousness of a planet through his simple meditation practice.

How can I make such claims? Because, before Maharishi left his native India in 1959 and stepped onto America's shores, "meditation" was a virtually unknown concept. By the time Maharishi died in 2008, his brand name "Transcendental Meditation" was as generic as Kleenex.

In India, the key to making a spiritual master is discipleship with his guru. Just as disciples sought Jesus as their mentor, likewise Indian *chela* seek and find their guru.

On January 12, 1918, Mahesh Chandra Srivastava (a.k.a. Mahesh Prasad Varma) was born in a mud house in Panduka village in Raipur, Madhya Pradesh (now known as Chhattisgarh), central India. His father, Shri Ram Prasad Srivastava, was a revenue inspector in civil service. Mahesh's siblings consisted of an elder brother and two sisters. His family name identified his caste as *kayastha* (scribe): public record keepers, accountants, writers, and administrators.

Sometimes Maharishi would describe how he met his guru, Swami Brahmananda Saraswati, whom he reverentially called "Guru Dev":

In his youth, Mahesh often visited holy men. During summer vacation, his uncle Dr. Varma told him about a saint in a remote area, unwelcoming to visitors, and difficult to approach. Mahesh and his friends conspired to slip in quietly around midnight.

The teenagers located the small house in the forest at about 11:00 p.m. An attendant on the ground floor asked impatiently, "How you are here? Who told you? You are not expected to come."

The youngsters replied, "Maybe we lost our way, and we are here. Tell us about the saint. We want to hear."

The attendant retorted, "Don't talk. Just sit quiet here."[57]

The attendant then disappeared upstairs. After half an hour, he returned and said, "Follow me very quietly." He led them upstairs to a small terrace. In the dark they could barely make out someone reclining on a chair. They silently took a place on the floor next to other men. No one made a sound. [58]

After twenty minutes, suddenly the headlights of a distant car lit up the porch for a moment. Mahesh caught a glimpse of the glowing face of a great saint. He described: "Then I saw *Guru Dev* and I thought, '*Here is the sun.*' This was the flashing moment of light, which decided my destiny."[59]

Mahesh later spoke with Guru Dev and asked to serve him. He was instructed to first finish his studies. After graduating in physics from Allahabad University in 1942, he joined his guru's monastery. By that time Guru Dev had been elected Shankaracharya of Jyotir Math. His winter residence was Allahabad, where Mahesh attended college.

In the tradition of the Swami Order established by Adi Shankara (509-477 BC), four Shankaracharya carry on as custodians of Hinduism in four monasteries: North, South, East, and West. Guru Dev served as Shankaracharya of the North, in Jyotir Math, Himalayas, from 1941 to 1953.

◇◇◇◇◇◇◇◇◇◇◇◇◇◇◇◇◇◇◇◇◇◇◇◇◇◇◇

Maharishi always described his guru with deep emotion, boundless love, and tenderness: "Everything regarding him was great, simple, innocent, complete. He was that perfect divine personality."[60] "His voice, the sight of him, even from a distance, inspired the people. His words had a soothing influence to the heart, mind, and soul. Even atheists became believers in God. We used to say, 'rocks are melting.' His divine presence had an overpowering spiritual influence."[61]

After one week in the ashram, *Bal Brahmachari* ("celibate since birth") Mahesh wasn't satisfied to bow at his guru's feet twice daily with other disciples. He realized the way to get close to Guru Dev was through work. When he noticed his guru's door open, he asked a brahmacharya, considered a great favorite, whether he could help. Disciples found Mahesh a willing volunteer and readily parted with chores like cleaning the floor.

When a pundit (Hindu priest) in charge of Guru Dev's correspondence returned home, Mahesh began reading mail to Guru Dev. One letter from an organization requested a blessing for a *yagna* (religious ceremony). Mahesh considered this important. He repeatedly asked Guru Dev for a reply, but was repeatedly ignored. Finally Mahesh asked whether he should write a draft. Guru Dev asked, "What you will write?"[62]

While Guru Dev rested after lunch, Mahesh took a bold step: *"I'll write a few lines myself."* He imagined, *"Now supposing if I was a Shankaracharya, what I'll say in that letter?"* That evening, in one breath, Mahesh read to Guru Dev the brief draft he'd written. Later Maharishi often recalled to us students: "And it sounded so apt, so appropriate."[63]

Guru Dev's response was, "Will these people get it if you write? Then send it."

Whenever Maharishi described this incident to us, he noted, with a sense of triumph: "Then I quickly wrote, and put a seal of Shankaracharya, and did the whole paraphernalia—and *sent* it."[64]

Maharishi described, "From the beginning, the whole purpose was just breathe his breath. Tune myself to Guru Dev. Fortunately, it struck me the only way to do this was to adjust my feelings to his feelings. Whichever way he sees, I want to see the same. Whichever way he thinks, I want to think the same."[65]

Mahesh would start an activity and then closely watch which way Guru Dev wanted him to go. If any time he felt Guru Dev wanted him to change directions, he would turn. He described, "Very precious activities I sometimes had to completely abandon. There were quite a few periods of test, but somehow I came through every one of them."[66]

Nancy Cooke, a TM Initiator from the early 1960s, said, "Apparently, from stories we heard, he had been a stern master to Maharishi, breaking his disciple's pride through countless tests, but at the same time earning his devotion."[67]

After about two and a half years, Mahesh began to think, *"Now the attunement is fairly well. I am making less mistakes now.* All that period of adjustment and readjustment, this was the impulse of my life. On this I was living, moving, breathing eating, and talking."[68]

After several years, Mahesh felt an "experience of complete oneness with Guru Dev, not in this isolated single body. And what I did from my side was, just on that first glimpse of the flashing light on him, the life was surrendered."[69]

Mahesh's lower caste birth prevented initiation into the Swami Order (a.k.a. Shankaracharya Order) of saffron-robed monks. Thus he wore white robes, indicating his lesser status. Even now he remains a thorn in the side of major religious leaders who give no credence to TM, since he wasn't Brahmin (priestly) caste, and therefore traditionally ineligible to dispense mantras and teach meditation.

In addition, Maharishi's notoriety caused political rifts, due to legal disputes concerning the viable successor to Guru Dev's office as Shankaracharya. Maharishi's greatest detractors harshly accused him of several crimes—even poisoning Guru Dev.

On May 20, 1953, Guru Dev was in ill health in Kolkata (formerly Calcutta). His doctors visited, issuing a good prognosis. He lay down, relaxed. Ten minutes later he said, "Help me get up." Seated in lotus posture and entering samadhi, he got up—up to God. He relinquished his mortal coil.

Singh Deo, Maharaja of Kanchi, was present when Guru Dev passed. He said that during his last minutes of life, Guru Dev pointed to Mahesh and called him near. As Mahesh bowed, Guru Dev placed his palms facing his own neck and ears and passed his hands upward near his own head, then above his head, making an arc toward Mahesh's head, and passed his palms down the sides of Mahesh's head. Singh Deo felt with this gesture Guru Dev transferred his power to Mahesh.

In India, great saints aren't cremated. Their bodies are believed sacred. Guru Dev's body, in seated position, was paraded amid throngs to a jam-packed railway station, to sounds of music, bells, conch shells, and hymns. The body was taken to Kedar Ghat in Benares (now Varanasi) and placed in an elaborately decorated stone box with his accouterments: *kamandalu* pot and *dandi* staff. The box was lowered into the Ganges.

In a dramatic act, Mahesh dove into the Ganges and held onto the container until it rested in the riverbed. When I visited the Shankaracharya ashram in Jyotir Math in 2011, the attendants told me Mahesh had remained underwater for twenty minutes. When he surfaced, he bowed in reverence.

After Guru Dev's death, Mahesh meditated in silence in a tiny cave below the ancient temple Gyan Mandir in Uttar Kashi for about a year. There his inner Voice repeatedly said, *Go to Rameshwaram* (in the southern tip of India).

Mahesh confided his wishes to an elderly *sannyasi* (renunciate) who advised him not to leave, because, beyond the Ganges, it is "mud." Six months later, when Mahesh still wished to go, the *sannyasi* suggested he go to rid himself of the desire.

In summer 1954, Mahesh accompanied an ailing elderly woman from Calcutta, said to be his aunt, to a medical facility in Madanapalle near Bangalore. Since no lodging existed in that town, he spent his days caring for her, and nights sleeping on a storage room floor off the kitchen in a small coffee house.

Bank manager T. Rama Rao, of State Bank of Mysore, visited the coffee house nightly with office colleagues. Their conversations continued on the steps of a nearby temple. The group noticed Mahesh on the steps, beaming. Impressed with his teachings, Rama Rao and coffee house proprietors Krishna and Narayana Iyer titled him "Maharishi" and declared him a great yogi. The title stuck, though no sanctioned religious body conferred it.

Within a few days, despite the best treatment at the hospital, the woman passed over. Maharishi traveled to the southern tip of India, to the holy sites Kanya Kumari and Rameshwaram.[70]

⊲×∞×∞×∞×∞×∞×∞×∞×∞×∞×∞×∞×⊳

After three weeks in South India, the thought came to Maharishi, *"It is not necessary for man to suffer. The Vedas say, 'All this is bliss. I am bliss, infinite, unbounded, eternal, non-changing.' But where is the reality of this in the day-to-day life of the people?"* A deep feeling arose in Maharishi's mind that something should be done so people wouldn't suffer.[71]

In Trivandrum, Kerala (now Thiruvananthapuram), Maharishi stayed in a small room. As he walked to the temple daily, a man living nearby asked him daily whether he lectured. Maharishi kept saying "No." After several days, finally Maharishi said, "I don't lecture, but if there are people to hear me I could give them some message."

A few hours later, that man stunned Maharishi by knocking on his door, saying, "Seven lectures have been prepared for you. Now I have to give them seven titles. And this will be a one-week program." Maharishi dictated seven topics.

The audience doubled every day he lectured at the library. The message was always the same: Life in its essential nature is bliss. Everyone can experience unbounded bliss consciousness and integrate it into daily life through his effortless "Deep Meditation" technique (later renamed "Transcendental Meditation").

Maharishi taught in Kerala for six months, then traveled two years throughout India, holding Spiritual Development Camps. In December 1957 in Madras (now Chennai), a three-day Seminar of Spiritual Luminaries celebrated the 89th birthday of Guru Dev, where ten thousand people gathered in a field.

At the microphone, Maharishi reviewed two years teaching this simple method, producing positive results: "In this small area of the world where the cultures are different, it has produced this effect, so why can't we spiritually regenerate the whole world through this technique?"

The crowd responded by clapping two to three minutes. When the clapping subsided, Maharishi said, "When this is the response from Mother Nature to the thought of spiritually regenerating the world through this practice, we'll inaugurate a world movement; we'll inaugurate the Spiritual Regeneration Movement here tomorrow evening."

Another set of clapping continued five minutes. Maharishi described, "There was such a joyous feeling in the whole atmosphere. The feeling suddenly rose, as if every heart was just enlivened with the thought. It was a natural consequence from the response of the people."[72]

Maharishi's goal was to teach Deep Meditation everywhere and solve everyday worries and miseries. Meditation was not just for reclusive monks. Householders could enjoy both material comforts and spiritual glory. He declared Deep Meditation "the simplest and fastest method of fulfillment in life."[73] His revolutionary message: to attain higher consciousness, it wasn't necessary to give up anything or accept any religious pathway or dogma. Just meditate twice a day.

On April 27, 1958, Maharishi wrapped into a carpet-roll his passport, silk dhotis, cashmere blanket, shawl, silk sheets, pillow, deerskin, picture of Guru Dev, brass puja vessels, alarm clock, fountain pen, and metal toiletry box. With no money and no timetable, he flew from Calcutta (now Kolkata) to Rangoon, Burma (now Myanmar).

He said, "It never came to my mind where I will stay and to whom I will talk and what will happen when I arrive there. I just started out."[74]

Then on to Thailand, Malaya, Singapore, Hong Kong, and Hawaii, where the *Honolulu Star Bulletin* reported: "He has no money, he asks for nothing. His worldly possessions can be carried in one hand. Maharishi Mahesh Yogi is on a world odyssey. He carries a message that he says will rid the world of all unhappiness and discontent."[75]

In 1959, Maharishi continued teaching in Honolulu, San Francisco, Los Angeles, Boston, New York, and London. On May 8 in Los Angeles, he moved into the home of Helena and Roland Olson, and daughters Theresa and Tina. The Olsons confided in me that Maharishi's presence was both a blessing and disruption. He took over the house, even appropriating the teenage Tina's forbidden, off-limits bedroom, leaving her in tears. He made constant demands, racked up outrageous phone and electric bills, entertained crowds nearly twenty-four hours a day, and generally wore down everyone to a pulp.

This set the standard for everywhere else he traveled.

Wherever Maharishi placed himself, there coexisted both the eye of the hurricane, in its center of deep silence, and also the rage of a surrounding tempest. Everyone nearby got stretched to his/her limit, making herculean efforts to fulfill impossible demands. No one could keep up with his extreme pace. He generally kept two or three secretaries busy at once. They seldom slept.

In 1959, Maharishi developed a three-year plan: 25,000 Deep Meditation centers manned by 25,000 meditation guides by the end of 1962. Then two more three-year plans to spiritually regenerate the entire world. After that, he planned to retire to the Himalayas.

In 1960 Maharishi held his first Teacher Training Course in Rishikesh, India under primitive conditions and suffocating 115-degree heat. Out of sixty-five attendees, he only allowed eleven to become Initiators. One was Beulah Smith of San Diego, California. It would be five years before Maharishi trained more. So Charlie Lutes, head of the Spiritual Regeneration Movement (SRM), kept Beulah busy.

From these humble beginnings, with a preposterous vision no one believed he would accomplish, the ever-enthusiastic, tireless Maharishi set out to change the world.

14

UNDER THE INFLUENCE

You swing with the wind and that's all you have to do. I blow the wind. Sometimes very fresh wind in the morning, sometimes a little warmer in the evening, maybe cold wind in the night. You go through the different values of knowledge and experience. The result will be, you will come out weatherproof. No weather will be able to upset you.

—Maharishi Mahesh Yogi

A typical day in the life of Maharishi—and us on International Staff:

He rose between 5:00 and 8:00 a.m., bathed, donned a clean white silk dhoti, and drank fresh-squeezed orange juice from a sterling silver cup. Then he met with devotees or talked on the phone with people from all over the world.

For hours, days, even weeks, people waiting to see Maharishi sat on the floor in the hallway near piles of stinky shoes belonging to those inside his room, while skin-boys ordered them to leave repeatedly. This test of determination quickly culled anyone bent on wasting his time.

With millions of meditators and thousands of TM centers, private meetings kept him busy. Then he would or would not meet those assembled in the lecture hall. Even if four thousand were gathered, or reporters were present, they might wait one hour or six hours.

When and if Maharishi arrived, he fully embodied his slogan, "Life is not a struggle; life is bliss." He frequently cracked jokes and laughed at himself. His joy was contagious. Much of the time, those in near vicinity were in stiches. He was bliss in the flesh.

The press dubbed him "the giggling guru." His robust laugh was described as "an irresistible invitation to join him in a huge joke—even if one was not at all sure what the joke was, whether it springs from his understanding of some sublime, specific truths or from his recognition of the idiocy of mankind in general."[76] Maharishi was the happiest person I ever encountered.

Maharishi loved ceremonies, celebrations, and pageantry, so excuses for special events were always being trumped up. At one point we started ringing little bells because he preferred bells to applause. He also favored alpenhorns and conch shells.

He never watched television or movies and was ignorant about pop culture. During music, dance, and magic performances, and most speeches, he closed his eyes and meditated.

1970, Rishikesh, India: Maharishi meditating on TM Teacher Training Course.

When Maharishi got down to work, he made notes on pads of paper with felt-tip pens, always handy on his coffee table. I collected over a hundred of these notes. A few are in this book in the photo insert.

Whatever task at hand, he glorified it the most vital responsibility in the cosmos, fraught with paramount significance, which must be completed this instant. By accomplishing it, we would save the planet and prevent unspeakable horrors.

In his presence, everything assumed a spellbinding golden glow. His unfathomable essence created an unparalleled corona of urgent immediacy. Fully absorbed in each moment, Maharishi's unwavering focus was 100 percent. Charismatic to the point of hypnotic, he exuded a spiritually charged magnetism—entrancing and inebriating. With his mere glance, I became the only person in the universe, and *now* the only time ever existing. The closer my proximity, the deeper I sank into timeless, spaceless infinitude.

There was *the silence,* his delicious, sweet serenity, physical and visceral, the unearthly quietude of the infinite—solid, dense, compact, and deep.

There was *the sound,* a heavenly vibrational resonance—distinct and recognizable. Was it the hum of creation, the primordial *OM, pranava,* or *nada?* When I asked him about it, Maharishi waved me off and said, "It's not important."

There was *the look,* whether infinite love, approval, anger, or disdain—vastly penetrating. The added bonus to every look was the attendant energy transmission, *shakti-sanchara,* transferred with a word, touch, or merely a glance. His piercing eyes of unimaginable intensity evoked an arcane priest, older than eternity. Other times, toying with a flower while shaking with easy laughter, his twinkling eyes beguiled us like an adorable child.

The Look.

There were *the words.* Maharishi's expressions wove tapestries of rich context, revelatory meaning, and hidden metaphor, while shattering all preconceptions and delusions. Though I observed him for years, I could never fathom the subtle nuances of his personal interactions and their enduring effects.

There was *the grace.* As I engaged in some mission assigned by Maharishi, whether nearby or continents away, a strange supernatural phenomenon occurred. Spiritual impulses would sweep over me like caresses of divine love, ecstatic blessings in waves of bliss. Was this tender, gentle sweetness the "love" extolled by the Apostle Paul?

Such energy flowing from a spiritual master might be expected. But strangely, in Maharishi's immediate proximity, I received one added dividend. What became acutely obvious was the utter futility and insanity of this world. Not by anything he said or did, but simply by his presence, it became clear nothing is real, all is transient and intangible, this entire world is an illusion, a mere puppet show.

◇◇◇◇◇◇◇◇◇◇◇◇◇◇◇◇◇◇◇◇◇◇◇

Maharishi worked on projects as a group and expected all to participate. He often spent two hours rewriting one sentence or paragraph. Such undertakings grinded on and on and on and on and on, with no break, increasing in intensity, until everyone was worn out, hungry, dehydrated, bored, and ready to jump out of our skin. This stretched us to our limit.

Under pressure to complete next-to-impossible deadlines, we toiled overnight. But when we reported to Maharishi, he often ignored us or waved us off until "later"— which never came. Thus our egos derived no gratification from accomplishments, and we developed nonattachment.

Invariably Maharishi requested the one thing that we forgot to do or that wasn't completed on time. He chastised us for whatever didn't reach his insufferable standard of impossible perfection. Our egos were prevented from indulging in "being right," since he often made us wrong.

In Rishikesh in 1969, boilers were acquired to heat the students' rooms. A British course attendee Tony Parker was assigned to draw up a plan. Pipes would carry boiling water into the rooms for steam heat, while laborers would feed coal into the stoves all night.

During construction, Maharishi watched the daily progress. Invariably he suggested the pipes were not the right height or placement, or some other madness. After holes had been punched through the walls, Maharishi stumbled around on the rocks behind the puris to inspect the pipes running along the ground.

Wherever pipes were placed, Maharishi said, "No, no, better to bring the pipe like this and across the wall like this."

After several senseless revisions by Maharishi, it was Tony's last straw. He trotted up the path to the smoker's dining room in a daze, grabbed the first guy he saw, and demanded, "Give me a fag, mate! He's making me crazy! Give me a fag!"

Maharishi's behavior seemed the height of perfectionism, breadth of control, or depth of insanity. He would reprimand us for things unknown to us, not our responsibility, or the very thing he instructed us to do. In this way he burned off our karmic seeds.

Occasionally he spoke in riddles or spewed incomprehensible gobbledygook. He would then ask a question about what he'd just said. We gaped at him with puzzled, blank expressions. He stared back with wild eyes slightly crossed, as though he'd gone mad. Thus we became confounded and more malleable to his guidance.

Maharishi pressed our buttons to the max. He deliberately tossed and stirred us into antagonistic brews and emotional boiling pots. With acutely heightened feelings, we would react to rebuffs with abnormal sensitivity. This nurtured emotional flexibility.

Craving the incredible love energy of Maharishi's darshan, timid devotees would suddenly shape-shift into shoving, scratching, cutthroat demons/demonesses, warring to get into his room. The brashest often received the most attention, by making the most noise.

Competition was extreme. Unless we captured Maharishi's attention, during the next personnel cut we would be expelled. Only the tough survived. I was one of a handful of sticky, immovable Staff that glued myself to him and remained year after year.

Maharishi fabricated and manipulated a rigid pyramid of hierarchy and status. Those on top received his lion's share of attention. Who ate in which dining room, who sat where in the hall, who got into his boat on the lake, who roomed in what building on what floor—all became nonstop button-pushing emotional boomerangs.

Maharishi's primary curricula seemed to include lessons in letting go, lessons in futility, in one-pointed resolve, and in egolessness.

To pulverize our egos and purify our minds, first he made us feel special, privy to his elite, clandestine exclusive conclave. If we bought the illusion, our ego would blow out of proportion. Then later we would become outcasts, banished from his secret inner circle, feeling small and ridiculous.

With a glance, gesture, or word, Maharishi alternately praised and demeaned us, while simultaneously swaying fellow disciples' opinions toward us. Ego balm rarely got dished out without ego blast in same measure. He would laud me for being "very creative," then dream up some excuse to humiliate me.

In the crystalline mirror that was Maharishi, we plainly saw our strengths and weaknesses. Like deep psychotherapy, our worst traits surfaced, then like psychosurgery, festering boils got removed. This painful process helped us develop compassion, nonjudgment, and humility.

<hr />

Sufi master Radha Mohan Lal said, "Saints are very cruel. It is because they want only the good of the disciple. That nothing should remain, no impurity, no obstacle; no defects to hinder them."[77]

Rhoda Orme-Johnson, wife of David Orme-Johnson (head of TM scientific research), while caring for her husband and kids, was reluctantly dragged into working for Maharishi. He put her in charge of housing. She found it unnatural and sometimes became severe and short with students. Maharishi sent her a message, "Don't be so mean."

Rhoda thankfully realized Maharishi was showing her to herself. It wasn't pleasant, but necessary. She recognized he was incinerating a rock in her heart. She said, "Today we might call it tough love. It *was* love and it was sometimes painful."[78]

Dr. Byron Rigby, Australian psychiatrist, on the MERU and MUM (formerly known as MIU) faculty for thirty-eight years, and leader of TM in Australia, said being around Maharishi was like "open-ego surgery."[79]

The great female "hugging saint" Ammachi said, "When the pus in a wound is squeezed out, it will cause pain; but will a good doctor refrain from doing this just because it hurts? Likewise, when your *vasanas* are being removed, you will feel pain. It is for your own good."[80]

Maharishi did whatever it took to cure our false egotism and awaken our true self. He followed no rules or polite social conventions. His erratic conduct seemed hot and cold, irrational, amoral, absurd, and agonizing. He might reward bad behavior or punish good behavior. Such Indian guru tactics are widely misunderstood.

One guru tradition is "burning off karma." The Sanskrit word *karma* means "action." Whatever we experience this lifetime is the consequence of past thoughts, words, and deeds—from this life and previous lives. Such consequences, both individual and collective, are inescapable.

However, some spiritual masters can, by a word, glance, touch, or intention, soften the intensity of karmic consequences. For example, a guru might harshly insult a disciple, thereby preventing a much worse, possibly physical blow, had the guru done nothing.

Or gurus might "take on" a portion of a disciple's karma, which causes the guru to become weak or ill. Christianity appropriated this uniquely Indian belief. Jesus is known as a sacrificial lamb for his disciples' sins, indeed for the entire world. He's a *jagadguru* (world guru), who "takes-on" karma for the masses.

Westerners generally can't handle guru methods. Maharishi's followers came and didn't stay long. In India, masters who employ guru devices get praised. But in the USA they get sued and slandered, as Maharishi did—repeatedly.

Yukteswar said to his disciple Paramahansa Yogananda, "You will go to foreign lands, where blunt assaults on the ego are not appreciated. A teacher could not spread India's message in the West without an ample fund of accommodative patience and forbearance."[81]

While Maharishi was performing his prestidigitations, our emotional pendulums swung between extreme heaven and hell. We barely hung on to brutal, maddening seesaws of radical polarities, from supremely sublime to radically ridiculous.

Though Westerners judge gurus' actions as abuse, sadism, mental illness, or downright stupidity, there is method to the apparent madness: The guru's senseless machinations literally drive us out of our minds so God can enter. This may sound insane, but it works. The world is so bound in ignorance that only extreme measures can wake us up.

Radha Mohan Lal said, "The *shishya* [disciple] is constantly kept between the opposite ups and downs; it creates the friction necessary to cause suffering which will defeat the mind. The greatest obstacle on the Spiritual Path is to make people understand that they have to give up everything. What is dearest to us must go."[82]

At the same time, no love can compare with a spiritual master's oceanic love. An ideal guru/disciple relationship is built on this immutable foundation. We on Staff loved and trusted Maharishi. While undergoing harsh ego blasts to burn off karmic seeds *(sanskaras)* and negative tendencies *(vasanas)*, we could handle the burn because of this divine love.

Like moths to a flame, we felt compelled to return again and again to that brightest of lights—the inferno that would ultimately mean certain demise. In our ego's death-throes, we clung to that fire, knowing full well it would burn us to ashes.

Maharishi said the path was easy. Yes, it was easy for those who stayed home, meditated twenty minutes twice a day, and never got involved with Maharishi. But the search for my Holy Grail seemed to have its share of pitfalls, more like caverns.

∞∞∞∞∞∞∞∞∞∞∞∞∞∞∞∞

By the time the curtain fell on Maharishi's masterful sleight-of-hand show for any given day, everyone had missed afternoon meditation. It was already 7:00 or 8:00 p.m. Dinner was cold in the kitchen, and Susan the Singer (chief chef) was tearing her hair out.

Maharishi would say, "Go and rest" (his favorite expression), or "Go and eat," or "Go and meditate," and then, "Come back at 9:00" (or whenever). Then Maharishi adjourned to his private quarters.

He took his second shower of the day, dressed in a fresh dhoti, and ate dinner prepared by his Brahmin cook. His diet consisted of North Indian vegetarian food served on a stainless steel *thali* (tray with little bowls). His favorite bread was *puri,* his oil was *ghee,* and his drink was water. No onions, garlic, meat, eggs, chocolate, caffeine, liquor, cigarettes, or drugs were present in his diet.

Before Maharishi ate, his cook poured water over his hands from a stainless steel pitcher and handed him a cloth napkin. Maharishi sprinkled Ganges water over his food with a spoon and silently repeated mantras. He ate with his right hand, without utensils. Afterward, the pitcher appeared again so he could wash his hands. He often ate just once a day.

Once Maharishi returned to the meeting room (if he showed up at all), he rarely stopped until well after midnight. We would troop to his private chambers late at night. If we were lucky, or if we could make up some good excuse, we would get in the door.

In Maharishi's bedroom or meeting room, there was his bed or couch, coffee table, night table, lamps, dresser, and altar with Guru Dev's picture. We would sit on the floor.

At some point he would lie down and nod off repeatedly. Each time he woke, he would say, "Go and rest." But no one budged. He rarely dismissed us until 4:00 a.m., when he said, with finality, "Now go and rest." At last he slept on white silk sheets under an undyed cashmere blanket. He slept in the silk dhoti he was already wearing.

In 1973 at Hotel Fira in La Antilla, Spain, Maharishi just finished his evening lecture. Crowds of devotees crushed, vying for attention. Throngs made a double-row corridor for him to pass through. Palms together, poised to say Jai Guru Dev as he strolled by, their gaze trained intently on him. All were hungry for a glance or word.

Arosa, Switzerland: Maharishi walking through the inescapable, ubiquitous corridor of devotees. The tall man to the left, behind Maharishi, is Bobby Roth, CEO of David Lynch Foundation (see page 220 for info). *Keystone Pictures USA/ ZUMAPRESS*

I stood in line with the ravenous pack. I had all the moves down, jockeying for position to catch his eye. I had years of practice. As he entered the elevator, maybe he would say, "Come, come," and I would ride with him. Or as he exited the elevator, I would talk to him on the way to his next meeting or car.

Sometimes he smiled, handed me a flower, and blessed me with waves of divine grace. Afterward I felt woozy, drunk, staggering from the wine of supernal love. Occasionally his glance was a scornful dagger, stabbing my heart with consuming shame.

Other times he ignored me, looking past my shoulder. Then I became a nonentity, without purpose or meaning. Nowhere. Nothing.

Sometimes I thought, *If I give him this flower, he'll smile at me. Better ask my question now. I may not get another chance.* Then, with his glance, my burning question would vanish and mind go blank.

That night I had no agenda. I was just waiting in line about fifty feet from the elevator. Jams of people blocked the elevator door. The moment he stepped past the threshold, people competed for attention.

Maharishi spoke to certain people in line. These words hit like arrows to bull's-eyes. So precise was his expression, suitable to each need. *How does he know what to say?* I wondered. *Does God whisper in his ear?*

One woman waited, holding a flower. Maharishi, whom she'd never met, took the flower and said, "Go home and take care of your mother. She needs you now."

Maharishi stopped before a balding middle-aged man with glasses. The man was holding back tears. Maharishi gazed at him with gentle, loving eyes and said, "How you are? Hmm? Come tomorrow at 10:00 and we'll see."

As Maharishi walked by a well-known devotee named Jim, he frowned and said, "Your face does not look like the face of a meditator." Jim's eyes widened in alarm, then lowered in shame.

As Maharishi continued down the line, he asked several people, "You are doing well?"

Strolling through the dense passageway of devotees, Maharishi spotted me from a distance. Something like a tunnel formed, as though we stepped beyond this earthly realm into an extra dimensional hallway.

As he drew near, he handed me a flower and hurled a rapturous bolt with inscrutable, abysmal eyes. He then declared, with gravity, "Don't look to anyone. When you don't look to anyone, then everyone will look to you."

It was an ecstatic blow that left me reeling. A moment later, as I regained presence of mind, I glanced at the flower in my hand. Then I looked around, stunned no one noticed what he'd said. This underscored my belief the message was for me, and me alone. But what was its meaning?

15

THE FIRST SHALL BE LAST

1975 TO 1976

Who is believing in me, I can trust. And more one is loving me, how much more bliss I can give him. You are all different flowers. And in my hand you are all together a bunch of flowers.

—Maharishi Mahesh Yogi

In November 1975, I wanted to ask Maharishi whether I could travel with him to the USA. Though Staff vacations weren't forbidden, no one ever took them. We ran the risk of never getting invited back. Anything less than 100 percent focus was viewed as meaningless diversion.

I was particularly apprehensive because Maharishi had already sent nearly all the Staff away. One night I summoned enough nerve to approach him. Steadying myself with a deep breath, I said, "Maharishi, I want to go to the States for a couple weeks while you're there. I want to initiate my parents into TM."

I could hardly believe my ears when he answered, "Very, very good. Fly with me and visit States. Then come back to Hertenstein."

He invited me to travel with him, and to return! I smiled and glowed with joy.

During my brief family visit, I convinced my parents to learn TM. But when I started the ceremony, my father cut me off and became hostile. My sister reacted similarly but more subtly. She sneered and rolled her eyes. Mother was more tolerant. She even practiced TM several times. She'd seen Maharishi interviewed by Merv Griffin and Johnny Carson. So, to her mind, it must be acceptable.

Most touching was initiating my paternal aunt with severe dementia. I did the ceremony in the nursing home and repeated the mantra for about half an hour. She tried to repeat it, unsuccessfully. But when I hugged her goodbye, I received the most powerful waves of celestial bliss ever.

∞∞∞∞∞∞∞∞∞∞∞∞∞∞∞∞∞∞∞∞∞∞

Back to Switzerland in December 1976—back to the bubble of Maharishi's enchanted chimera, back to more emotional roller-coasters. More hocus and more pocus. More Sturm und Drang in the Guru Reality Show. As I endeavored to get closer to him, to my mind, department heads were getting all his attention—not me.

Autumn and winter consisted of a blur of dreamlike glass-top boat rides—almost daily. Happily, I was always assigned to Maharishi's boat. We then took silence with him the first eight days of 1976 in Hertenstein, on water's edge of a lake of dreams—a sphere of heaven on earth saturated with his glowing aura. Much of that time I spent compiling quotations I'd gathered at Zentralbibliothek Zürich for the Vacuum State book.

With a handful of other fortunate souls, I met Maharishi as he emerged from silence, midnight January 8. He declared, "Now we will inaugurate the World Government for the Age of Enlightenment to perpetuate the Age of Enlightenment for all mankind."

I showed Maharishi my project about the vacuum state of modern physics illuminated by world scriptures, constitutions, literature, arts, and sciences. He seemed astonished. "You did this by yourself?" I nodded. He smiled and darted a profoundly intense glance of divine grace my way. "Good. Very, very good. Later I will see."

Maharishi assigned me to make an elaborate chart to display the World Government's structure. Arthur Wellington, a tall, skinny British designer with a small frame, close-set turquoise-blue eyes, and chock of wavy auburn hair, worked with me day and night on it.

Halfway through Maharishi's birthday celebration and World Government inauguration on January 12, 1976, we finally finished the chart and caught up with the steamship. Since I was carrying the chart, I got into the meeting hall. Arthur didn't. Guards blocked him. The little guilt monster in my brain reared its ugly head. The hurt on Arthur's face, furrowed brow, and teary eyes, haunts me still. After all, he'd done most of the work.

∞∞∞∞∞∞∞∞∞∞∞∞∞∞∞∞∞∞∞∞∞∞

On the birthday of International Staff members, we would perform private puja with Maharishi. This was my chance to speak with him.

After my birthday puja in 1976, I said to Maharishi, "I want so much to be close to you. But it's difficult with so many people trying to get your attention."

"What goes on around me is not important," he answered. "People think that a man who is always hanging around me is so special. But I may all the time be trying to get rid of him." He giggled.

Maharishi picked up a blue felt-tipped pen. In the center of a piece of paper, he drew a big dot like a bull's-eye, with concentric circles around it. Then he scribbled around the circles. "The external things are not important," he said. "The inner feeling is what's important. I love a man by how simple and natural he is on the inside."

He drew an arrow pointing to the dot in the center.

"Sometimes it's so difficult," I said. "Are you testing me?"

"It's not testing," he replied. "It's a man's karma. The master is purifying a man."

"But there's so much competition around you," I looked at Maharishi with an expression that undoubtedly conveyed my anguish.

"Competition is all right, but it doesn't work on this level." With his pen Maharishi pointed to the scribbles to the right of the concentric circles and drew a tiny oval with a tail.

He continued, "I don't think about what people say about a man or anything. I don't work on that level. It is a man's inner focus of attention. The level of feeling for the master. The inner feeling is what it important, adjusting one's thoughts and feelings to the master. What I love is the quality of *sattwa* inside a man, the quality of simplicity."

"I want to be near you, to have a job that brings me closer." My words got stuck in my throat.

Beneath the concentric circles, Maharishi drew a rectangle with curved edges and little circles and dots inside it. He pointed to the rectangle with his pen. "We have a world plan. That's what we want. If everyone does some little thing, then we will accomplish it."

"I want a job with more responsibility," I entreated.

"High school isn't responsible?" He drew lines from the bull's-eye down to a spot near the box, where he drew a star. "Anything you want to do. High school curriculum, accounts, initiating in the field, anything. If you get bored, then tell me, and you can do another thing. High school curriculum is good. You are good at that."

I was so sick of my second-class status. My Pollyanna-eyed notion was I should have great authority. I didn't grasp the obvious—young women had no chance for advancement in Maharishi's male-dominated organization.

Maharishi drew another dot on the right side of the page, surrounded it with a spiral, and drew a check mark. He pointed to it and said, "Distance doesn't matter. It's my feeling for a man."

"You've been angry with me sometimes," I said.

"I may be angry on a man because I love him . . . Or because he is horrible!" Maharishi chuckled. He drew a slanted line on the right side of the page, scribbled many lines over it, in a violent motion, and circled it with an elongated oval.

He continued, "I may be very angry because I love him and I want to teach him something." Below the elongated oval, he drew a circle with tails and surrounded it with sunrays.

"It would get complicated if I have to make my own decisions," I said.

"Then don't make decisions. Just simple, natural," Maharishi replied.

"Maybe I analyze too much," I said.

"And this is the analysis," Maharishi said. He looked at me and drew my eyes to his marking pen, which was pointing at the dot in the center of the big circle. "Everything easy, simple, natural."

My immature mind viewed the page, but with scant comprehension of his meaning. Mostly I felt agony that his favored disciples were always in his room, while I slaved away at some menial task, feeling utterly worthless.

As if he could read my mind, he drew an oval on the left of the page with dots in it and said, "I know what happens around me. I see everyone's heart. There's nothing I don't notice . . . Now, Susan, go and rest."

"Jai Guru Dev," I said. Awkwardly, I rose and left the room in a daze. That night I longed for sleep's blessed oblivion. It didn't come. Instead there was the torment of fearing I would never return to his inner circle of magical grace.

Maharishi had said, "In the relationship of the disciple and the master, it's very natural, very simple, very thorough, very perfect. There is no 'if,' no 'but.' Nothing. Innocence, naturalness, complete freedom. Anything you can ask and receive an answer. If there is a doubt, then ask again, ask again, ask again. No maneuvering, no fear. The disciple never feels, 'Oh, if I say this . . .' Such complications never exist. He says what he feels. It is the most innocent, spontaneous relationship on earth."[83,84]

I longed for that ideal relationship. But so timid, insecure, and self-doubting, I rarely could speak openly. Ah, if I only knew then what I know now. There's such wisdom in the expression, "Youth is wasted on the young"! Painful regret yearns for a do-over.

∞∞∞∞∞∞∞∞∞∞∞∞∞∞∞∞∞∞∞∞∞∞∞

The most luxurious, picturesque hotel on Lake Lucerne was the grandiose Park Hotel Vitznau. From February to April 1976, women were staying there. Maharishi was in Weggis, seven kilometers away.

"Work with Clarissa. Write high school," Maharishi told me. But my mind rebelled. *I'm not qualified to write the curriculum,* I thought. *I know nothing about educating kids.* Clarissa Aldridge tried to convince me to write, but inadequacy prevailed (perhaps my mother incinerating the only copy of my best-written story and calling it "filth" had something to do with it).

Instead I traveled to Weggis daily and hung around Maharishi. Whatever projects were on his mind, I depicted on a large newsprint pad. This was Reginald's job, but he was rounding. I lugged my father's heavy, beat-up metal toolbox, stuffed with art supplies, to every meeting.

One night, as I reluctantly headed toward the last car to Vitznau, I came across Reginald. "I see you're busy with Maharishi these days," he said. "You're doing charts for him. That used to be my job." I actually detected hints of insecurity—something I would never expect from him.

"It's still your job," I said. "You're just rounding now, temporarily."

Every day I rode from Vitznau to Weggis in a Mercedes with Maharishi's current favored disciple Mindy Leibowitz and her minions of guardettes and slavettes. I mentally named them "Mindy and the Mindettes." One day Mindy expressed how exhausted she was.

"Why should you be exhausted? All you do is sit with Maharishi and take dictation all day writing the World Government book" was my snotty retort. "I work really hard making charts."

"Take dictation!" Mindy exclaimed, clearly affronted.

Beverly Stein, one of Mindy's ladies-in-waiting, jumped in, "How could you say such a thing, Susan? We use every bit of our creativity and intelligence all day."

Mindy and her entourage of prima donnas—so affected, strutting in their jewels, makeup, and gold-embroidered saris (gifts from Maharishi). Feasting in their elite dining room with linen tablecloths, gold plated flatware, gilded porcelain, crystal goblets, on gourmet meals au gratin, al dente, à la mode, à la bullshit.

I detested their disdainful, ugly power plays, intrigues, and subtle cruelties—tossing crumbs from their lofty pedestal, striking artificial poses with limp wrists. Such pretentious little snobs. They made life hell for every female not in their inner circle.

Okay. I might as well admit it. I was insanely jealous of Mindy.

Why does he give her so much power? I wondered. *Doesn't he see through these affectations?* Years later I realized there *was* something special about Mindy—her quality of unwavering attention, her intensely focused mind.

One night Maharishi said, "Susan, on Thursday at 6:00, you will present your Vacuum State book to Purusha. Come then." Purusha group comprised a few dozen celibate men in Weggis on an advanced course.

My "book" consisted of longhand notes on messy, taped-together paper scraps. When I told Patsy Lindberg, the Staff typist, we needed to work day and night to finish by the deadline, she replied, "No, Susan. I don't work at night. Only ten to five."

When I protested, she insisted, "Susan, those are my hours." *Typical*, I thought. *These useless people aren't devoted to Maharishi. It will never get done on time.*

I worked furiously to complete the impossible task. But even with my heroic effort, it wasn't done. Predictably, Patsy was way behind. Maharishi happened to be in Vitznau that afternoon. He spotted me and said, "Come with me to Weggis when I leave at 3:00 and present your book to Purusha at 6:00."

At 3:00 p.m. the driver phoned my room. "Maharishi's looking for you to come with him in the car to Weggis."

I answered, "I'm not quite done. Tell him I'll come soon. I'll call for a car."

Instead of riding with Maharishi, I persisted in finishing my typed draft—three hours late. Half an hour later, the driver conveyed Patsy and me to Weggis, where Maharishi was working on some project or other. No discussion of my book. After a couple of hours, still nothing.

Finally I said, "I brought the Vacuum State book, Maharishi."

Maharishi glared at me. "The meeting is already over. Purusha was here at 6:00 and they discussed the project without you. Why you didn't come with me in the car, hmm?"

"It wasn't typed in time," I said.

"Why you didn't bring it anyway? It didn't have to be typed," Maharishi snapped. "Now go and rest."

To teach a lesson about my obsessive behavior, Maharishi never gave me a second chance. This lesson revealed to me one of my subconscious patterns—I couldn't receive love without being perfect.

Even so, later that year, a preliminary draft of the Vacuum State book did get produced in whiteprint, eleven and a half by sixteen inches.

<hr />

The contract on Park Hotel Vitznau ran out in April. Some of us Staff were deported to the top of the world above the timberline—Melchsee-Frutt, where automobiles were banned. I tromped from the cable car to Hotel Posthuis, dragging my suitcase through deep snow. Cleats attached to my boots prevented slipping on ice.

The Swiss Army was ensconced in the hotel. Loud voices, stomping boots, cigarette smoke, and gruff hairy soldiers became my companions. *This is what I get for my foolishness,* I figured.

After the soldiers left, Melchsee-Frutt became the most silent ski village in the Alps. Its starkness and spectacular view were electrifying. *This place is quite heavenly. The air is fine. The wind is purifying. It's touched by the Gods!*

I began editing the high school curriculum book. Though Maharishi couldn't talk me into writing, he had persuaded me to edit.

One day I received an unexpected message, "Come to Weggis. Bring your painting of the trees in India, and the commentary." I took a cable car and train through the white landscape, painting in tow.

"Read the commentary," Maharishi said. After I read it, he declared, "This will be printed in a book." He picked up a felt-tipped pen and drew a line down the center of a piece of paper. He pointed to the right side. "On this side will be the painting." He then pointed to the left side. "This side will be the commentary."

I was puzzled. "Maharishi, what book? Don't you mean a poster or pamphlet?"

"No. A book." He then dropped the subject.

So in 1976, decades ago, Maharishi knew the painting would be printed in a book. *This* is that book.

In the lecture hall the following day, Maharishi beamed at me. "Come, sit here in your special chair each day and make charts." *Wow, my own chair,* I thought. *This is a chance to be near him again.* Daily I showed up, tackle box in hand, ready to make charts about the proceedings.

I took copious notes about everything Maharishi said, made outlines, and created charts. Whatever publications or designs he concocted, I put on paper for Reginald to design posters, pamphlets, and books.

One day I arrived late. My special seat was taken. *No problem, I'll just sit over here.* After a while Mindy showed up and sashayed over to me. "You're sitting in *my* chair," she bellowed, gesticulating with limp-wrist mannerisms.

I replied, "There's nowhere else to sit. All the chairs are taken."

"But that's *my* seat Mahaaaashi assigned to *me.*"

"If Maharishi wants you to sit here, he'll move me. But right now there's nowhere to sit. I didn't know you were coming. Why are you so late?" I asked.

"It's *my* seat," Mindy repeated.

Maharishi appeared. The throngs stood to greet him. "Jai Guru Dev."

Mindy approached Maharishi and whispered in his ear. He looked at me and smiled lovingly. Then he pointed to the first row. "Mindy and her girls will sit there."

Maharishi's skin-boy shooed away some people so Mindy and Mindettes could park their satin-sari-clad fannies a few feet from their usual spot. Tears rolled down Mindy's face. *Is she so attached to this chair?* I thought. *She seems inconsolable. She's still in the front row, right in front of Maharishi. What's her problem?*

Though I couldn't decipher what upset Mindy, perhaps Maharishi had hurt her feelings. The next day I found myself on a train back to Melchsee-Frutt with a message from Maharishi—"Go and edit high school." It was obvious who was behind my abrupt dismissal.

June 1976 arrived with International Staff back in Arosa. We high-school-group wom-en got dispatched to Suvretta, a small, dumpy hotel in the valley, far from Maharishi's lofty, sun-drenched Prätschli Hotel on the ski slopes.

Women assigned to Suvretta considered ourselves abandoned, second-rate out-casts. But I conjured a grand plan. I tried to persuade them, "Have faith. Maharishi will visit us. We can attract him with the right atmosphere. Thoughts are powerful. Mahari-shi says, "Whatever you put your attention on grows stronger in your life."

"Maharishi—here?" They all laughed at me.

"You'll see. He'll come. We have to take the leap of faith. Leap before we look."

In the only public room in the hotel, I placed a riser with a makeshift step leading up to it, found a couch and covered it with a sheet, arranged potted plants, placed flow-ers and a clock on a coffee table, and arranged chairs in a semicircle.

After I managed to get everyone fired up about inviting Maharishi, I phoned his skin-boy. Sure enough, a few days later I got a call. "Maharishi's coming to your hotel. He'll be there in an hour."

I greeted Maharishi at the door. He smiled and gave me a flower. I escorted him to his platform. The steps were shaky and he nearly slipped, but he held onto my arm, made it to his couch, and sat down. "Very good," he said. "Very, very good." He looked at the eager faces. "Now, what you have been doing?"

Maharishi met the women in the Suvretta for two days in a row.

I felt I'd achieved a breakthrough. By taking initiative, I created what was essential-ly a miracle. After so many years on Maharishi's personal Staff, I could make something happen by myself. As Maharishi said, "Know what you want, decide when you want it, figure your plan of action, follow through on it, and never doubt."

One time I asked Maharishi whether Clarissa, Julie, and I (high school curriculum women), could round on the AEGTC Sidhi Course. That was a mistake. In August he packed us off to Leysin, near Lake Geneva, to "round" in the same hotel as women taking AEGTC. Adding scorn to shame, he made a public mockery of our group, an-nouncing to all attendees that we were outcast from the secret AEGTC club (not in those words, but you get the idea).

After a month, Maharishi returned to Leysin and stayed two months. He called me to his room and said, "The three high school curriculum ladies will take care of a lady on AEGTC. She should never be left alone."

Our assignment was to babysit Nancy Raymond, a "heavy unstresser." I told Claris-sa and Julie, "We have to move her to the ground floor. That's the first thing Maharishi does with problem cases. In Mallorca, a female course participant seduced by a lustful male committed suicide by leaping off the balcony. And a mentally ill guy jumped off a rock into the ocean and washed up on the beach."

"Oh my God! How horrible!" Julie exclaimed. "I'm a registered nurse. Maybe that's why he asked me to look after her."

Nancy told us, "I'm having experiences of sidhis, and they don't believe me. This is the TM-Sidhi Course, right? So if I'm getting sidhis, wouldn't that be the proper experience?"

"What are your experiences?" I asked.

"When I do the flying *sutra,* I levitate. I float up to the ceiling. I told the course instructor, Mindy Leibowitz. But she didn't believe me. She was really mean." Nancy sobbed.

Julie sat next to Nancy on the bed and put her arm around her. I went for a tissue in the bathroom. "Hush. It's okay," Julie said. "You're safe with us. No need to be afraid of anything. We'll take care of you."

I handed her a tissue. "We're going to have a good time. You'll see."

The following two months Julie, Clarissa, and I took turns babysitting Nancy. Sometimes she had clarity, other times instability. I was always cracking jokes, getting her to laugh. Clarissa fed her philosophy and inspiration. Julie gave her comfort. We made a good team, taking her on walks and lifting her mood.

Maharishi occasionally called us in for a report. He cut Nancy's meditation down to nearly nothing. Soon she was okay—and grateful to her three angels of mercy. But she still contended she floated up to the ceiling during meditation. I figured she was probably astral traveling.

<hr />

The course was finally over in October. Clarissa, Julie, and I traveled to Mürren with ladies from Leysin, including our charge, Nancy, who was ready to go home.

We got a feeling our days were numbered, as we waited anxiously to hear news from Maharishi. We were petrified he would send us away. All the signs were there. I feared he would say any day: *"Go back to the States and initiate the people."*

We never discussed the grim topic—like we would jinx ourselves if we did. We pretended everything was okay. Finally a message came from Seelisberg via his skinboy. "Maharishi says, 'Come to Seelisberg. Then go to Gersau and work on high school curriculum.'" *Gersau?* I thought. *That's not what I expected.*

We traveled to Seelisberg, where Clarissa said, "I'm taking the ferry to Gersau and I'm not gonna ask him. I'm not even gonna see him. I'm just *going.* I'm grateful to have a job. Are you coming?" I told her I would talk to Maharishi first.

One hour later I got a knock on my door. "Maharishi wants to see all the high school curriculum girls. You and Clarissa and Julie. Come now." Panicky, dreading the inevitable, expecting the worst, I entered Maharishi's room, palms together in Indian greeting, head bowed in reverence. *Will this be my appointment in Samarra?*

He greeted me with a scowl. "Where the other two high school girls are? Clarissa and the other?"

"They went to Gersau. They left on the ferry this morning."

"Why they left for Gersau?"

"Maharishi, we got a message that you wanted us to go to Gersau and work on high school curriculum. Is that what you want?"

Maharishi snapped, "It's time for you to go to the States and make a lot of money."

Make a lot of money? I thought. *What about initiating?*

"You want me to leave?" I asked.

"This is due to your impatience," Maharishi scoffed.

I was confused. *Impatience? Why didn't he tell me to go to the States and initiate the people?*

"But Maharishi, I don't want to leave the TM Movement. I would never want to work for anyone but you."

"You are a very good artist. Make a lot of money and then take the six-month course." Now I was more befuddled. *Why would I leave the organization just to make money? Does he want me to become a householder and abandon the whole recluse lifestyle? Is that why I should make a lot of money?*

"Maharishi, do you want me to get married?" my voice cracking.

"You always have to be dependent on someone," he snapped.

This sounded like an insult, but I thought, *I suppose I've always been dependent on someone—on Hannah, on Reginald, on Clarissa. Always someone. But I want to be celibate, which I've been for seven years. I don't ever want to leave the TM Movement. Why money? That's the last thing I care about.*

"Maharishi, when you were with Guru Dev, you were dependent on him—"

"Don't compare yourself to *me*," Maharishi barked in an angry, arrogant tone. "Pshaw," he sneered.

Oh my God. What a jolt! My mind whirled. I felt sick to my stomach. Everything I'd believed seemed to be collapsing.

But I've tried to model my life after you all these years, I thought. *Every moment has been for you. Why did you tell us about Guru Dev unless you wanted us to emulate you?* My throat choked with emotion. Tears filled my eyes and Maharishi's face began to blur. The room started to spin.

Suddenly, inexplicably, Maharishi's tone softened. "You are too much dependent upon me as a person. I won't always be here."

Confused and bewildered, I groped for words. What could I possibly express, with my mind a jumble? What I didn't say but might have been appropriate, even eloquent, would have been some measure of gratitude—counting the innumerable gifts he'd given me, or extending thanks for the value he had ascribed to me. For by accepting me, sheltering me, and transforming my life, he had bestowed value on it. I wished it were a currency I knew how to spend, with wisdom.

Though all these fragments of truth lay hidden somewhere in my heart, the words weren't there. In my state of utter confusion, I mumbled, "Uh, I, I want to tell you how grateful I am. Uh, how much I've benefited from being near you all these years." I spoke just to say something, to say anything, as I felt completely lost.

Maharishi looked down his nose and scoffed at me as if to say, *You aren't worthy of my love.* Then his face changed again, like a chameleon. Suddenly it softened. "Good. Go back to the States. Make a lot of money as an artist and then come back and stay."

"What should I do with the Vacuum State book? Should I work on it in the States?" I felt like a hopeless, drowning person, grappling for a lifeline.

"Give all your notes to Mindy," he barked.

No words could have ever been more shattering than these. My mind screamed. *Mindy! My precious book—to Mindy! I'll never see it again. It will never get published.*

"Now go," Maharishi snapped.

"Jai Guru Dev," I said.

"Jai Guru Dev," Maharishi replied, lovingly and sweetly.

Dazed, baffled, utterly broken, I stumbled out of the room, feeling quite like Arjuna in the first chapter of the *Bhagavad Gita.*

August 26, 1967, Bangor, North Wales: Sitar concert by George Harrison: counterclockwise: Maharishi, John Lennon, Paolo Ammassari, Ringo Star, Maureen Starkey, George Harrison, Pattie Boyd. © *Colin Harrison-Avico Ltd.*

Serenade at the Beatles' quarters in Rishikesh: l. to r.: Back row: Sarah Sadowski, Jenny Boyd, Donovan, Windy Winkler, Joe Lysowski. Front row: Edna Linnell, Rosalyn Bonas, John Lennon, Sundar Singh, Mike Dolan. © *BeatlesPhotos.de.*

Above: August 26, 1967, Bangor, North Wales: George Harrison practicing sitar. He'd been studying with famed sitar player Ravi Shankar. © *Colin Harrison-Avico Ltd.*

Left: Donovan and Paul sing in "Silence Zone" at Maharishi's ashram, Rishikesh. Terry Gustafson (Jojo in Beatles' "Get Back") in background. © *Colin Harrison-Avico Ltd.*

February 1968, Teacher Training Course, Rishikesh, India: front row: l. to r.: Ringo Starr, Maureen Starkey, Jane Asher, Paul McCartney, George Harrison, Pattie Boyd, Cynthia Lennon, John Lennon. © *Paul Saltzman / (Contact Press Images)*

Beatles Ringo, John, and Paul sing on steps of their quarters in Rishikesh, photographed through chain link fence. © *Paul Saltzman / (Contact Press Images)*

Mia Farrow holding puppy Arjuna.
© *Colin Harrison-Avico Ltd.*

Eating lunch in Rishikesh: l. to r.: Rosalyn
Bonas (see page 177), and Mia Farrow.
Saturday Evening Post

Sing-along on Ganges bank: front row: l. to r.: Mia Farrow, Pattie Boyd, Jenny Boyd, Donovan, George Harrison. *Pictorial Press Ltd / Alamy Stock Photo*

February 10, 1968: Mia wearing silver crown, holding puppy Arjuna: l. to r.: Walter Koch, Maharishi, Mia Farrow, Gerd Hegendörfer. © *Colin Harrison-Avico Ltd.*

Beatles John and Paul compose most of the White Album in India. © *Paul Saltzman / (Contact Press Images)*

Sing-along on Ganges bank below ashram: l. to r.: Richard Blakely, Mia Farrow, Terry Gustafson (Jojo in the Beatles' "Get Back") Donovan, George Harrison, Mike Love, Maharishi, John Lennon, Cynthia Lennon, Paul McCartney, Jane Asher. Front of Donovan: Pattie Boyd. © *Colin Harrison-Avico Ltd.*

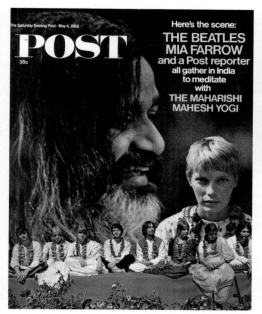

Above: Socialite Nancy Cooke in a sari, and Beach Boy Mike Love in his designer outfit, meditating on the bluff overlooking Ganges River in Rishikesh. *Marvin Lichtner / Saturday Evening Post*

Left: Maharishi, The Beatles and wives, and Mia Farrow on cover of *Saturday Evening Post*, May 4, 1968. *Marvin Lichtner / Saturday Evening Post*

Celebrities in Rishikesh, February 1968: front to back around circle: Paul McCartney, Jane Asher, George Harrison, John Lennon, Cynthia Lennon, Maureen Starkey, Ringo Starr, Mike Love, Maharishi. *Saturday Evening Post*

Left, top: February 1968: l. to r.: George Harrison, Cynthia Lennon, Maureen Starkey. © *Paul Saltzman / (Contact Press Images)*

Left, middle: February 25, 1968: George Harrison buried in garlands on his birthday: l. to r.: Ringo Starr, George Harrison, Pattie Boyd, John Lennon, Paul McCartney, Jane Asher, Mal Evans (Beatles road manager). © *Colin Harrison-Avico Ltd.*

Below: George plays organ on rooftop. (See page 167.) © *Colin Harrison-Avico Ltd.*

Left bottom: 1968, Rishikesh: Mike Love, Pattie Boyd, and John Lennon outside the Beatles' quarters. © *BeatlesPhotos.de*

1969, Rishikesh: l. to r.: Maharishi holding pink flowers, Tat Wale Baba with umbrella and staff, brahamacharya holding Tat's hair to prevent dragging on ground. Brahmachari Dherendra behind Tat. Brahmachari Shankar Lal with white hair and beard: direct disciple of Guru Dev.
www.gutenberg.org / Tat Wale Baba-Rishi of the Himalayas by Vincent J. Daczynski.
Copyrighted: Free Use

April 13, 1968, Rishikesh: Holy men visit the ashram. Satchadananda in saffron robes holding staff, left of Maharishi. Tat Wale Baba with long dreadlocks, right of Maharishi. Westerners include: l. to r.: Gerd Hergendörfer bearded, Charles F. Lutes below Satchadananda, and Jerry Jarvis below Maharishi. On this occasion, Satchadananda said, "The Almighty created only bliss; man created everything else." *Photo courtesy of Paul Mason*

1970, Rishikesh: Maharishi and Devendra in back seat of India-built Ambassador taxi. Maharishi's cook Hari Har Khan on right holding car door. *Photo courtesy of Jared Stoltz*

1970, Rishikesh: Prudence Farrow and Jerry Jarvis on my TM Teacher Training course. *Photo courtesy of Jared Stoltz*

1970, Rishikesh: Maharishi walking on the ashram path. Behind Maharishi: l. to r.: Turkish guy: possibly Kyani, Judith Bourque in purple, Brahmachari Satyanand in white robes, Dick Britton-Foster behind him, Mrs. Paul Levine, Nini White, Maharishi, Jane Hopson, Carole Hamby, German in blue: possibly Elsie, Helga Fiernow, Jerry Jarvis, Turkish TM leader: Madame Kaivani. *Photo courtesy of Jared Stoltz*

1969, Pahalgam, Kashmir: Maharishi (l. on couch) debates spiritual master Rajneesh (r. on couch). (See page 206.) *Photo courtesy of Jared Stoltz*

Maharishi performs puja ceremony in India. *Photo courtesy of Fred den Ouden*

March 6, 1970, Rishikesh: Maha Shivaratri (Great Night of Lord Shiva) puja ceremony: l. to r.: Maharishi, Brahmachari Devendra, Brahmachari Satyanand. *Photo courtesy of Fred den Ouden*

**A Vision of Cosmic Consciousness, God Consciousness, and Unity Consciousness
On a Moonlit Night with Maharishi** *(painted by Susan Shumsky)*

As we sat on Maharishi's terrace that moonlit night of 16 April, 1970, he gave us a vision of the three higher states of consciousness.

"Look, you have behind you all the higher states of consciousness in one glance.

"The two trees seen distinct from the clear blue of the sky present creation appreciated as separate from the self in Cosmic Consciousness. When the light comes from this side and illumines the tree, it pictures God Consciousness, in which creation is viewed in the celestial light with the blue of the unbounded self. The vision of a tree almost one with the blue presents the state of unified consciousness, in which everything is cognized in terms of the self.

"From left to right the sequence shows the development of consciousness. Cosmic Consciousness establishes the infinite splendor of the self as separate from the finite values of the world whilst yet engaging it in the mastery over the entire creation. God Consciousness experiences the world in the celestial value along with the infinite value of the self—the self enjoys the resplendent glories of the celestial light. When this state of God Consciousness is a living reality of day-to-day life, the cognition rises naturally to the infinite value. The infinite self finds everything in terms of himself.

"This is how the finite values of Cosmic Consciousness find fulfillment in the infinite value of the self in Unity, the state of Supreme Knowledge. Through this sequence of the evolution of consciousness, Transcendental Meditation brings fulfillment to the infinite possibility of everyone's life."

The trees of the Academy stand to illustrate Maharishi's words.

My original painting of Adi Shankaracharya and four main disciples: Padmapadacharya, Hastamalakacharya, Trothakacharya, and Sureshwaracharya. Section of Holy Tradition painting I worked on with Maharishi. (See page 124.)

Original painting I made of Guru Dev.

1970, Rishikesh: Maharishi on Ganges riverbank. *Photo courtesy of Colin Harrison*

1970, Rishikesh, India: Maharishi (rear, slightly right, seated on a chair) personally directs workers in construction at the ashram. (See page 43.)
Photo courtesy of Jared Stoltz

1970, Rishikesh, India: Maharishi (third from left) seated in the ashram garden with Sama Veda pundits, who chant ancient Vedic scriptures in an oral tradition.
Photo courtesy of Jared Stoltz

June 1970, Livigno, Italy: r. I am wearing a ring gifted by The Doors' lead guitarist Robbie Krieger; l. my Dutch friend "Lars." (See page 62.)

June 1970, Livigno, Italy: l.: Mr. Roy, a banker who sold gemstones on the side, r.: Maharishi.
Photo courtesy of Jared Stoltz

April 1976, Opera House, Lucerne, Switzerland: Spring Festival of the Age of Enlightenment, attended by participants of six-month TM-Sidhi Course and Teacher Training Course.
Marcus Brierley / Alamy Stock Photo

Above: TM Movement headquarters in 1970s: Hotel Sönnenberg, Seelisberg, Switzerland. (See page 96.) *Ringier AG*

Left: Maharishi in lecture hall, Sönnenberg, seated below Holy Tradition, painted by Frances Knight. (See page 81.)
Régis BOSSU / Sygma / Getty Images

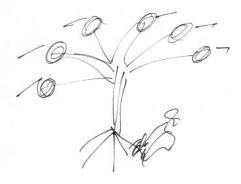

Maharishi often said, "Water the root to enjoy the fruit." Watering the root means meditating. Enjoying the fruit means a successful, happy life.

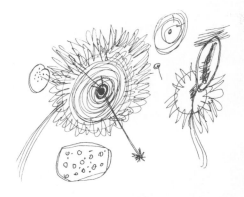

Maharishi made this drawing during our conversation on my birthday in 1976. (Read what he said on pages 139–141.)

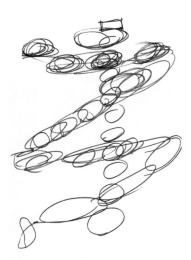

For the Holy Tradition painting design, Maharishi first drew circles to represent the masters in a vertical straight line. Then he changed his mind. He placed the masters along a meandering stream. (See page 82 and pencil sketch on page 83.)

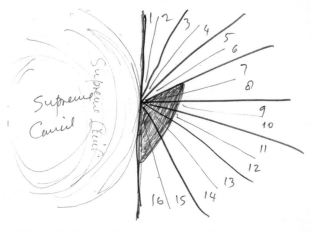

Maharishi's design for a poster he asked me to create. It depicts the Supreme Council of the World Government of the Age of Enlightenment with sixteen Ministries. (See pages 99–101.)

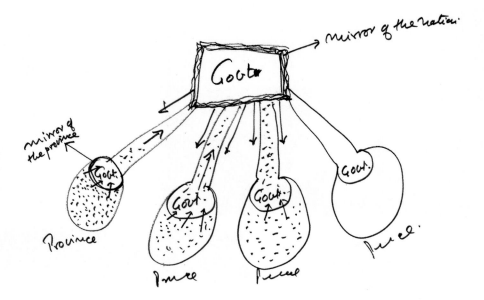

Maharishi often stated, "Government is the innocent mirror of the nation."
He believed government perfectly reflects the collective consciousness of any population.

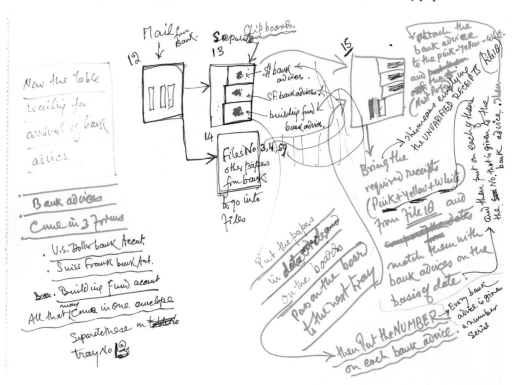

Maharishi made loads of notes like this during our Finance Office marathon
while my parents visited Seelisberg. (See page 99–101.)

Andras Nevai

Photos of me: Top l.: 1988: In front of my home in Fairfield, Iowa. Top r.: 1984: Wearing sari. Middle l.: 1983: Wearing "Sidha Dress." Lower l.: 1996: On book tour pumping fuel at truck stop. Lower r.: 1997: Promoting book at International New Age Trade Show.

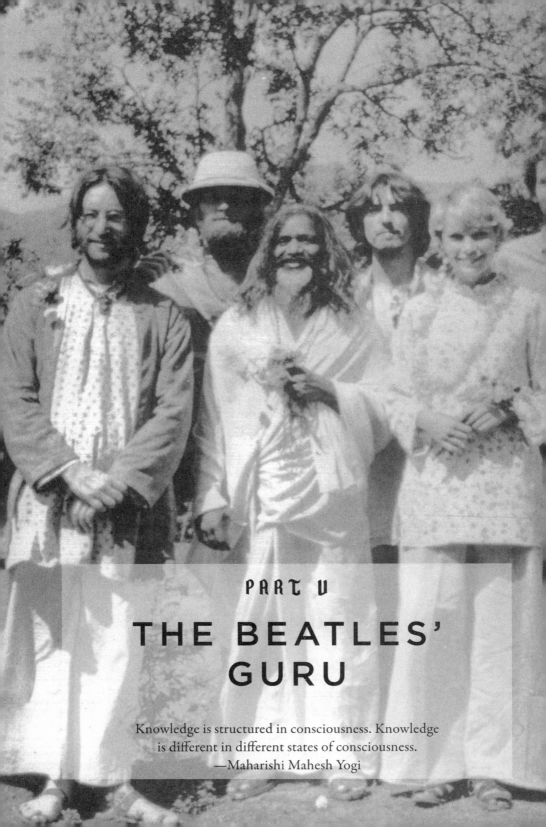

PART V

THE BEATLES' GURU

Knowledge is structured in consciousness. Knowledge
is different in different states of consciousness.
—Maharishi Mahesh Yogi

THE BEATLES INVADE INDIA

FEBRUARY TO APRIL 1968

Do less and accomplish more. Do nothing and accomplish everything.
—MAHARISHI MAHESH YOGI

In 1968, the shock waves hitting Rishikesh, India reverberated around the world. When Mia Farrow, the Beatles, Donovan, and other celebrities visited Maharishi's Meditation Academy, the planet paused for a moment, then changed orbit.

Though struggling to keep his sparsely constructed ashram solvent, Maharishi provided his famous guests double beds with mosquito netting, sit-down toilets, rugs, curtains, and bathtubs with water heated by staff in disused oil drums.

Maharishi covered airline, hotel, taxi, and sightseeing expenses for film star Mia Farrow and sister Prudence, who traveled with him on January 24, 1968, from New York to London, Bombay (now Mumbai), New Delhi, and Rishikesh.

January 1968, London: Mia Farrow and sister Prudence Farrow at Heathrow Airport on their way to India.
Howard/Associated Newspapers/ REX/Shutterstock

On their way to Rishikesh, Maharishi initiated Mia into TM in Bombay. As he imparted the mantra, she sneezed. When she said, "Excuse me, I don't think I quite heard you," Maharishi refused to repeat it. Later, whenever she brought it up, he waved her off. She felt this prevented her reaching the "field of pure Being." [85]

Sixty-two course participants waited for a week, as Maharishi held a conference, and Mia enjoyed sightseeing at Maharishi's expense. Finally, on January 31, all were assembled in Delhi to leave for Rishikesh—all except Mia, that is. Six hours later the sisters finally boarded their car, and at 3:00 p.m. the procession began.

The group reached Rishikesh too late to catch the ferry to the ashram. Both young and elderly teetered across the wobbly bridge over freezing Ganges rapids in the dark and hiked two miles to the Meditation Academy.

∞∞∞∞∞∞∞∞∞∞∞∞∞∞∞∞∞∞∞∞∞∞

The outgoing, vivacious Mia became the center of attention. Maharishi catered to her every whim. Students resented her preferential treatment. When warned his coddling might backfire, Maharishi insisted, "An international star like Mia can bring good publicity. We must treat her special." [86]

Maharishi often invited Mia to his cottage for an afternoon talk and mango snack. He singled her out and asked her questions during lectures, making her feel awkward. Maharishi appeared oblivious and continued to pile it on.

Mia's impression of the ashram: "It was a strange and colorless place. We moved as if in a dream and spoke only where necessary, in the respectful, hushed tones of visitors to a graveyard." [87]

Mia had just learned TM and wasn't practicing hours of meditation. She often wandered off to read by the Ganges. When Mia went shopping in Rishikesh, Maharishi, concerned for her safety, sent a brahmacharya after her. Mia was simply "bored out of her skull," trying to occupy herself. [88] Maharishi's concern amused and annoyed her.

Mia brought back an emaciated, floppy-eared black puppy from one outing. Maharishi named it Arjuna. When Mia played hooky, Arjuna, with free reign, nipped and yapped at students as they meditated in the lecture hall.

Maharishi acted starstruck over Mia, who seemed to play him with her baby voice and wide-eyed look. The operative expression is "acted." It's hard to imagine him starstruck over anyone. However, the more Maharishi showered favor on Mia, the more condescending and hostile she became.

Disgusted with Maharishi's apparent sycophancy, Mia dictated a cable for ex-husband Frank Sinatra (who deemed meditation "pagan") in Miami: "Fed up with meditation. Am leaving ashram. Will phone from Delhi." [89] The cable wasn't sent, because Mia was persuaded to take a safari with course participant Nancy Cooke (assigned by Maharishi to look after Mia) and return for her birthday.

On Mia's birthday, February 9, lavish flowers, balloons, pennants, candles, and incense festooned the hall. Maharishi placed a silver paper crown on her head. Students presented fifty gifts provided by Maharishi, which Mia accepted with smiles and variations on "Wow, just look at that!" A decorated carrot sheet cake was served. The celebration ended with an inept fireworks display of misfired rockets, bloodcurdling explosions, alarming cries, close calls, and students ducking for cover. Maharishi laughed uproariously and Mia seemed entertained. When a rocket hit a German's foot, festivities ended abruptly. The doctor was summoned.

Afterward at a private party, in an abrasive tone, Mia vented uncensored feelings: "I'm so fucking mad! Have you ever seen anything like it? I felt like an idiot up on that stage, with everyone bowing down to me!"[90]

She forcefully demanded a ride from an Indian guest leaving the following day and raised a glass of champagne: "To the last night in this holy place. Hah. That's a laugh. Maharishi's no saint. He made a pass at me when I was over at his house before dinner."[91]

Stunned, Nancy Cooke asked how she could say such a thing. Mia insisted, "Look, I'm no fucking dumbbell. I know a pass when I see one."[92]

Mia described to incredulous onlookers how Maharishi made her kneel on a small carpet before an altar. He performed puja to Guru Dev and placed a garland around her neck. Then he made the "pass." When asked what he did, Mia replied, "He started to stroke my hair."

Observers tried to convince her this was an honor, Maharishi was blessing her, and she misconstrued his intentions. She insisted, "Listen, I know a pass from a puja."[93]

Next morning, Maharishi placed Mia front and center in a group photograph, wearing her silver crown. She feigned a happy face (she *was* an award-winning actress) and promised to return after visiting Kathmandu and Goa, where drugged-out European hippies (and her brother John) camped out.

Was Maharishi oblivious to Mia's feelings? My guess is he was keenly aware. Everything he did was with intention. I believe, as a mirror to her, he parodied the kind of adulation she expected. That pressed her buttons and pushed her to react.

After Mia's travels, Maharishi asked Prudence to ride to Delhi, pick up Mia, and bring her back to Rishikesh. Prudence resented breaking her long meditations for her privileged sister. Her plan was to meditate in the taxi and continue all night at their hotel. At 3:00 a.m. the phone rang. It was Maharishi for Prudence: "Stop meditating! It's time to rest now."[94]

Next morning on February 16, John Lennon and George Harrison arrived in Delhi. At the airport Brahmachari Satyanand and Malcolm "Mal" Evans (Beatles road manager and Apple Records president) greeted John and Cynthia Lennon, George Harrison and Pattie Boyd, and Pattie's younger sister Jenny Boyd.

Mia Farrow greets John and Cynthia Lennon at Delhi Airport. *STARSTOCK/ Photoshot/Newscom*

When Mia discovered the Beatles were slated to arrive, she asked her driver to swing by the airport on the sisters' way to Rishikesh—or so Prudence thought. Instead, at the airport Mia bolted from their taxi straight toward John Lennon, deserting Prudence. From afar, Prudence watched Mia ride off in the Beatles' entourage without even a wave goodbye. Prudence rode back to Rishikesh alone, relieved to return. Three taxis, circa 1955 vintage, conveyed the Beatles' entourage (including Mia) on the bumpy road to Rishikesh.

The woman who'd spewed hideous expletives about Maharishi last week and fled in a rage, now (with worldwide press focused on Rishikesh) suddenly became an ardent devotee with rekindled enthusiasm about meditation, exclaiming, "Good to be back, believe me."[95]

Paul McCartney and fiancée Jane Asher, with Ringo Starr and wife Maureen, arrived three days later, February 19. Brahmachari Raghvendra garlanded them with red and yellow marigolds at the airport.

Ringo and wife Maureen foreground, Paul and Jane Asher background, walk over Lakshman Jhula footbridge to ashram. *Bettmann/Getty Images*

Though Maharishi offered the Beatles private dining, they elected to eat outdoors at cliff's edge with other students, seated on benches at long tables covered with plastic tablecloths held down by jelly jars and fruit bowls. A creeper-covered wooden trellis provided scant shelter from rain and wind. Occasionally monkeys dropped by to snatch a piece of toast or two.

Maharishi asked students to respect the Beatles' privacy and treat them like everyone else. But he didn't take his own advice. They received private lessons on his bungalow roof or inside his meeting room. The Beatles propped themselves on pillows. Mal Evans got a chair, since he found crossed legs difficult.

John and George were more absorbed in Maharishi's teachings than the other Beatles. "Whenever I meditate, there's a big brass band in me head," John told Maharishi.[96] "When I'm deep in meditation, I start writing songs. What should I do?"

Maharishi replied, "When you are deep in meditation, and you feel a song, come out of meditation, write down the song. After you have written the song, go back to the meditation."

John said, "You mean that simple?"

Maharishi said, "That simple."[97]

George said, "It's the only place to be. It's a quest to find the answer to 'Why are we here? Who am I? Where did I come from? Where am I going?' That became the only important thing in my life."[98]

During meditation Paul experienced this: "It appeared to me that I was like a feather over a hot-air pipe. I was just suspended by this hot air. And I thought, *Well, hell, that's great, I couldn't buy that anywhere*. That was the most pleasant, the most relaxed I ever got, for a few minutes I really felt so light, so floating, so complete."[99]

Jenny Boyd said, "I'd been in San Francisco taking acid and all that stuff and it had made me question a lot of things. I was very confused, so going to India was absolutely right for me at the time. George knew I'd had some kind of spiritual awakening and invited me. It was wonderful because there was nothing, just meditation and it was so beautiful. I loved it there."[100]

Cynthia Lennon said Maharishi's talks were humorous and enlightening: "John and George were in their element. They threw themselves totally into the Maharishi's teachings, were relaxed and above all had found peace of mind that had been denied them for so long."[101]

○○○○○○○○○○○○○○○○○○○○○○○○○○○○○○○○

On George's twenty-fifth birthday, February 25, a turbaned musician decked in neon crimson satin performed with his band. George played the sitar. Everyone enjoyed a seven-pound cake and fireworks. The Beatles' foreheads were smeared with red *kumkum* powder and yellow sandalwood paste.

Students buried George in garlands. Maharishi presented a book and plastic globe with the Southern Hemisphere on top, saying, "This is what the world is like today—upside down. It is rotating in tension and agony. The world waits for its release and to be put right. Transcendental Meditation can do this. George, this globe I am giving you symbolizes the world today. I hope you will help us all in the task of putting it right."[102]

George turned the globe over, saying, "I've done it!" The crowd cheered.

On his birthday, George Harrison places a marigold garland over Maharishi's head.
Cummings Archives/Redferns/Getty Images

Maharishi presenting a globe to George Harrison.
Cummings Archives/Redferns/Getty Images

Mia Farrow spent most afternoons on the puri roof watching George Harrison practice sitar. But once Donovan arrived on February 26, she followed him like a shadow. Mia's and Donovan's next-door huts overlooked the Ganges. He found her "an innocent and charming girl." His obsession with Jenny Boyd ("Jennifer Juniper") quickly vanished.[103]

Upon arriving, Donovan met Maharishi in his bungalow with Mia and the Beatles. Seemingly dumbstruck, everyone remained mute. To break the awkward silence, John patted Maharishi on the head, and said, "There's a good little guru." That cut the ice. Laughter erupted all around.[104]

Donovan said, "Before each concert I'd meditate for half an hour and go out on stage relaxed and totally refreshed."[105] Donovan composed the song "Maharishi" while in Rishikesh, which he performed for a handful of students in the guru's garden.

When Mia's brother John Farrow handed Donovan a lump of hashish, he was shocked and concerned about the press getting wind of it, since no drugs or alcohol were allowed in the ashram. Donovan promptly flung it into the Ganges.

But when *Wonderwall* film director Joe Massot showed up with hashish he'd smuggled in, John Lennon didn't hesitate to imbibe as they played Otis Redding's "The Dock of the Bay" twenty times. John asked Joe to keep it secret from George. John Lennon also demonstrated to Joe his awe-inspiring, spine-tingling trick of lighting a cigarette during meditation.

Ringo Starr and wife Maureen didn't fare well in Rishikesh. His allergies and peritonitis caused problems with ashram food. One suitcase was filled with clothes, the other, Heinz beans. Terrified of insects, Maureen demanded "Ritchie" kill them all and dispose of the carcasses. A single fly held Maureen hostage until Ringo returned hours later.

"You'd have to fight off the scorpions and tarantulas to try to get in a bath so there was amazing noise in the bathroom," Ringo said. "To have a bath you'd start shouting, 'Oh yes, well, I think I'll be having a bath now' and banging your feet. Then you'd get out of the bath, get dry, and get out of the room before all the insects came back in."[106]

Eggs and meat were banned in Rishikesh, but Mal smuggled in contraband eggs for Ringo's breakfast. When the staff was caught burying eggshells, Ringo said, "What do you mean, you're burying the shells? Can't God see that too?"[107]

Ringo recalled, "I wasn't getting what I thought I would out of it . . . We came home because we missed the children [three-year-old Zak and six-month old Jason]. It was a good experience. It just didn't last as long for me as it did for them."[108]

After ten days, on March 1, 1968, Ringo and Maureen left in a taxi with Donovan's companion Gypsy Dave and wife Yvonne Mills (whose temporary visa expired). Mal Evans left one week later, March 8.

Ringo said, "We were in this really spiritual place, and we were meditating a lot, having seminars by Maharishi. It was pretty far out."[109] "The Maharishi shows you that, through meditation, you achieve a sort of inner peace. I've found it works, anyway. So have the others. We all feel so much better for it."[110]

His Holiness Ravindra Damodara Swami, one of the brahmacharyas, noted in his diary Maharishi's impressions of the Beatles: "Ringo is always in meditation and goes by feeling and heart, but as for the other Beatles, too much brain is in the way. Of all the Beatles, George is the most advanced, and this is his last life. John has many more to go and must not give in to his weakness for women or it will ruin him."[111]

George Harrison, Mike Love, and John Lennon strolling on ashram grounds. *Bettmann/Getty Images*

Beach Boy Mike Love, initiated into TM by Maharishi in Paris in 1967, arrived in late February with TM Teacher Paul Horn, jazz flutist, who learned TM in 1966. Mike was delayed because his tailor at Profils du Monde in Beverly Hills hadn't finished his wild-looking course wardrobe. (Must dress *en vogue* in "Maharishiville"—Mike's pet name for the ashram.) Rumor had it, Mike smuggled hashish into the compound. But his only real contraband was beef jerky.

Mike's scheme was to build a "fan-fucking-tastic" World Capital of Transcendental Meditation across the river in Rishikesh, complete with stadium, airport, train station, skyscrapers, parks, and freeways.[112]

While at the ashram, Mike overcame his irrational phobia of knives: "Death by stabbing, I thought, was the absolute worst way to go. One day when I was meditating,

I felt this intense pain in my thigh, as if I were being stabbed. I kept meditating, kept going deeper into myself until finally, slowly, the root of the problem was resolved, the pain left my body, and the fear of blades was gone forever."[113]

On Mike's twenty-seventh birthday, March 15, the Beatles and Donovan composed and sang a birthday song that referred to Maharishi's Spiritual Regeneration Movement (SRM). It was patterned after the Beach Boys' "Fun, Fun, Fun." George Harrison gifted a painting of Guru Dev to Mike. John presented a handmade circular card scrawled with a nude self-portrait and farewell message, since Mike left for the USA shortly afterward, in time to begin his concert tour April 7.[114]

March 15, 1968: Mike Love's birthday celebration: l. to r.: Mike Love, Maharishi, Brahmachari Shankar Lal (direct disciple of Guru Dev.) © *Colin Harrison-Avico Ltd.*

Later that night in his basement cave, Maharishi performed private puja for Mike, who expressed devotional feelings: "At the end of the puja, Maharishi bowed toward Guru Dev. I bowed as well. After about a minute, I sensed Maharishi rising, so I lifted myself, except I couldn't. I fell back down, dazed. My heart was overwhelming me. Maharishi reached over and patted me on my neck three times, and I'll never forget what he said. 'You will always be with me.'"[115]

Mike planned a television show and tour featuring Maharishi and the Beach Boys. Paul McCartney, sniffing disaster, attempted to dissuade Maharishi from the hapless tour, albeit unsuccessfully.

Mike continued practicing TM throughout his life. He attended Maharishi's Humboldt course in August 1971, and in January 1972 took TM Teacher Training in Mallorca and Fiuggi. He and Al Jardine became initiators in 1972. Maharishi advised Mike would do more good spreading positive messages through music rather than teaching TM full-time. He said, "Live your own life, but stay in the group."[116] Later Mike attended more advanced courses, including the TM-Sidhi Course in 1977 in Vittel and Leysin, Switzerland.

During a tedious lecture by Maharishi, George Harrison stood up and said it was unbearably boring. All laughed uproariously, including Maharishi. Occasional diversions included visits by holy men, torchlight processions and full moon boat rides, sing-alongs on the riverbank, traveling cinema-in-a-truck, and trips to Dehra Dun—the closest large town. Secret indulgences included smokes, card playing, and dreadful hooch smuggled into the ashram.

Students gradually increased their meditation time and discussed experiences daily with Maharishi. After a few weeks he announced, "Now go to your rooms and meditate as long as you can. For the time being we will cancel all lessons, but remember one thing is important—if you want to talk to me about anything, come to me, even in the middle of the night."[117]

Beatles John Lennon and George Harrison meet Maharishi on his bungalow rooftop. *Kobal-REX-Shutterstock*

The Beatles and wives competed over length of meditation. Debates raged about who was "getting it," who wasn't, and "who was going to get cosmic first." John and George meditated eight hours daily. Pattie Boyd reached seven hours. George disapproved when she escaped to Dehra Dun or Mussoorie to shop at Tibetan trading posts, or to swim in the Ganges. While swimming, she dropped her wedding ring into the rapids. But luckily John Farrow (Mia's brother) retrieved it.

George said, "The goal is to plug into the divine energy and raise your state of consciousness. All those things, like walking on water and dematerializing your body at will, are just the sort of things that happen along the way."[118] John said, "The way George is going, he will be flying on a magic carpet by the time he is 40."[119]

Many students, including George and John, stayed inside their rooms for two or three weeks. Order forms were distributed for food deliveries. Long meditations brought dramatic improvements in health, well-being, and physical appearance. Chronic aches and pains disappeared. Long-term psychological hang-ups vanished.

But the road to well-being was rocky for some who experienced psychological distress, oversensitivity, frightening past-life flashbacks, astral travel, and other challenging phenomena.

Big surprise? . . . Not so much.

To resolve the crisis, Maharishi convened an emergency meeting where he explained "unwinding" (a.k.a. "unstressing"): Deep stresses from past traumas are like icebergs, appearing small on the surface but massive underneath. As stresses release, students might feel discomfort. Whenever such distress arose, Maharishi would say, "Something good is happening, hmm?"

February 1968, Rishikesh: Maharishi meets Beatles at ashram: l. to r. Pattie Boyd, George Harrison, John Lennon, Cynthia Lennon, Maureen Starkey, Maharishi.
Pictorial Press Ltd / Alamy Stock Photo

Michael, an Australian, stricken with childhood polio, walked with a cane and wore leg braces. During meditation in the lecture hall, he let out several screams. With eyes wide open, he stared at something and sobbed about a snake wrapped around his leg. He pointed his cane at arm's length to keep the monster at bay, and yelled again. Maharishi said loudly, "Don't anyone touch him."

Michael jerked and convulsed like a marionette, arching and twisting his back, grabbing his throat, flailing and dropping his cane. He yelled, "No, no, don't!" Maharishi asked where the pain was in the body, and Michael shouted, "When I close my eyes, I feel it crushing me!" It was in his feet, legs, and thighs. Maharishi told Michael to close his eyes and feel the pain. He assured Michael everything was all right and "it was going to come out."

Within a few minutes, Michael was okay but had no memory of the experience. Maharishi called it "a severe case of unstressing."[120] After one week, Michael's leg braces disappeared. He emerged renewed and restored.[121]

<hr />

Paul McCartney told Donovan that in India the Beatles hoped to get answers for personal and world peace. However, their towering expectations included the secret of life, astral magic, supernormal powers, and global peace—all in one month.

George Harrison said, "I believe that I have already extended my life by twenty years. I believe there are bods up here in the Himalayas who have lived for centuries. There is one somewhere around who was born before Jesus Christ and is still living now."[122]

Paul asked Maharishi about the Indian rope trick, "Did they do that? Was that just a magic trick? Do they really levitate, Maharishi?"

Maharishi replied, "Yes it is. There are people who do it."

Assuming some local fakir could pop over and demonstrate, Paul answered, "Great. Give me one photograph and I'll have you on the *News at Ten* tonight, and you'll be a major source of interest to the world and your organization will swell its ranks."[123]

John Lennon believed there was some secret to get—then he could just go home. He suspected Maharishi's disciples knew the secret but were holding out. When industrialist K. S. Cambata loaned Maharishi a helicopter, John volunteered for a ride. He figured, "Maybe if I go up with him in the helicopter, he may slip me the answer on me own."[124]

Donovan took a more sensible approach: "I wasn't really looking for any answer to a problem. Other people used to ask him for secrets like 'Can men really fly?' I asked him if I could have some more mango juice. Meditation doesn't mean you are going to get rid of all your pain so that you'll only feel joy all the time. It's just a way back to God."[125]

March 1968: Maharishi with celebrity guests at the ashram: l. to r.:
Pattie Boyd, John Lennon, Mike Love, Maharishi, George Harrison, Mia Farrow,
John Farrow, Donovan, Paul McCartney, Jane Asher, Cynthia Lennon.
Keystone Features/Hulton Archive/Getty Images

Mia Farrow left India on March 7 to make a film, *Secret Ceremony*, in England with Elizabeth Taylor. She abandoned sister Prudence with no money or return plane ticket. Maharishi was stuck with Prudence's travel and health-care tab. After the course he personally escorted her to Italy, where she flew to England and the USA.[126,127]

March 17 was Pattie Boyd's twenty-fourth and Paul Horn's thirty-eighth birthday. Paul presented Pattie a stringed instrument, *dilruba,* with bird's head engraved at the neck. John drew a picture of the Beatles and wives meditating and wrote "Happy Birthday Pattie love from John and Cyn." Cynthia gave her a handmade painting.[128] Paul Horn received a kurta (shirt) from Paul McCartney and Jane Asher with the word "Paul" hand-painted on the front and "Jai Guru Dev" on the back. The evening ended with a magician's performance and fireworks display.

On March 18 Donovan flew back to England. John Lennon gave him a picture he drew of a girl with long dark hair making a secretive hand gesture. Later Donovan recognized the image as Yoko Ono. On March 21 at Royal Albert Hall in London, a reporter found Mia Farrow sitting in Donovan's dressing room at his concert. Apparently their friendship continued after they met in India.

<hr />

While in Rishikesh, John and Cynthia's son Julian stayed with Cynthia's mother in England. For Julian's fifth birthday, Maharishi gifted the couple many tailor-made Indian clothes and hand-painted jungle animals and hunter figures. While leaving Maharishi's quarters, John held Cynthia's hand and said, "Oh, Cyn, won't it be wonderful to be together with Julian again? Everything will be fantastic again, won't it?"[129]

Such bursts of affection were rare. Two weeks into their stay, John moved into separate quarters, where he reveled in secret telegrams and letters from Yoko Ono.[130] "She would write things like, 'I am a cloud. Watch for me in the sky.' I would get so excited about her letters," said John. [131] Though Cynthia hoped for a second honeymoon, John ignored Cynthia virtually the entire time.

John had wanted to bring both Yoko and Cynthia to India but couldn't figure out how. John and Yoko were both married to people other than each other, and were both parents. Were they our ideal free-love-generation role models? Maybe not so much.

<hr />

Kumbh Mela is a religious festival held every twelve years where thousands of holy ascetics and millions of pilgrims bathe in the Ganges at auspicious astrological times. George Harrison wanted to attend the fair in nearby Haridwar. Maharishi insisted the Beatles ride in on elephants. George argued, "Being a Beatle is already seeing life from the back of an elephant. We want to mix with the crowds. Maybe I'll find Babaji sitting under a tree."[132]

In the end, The Beatles never made it. Neither did Maharishi.

17

AND THEY WRITE A LOT OF MUSIC

FEBRUARY TO APRIL 1968

Come on.
It's such a joy.
Take it easy. Take it as it comes.
Enjoy!

—MAHARISHI MAHESH YOGI

In the ashram, the musicians made music—*noisy* music. Students who came for deep meditation became resentful. Initially, the afternoon songwriting activities were clandestine, inside the musicians' rooms.

"I wrote quite a few songs in Rishikesh and John came up with some creative stuff," Paul McCartney said. "George told me off because I was trying to think of the next album. He said, 'We're not fucking here to do the next album, we're here to meditate!' It was like, 'Ohh, excuse me for breathing!'"[133]

Ironically, soon afterward George began singing and guitar playing for elderly female course participants and those on meditation meltdown. He played organ or guitar on the lecture hall roof in a daily mini-rock-festival for twenty-somethings. They envisioned a TM hippie revolution, without course fee, puja ceremony, or drug ban. The group pleaded their case to Maharishi, who responded with his usual evasive giggles. Eventually more musicians led jam sessions in the dining room.

George converted a hut overlooking the Ganges into a music room, lined with carpets, cushions, and Indian musical instruments. He extended an open invitation for anyone to listen or learn to play. The hut became Donovan's crash pad. Pattie Boyd played the *dilrubha* and Jenny Boyd, the *veena*. George gave Donovan a *tambura*. Maharishi hired a sitar teacher to instruct Donovan and George, who believed Indian ragas attuned listeners to natural rhythms and altered consciousness.

Just before his trip to Rishikesh, Donovan, who had a crush on Jenny Boyd, released "Jennifer Juniper." He also composed a ditty about TM, "Happiness Runs." For Donovan's "Hurdy Gurdy Man," a song about Maharishi, George wrote the third verse about past ages of unenlightened souls.

Donovan suggested since the Beatles were so famous, they didn't need a photo on their next album. It could be plain white and nameless. He taught John and Paul clawhammer guitar, an old-time banjo finger-picking style—used on the Beatles' White Album.

In December 1967 Donovan had released a boxed set album, *A Gift from a Flower to a Garden*, with Maharishi's photo on the back cover. Paul Horn recorded a flute solo album in the Taj

Paul Horn playing clarinet.
© Paul Slaughter/mptvimages.com

Mahal and later toured with Donovan. In 1968 the Beach Boys recorded their album *Friends*, influenced by Maharishi. "Transcendental Meditation" was one of the tracks.

⚬⚬⚬⚬⚬⚬⚬⚬⚬⚬⚬⚬⚬⚬⚬⚬

Out of forty Beatles songs written in India, one was about Mia's sister, Prudence Farrow. She said, "Being on the course was a dream come true—more important to me than anything in the world."[134] "I would always rush straight back to my room after lectures and meals so I could meditate. John, George and Paul would want to sit around jamming and having a good time."[135]

Prudence told Maharishi about her susceptibility to drug flashbacks. He reassured her meditation would dissolve stones in her heart and fears would disappear. He placed her in a discussion group with John and George. "We talked about the things we were all going through," Prudence said. "We were questioning reality, asking questions about who we were and what was going on."[136]

In the discussion group, George said this generation was heralding a new time, the beginning of an even more powerful wave to follow. He felt he needed to be part of it, and his music would awaken people's consciousness.

When Maharishi asked Prudence which Beatle she liked most, she said George had most in common with her. Maharishi replied that was because he was most Indian.

John said Prudence went slightly "barmy" locked in her room for three weeks, "trying to reach God quicker than anybody else."[137] John and George were bidden to nudge Prudence out of her room. "All the people around her were very worried, because she was going insane," John reported. "So we sang to her."[138]

Prudence remembered them bursting into her room, singing "Sergeant Pepper's Lonely Heart's Club Band," and "Ob-La-Di, Ob-La-Da." She was grateful and thought they were sweet, but she just wanted them to disappear. She detested the celebrity circus and asked Maharishi to move her from the noisy Beatles' building. But the ashram was full.

One afternoon Prudence waited at Maharishi's doorstep, distraught, pacing back and forth. When she finally got in, she declared, "I am doomed. I lost my soul." She'd suffered a terrifying LSD flashback of merging with the devil. But she regained composure quickly when she noticed Maharishi restraining himself from bursting into laughter.

In early March, Prudence sat in meditation without moving for five days, without food, sleep, or water. On the fifth day she returned to a hellish LSD flashback and screamed, "Get Maharishi! I need him. Only he can help!" John fetched Maharishi and Prudence cried, "I am in hell again! It has come back! Please help me!" Maharishi calmed her down.

One night in late March, George Harrison and another student, Richard Blakely, chatted with Prudence in the garden. Her withdrawn demeanor prompted Richard to ask, "Prudence, are you okay?" Staring down at her white-knuckled clenched fists, she expressed she was afraid, but there were no words to say of what.

They offered to take her to Maharishi or get help. She refused. They asked if she wanted to be left alone. She answered, "Then I would be alone with all my fright." George gently touched her knee. She jumped in fear and began sobbing. George put his arm around her and led her back to her room.[139]

That night Prudence started screaming and throwing things around her room. She woke up everyone within earshot. She was led to Maharishi's bungalow and he tried to comfort her. Finally the doctor injected her with a sedative.

Maybe "something good was happening . . . hmm?"

Maharishi escorted Prudence to newly built quarters, a cell blocked by bamboo bars (the previous occupant relocated to an unused laundry cubbyhole, accessed by jumping over a wall). A course attendee trained to handle mental illness volunteered to stay next-door. Students took shifts outside Prudence's door. Two nurses from Delhi took turns sleeping inside her room.

At this point Prudence didn't recognize her own brother John, who was on the course. Screams ripped through the night air. When she tried to escape, she was cornered by guards and dragged back, moaning.

Students asked Maharishi what happened to Prudence. He said her nervous system was damaged by drugs, she hit an "iceberg" during long meditations, and it was good it happened here, because healing would be speedy. Soon afterward, Maharishi told students to get massages as often as once a day and never meditate more than thirty minutes without breaking for asanas and pranayama.

The staff and nurses ushered Prudence, who resembled a sleepwalking zombie, to Maharishi's bungalow daily, where he directed her to do asanas in the corner of his room. If her mind wandered, he tapped on his coffee table with a pen to get her attention and said, "Continue, continue."

Maharishi asked Prudence to sit facing him while a British naturopath sat behind her. As she meditated, Maharishi blasted her with tidal waves of energy. She felt as though an interior bodily lining was ripped out through her back. She sensed coolness, then burning. Then she lost consciousness.

Within three weeks of daily massages and daily visits with Maharishi, Prudence returned from the abyss of madness. She became responsive and happy. Maharishi said the stones in her heart had been healed and she would never have flashbacks again. It was true. Prudence returned to India for the course I attended in 1970, plus many others.

Just before leaving Rishikesh, George Harrison sent Prudence a message that John had written a song for her—"Dear Prudence."

∞∞∞∞∞∞∞∞∞∞∞∞∞∞∞∞∞∞∞∞∞∞∞∞

It seemed Prudence wasn't the only "barmy" course participant. John wrote "I'm So Tired" three weeks after arriving. The song described his insomnia and avalanches of thoughts continually cycling through his mind, driving him bonkers.[140] He wrote hundreds of songs in Rishikesh about how he was feeling. He described:

"Although it was very beautiful and I was meditating about eight hours a day, I was writing the most miserable songs on earth. In 'Yer Blues' when I wrote, 'I'm so lonely I want to die,' I'm not kidding. That's how I felt. Up there trying to reach God and feeling suicidal," said John.[141] "I couldn't sleep and I was hallucinating like crazy."[142]

Perhaps "something good was happening, hmm?"

"We got our mantra, we sat in the mountains eating lousy vegetarian food and writing all these songs," John said.[143] "I was going humity-humity in my head and the songs were coming out. For creating it was great. It was just pouring out!"[144] "I did write some of my best songs while I was there. It was a nice scene. Nice and secure and everyone was always smiling."[145]

One of Maharishi's lectures about the unity of nature and mankind touched John and Paul deeply, inspiring "Mother Nature's Son" by Paul, and "Child of Nature" by John, which mentioned Rishikesh in the lyrics.

Among other songs written in Rishikesh, the lyrics of "Everybody's Got Something to Hide Except Me and My Monkey" consisted of Maharishi's favorite expressions and portrayed meditation experiences. John said the "monkey" was Yoko Ono. "Revolution" originated from Maharishi's philosophy that the only way to attain world peace is for individuals to achieve peace through meditation—not political revolutions. "Julia" was written for John's mother and also for Yoko, whose name means "ocean child."

∞∞∞∞∞∞∞∞∞∞∞∞∞∞∞∞∞∞∞∞∞

Six feet tall, with crew cut hair and dressed in white, Richard A. Cooke III (Rik) was the textbook Ivy League American jock. On a jungle safari, Rik and his mom Nancy Cooke rode one of eight elephants that drove tigers into a kill zone. Observing from a small machan (high platform in a tree), Nancy spotted the tiger and Rik shot it in the head.

John, Paul, George, and Jane Asher happened to be in Maharishi's bungalow when the hunters described their tiger kill, while Maharishi glared silently at Nancy. Rik said it was the only time he ever saw him angry. What's bizarre was Nancy and Rik expected the vegetarian Hindu yogi would react differently.

Maharishi asked, "You had the desire, Rik, and now you no longer have the desire?"

Rik answered with regret, "I don't think I'll ever kill an animal again." He then asked Maharishi, "Am I just a part, an agent of change? Am I just part of this bigger dance?"[146]

John Lennon piped in. "Don't you call that slightly life-destructive?"

Nancy said, in defense, "Well, John, it was either the tiger or us. The tiger was right where we were."[147]

Maharishi said coldly, "Life destruction is life destruction. End of story!"[148]

John's answer to Nancy's paltry excuse was the song "The Continuing Story of Bungalow Bill," which John described as "written about a guy in Maharishi's meditation camp who took a short break to shoot a few poor tigers, and then came back to commune with God."[149]

∞∞∞∞∞∞∞∞∞∞∞∞∞∞∞∞∞∞

Terry Gustafson, originally from Tucson, AZ, was a Ranger in Sequoia National Park. A bitter divorce and tough years drove him to LSD, which he took weekly for six months—enough to realize drugs weren't the answer. In January 1967, he learned TM from Jerry Jarvis in Berkeley, and at the end of 1967, he quit his Park Service career and flew to Rishikesh.

Terry came across John Lennon outside the lecture hall one night. Terry was dressed in short hair and khakis. John wore a flowing paisley cape, Indian shirt, red sash, white bell-bottom pants, and green Egyptian slippers with curled-up toes. His hair was dyed five different colors. Strobe lights built into his eyeglasses flashed on and off.

"Look at you!" "Look at me!" John exclaimed. "One of us don't belong 'ere. Get back to the forest! Get back to Tucson Arizona! Get back where you belong!" After that, John often told Terry to "Get back!" when their paths crossed. This was how the song "Get Back" was conceived.

Paul McCartney wrote "Cosmically Conscious" because Maharishi talked endlessly about Cosmic Consciousness, and also often said, "It's such a joy." When Paul heard loud crowing in the early morning, he wrote "Blackbird." Paul wrote "Why Don't We Do it in the Road?" after he saw two monkeys copulating. It occurred to Paul that people's sexuality should be natural, simple, and free as animals.

Paul composed "Rocky Raccoon" while playing acoustic guitar with John and Donovan on their puri roof in Rishikesh. One day at breakfast, Beach Boy Mike Love helped Paul with "Back in the USSR," with its Beach Boys sound. Mike suggested the mention of girls from Moscow, Ukraine, and Georgia.

Paul said about "Fool on the Hill," "I think I was writing about someone like Maharishi. His detractors called him a fool. Because of his giggle he wasn't taken too seriously."[150] "The Long and Winding Road" was about the path to spiritual enlightenment.

In "My Sweet Lord," George Harrison sang words from the puja ceremony chanted during every TM initiation. Here's the translation of the Sanskrit words, which Maharishi borrowed from the ancient *Guru Gita* (Song of the Guru): "The guru is Brahma, Vishnu, and the great Lord Shiva. The guru is the eternal Brahman, the transcendental absolute. I bow to the supreme guru, adorned with glory."

George's song "Dehra Dun" was a commentary on students running off to shop for meat and eggs in Dehra Dun, twenty-eight miles away—far from the spiritual riches of Rishikesh. George's "Long, Long, Long" was about tears shed in losing and finding

God. His "Sour Milk Sea," written in ten minutes one evening, promoted the simple process of TM as the way to overcome dissatisfaction and limitation.

Flutist Paul Horn said, "Look how prolific [the Beatles] were in such a relatively short time. They were in the Himalayas away from the pressures and the telephone. When you get too involved with life, it suppresses your creativity. When you're able to be quiet, it starts coming up."[151]

Beatles fans, music critics, and audiophiles laud The Beatles (a.k.a the "White Album"), consisting mostly of songs written in Rishikesh, as a masterpiece. Thanks to Maharishi's influence on the band.

18

DROPPING THE BEATLES BOMB

MARCH TO APRIL 1968

The knowledge from an enlightened person breaks on the hard rocks of ignorance.

—MAHARISHI MAHESH YOGI

Maharishi offered The Beatles' company, Apple Corps Ltd., exclusive rights to produce a movie about TM and Guru Dev, with John Farrow as director and music by the Beatles, Mike Love, and Donovan. It would star Maharishi, the Beatles, and Mia Farrow.

However, Maharishi had made the same promise to someone else.

In August 1967, Charlie Lutes (president of Maharishi's Spiritual Regeneration Movement—SRM) gave TM meditator Alan Waite permission to film in Rishikesh, under the assumption the Beatles would be there. Alan contracted the rights to David Charnay of Four Star Productions of Hollywood.

Guru-who-knows-all-but-blatantly-ignores-the-obvious, Maharishi rebuffed warnings from sensible people who saw blinding, flashing red flags. He seemed to be setting the scene for an interesting drama.

On March 20, Neil Aspinall (manager, Apple Corps) and Denis O'Dell (producer of *A Hard Day's Night* and *Magical Mystery Tour*) arrived in Rishikesh to negotiate the Apple Corps film contract. Aspinall's agenda was to thwart the project, since the Beatles were under contract with United Artists for a third picture. O'Dell's agenda was to convince the Beatles to make *The Lord of the Rings* (John wanted to play Gandalf).

During the meeting Aspinall noticed this little bearded man in a robe haggling about his 2.5 percent. *Wait a minute*, Aspinall thought, *Maharishi knows more about making deals than I do.* [152]

On March 26, Aspinall, Paul McCartney and Jane Asher left Rishikesh for Jane's theatrical commitment in England. Paul expressed gratitude to Maharishi and told a student, "I'm going away a new man."[153] He said, "I will continue to meditate and certainly feel it was a very rewarding experience."[154]

∞×∞×∞×∞×∞×∞×∞×∞×∞×∞×∞

John Lennon and George Harrison, the two Beatles remaining in Rishikesh, proposed a musical event in New Delhi starring sitarist Ravi Shankar, Donovan, and the Beach Boys. A Festival of Peace in Britain was planned for May 1969, featuring the Beatles and Maharishi.

A cable was sent to London telling Aspinall to return to Rishikesh, bring a film crew, and begin shooting the Beatles' Apple film. Again Maharishi received warnings about conflicts of interest. But he paid no mind: "If Charlie has a contract, then they can all work together for the glory of Guru Dev. There will be enough work for all,"[155] Maharishi said.

Though Maharishi had been warned that contracts didn't quite work that way, he appeared determined to incite the kind of pandemonium that seemed like an average Tuesday in his mad, mad world.

One of Maharishi's mind games was stirring competition by assigning two people to the same project. Was this why Charlie Lutes arrived on April 4 with a Four Star Productions lawyer and contract he'd signed as Maharishi's power of attorney? His contract granted Four Star exclusive rights to film Maharishi for the next five years!

Gene Corman, executive producer, arrived in Rishikesh to meet Maharishi, George Harrison, John Lennon, and Joe Massot about the Four Star film. Gene's fifteen-man team, including cameramen from Britain and France and Mia Farrow's brother John Farrow, were standing by in New Delhi.

On April 9, the Four Star movie crew arrived in the middle of the night, cutting out Beatles colleague Joe Massot as well as Apple Corps. At dawn, in the Beatles courtyard, the bed-headed, bleary-eyed, half-asleep John Lennon opened his door to a cameramen and director yelling "Action."

Now the Beatles were expected to be two-bit players in the Four Star film. John and George avoided the lecture hall, where lights and cameras were installed. They refused to leave their rooms.

∞×∞×∞×∞×∞×∞×∞×∞×∞×∞×∞

The Beatles had basked in glorified self-aggrandizement in Guruville as honored guests of what they'd considered a great spiritual master. Ringo declared, "We never did anything for him. We never paid him one penny."[156]

Now John and George suspected Maharishi's motive was exploiting them for publicity, beginning with his vinyl record by "The Beatles' Spiritual Teacher" in 1967. Maharishi persisted in promising ABC a television special with the Beatles, though the band refused repeatedly. The Beatles were also requested to tithe 10 percent or more of their annual income to the Movement. Mal Evans noted John's reaction: "Over my dead body."[157]

When Charlie Lutes (whom John nicknamed "Captain Kundalini") railed against the 1960s hippie culture in the lecture hall, John stood and said, "Anyone who believes that has his 'ead up his arse!"[158] As John perceived Maharishi in cahoots with Charlie's back-alley movie deal, John discounted Charlie's miraculous tales about Maharishi as fantastic lies.

John's suspicions might have arisen from naïveté, gullibility, unrealistic expectations, meditation inexperience, inconstancy, insincerity, or all of the above. However, many forces were at work, manipulating the Beatles. Their disenchantment over the film contract was the first rumble in a coming volcanic eruption. More heinous powers churned in the molten crucible below.

<hr />

Enter Johan Alexis "Magic Alex" Mardas—a Beatles associate who arrived in Rishikesh the last week in March. John Dunbar, Marianne Faithfull's ex-husband, had introduced Alexis to John Lennon on an acid trip. Dunbar extolled the Greek as Marconi/ Edison/ Bell in one convenient package. Alexis had made a seldom-functional psychedelic light box for the Rolling Stones, but Brian Jones was charmed by his banter.

Soon after meeting John, the unshakeable Alexis seemed to have surgically attached himself to John's hip. Cynthia was alarmed at his Svengali-like influence over her husband. She declared Alexis "made her skin crawl."[159] John introduced Alexis to the other Beatles as "my new guru Magic Alex."[160] Alexis's harebrained schemes included drilling the Beatles' skulls at their foreheads—trepanning to open the third eye.

Alexis had convinced the Beatles of his genius, claiming to be designing a solar-powered electric guitar (for daytime rock concerts?), a force field to keep fans away, wallpaper that doubled as a stereo speaker, paint that made objects invisible, and a flying saucer. But his most improbable device would power a radio station, broadcast Maharishi's message worldwide, plus supply electrical power to the entire region. The size of a trash can lid, it would consist of electronic parts from the local equivalent of Radio Shack (as if such thing existed in 1968 rural India).

Reality check—Alexis was a TV repairman.

"Magic Alex" described the students at the ashram as "second-rate American actresses,"[161] "mentally ill old ladies, and a bunch of lost, pretty girls."[162] Yet he had no compunction about having sex with one—a short-haired blond schoolteacher from Brooklyn in her late twenties, Rosalyn Bonas.[163] She'd been meditating a year. Spending her savings on the course, she hoped to become a better schoolteacher, spread TM to the world, get close to Maharishi, and absorb his vibrations, which had made her meditations deeper after she saw him at a New York lecture.

Two Hollywood actors were course attendees: Tom Simcox and Jerry Stovin. Before Rosalyn hooked up with Magic Alex, she had an affair with Tom. Maharishi told Rosalyn to socialize less and meditate more, and then after long meditation socializing would be more enjoyable. She claimed she found this to be true.[164]

Jenny Boyd said Alexis Mardas came to Rishikesh "because he didn't approve of the Beatles' meditating, and he wanted John back." She noted Alexis "made friends with another girl in our party [Rosalyn]." Jenny watched them "walking the grounds of the ashram together, obviously cooking something up."[165]

No one ever reported Alexis meditating—quite the opposite. Alexis's expressed motive for coming to Rishikesh was to end the Beatles' obsession with this Indian guru. Maharishi was a threat to Alexis's gurudom status. Determined to undermine Maharishi's influence, Alexis's first move (according to Beatles manager Peter Brown) was smuggling wine into the ashram and drinking with Cynthia, Pattie, and some Americans.

Mike Dolan, Rosalyn's next-door neighbor at the ashram, described her as "perkily attractive, very funny, and at times combative. She would interrupt Maharishi with pointedly uncosmic questions during his lectures."[166] Though Maharishi was a Hindu yogi in an ashram in India, she was astounded to discover Hindu beliefs underlying TM. Mike claimed Rosalyn stopped attending Maharishi's lectures, became increasingly hostile toward meditation, and wanted to go home. But her plane ticket restricted her from leaving early.

At night Mike overheard Alexis and Rosalyn next-door through the thin walls, practicing the *Kama Sutra*—apparently her definition of taking Maharishi's advice to "socialize less." Whiffs of a distinct herb wafted from her room, and bottles of fermented brews appeared—definitely not on the course agenda. This behavior caused a rumble. Brahmacharya Rhaghvendra informed Mike that Rosalyn would be expelled from the ashram.

In a statement to the *New York Times* in 2010, Alexis Mardas reported: "About three to four months after I had arrived at the retreat, we were attending a lecture given by the Maharishi. Also present was an American teacher, whose name I now know to have been Rosalyn Bonas. I remember the Maharishi saying that this lady had an 'iceberg' in her brain and was unable to understand what he was saying. In the presence of everyone there, he told her that she should come to his villa after the lecture for private tuition."[167]

Alexis further stated that a day or two later, Rosalyn approached Alexis and John on the porch of the Beatles' bungalow, saying Maharishi had made sexual advances. Alexis also claimed Maharishi offered her chicken and invited her to return. The following night, John, George, and Alexis purportedly hid in the undergrowth at Maharishi's bungalow to catch Maharishi and Rosalyn in flagrante delicto. They supposedly spied Maharishi trying to hug Rosalyn (who were both fully clothed) and were very upset by what they saw.[168]

Was Alexis hallucinating or just drunk when he made these statements? Firstly, he feigned unfamiliarity with Rosalyn—or did he ever bother to ask the name of the woman he was having sex with? Secondly, John and George never claimed to have seen any alleged tryst. Peter Brown reported that when Alexis hatched a plot to spy on Maharishi, the Beatles wanted nothing to do with it. After Alexis and Rosalyn claimed they went through with the plot anyway, the Beatles argued with Alexis about what he allegedly saw. Third, Maharishi never offered Rosalyn chicken. The entire "chicken" controversy, which spread throughout the ashram, was fabricated. Fourth, Alexis claimed to stay in Rishikesh three or four *months* yet never saw Paul, Ringo, Donovan, Mia, or Prudence. That was impossible. Figuring the dates the celebrities arrived and departed, and assuming no one ever saw Prudence anyway, Alexis couldn't have stayed more than two weeks.

Some course participants believed Alexis conspired to entrap Maharishi in a sexual scandal to split the Beatles from Maharishi. Others believed Alexis concocted the scandal to avoid Maharishi's pressing questions about the proposed radio station. Was this how Alexis escaped the humiliation of the Beatles discovering the truth about his spurious "inventions"?

Whether anyone actually saw the purported "hug" is immaterial. What *is* real—Rosalyn reported to Cynthia, Pattie, Alexis, and Tom that Maharishi made a pass at her. The result: her accusation exacerbated John and George's disillusion about Maharishi's exploitation of them—a wound still bleeding fresh blood.

Paul Horn described, "She [Rosalyn] starts all this crap about Maharishi making passes at her. Basically, there were a lot of rumors, jealousies, and triangles, and she got back at The Beatles through saying this about Maharishi."[169]

Cynthia Lennon thought Alexis had put the "young and impressionable" Rosalyn up to it.[170] She said Mardas had accused Maharishi of being a blackguard, "without a single shred of evidence or justification. It was obvious to me that Alexis wanted out and more than anything he wanted The Beatles out as well."[171]

The Beatles and wives, hypersensitive and highly suggestible after two months of constant meditation, stayed up all night debating the allegation. George didn't believe a word of it and was furious with Alexis. But Alexis swore to its veracity and insisted they all leave immediately. He warned the evil Maharishi might hex them with black magic. Finally, when George started to believe the rumor, John thought, "Well, it must be true; because if George started thinking it might be true, there must be something in it."[172]

Cynthia Lennon said, "To me it was tragic—hearsay, an unproved action and unproved statements. The finger of suspicion pointed at the man who had given us all so much in so many ways—Maharishi. Alexis and a fellow female meditator began to sow seeds of doubt into very open minds."[173]

Early morning April 10, Alan Waite and Paul Horn were meeting Maharishi in his bungalow. Alan said John and George arrived and asked to see Maharishi, who took them into his bedroom. After twenty minutes, they came out, shook hands with Alan and Paul, and said they were leaving. No one knows what happened in that room other than John, George, and Maharishi. Alexis claimed to have been in the room, but there's no evidence he was.

Here's what eyewitnesses John Lennon and George Harrison reported:

John announced to Maharishi, "We're leaving."

Maharishi asked, "Why?"

George, who'd already made a commitment to travel to South India to make a film called *Raga* with sitar player Ravi Shankar, said, "Look, I told you I was going. I'm going to the South of India."[174]

Maharishi, obviously not buying this explanation, asked, "What's wrong?"

Since Charlie Lutes often hinted that Maharishi performed miracles, John responded sarcastically: "Well, if you're so cosmic, you'll know why."[175]

Maharishi responded, "I don't know why. You must tell me."[176]

John said, "Well, you're supposed to be the mystic. You should know."[177]

Then Maharishi shot John an intense, piercing glare, which John interpreted as saying, with his eyes, "I'll kill you, you bastard."[178]

Maharishi then told the Beatles the truth was like an iceberg with only 10 percent showing. But with Maharishi's scorching look, John was struck with what he considered an epiphany. To his mind, he'd called Maharishi's bluff. His reasoning was, if Maharishi knows all, he should know this. John recalled later, "I was a bit rough with him."[179]

But should Maharishi really "know all"? Are gurus gods? Such unrealistic expectations characterize naïve guru chasers. They assume silk-robed men should fulfill their ridiculous fantasy of saintly behavior: all-seeing, all-knowing, all-powerful, godly, pious, virtuous, flawless, and chaste.

Maharishi never claimed supernormal powers, and, if he indeed possessed them, he wouldn't prove them on a dare from a cynic. Those who attempted to worship Maharishi, he quickly dismissed and sent packing on the next plane home.

John Lennon returned to his bungalow. He ripped up his poster of Maharishi and tossed it, face down, onto the cement floor. Alexis scrambled to find taxis in Dehra Dun to speed the group to the airport, before anyone changed his or her mind. The entourage packed in a flurry.

Cynthia recalled, "I never packed my belongings with such a heavy heart. I felt that what we were doing was wrong, very, very wrong." "The Maharishi had been accused and sentenced before he even had a chance to defend himself."[180]

On the morning of April 10, the distraught group ate breakfast in whispers, surrounded by a ghostly mist blanketing the morning air, while faint chants of mantras and tinkling of bells wafted across the river from the Sivananda ashram on the far riverbank.

Maharishi's robed form, clouded by fog, emerged like a specter from the gloom, seating itself silently in a small wooden shelter with a grass roof, about a hundred yards from the dining area. Jerry Jarvis approached the Beatles and requested on behalf of Maharishi "to talk things over properly." He said Maharishi is "very sad and wants desperately to put things right" and wanted to convince them to stay.[181]

"I wanted to cry," Cynthia said. "He looked very biblical and isolated in his faith. To me he was a man with a quest, a dream for a better world and here were we, a group of people who had the power to influence the youth of the world, possibly squashing all the good work he had done."[182]

John and George denied Maharishi's request to talk with them. They stood up from the table and filed past him without making a sound, as he stood under an umbrella at the ashram gate. "Wait," Maharishi said. "Talk to me."[183] Alexis, with steely determination to win, was not about to let that happen.

As the Beatles loaded taxis, with wives in tow, the weeping, shaken women pleaded with John and George to reconsider. Alexis got what he wanted—his Beatles back. Did Rosalyn get what she wanted?

She said, "I left the ashram the day after I was totally disillusioned with my guru. Up until that point I believed every word Maharishi said, and I was determined to make a difference in the world by teaching his meditation. Yes I might have missed but a few lectures because I found Alex to be quite an interesting character, but other than that I was a devoted student meditating several days at a time, studying and reading daily."[184]

However, decades later, there is evidence to support Maharishi was actually the one who got what he wanted—no more disruption of the serene atmosphere of his Teacher Training Course (see page 218).

<hr/>

As they were about to leave, John sensed, "Even then, [Maharishi] sent out so much power that he was like a magnet, drawing me back to him. Suddenly I didn't want to go at all, but I forced meself to carry on before it was too late."[185]

John described, "We thought: 'They're deliberately keeping the taxi back so as we can't escape from this madman's camp.' And we had the mad Greek with us who was paranoid as hell. He kept saying, 'It's black magic, black magic. They're gonna keep you here forever.'"[186]

While waiting for taxis, John took out vengeance on Maharishi, singing "Maharishi, you little twat. Who the fuck do you think you are? Oh, you cunt."[187]

When George objected, "You can't say that. It's ridiculous," John changed the lyrics.[188] "Sexy Sadie" became the seductress in his song that appeared on *The Beatles* (White Album).

The Beatles' entourage arrived in Delhi after a harrowing journey. The Lennons' taxi got a flat tire and the driver abandoned them. They were forced to hitchhike in the dark. They speculated Maharishi had put a curse on them.

In Delhi, John and George told reporters they had urgent business in London and didn't want to appear in Maharishi's film. George Harrison traveled to South India, where he contracted dysentery, which he suspected was a spell cast by Maharishi. He was given amulets by famed sitar player Ravi Shankar, and recovered.

Meanwhile, the Lennons caught the first plane back to London, where in a drunken stupor, John confessed to Cynthia his infidelities with hundreds of women. She was heartbroken. Incredibly, she never dreamt John had been unfaithful.

Maharishi used various tricks and traps to weed out those not ready to commit to spiritual development, receive his teachings, and remain steadfast. Had this been a test of the Beatles' faith and sincerity of intention? Could superstars like the Beatles ever be serious disciples of this strict, relentless, exacting, spiritual master? George Harrison said, "Being in The Beatles did help speed up the process of God-realisation, but it also hindered it as there were more impressions and more entanglements to get out of."[189]

※※※※※※※※※※※※※※※

On May 11, 1968, *Billboard* reported Verite Productions, founded by Paul Horn (producer and score composer), Alan Waite (associate producer), and Earl Barton (director) would make the feature titled *Maharishi*. Four Star paid $80,000 to SRM, $6000 each to Alan, Paul, and Earl, and $300,000 to cover production expenses.

Paul, who characterized executive producer Gene Corman a "total drag," was responsible for getting the film made, but possessed no decision-making power. Paul envisioned cinema verité, but Gene demanded everything scripted. Gene disliked Maharishi, bossed him around, and spoke rudely to him. Gene and Paul clashed on nearly everything. The film imploded.

On May 3, 1968, Maharishi appeared in Washington, DC, with the Beach Boys as their opening act. But the auditorium was half-full, and Maharishi was booed off the stage by hostile Beach Boy fans. The "Maharishi Tour" folded in less than a week.

Magic Alex ended up wasting an estimated £180,000 in Apple funds inventing products that never saw light of day. Of one hundred patents filed by EMI's patent attorneys for Alexis, every one was declined as previously invented. He was responsible for the disastrous construction of Apple's studios. The eight-track tape recorder had no mixing desk, no soundproofing, and no way to run cables from the studio to the control room. All this junk was sold for scrap. It seemed Magic Alex subscribed to *Popular Science* and the Beatles didn't, so he enthralled them with his vast erudition.

Jenny Boyd, who platonically shared a flat with "Magic Alex" in London in 1968, termed him as "Not very magic at all."[190] John Lennon commented, "He was just another guy who comes and goes around people like us. He's cracked, you know."[191]

Charlie Lutes said Alexis admitted in Rishikesh, "I came to India to get the boys out of India, away from Maharishi." When Charlie asked, "Why do you want to do this?" he answered, "We don't want Maharishi to have this much control over the boys."

While the Beatles were in India, Maharishi prophetically warned them: "If you don't continue your meditation practice, your singing group will break up."

PART VI

INEVITABLE AND INESCAPABLE

We must take situations as they are. We must
only change our mental attitudes towards them.
—Maharishi Mahesh Yogi

WORLD
ASSEMBLY
OF
GOVERNORS
OF THE AGE OF
ENIGHTENMENT

19

SHATTERED, SHAKEN, AND STIRRED

1976 TO 1978

These are the days of wireless connections from anywhere to anywhere. The relationship between the master and the disciple is not restricted to physical nearness. The link is between heart and heart.

—MAHARISHI MAHESH YOGI

It was October 1976. Maharishi told me to go and make money—the last thing I would ever want to do. I staggered to my room on unsteady legs. Once safely inside, away from prying eyes, it hit like a guillotine. Even though I'd seen the signs, when it finally came, the pain cut with piercing cruelty. I construed Maharishi's brutal expulsion as proof I'd failed his tests and was banned forever.

I curled up on the bed in a daze and pulled the covers over my head. Hours went by as my mind echoed Maharishi's words. I counted Staff members I'd made mad or jealous. I regretted my long list of mistakes. After hours of self-recrimination, I welcomed sleep's sweet oblivion.

Something startled me awake. I bolted up and cried, "Oh God, what will I do without Maharishi?" Terror shot through my body. Nothing could stop the avalanche of loss, the hopeless emptiness. After a fitful night, I woke, desperate and inconsolable.

I didn't leave my room all day. I felt nauseous and couldn't eat. Then I realized, *No, I have to get out. Better find Mindy and give her my precious book. Must see Prakash to get money for plane fare.*

It was hard to wrap my sari that night. My fingers faltered. My feet ventured tentatively toward Mindy's office. I paused, wondering whether to return to my room and keep the manuscript. *What will Mindy do with it? Who'll be the wiser if I keep it?*

But disobedience to Maharishi never ended well. So, carrying dread and emptiness in my heart, and the folder in my hand, I forced myself to trudge toward the office. Beverly answered the door. I thrust the voluminous notes in her direction.

"Here. I'm leaving for the States. Maharishi told me to give this to Mindy." Beverly, speechless, stared at the folder, a blank expression on her face.

I turned and walked away.

"But Susan, Susan . . ." Beverly called after me.

I didn't respond. I just kept walking.

Next stop: Prakash Srivastava, Maharishi's nephew. It seemed his relatives were taking over accounts. I said, "Maharishi's sending me to the States. I need a plane ticket."

Prakash replied with utter contempt, "We'll just forget about that."

"What?" I said.

"We will not be having any plane ticket for *you,*" he said in a Hindi accent.

"But I've been working for Maharishi for six years."

"No. No ticket. No money."

I said nothing. What would words do? I despised him violently. An animal trapped in a cage, I glared out through the bars, poised to attack my jailer. But the cage was locked.

When I returned to my room, I had to scream. The pillow fell prey to my abuses. "Damn them. Damn them all!" *I don't have money for plane fare, let alone to live on. I've subsisted for years on $25 a month. $25!*

∞∞∞∞∞∞∞∞∞∞∞∞∞∞∞∞∞∞∞∞∞∞∞∞

The next morning I woke to what hell really was. *How will I get back to the States? No money. No way to earn a living.* Though I felt like a palm frond thrashing violently in a hurricane, I fought the gale and struggled to move in the direction of lunch. There I feigned a calm face. I attempted to eat without revealing the overwhelming panic and adrenaline-freak-out churning inside.

One of the friendliest women from the "108," Veronica Foster, sat beside me. "I heard you're going back to the States."

"Bad news travels fast," I replied, staring at my soup.

"You know why he did it, don't you?" Veronica asked.

"Because I screwed up royally, that's why."

"No. Because he wants you to realize where God really is."

"What do you mean?" I asked.

"Time to discover God is within you," she said.

"Well . . . he *did* say, 'You are too much dependent upon me as a person. I won't always be here.'"

"Doesn't surprise me at all. Could have guessed. You're very talented, Susan. You're gonna do just great."

My throat tightened. I grabbed my napkin and covered my face. Veronica tried to put her arm around me. But I wrenched away and fled in shame.

By the time dinner rolled around, with as much dignity as I could muster, I began quietly soliciting funds. I entreated wealthy friends, engendering sympathy. A kindly lady "108" from Kansas City took pity and gave me a generous $400. Another charitable "108," whom I'd known since childhood in Colorado, gave me $300. With $700 in my pocket, I would get a plane ticket, settle in the USA, and ostensibly take on the world.

A few days later, the night before my flight, I spent hours packing. At 1:00 a.m. I entered the elevated glassed-in walkway—borderland between the Sönnenberg, where women stayed, and forbidden territory of the Külm, where Maharishi and male devotees lived. German WYMS guarded the doors like Gestapo.

In their private wing of the Külm, Karl Werner and his WYMS Wehrmacht played Wagner operas, dressed in formal attire, and dined with their evening-gown-bedecked high-heel-clad lovers. Under a gilded domed ceiling and crystal chandeliers, the lavish banquet hall was adorned with garish oil paintings, tapestries, foliage blinking with white Christmas lights, and faux-Roman statues. A long banquet table held a lacey tablecloth, porcelain china, sterling silverware, and candelabra. Starched waiters filled crystal goblets with wine and served calorific seven-course meals of lamb, duck, roast beef, Coupe Dänemarks, bonbons, brandy, and more.[192]

It was a far cry from our International Staff dining room, where we wore saris and sandals and ate basmati rice, zucchini, salads, minestrone soup, bread, butter, yoghurt, and fruit. Not that meat ingestion or luxury dining interested me. For a decade, my culinary tastes had been simple vegetarian fare.

Gone were the glory days of women visiting Maharishi privately without permission from layers of guards through tiers of fortifications. At the barricaded gate to the Külm, I phoned the current skin-boy, a Canadian, on the intercom. "I'm leaving for the States in the morning," I said. "I want to see Maharishi."

"I think he just went to bed," he replied. "Let me go check."

Moments later he returned to the intercom. "Too late. Maharishi has gone to bed. Come in the morning at 9:00."

"But I'm leaving at 7:00."

"I'm so sorry. Can't help you now. Wish you'd come earlier. I would have told him. Now it's too late. Call him when you get to the States. I'll give you his phone number."

My first thought was, *He's lying. Maharishi never retires this early.* Then it felt like someone hurled a cannonball at my stomach, and panic set in. *No. This can't be real. Oh God, no. Now I've really blown it!* No one had ever left Staff without seeing Maharishi.

Next morning, Erich Buchman, a kindly young Swiss meditator who was Maharishi's driver, loaded my luggage into a Mercedes. When he opened the trunk, it looked like a junk pile—papers scattered everywhere, haphazardly, apparently discarded.

Erich piled my luggage on top of the refuse. He tried to squeeze the final suitcase into the trunk. It wouldn't fit, so he packed it into the back seat. As I walked around the car, I got a closer look at the trunk and picked up a castoff page.

A strange sight emerged.

Oh my God! The loose notes of my precious Vacuum State book, strewn about the trunk of this random Mercedes. I didn't know how they got there, but there they were! I gasped in dismay. Erich asked, "What's wrong?"

"It's the notes for my Vacuum State book!" I cried. "Maharishi told me to give them to Mindy! I don't know why they're in this car!"

Erich asked, "Do you want to take them with you?"

"No," I replied. "Let's get the hell out of here."

<hr>

I arrived in Manhattan, in culture shock and bliss-withdrawal trauma, alone and penniless in a threatening world. I'd just spent seven years cloistered with a guru who convinced me, with great effectiveness, that without his direct care I was nowhere, and life was dangerous. While he touted self-sufficiency, he also made us fear everything outside his insular walls. Now, expelled from heady heights of his paradise, nothing seemed real. I had no context for a new life.

Ten years earlier, I'd introduced Gloria Zimmerman to TM. Now she was the New York TM Center Chairman. *Surely Gloria will find me a place to stay.* "No," was her answer. "Everyone always asks for a place to stay in New York. I can't help you." In her world, I was nobody.

After phoning everyone I could conjure, a generous woman, Angela, whom I'd met while on International Staff, and her husband Ralph Radetsky, took me in. I slept in their storage closet for two weeks. Then I moved into a furnished room at $250 per month in a high-rise in Flushing, Queens, with an elderly Jewish couple.

After seven years of seclusion, ingesting daily doses of heavenly bliss, the noises, vehicle exhaust, subway slime, weird street people, and crushes of negative vibes assaulted me. Everything about Switzerland was refined. In New York, whenever I walked down the street, I wanted to shower off its gross energy.

Fractured and dispossessed, I flopped around like a crustacean without its shell. Devoid of social or survival skills, I could barely finish a sentence. I was incapable of relating to anyone, not even meditators or TM Teachers. In Switzerland all we ever talked about was what Maharishi said or did that day.

What can I possibly say to these people? How do I try to make small talk when Shangri-la is my home? My universe isn't here. Utterly addicted to Maharishi's darshan—breaking this dependency was like drug withdrawal.

In culture shock, devoid of television, radio, movies, or entertainment for ten years, I was a displaced refugee from a remote planet, with alien language and civilization. I spoke a foreign tongue: Maharishi-speak.

An entire decade of American culture was absent. I pondered how to open a soda can and asked for a can opener from a puzzled cashier. To define me, "introverted" was an understatement. "Paralyzed" was more accurate. An appalling sense of helplessness overtook me.

Nothing could stop the excruciating pain—no cure for the grief and rejection. My connection with Maharishi felt broken and my only chance for spiritual enlightenment in ruins. With nothing but regrets for friends, life seemed meaningless. And I felt it was my own fault.

∞∞∞∞∞∞∞∞∞∞∞∞∞∞∞∞∞∞

The *New York Times* listed positions for book designers, graphic artists, paste-up, and so forth. But no one wanted a designer whose only job experience was a non profit in Switzerland that printed everything with Victorian flourishes and masses of gold ink.

I dragged my heavy portfolio in the snow from packed, stifling subways to dozens of magazines, book publishers, and ad agencies to try to get freelance illustration work. My arms ached. My shoulders hurt. I was cold. Tears filled my eyes. No money to live on. No money for subway tokens. My rent was overdue.

After agonizing months of defeat, I got a pitiful assignment from Health-Tex children's clothing manufacturer in the Empire State Building. I designed hanging tags and woven labels. Then a new magazine, *Entrepreneur,* hired me to illustrate a few articles. It took seemingly forever to execute these illustrations, for which I received $150 apiece—long hours with little pay. But my luck improved when a TM meditator asked me if I could design jewelry.

"Sure. Why not? I can design everything else," I replied.

After designing a line of jewelry for them, they promptly went bankrupt. However, it whetted my appetite. I could draw a jewelry design in thirty minutes and sell it for $30. In 1976, that was serious pay. Maybe this was what Maharishi meant by, "Make a lot of money as an artist."

I created a portfolio and hawked my wares on Forty-Seventh Street, the jewelry district. To my delight, I actually sold some designs. Moreover, I could pay rent and buy pizza at a dollar a slice, and a Papaya King once in a while.

A year went by while I struggled to save money. I was encouraged by design sales, but it wasn't enough to return to Switzerland.

I lugged my portfolio to the biannual jewelry trade show, held at the Hilton and Sheraton. Sam Ziefer, president of Meyer's Jewelry, a large diamond jewelry manufacturer, and his consultant Al Jaffee, perused my portfolio in their suite, amidst hors d'oeuvres and booze. "There's nothing here I can use, but I'm impressed with your talent. I think we can work together," Al said.

"If you're so impressed, why don't you buy something?" I scoffed. Seven years in the ashram with closed eyes hadn't improved my tact.

"Okay, I'll buy a couple of designs, just to show I'm serious. But once you understand what I want, we'll develop a jewelry line together." That's how I ended up designing line after line for Meyer's Jewelry for two decades.

∞∞∞∞∞∞∞∞∞∞∞∞∞∞∞∞∞∞∞

TM had become wildly popular, especially after Maharishi appeared on *The Merv Griffin Show* three times, along with celebrity meditators—on April 14, 1975 with Ellen Corby of *The Waltons,* October 31, 1975 with Clint Eastwood and Mary Tyler Moore, and December 14, 1977 with Burt Reynolds, Squire Fridell, and Doug Henning. Clint had learned TM during Maharishi's 1970 course at Humboldt. A long list of celebrities became TM meditators, including film director David Lynch, who started in 1973.

In November 1977 I moved to The Cenacle, formerly a convent in Armonk, New York, where "Executive Governors of the Age of Enlightenment" (Maharishi's hyperbolic title for Initiators who'd graduated from the AEGTC Course) were teaching residence courses.

Richard Chamberlain, television star of *Dr. Kildare,* showed up for a course. He was often spotted on the patio strutting around bare chested. Aspiring radio personality Howard Stern was staying there while hosting the morning show at WRNW in nearby Briarcliff Manor.

I became infatuated with a so-called "Governor"—Robert Schumacher, from Glen Cove, Long Island. I imagined him the man of my dreams—a Jewish-TM-John-Travolta-lookalike, talk-alike, act-alike. He stopped by my design studio for our daily walks in the crisp autumn air—he in his three-piece suit, I in my sari. Our footsteps crunched the rainbow of leaves blanketing the near-frozen ground.

"Susan, what was it like around Maharishi?" Robert asked.

I paused to consider the yellow, orange, and red leaves strewn about my feet. "The master-disciple relationship is difficult to fathom. It's easily misinterpreted," I said.

"Please, try. Try to explain," Robert urged.

"A combination of heaven and hell," I stated. "Very personal and felt deep within my heart. Maharishi helped me develop inner strength, flexibility, one-pointed perseverance . . . and deep silence in awareness."

"What about heaven and hell? What do you mean?"

"One day heaven, next day hell." I dropped the subject. *He'll never understand.*

However, when Robert continued to press me day after day, I realized I might try to explain it as Maharishi did. So I asked him, "You've read the *Bhagavad Gita*?"

"A while ago," he answered.

"Krishna teaches his disciple Arjuna similarly to how Maharishi trains his disciples," I said. "Prince Arjuna is a strong, mighty, seasoned warrior. But his chariot driver Lord Krishna says *one simple sentence* that sends him into a tailspin. That sentence is this: 'Just behold, Partha, all the Kurus who are assembled here.'

"With this statement, Krishna reminds Arjuna of his family name and thereby draws attention to the cruel, immediate reality: With nearly four million soldiers arrayed to fight this war between forces of light and darkness, Arjuna's kinsfolk, the Kauravas, are lined up with swords drawn—*on the other side of the battlefield.* Arjuna is about to slay his own cousins, teachers, and loved ones.

"This realization hits Arjuna like a bombshell. He reacts with fight-or-flight response. His heart pounds, body quivers, mouth dries up, hair stands on end, skin burns, and mind reels. He was so sure of himself, prepared for battle. Then Krishna throws him for a loop, and he falls into what Maharishi calls a 'state of suspension,' meaning frozen and unable to act."

"Was that the same *Gita* I read?" Robert laughed.

"Yes, in the *first chapter*," I said unequivocally. "Arjuna gets shaken and foresees only hell resulting from the battle. His mind is overcome with compassion and grief. His eyes brim with tears.

"So then what happens?" Robert asked.

"Well, in the second chapter, Krishna insults Arjuna, branding him impure, degraded, lamenting, impotent, with petty weakness of heart. Yet in the same breath, Krishna lauds him as 'chastiser of enemies.'

"After Krishna has artfully confused his disciple and diminished his confidence, Arjuna becomes putty in Krishna's hands. Arjuna ultimately concedes: 'Inflicted by this miserly weakness of mind, bewildered in my heart about my dharma, I am your disciple, I am surrendered unto you. Please instruct me clearly what is best for me.'"

"So Krishna pressed Arjuna's buttons until he finally broke down and asked for help," Robert said. Then he paused. A light seemed to switch on. "This is what Maharishi does?" he asked.

"Yes, and with Maharishi it was incredibly intense, because he did it over and over. Like combination heaven and hell," I said. "Once Arjuna surrendered, then Krishna's teaching could begin. The rest of the *Gita* is that teaching—most importantly, the verses that said, 'Be without the three gunas, freed from duality, ever firm in purity, independent of possessions, possessed of the Self,'[193] and 'Established in Being, perform action.'"[194]

"Wow. Amazing. I've got to read the *Gita* again," Robert said.

I was bewitched by Robert—his eyes, the sound of his voice, his muscular, tall body, his scent. I took a 180-degree turnabout. No longer did I want to be a recluse. I wanted a relationship. My infatuation for Robert persisted, even after he became bored of our walks and began chasing Tinker Lindsay, daughter of New York City ex-Mayor Lindsay.

∞∞∞∞∞∞∞∞∞∞∞∞∞∞∞∞

One day Robert knocked on my office door, out of breath. "Just heard. Maharishi's in South Fallsburg at a conference. Can't promise we'll get in. We're leaving in a few minutes. Hurry." My heart beat fast. *Maharishi!* I ran to my room, grabbed my coat, combed my hair, and was out the door in a flash.

We pulled up to the TM residential facility, an imposing group of white-stucco red-roofed buildings nestled amidst maples and oaks near South Fallsburg. It was known as Windsor Hotel in the Borscht Belt Catskills' heyday, twenty years previously. We entered the lobby. "Only Executive Governors allowed," someone announced.

All the way from Armonk, a two-hour drive, and I'm not an Executive Governor. At that devastating moment Helene and Luther Koffman happened by. I knew them from the "108." He was a chief surgeon's son, she a Campbell's Soup heiress. After waiting an agonizing hour, finally I got permission from Luther to enter the hall.

I tiptoed in, trying to remain invisible. *I don't belong here.* Maharishi was addressing a group from the Pentagon, lecturing on defense. A few hundred Executive Governors were present, attending a one-month conference.

Maharishi eyeballed me. *Will he throw me out, as he did one time in Vitznau?* My face blushed and palms got clammy. I tried to blend into the wallpaper. I breathed a sigh of relief when no one seemed to care I was there.

Next day, some conference attendees got on the mike and described their projects. I was sitting in the back row, and "the back row" was exactly how I felt. After a few hours of feeling too insignificant to exist, something extraordinary happened.

Three women ascended the stage. They were describing children's stories to Maharishi in what seemed an overbearing manner. As they showed puppets and told stories, he appeared woefully unimpressed. "These stories are too complicated for children," he said. "They should be simple and to the point. Just a few words, hmm? No rambling stories that go on and on. Children should not have to follow complicated logic of a story."

I wish I were an Executive Governor. Then I could tell Maharishi about the two children's books I wrote—I Can Do Anything *and* Age of Enlightenment Alphabet Book. *But I can't. I don't even belong here.*

Maharishi grew impatient. He waved the women off the stage. Then he announced in a booming voice, "There should be different kinds of stories. There should be *Age of Enlightenment* and there should be *I Can Do Anything.*"

What? What did he just say? I turned to a woman seated next to me. "Did he just say *Age of Enlightenment* and *I Can Do Anything?*"

"That's exactly what he said," she affirmed.

This is just too Twilight Zone. I raced forward and grabbed a microphone. "Maharishi," I said, "I've just written two children's books. One is called *I Can Do Anything* and the other is *Age of Enlightenment Alphabet Book.*"

Maharishi laughed. "You see, how Mother Nature supports? She fulfills our every desire."

I said, "Should I go ahead with these books?"

"Yes. Get them published." Maharishi said, smiling, darting a powerful glint of divine love energy toward me.

I felt deeply touched. Tears of joy welled up, and waves of divine energy coursed through my body. *Such infinite compassion,* I thought. *Maharishi is indeed unfathomable.*

∞∞∞∞∞∞∞∞∞∞∞∞∞∞∞∞∞∞∞∞∞

Due to my efforts in designing jewelry, two years after departing Switzerland I finally saved enough for the six-month AEGTC Course.

In July 1978 I took the plane to Zurich and train to Brunnen and arrived a day early, hoping to see Maharishi before the course. I stepped onto the ferry. The sight of the lake, swans, sun streaming onto snow-capped peaks, Seelisburg atop the cliff, it was all too much. I broke down in sobs. *Home again. Home.* I took the funicular railway and trudged up the incredibly steep road toward the Sönnenberg.

The crystalline blue lake, bordered by sun-laden peaks, taunted me, recalling another time—a time when I had everything. *I used to be on top of the world. Now what's my life? Designing jewelry? Being obsessed with a John Travolta lookalike? I'm nothing.* The lake morphed into a gigantic mouth lined with hideous white teeth, mocking me as I dragged my burdensome suitcases uphill.

Short of breath, I entered the Sönnenberg lobby. WYMS Nazi types, guarding the place like SS troopers, stopped me from ascending the imposing double staircase.

I remembered the code for Maharishi's meeting room and used the intercom. Brahmachari Nand Kishore, whom I'd known since 1970, answered.

January 12, 1991, Maastricht, Holland: Maharishi Mahesh Yogi and Brahmachari Nand Kishore at World Peace Assembly Hall.
CC-BY-SA-3.0: Centre Védique Maharishi

I identified myself as Susan the Artist, and he remembered me. I asked if I could stay here until my AEGTC course started. He said he would check. Then I waited—all day.

People on Staff came and went. Some were friendly. Others ignored me. The kindly Hannah asked if she could help. Reginald walked by, gave me a toothy grin, and we exchanged a few words. He said he'd taken the AEGTC course a year before. We reminisced about sneaking out for *Coupe Dänemark* sundaes.

How did I ever leave? This is my home. But where's the welcome for the prodigal daughter? Oh, God. This is agony.

That evening I used the intercom again. "Did you talk to Maharishi?"

Nand Kishore's voice replied, "Yes. He said you should not be in Seelisburg. Go to Weggis. Come to Seelisberg later, after the course."

"What do I do tonight? I've got nowhere to stay," I said.

"Susan."

"Yes?"

"Remember. God Consciousness."

The intercom clicked off.

20

FROG-HOPPING TO ENLIGHTENMENT

1978 TO 1980

Life is not a struggle. Life is bliss.
The natural state of man is joy.
The highest state is laughter.

—MAHARISHI MAHESH YOGI

Demoralized and desolate, I checked into a cheap hotel down the road in Seelisberg. The curtains and bedding reeked of cigarette smoke. I tucked myself into a feather-bed but couldn't sleep. *What should I expect? After all, I'm a nobody,* I thought.

The next morning, heavyhearted, I dragged across the lake to Weggis and checked into Hotel Alexander, where I'd often stayed with Maharishi—when I used to be somebody. Five people attended my AEGTC Course: three women and an octogenarian couple, Arthur and Christina Granville from Santa Barbara, old-time devotees since Maharishi first arrived in the USA. Nearly every other Initiator had already taken the course.

Suddenly Jerry and Debby Jarvis showed up at our hotel. *Why aren't they in Seelisberg?* I was floored to hear Jerry and Maharishi were on the outs. Apparently Jerry had become somewhat rebellious. He opposed course fee increases and didn't like the TM-Sidhi Program. But the last straw was Jerry pushing to fight and appeal the case *Malnak v. Yogi,* though Maharishi told Jerry to drop it.

SCI (Science of Creative Intelligence) curriculum was being taught at five New Jersey public high schools. The course book I edited and illustrated while on International Staff was used as evidence that "Creative Intelligence" was a religious concept. And puja ceremony was deemed "student offerings to Hindu deities." The District Court of New Jersey (and later United States Court of Appeals, Third Circuit) ruled

1978, Weggis, Switzerland: AEGTC Course. I am at upper right, Granvilles seated.

that teaching SCI/TM violated the first amendment of the US Constitution, because SCI/TM is a religion, prohibited in public schools. So much for TM being a mechanical, scientific technique, and Creative Intelligence being a "field."

When the plaintiffs prevailed and TM lost, Jerry paid the lawyers one million dollars, though Maharishi told Jerry not to pay anything. As a result, the Advanced Training Resources (ATR) fund, earmarked for Initiators to take Advanced Training Courses (ATC), was depleted.

It seemed impossible to imagine Jerry no longer on Maharishi's A-list. His closest disciple for decades wasn't immune to baseless blame and ego bashing. He was treated like the rest of us, crushed into oblivion like insects.

After years of anticipation, it was depressing to find Maharishi no longer taught AEGTC. Instead his videotaped image on a screen said, "The TM-Sidhi Program is an advanced meditation practice that cultures the ability to think and act from the most powerful and unified level of consciousness—Transcendental Consciousness. It was brought to light from the Yoga Sutras of Patanjali, from the ancient Vedic tradition. The word siddhi means perfections . . ."[195]

Adding to the letdown, my nemesis Mindy Leibowitz and her Mindettes, complete with nauseating pretentions, facilitated our TM-Sidhi Program initiations by playing videotapes. We boarded the ferry to Seelisberg for our first initiation, July 19, 1978, while I tried to quell the revulsion of reunion with not-so-kindred spirits.

Some consolation—*Guru Purnima* (full moon of the guru) happened to correspond with that day. Since the Granvilles were present, Maharishi invited us on a full moon boat ride. After that happy coincidence, we settled into our course routine— rounds of asanas, pranayama, TM, TM-Sidhis, readings from *Rigveda* Ninth Mandala, repeated all day. After meals was "walk and talk" with our "buddy." (Maharishi had instituted his "buddy system" at the Rishikesh Beatles course, a decade earlier.) At night we watched videotapes.

To soften buttock blows, we three women practiced "flying" on thick foam mattresses covered with cotton sheeting in the hotel basement. Powerful wave upon pulsating wave of energy surged through our bodies, and rapturous exhilaration coursed through our minds, suddenly, strangely, lifting us off the ground.

In loose white cotton pants and shirts, seated in lotus posture, looking ridiculous, we hopped across the foam like frogs jumping across a shallow pond, squealing, laughing, and shouting. I had never had so much fun. The fun wasn't in hopping, though. It was the inner experience of indescribable bliss.

According to Patanjali's *Yoga Sutras,* the first stage of levitation is bodily shaking. The second is hopping like a frog, and third is hovering in the air. So we achieved frog-hopping stage—lifting into the air, then falling right back down. That was actually impressive, considering we did the impossible—overcome gravity.

After "flying," we lay down on the foam for fifteen minutes, bodies charged with electric energy, flooded with intense feelings of joy and integrity in our higher self. Then we read from *Rigveda:* "Flow, Soma, in a most sweet and exhilarating stream, effused for Indra to drink,"[196] and so on.

During course meetings we discussed mind-blowing spiritual experiences. As the course progressed, we took the steamship to Seelisberg five times to get more sutras. After each initiation by Mindy and her Mindettes, the "TM-Sidhi Administrators," we visited Maharishi in the lecture hall.

The press didn't report Maharishi's "yogic flying" in enormously favorable light. That's an understatement. Hopping across foam rubber didn't make a graceful or believable impression, though Maharishi invited reporters to film it. However, when strong professional athletes tried to duplicate yogic flying, they were incapable of achieving more than a few hops. Yet sedentary TM-Sidhi meditators effortlessly hopped for an hour with increasing energy.

Seelisberg lecture hall: l. to r.: Charles F. Lutes (SRM president), Praveen Srivastava (Maharishi's nephew), Pundit Parameswar Iyer, Maharishi, Acharya Ram Vilas Shukla, M.V. Mahashabde, Hans-Peter Ritterstadt (TM leader), Vesey Crichton (TM leader) at podium.
Keystone Pictures USA/ZUMAPRESS

I engaged in a little secret project during the course, fabricating a cardboard model of intertwined discs that represented ten mandalas ("circles")—chapters of the Vedas. These mandalas supposedly structure all life in the universe. Maharishi often described them fitting together in a configuration resembling a mosquito.

At the end of the course, we took a final boat ride. As I boarded the glass-topped boat, I showed Maharishi my bizarre-looking model. He smiled, exclaiming, "The mosquito!" and darted his glance of divine love. He displayed the mosquito enthusiastically to the passengers, explaining how the mandalas fit together.

"This should be done in plastic," he said. As always, he wanted a better, improved version. "Sit here, Susan." Overcome with joy, I took the seat right next to him.

Whenever near Maharishi, I entered an alternate reality. My mind became either amazingly still, or exceedingly jumbled—either blanking out or freaking out. Occasionally I would forget why I was there and what my question was.

This time my mind spun like an Osterizer, calculating every possible repercussion of the "mosquito." *He asked for it in plastic. Was that an invitation to stay and work on it? Maharishi had said, "Make a lot of money and then come back and stay." Nand Kishore had said, "Come to Seelisberg later, after the course." There I was. I'd created the mosquito. Maybe I could stay.*

Then I argued with myself: *But I don't know how to fabricate it in plastic. What about my jewelry business? What about the stuff I left in New York? What about Robert?*

The boat reached Weggis—too soon. *I thought we were returning to Seelisberg. But he's letting us off in Weggis!* I panicked. Reacting without reason, I blurted out, "Maharishi, do you want me to go back to the States?"

Maharishi snapped, "Yes, you should go back to the States," in such a condescending tone that conveyed how utterly insignificant I really was, confirming my worst fears.

One minute later, floods of regrets engulfed me: *I could have asked whether I could stay and work on the mosquito. I could have asked permission to go and come back.* But it was impossible to think straight in his presence. My shyness, powerlessness, frozen mannequin-like veneer, and failure to communicate blocked me from so many precious opportunities.

Don't worry, Susan. It doesn't matter. It was just the most precious opportunity of your life, which you screwed up royally.

Frankly, I never got over it.

I foolishly returned to the USA in November 1978, to my jewelry design business and idiotic obsession with a John Travolta lookalike fantasy man. Of course, returning to Robert proved futile. For a couple of years, I bumbled around chasing him like a pathetic fool with zero self-esteem.

In August 1979, Maharishi called an emergency one-month meeting in Amherst, Massachusetts—his first "World Peace Assembly." Twenty-six hundred meditators showed up.

At the end of the course, Maharishi recalled Guru Dev in an emotional, nostalgic, dreamy voice. That got us into a receptive mood. He moved on to the responsibility of Citizens and Governors as guardians of the Age of Enlightenment. That made us feel guilty. He then conveyed Mother Divine had told him there was too much crime, war, and pollution. Maharishi's "World Plan" wasn't working fast enough, and Mother Divine's patience was running out. She was going to destroy the entire earth. That made us terrified.

Maharishi said, "I begged and pleaded with her, 'Mother Divine, please, just give me one more chance,' until she finally agreed, 'All right, just one last opportunity to save the world from complete annihilation.' How fortunate it is she has given us this one chance, hmm?"[197]

Maharishi then declared a state of world emergency—a perilous juncture. We must immediately create a critical mass of two thousand who practice TM-Sidhi Program together permanently to counteract the stress of two billion people. He saddled us with the added burden that each of us was responsible for one hundred thousand people.

His tirade concluded with announcing the first "Creating Coherence Course" at MIU in Fairfield, Iowa beginning in one week. We must pack our bags and relocate our families immediately, as time has run out. He promised us "wealth and wisdom squared" in Fairfield.[198]

As master manipulator of fear-for-motivation, a guilt-inducing, coercive Jewish mother par excellence, Maharishi persuaded about a thousand of us to move to Fairfield in September, to ostensibly prevent certain global annihilation.

Maharishi was not the only seer predicting earth changes and global disasters. Others with similar visions included Yogi Bhajan, Vishnudevananda from Sivananda's ashram, Hilda Charlton, Edgar Cayce, Elizabeth Claire Prophet, Gordon Michael Scallion, Yogananda's book of predictions, Hopi Indians, Mayan predictions, and Lori Toye.

❈❈❈❈❈❈❈❈❈❈❈❈❈❈❈❈❈

Maharishi had asked Keith Wallace, president of MIU in Santa Barbara, to locate a new campus for the college. In August 1974, Keith found Parsons College in Iowa, a "party school" that lost accreditation and went bankrupt. On the market for over a year, it was fourteen million dollars in debt and a bargain at three million. I was in the meeting room to hear Maharishi's reaction to Iowa: "Can't we do better than this?"

Rolling hills and fields of corn, soybeans, hogs, and cattle surrounded the Jefferson County seat, Fairfield, in southeast Iowa, a one-stoplight town of six square miles near the Missouri border. A white gazebo in the town square was circled by farmhouses, Victorian homes shaded by indigenous oaks, and trains whistling through but never stopping. Fairfield was the poster child for Grant Wood's "American Gothic."

The town's claim to fame was the first Carnegie Library outside Pennsylvania or Scotland, and a prototype for twenty-seven hundred others, plus some defunct factories, including Louden Machinery, which manufactured farm equipment and ammunition.

Making immediate enemies of all Fairfield native sons, the "ru" invasion began. Coined by locals, our derogatory nickname was "ru" for "guru," or "tater" for "meditator." The ever-optimistic Maharishi named us *sidhas,* but we weren't even distant cousins thereof. *Siddha* means "perfected being"—in command of all laws of nature. Did the missing "d" from Maharishi's version of *siddha* characterize our level of consciousness—"designated deficient"?

Twice daily I walked from my miniscule dorm room in a hexagon-shaped "pod" to the college fieldhouse where we frog-hopped to enlightenment on foam rubber. Men on one side, women on the other, separated by what I guess was a celibacy curtain.

Every male meditator in Fairfield was recruited to erect the foundation for a geodesic dome, which would become a "flying hall." Within a few months, a giant concrete slab was poured and the skeleton structure for a giant dome raised: a dome built on guilt, fear, and manipulation—but with best intentions.

In December 1979, Maharishi arrived to inaugurate the dome. His worker-bee army managed to finish before the bitter freeze. The dome was about two hundred feet in diameter and thirty-five feet high. The roof was sprayed with polyurethane foam coated with miles of yellow ochre paint, later replaced by metallic gold developed exclusively for MIU.

Massive plastic sheets covered twenty-five thousand square feet of cement. Truckloads of foam mattresses blanketed the plastic. Legions of female meditators sewed giant fireproof coverings. The interior recalled the Sönnenberg, with a painting of Guru Dev, gold drapery, red carpeting, and world flags.

In this "Golden Dome for the Age of Enlightenment," men practiced the TM-Sidhi Program together. Women, second-class citizens, were relegated to the drafty fieldhouse.

∞∞∞∞∞∞∞∞∞∞∞∞∞∞∞∞∞∞∞∞

The snow didn't thaw all winter. To protect myself from minus 20 degree temperatures with wind chills of minus 50, I wore a parka with a hood resembling a periscope. After the thaw, the campus became mud hell where our boots sank six inches into sludge.

Morning and evening TM-Sidhi Program took about five hours per day. During the three remaining hours, we thousand sidhas were free to figure how to survive in this God-forsaken poverty-stricken hellhole of baking steambath summers and frozen Arctic winters.

I was incredibly lucky to have my jewelry design business and could work with clients through the mail. However, as fast as I raked in money, I spent it on the TM dome entry badge, TM advanced techniques, TM courses, TM products, and spiritual *tchotchkes*.

In March 1980 an announcement was made at the fieldhouse. Those who wanted to be "single" (Maharishi's euphemism for "celibacy") could take a special course in the Catskills—men in Livingston Manor and women in South Fallsburg. A handful of people, including Robert Schumacher and his entire oil-brokerage firm, jumped at the chance.

So did I.

If I could operate my business from Nowheresville-Hellsville, Iowa, then I could certainly do it from the Catskills—two hours from New York City.

I'm gonna leap before I look.

∞∞∞∞∞∞∞∞∞∞∞∞∞∞∞∞∞∞∞∞

The TM nunnery was paradise. No men. My personal dictionary-in-my-head defined the word "men" as "source of great pain." In the quiet, hilly forests of upstate New York, I could relax completely, free from pretenses and hierarchies. Unlike Switzerland, all traces of highfalutin Mindy and smug Mindettes were visibly absent. Only loving, unassuming women dwelt in the gentle South Fallsburg atmosphere.

My jewelry design business made me independent, while enjoying companionship of lovely women. I felt nurtured, loved, and cared for. Something was uniquely special about energies of my own sex. I could sense a tangible feminine power. Softness and sweetness filled the air.

In South Fallsburg, during our menstrual period we stayed in bed, ingesting only fruit, water, and tea for three solid days. We weren't allowed anywhere near men, especially not Maharishi. The phrase "I'm resting" took on a unique connotation—a monthly mandatory three-day vacation.

I followed the "resting" program religiously. Now that I knew how women were "supposed to" behave during our period, I came to some revelations about how Maharishi treated me in Austria (assigning me to ride with a bitch in heat bleeding on me). Apparently every twenty-eight days women became contagious to men and had to be quarantined because we might infect some man with female menstrualpathic disease.

In 1983 Swami Muktananda (Siddha Yoga founder), bought our TM nunnery, augmenting his "Syda Yoga Foundation" real estate holdings in South Fallsburg. In autumn 1976 Muktananda and his retinue visited Maharishi in Seelisberg. He gabbed nonstop and his followers chanted nonstop. Maharishi spent the entire time in meditation. We gasped as Muktananda suddenly jumped onto Maharishi's couch and engulfed the tiny yogi in a bear hug. The Attack of the Killer Swami! When asked how Maharishi felt about the hug, he answered, ever a diplomat, "I just stayed on my self."

Muktananda hugging Maharishi.

When Muktananda visited Melbourne, Australia, Maharishi requested a group of sidhas pay their respects and express his regards. In a private meeting, Muktananda said, "Maharishi has given you a technique to cleanse and purify not just yourselves; it is a technique to cleanse the whole world. Maharishi's path is unique. You only need to do what he has asked. It is glorious but not easy to be self-sufficient. Devotion must be in the heart rather than sitting at the foot of the Master, because Maharishi is here for the whole world."[199]

Osho was an entirely different story. In 1969 in Pahalgam, Kashmir in the Himalayas, Maharishi met with Bhagavan Shree Rajneesh (a.k.a. Osho) to debate merits of their respective systems. Maharishi warned his students Rajneesh was a college professor with a keen mind, so be careful how you respond.

The two gurus sat on a couch on the lawn surrounded by their students. Maharishi described TM as a technique that takes the mind from the surface to subtler levels into the state of transcendental pure consciousness, the absolute, which is everywhere present and the basis of everything.

Rajneesh disagreed. "There is no validity to this whatsoever. How can you have a technique to go somewhere that is everywhere? If it's already everywhere, where is there to go? Why would you need a technique to go there?"

The two gurus got into a heated debate. They denigrated each other's methods, cringed, and made faces at each other. Students got restless and felt the need to defend their respective gurus. Not realizing it was just a game, they became agitated, stood up, and started arguing.

Then the two gurus stood up, hugged each other, and walked off arm in arm.

∞∞∞∞∞∞∞∞∞∞∞∞∞∞

In summer 1980, Maharishi suddenly sent word to South Fallsburg and Livingston Manor. All Governors of the Age of Enlightenment should form "Vedic Atoms," which will travel to TM Centers and purchase large buildings for "Capitals of the Age of Enlightenment." In August my Vedic Atom of five women was dispatched to Wellesley, Massachusetts—one of the rare TM Centers that already owned a building.

Our group was first to locate a suitable new property. However, financing became impossible because the current TM Center was encumbered with liens. A shady character, disguised as a benefactor, managed to finagle his way into TM teachers' graces, get his name on the title, then mortgage the TM Center to the hilt. He used his ill-gotten gains to finance his own enterprises. Though I was enraged, my Vedic Atom partners and local TM teachers couldn't see it—or didn't want to.

I confronted the malefactor and pointed at paperwork clearly showing his private properties using the TM Center as collateral. His lame excuse was his actions were, in some warped way, of benefit to TM. When I reported this travesty to national and international TM officials, even phoning Maharishi's private line in Switzerland, I was stunned that no one was interested. Nothing ever got done without Maharishi's specific instructions. So nothing got done.

Meanwhile our dreams of a Capital for Wellesley flushed down the toilet. And sadly, within one week of my appalling discovery, our Vedic Atom suddenly received free plane tickets to Delhi, India, with three days' notice to pack for a colossal World Conference on Vedic Science. This turn of events was lucky for the conman, but not so lucky for Wellesley. Without me to follow up, who knows what happened to Wellesley TM Center.

∞∞∞∞∞∞∞∞∞∞∞∞∞∞∞∞∞∞∞

Maharishi arrived at Palam Airport, New Delhi, on November 5, 1980. His Staff from Switzerland and sidhas from far and wide trailed behind. My arrival was November 11. Newspaper magnate Ramnath Goenka, patriarch of *The Indian Express* empire, hosted 3470 people in his gargantuan building, covering a city block on Bahadur Shah Zafar Marg.

I traveled in a motorized rickshaw from my guesthouse to the conference daily. Thousands of meditators rushed up the stairs to a giant air-conditioned lecture hall, carpeted wall-to-wall in foam mattresses covered with white cotton sheets, where we sat cross-legged before Maharishi.

Goenka remarked, "I see these 3000 people flying in the air every morning and evening right here in this building. I don't require any proof, nor do I have any doubt that I too will be able to fly in a month or so."[200]

German WYMS guards strictly enforced the pecking order. International Staff sat in front. Then came Executive Governors, Governors, and Citizens. Maharishi's rigid hierarchy was firmly fixed. My Vedic Atom sat back in some corner beyond the edge of nowhere.

Maharishi began his Vedic Science Course with a story: "One king was so affluent that he was famous for fulfilling anyone's desire. A dwarf asked, 'I want some space. Just give me three steps.' A wise man warned the king, 'Be careful. What you see is not reality. What you don't see is reality.' The dwarf suddenly grew into a giant. He put one foot on the earth, one on heaven. There was no space for the third foot. He put the third foot on the heart. So the dwarf got the full range of satisfaction.

"The three steps represent the three levels of knowledge. The knower, the known, and knowledge merge into one wholeness in Unity Consciousness. Vedanta establishes the self as an all-time reality."[201]

Maharishi spent three months delving into all areas of Veda through the entire gamut of knowledge and experience of unmanifest and manifest creation—how the uncreated creates creation, how from nothing comes something, and then everything.

He equated the Veda to the superparticle, the basic unit in supergravity theory. Maharishi was fascinated by quantum electrodynamics, quantum chromodynamics, geometric dynamics, and gauge theory. He relished unearthing modern physics from the ancient Vedas.

After investigating the makeshift outdoor "kitchen" at the Express building, replete with untold vermin and grubby teenage boys, I opted to pass up that fine culinary opportunity. Instead I lunched at my guesthouse or hotels Oberoi or Ashoka on the way to the conference. However, I ingested dinner daily at the Express feeding trough, served on stainless steel *thalis*—trays divided into sections for rice, dal, veggies, and chapattis.

I practiced the afternoon TM-Sidhi Program with thousands of women in a giant foam-carpeted room at the Express, one floor above the men's flying room.

At one point I created an enormous poster, representing all branches of Vedic literature, organized systematically, as explained by Maharishi on the course. I brought it near the stage, in front of the meeting hall of four thousand people, and tried to show it to him.

Maharishi totally ignored me.

2 1

RIDING THE INDIAN EXPRESS

1981

> Knowledge is always drawn. It is never given. The master-disciple relationship is always one way. The ocean is always there.
>
> —MAHARISHI MAHESH YOGI

When I tried to show Maharishi my Vedic Science poster, he snubbed me. When the lecture ended, I neared the stage and tried getting his attention by placing the poster in his direct line of vision and talking to him. He still ignored me. In fact, he ignored me so vehemently that several people approached me afterward.

A whole cheerleading section started up. Even Reginald joined in. However, by that time I was so humiliated that I sank into nothingness. I tried to become invisible.

Despite this slight, when I noticed several course participants reading poems to Maharishi, I decided to queue up to read my children's book to him. Intimidated and terrified, I neared the microphone. My heart beat faster and face turned red. Adrenaline shot through my veins. My limbs trembled. *I can't do this. I've got to go back to my seat. No. I must do this.* The paper I was holding started shaking.

Finally it was my turn. I cleared my throat, but no sound emerged. Then a teeny voice, barely audible, squeaked out. "Maharishi, I have a poem to read."

Maharishi said, "Poem? What it is?"

With voice shaking, legs unsteady, knees visibly knocking together, and bladder barely keeping control, I said, timidly, "It's called *I Can Do Anything.*"

"Read," Maharishi said.

"Now my name is Sidelle and I tell you it's true; I can do anything that I'd like to do. I can play with the earth, water, space, or the air; Just as if they were toys from my own toy

chest there. I can juggle a car and a bus and a horse; Just as strong as an elephant; that's me, of course."

Maharishi giggled. Thousands of people laughed.

I continued, *"I can be just as fat or as thin as I please—Grow the size of a mountain or turtle with ease. If you want, I can turn myself into a bird; Or a fish or rhinoceros, just say the word."*

More laughter.

Trembling uncontrollably, knees colliding, I continued until I read all fifty-four couplets of the poem. At the end Maharishi laughed. "Good. Very, very good, hmm?" he said.

Sweating, shoulders hunched, staring at the ground, averting the gaze of thousands of eyes, I wobbled back to my seat, shaking like a bowl of Jell-O. I sat down, stunned by my extreme physical reaction. Never had public speaking so physically shaken me. I didn't know whether to laugh, cry, vomit, or pee myself.

After previous encounters with Maharishi that ended badly, it was a huge gamble to expose myself to him and four thousand others who knew me. After this episode, my stage fright significantly lessened. Perhaps this incident proved a blessing.

∞∞∞∞∞∞∞∞∞∞∞∞∞∞∞∞∞

I became increasingly depressed about my crappy seat in the lecture hall. I still wasn't over the fact that Maharishi ignored my poster. Restless, ever seeking more, I was determined to change my lot.

Spiritual masters never project. They only reflect. In every situation Maharishi's mirror reflected how much I was capable of receiving. Like a game of hide and seek, my true nature of infinite love hid behind a mask of rejection and inadequacy—all my childhood baggage. If I could overcome these limitations, I would be an ocean of love.

Maharishi often said the master-disciple relationship is one way. The guru's love for the disciple is already unlimited and therefore never increases. Over time the disciple increasingly opens to the guru: "Water in a lake will not flow out, but if a pipe is brought up to the level of the water, it will naturally flow. This is how wisdom flows from master to disciple."[202]

Maharishi was like a deep well, available to draw from. When I opened my heart and attuned my mind to him, I received the blessings. If I withdrew and sabotaged myself, I got nothing. *How can I draw the water if I don't let down the bucket? I must surrender. No other way. I can't go on like this. I'm dying of the pain of separation.*

I don't know what came over me, but the day after Christmas in 1980, I proclaimed to my Vedic Atom partners at lunch, "From tomorrow my karma is going to improve. You'll see. My karma will change dramatically, as of tomorrow."

The next day I woke up determined to speak to Maharishi. *Tonight I'll go to his suite and speak with him privately. I must tell him my inner feelings. Must have everything clear in my mind. I'll write a list of questions.*

That day I approached Wolfgang Keller, a German artist who'd served on Staff in Semmering, Austria. He seemed to be in charge of making charts.

"I want to make charts. I'd like to help you."

"Good, Susan. Here's the layout of a chart about how Vedic Science relates to quantum physics, Schrödinger wave mechanics, and Heisenberg matrix mechanics. You can start on that."

Not more than fifteen minutes later, someone caught the corner of my eye. It was Amber O'Connell, a TM-Sidhi Administrator I'd known from the "108," now one of Maharishi's favorites. She seemed to be wandering around the lecture hall, lost.

A powerful thought suddenly overtook my mind: *Amber is looking for me to give me a message from Maharishi. She's going to call me to the back of the hall and give me a message.* I stared intently at her. *I'm over here, Amber.* Sure enough, Amber spotted me and headed straight toward me.

"Susan, I need to speak to you in the back of the hall."

"Sure, Amber."

I trotted behind her. *I knew something was going to happen. I knew my karma was going to change. I knew she was looking for me. I don't know how I knew, but I knew.*

"Susan, I mentioned your name to Maharishi today. I suggested you as one of the artists to make textile designs for ladies' dresses that Sidha Corporation will manufacture. A room is being built now in the back of the lecture hall for three lady artists to work on this project."

I smiled at Amber. "Thank you."

Meanwhile, inside, my heart burst with joy.

~~~~~~~~~~~~~~~~~~~~~~~~~~

Maharishi was looking for ways to support TM teachers financially. That was his expressed motive for founding Sidha Corporation International—a private corporation that would hire sidhas (though there's no evidence anyone ever got paid). One harebrained scheme was Sidha Corporation's designer dress line. Silk fabrics would be designed by us amateur volunteers in India and printed in Italy. Then dresses would be designed by unpaid, inept, but sincere devotees, then manufactured and sold as "designer dresses."

What?

Delighted to be doing artwork for Maharishi again, I diligently designed lovely fabrics with floral motifs. Reginald supervised, along with Sidha Corporation board members Helene and Luther Koffman and Marlene Cummings. Unwittingly and regrettably, at one meeting I criticized one of Reginald's designs.

Open mouth. Insert foot. Choke.

Our textile design group continued designing fabrics for two months. Then Marlene phoned me at my guesthouse. It was the first day of my menses, so of course, all good little South-Fallsburgians "rested."

"Where are you, Susan? Maharishi asked about you," she said. "We want to go over some designs."

"I'm resting. It's my first day," I answered.

"Well you better come here the day after tomorrow. You've got to be here."

"Why?" I asked.

"Just take it from me, you better show up."

The next day I stayed in my room. I couldn't go to the Indian Express. I was "resting." The day after that I didn't go either. *All ladies must rest the first three days of our period.*

I got a call at my hotel. It was Marlene. "Maharishi wants to see all the fabric design group today at 4:00."

"I'm resting. Please tell Maharishi I'm resting. He'll understand. Be sure to use the name 'Susan the Artist.' Would you? Though he sometimes calls me Susan Shumsky, usually he calls me 'Susan the Artist.'"

"Okay, we'll tell him," Marlene promised.

I was in agony. *Oh, God. Four years have gone by. My only chance to meet Maharishi privately, now thwarted by my #@%*&! period.*

⋘⋘⋘⋘⋘⋘⋘⋘⋘⋙⋙⋙⋙⋙⋙⋙⋙⋙

The following day, I showed up at the meeting hall to work on designs. A big stir was in the air. Maharishi sat on stage, directing a chaotic scene. People stood in line, waiting to talk to him privately. Others rushed to and fro.

"Susan," Helene said. "We've been looking for you. Maharishi was calling for you last night. Why didn't you come?"

"I was resting," I said. *Didn't Marlene tell him I was resting?* I thought.

"Maharishi says you must go back to the States, back to your Vedic Atom. He says you must leave tonight with the rest of the course participants."

I was utterly aghast. "Leave tonight?" *My infernal period. Argghhh!*

"Yes, tonight," Helene said.

"My Vedic Atom? But my Vedic Atom doesn't exist. They all resigned," I informed her. "Did Maharishi say anything about the fabric designs?"

"He liked yours very much. He said all ladies should wear roses."

"Did you tell him who designed the fabric?"

"Reginald told him."

"Did Reginald call me 'Susan the Artist'?"

"No. I don't think Maharishi realized who you were. He confused you with Susan Ballantine who runs the kitchen," Helene said.

Susan the Singer, I thought. Helene continued, "Once we explained that you're not the Susan who runs the kitchen, he didn't remember you, and said you should be sent home. You've got to leave tonight. Do you want me to ask Maharishi if you can go back to South Fallsburg, since your Vedic Atom no longer exists?"

But he knows me. And Marlene promised she would say Susan the Artist!

"Thank you, Helene. I would love that," I said. "I could work on fabrics there."

"Good idea. Wait here. I'll ask."

My fate was being sealed. Helene and Reginald approached Maharishi. Then Helene headed toward me. "Maharishi says you can go to South Fallsburg and work on fabrics and also design Sidha dresses."

Flabbergasted by the sudden expulsion from my presupposed glorious reinstatement to International Staff, that night of March 8, 1981, I found myself abruptly thrust onto a jet headed toward the USA. *Why should this surprise me? I know the competition around Maharishi and what it takes to stay.*

I surmised it was Reginald's doing, because I lambasted his horrid design, or didn't participate in the compulsory bootlicking, or threatened his position years ago. Tears welled up in my eyes. My heart was shattered.

Futile regrets beg some questions: Why didn't I just get in line and ask Maharishi whether I could stay on Staff? He was right there, a few feet away, taking questions from everyone. And why did I blame Reginald?

I suppose answers could be found in my paralyzing, helpless powerlessness provoked by Maharishi rejecting my poster. And despair from past perceived slights from Reginald. Ah, the foolishness of youth and wisdom of old age.

Oh well. It's not important, Susan. Who cares that for four long years you put all heart and hopes into returning to Maharishi, only to be sent packing PDQ? Don't worry. You're never really alone. You've got a big pile of regrets to keep you company.

Back in South Fallsburg, I started designing dresses according to Maharishi's long list of edicts, which included no low necklines, no short sleeves, loose fit, no figure flattering, no dark colors, no red or black, gold lamé is good. The fabric design motif should match jeweled buttons, parasol or handbag. Translation: make beautiful young women look like great-grandbags-in-a-bonnet.

I studied *Vogue* and *Bazaar* and came up with an entire collection, in line with current trends. In 1981, ethnic prints, mandarin collars, brocade jackets, and cuts from India, China, and Arabia were stylish. That seemed great for what I envisioned.

It took several months to design eleven day-dresses, four two-piece knit suits, one knit dress, four two-piece suits, two cocktail dresses, nine evening gowns, two two-piece evening gowns, one elegant evening cape, and a gorgeous wedding gown. Many of the designs used elaborate oriental or floral prints.

In high school I'd studied fashion design, and at age seventeen won a contest. In the Miss Universe pageant, Miss Colorado USA wore a gold and silver lamé dress I designed to represent coins from the Denver Mint. An article in *The Denver Post* showed me wearing it. Plus during my hippie years, I designed and sewed flower child costumes. So I knew a bit about clothing design.

I sent my designs to Maharishi via Reginald in Switzerland.

That was the last I ever saw or heard of them.

In October 1981 I was assigned to run the showroom in New York City for the "Sidha Dresses" line of clothing. Two meditators I knew were professional models. One was a Revlon "Charlie Girl" who still called herself Charlie ten years later. The Sidha Corporation board bullied the other model, Sheryl Lund, a tall brunette, into organizing the Sidha Dress fashion show at the Pierre Hotel.

Although Sheryl arranged the show, she was not entitled to any privileges. Sidha Corporation officials Marlene and Helene stayed at the five-star Pierre on Central Park. However, Sheryl flopped on a meditator's couch. None of her expenses were paid.

The hotel ballroom rental cost thousands of dollars. But Sidha Corporation wouldn't spend a few hundred dollars to hire models. Sheryl was forced to recruit random women who happened to show up at the TM center.

Sheryl received strict orders. "Models" just walk down the runway, turn around, and walk back. No hands on hips, dancing, or "provocative, enticing" movements. Most so-called "models" never showed up for rehearsals. Others flaked out at the last minute.

The fashion show ended up a sad, miserable joke. The editor of *Vogue* magazine attended. So did other top industry professionals whom Sheryl had invited. It was a humiliating nightmare for Sheryl, obliged to explain why her models looked like Amy Farrah Fowler had time-traveled back to the 1980s to model Ugly Betty Couture—and why the designs looked like a teen crafts project glued together at summer camp.

I modeled at the show. I was tall and thin, not that it mattered. I still looked like a homeless vagrant, conscripted at the last minute while aimlessly wandering down

Seventh Avenue. Unprofessional, unrehearsed, unstyled, and unkempt, I felt like a hippie ashram fugitive. The press described the fine, high-quality, attractively designed fabrics, but the dresses as matronly, poorly conceived, and decidedly unstylish.

After this bloodbath, I was assigned to live in New York City (sleeping on someone's couch, without pay) and babysit the astronomically high-rent Sidha Dress showroom in the Halston building. I "modeled" dresses there—a loose term, since 1) I never wore makeup, 2) My hair was frizzy and feral, and 3) No buyers ever came. Gee whiz. Imagine that!

Though the fabrics, printed in Italy, were gorgeous, we tried to pass off as "designer dresses" pleated or A-line skirts with hemlines below the knee, baggy, blousy button-up bodices with covered buttons, gathered shoulders, long sleeves, big cuffs, and a big bow at the neckline and/or ruffles down the front. To fit me, these so-called "couture creations" would require significant alterations. Since no alterations were made, they just hung like potato sacks.

The only redeeming feature were gorgeous cashmere-silk blend scarves that could be draped over the dresses to hide their hideousness. These deadly dull dress silhouettes made any woman, no matter how beautiful, look like a constipated Victorian spinster who just swallowed a turd.

<hr />

I believe one of Maharishi's favorite games was what I dubbed "lessons in futility." He would conceive an utterly meaningless project (such as amateurs designing absurdly styled dresses). It would, of course, be doomed to failure. Devotees would toil day and night for months, only to be censured for its flaws and requested to rework it over and over, ad nauseam. The project would never get finished, or would fail, or be abandoned.

Which reminds me of Tibetan yogi and poet UJetsun Milarepa (1052–1135 AD), disciple of Marpa Lotsawa, of the Kagyu School of Tibetan Buddhism. Marpa repeatedly chastised and insulted his disciple Milarepa while breaking every promise to instruct him into the secret teachings. Marpa asked Milarepa to construct several large towers, only to tear them all down and return all the earth, stones, and boulders to their original positions.

It mattered not to Maharishi whether a project was preposterous or whether it had merit. Before its completion he would often end it abruptly. Any attachments and expectations we clung to regarding anticipated outcomes would be squashed. We would thereby learn nothing in this world is real, nothing lasts, all is ephemeral, and all is but dust.

When the young Mahesh was in Guru Dev's ashram, he was sent to travel throughout India to visit various holy men. Guru Dev gave Mahesh important notes in envelopes to carry and deliver to them. One day Mahesh dropped one of the notes and happened to read it by accident. The note read, "Please send this man back to me."

Maharishi's "lessons in futility" resemble Tibetan Buddhist monks' sand mandalas, or *alfombras* (sawdust street carpets) of Guatemala during Easter week. Magnificent, intricate, painstaking designs take days to create—only to be ceremoniously dismantled. Such rituals are known to symbolize life's transitory nature.

Maharishi taught us to let go of anticipation. As stated in the *Bhagavad Gita,* "You have control over action alone, never over its fruits. Live not for the fruits of actions, nor attach yourself to inaction."[203] For there is only one lasting thing: the unchanging, unmanifest reality beyond relative existence—absolute pure consciousness.

<hr />

Needless to say, none of my beautiful dress designs was used. Knowing Maharishi's so-called fashion sense, I believe he wanted all "ladies" (females were never "women") to either dress in saris or like British royalty—only radically less stylish. He preferred lady-like attire. I imagine Queen Elizabeth II was his primary fashion icon.

Only Maharishi would waste hundreds of thousands on such idiotic, hopeless schemes, just to teach us how meaningless this material world is.

22

GURU TRICKS AND CELEBRITY TREATS

Thin wires allow electricity to pass through, but if we want more electricity, we have to make the wire thicker. Every contact of activity around the master is adding one more wire for more power, more love, more intelligence, more being to flow.

—MAHARISHI MAHESH YOGI

The actions of spiritual masters arise from cosmic perspective rather than individual ego. Their motive is freeing people from the stranglehold of illusion. They don't follow social conventions. Some pass their tests. Others fail. Celebrities are not exempt from such tests.

In December 1969, eight months after John Lennon left India in a tizzy, a handful of students met Maharishi in his simple brick, concrete, and stone bungalow in Rishikesh—far from the "villa" or "air-conditioned mansion" described by the media, or "million-dollar" "very rich-looking" house professed by John Lennon, though he'd visited the modest quarters numerous times (see page 55 for a photo).

A USA map was propped against the wall. Maharishi was discussing a place to hold a Teacher Training Course for at least a thousand students, since the ashram was too small.

Suddenly Kathleen Chambers, serving as Maharishi's secretary, burst into the room and announced there was an important telegram. Maharishi asked, "Yes, who it is from?"

Kathleen said, "It's from John Lennon. He's in New Delhi, and he's asking if he can come and see you."

Maharishi looked at her with a blank expression. His response was "Who?"

Kathleen replied, "John Lennon, Maharishi, who was one of the Beatles who were here."

Again Maharishi asked, "Who?"

Kathleen replied, "Maharishi, it's John Lennon from the Beatles. He flew into Delhi, by himself, and he very much wants to come and see you."

Maharishi turned from her, and declared, with disgust:

"I do not know a *John Lennon*."

<hr />

On February 15, 2006 and again right after Maharishi's death on February 6, 2008, Deepak Chopra reported to the press:

"The Beatles, along with their entourage, were doing drugs, taking LSD, at Maharishi's ashram, and he lost his temper with them. He asked them to leave, and they did in a huff."[204] Deepak said Maharishi never encountered anything like that before, and he strongly opposed it.[205]

Deepak explained that in September 1991, George Harrison asked him to arrange a private meeting with Maharishi in Vlodrop, Netherlands. Deepak was in attendance. As the meeting began, George presented Maharishi with a rose, followed by a long silence.

Then Maharishi asked, "How have you been?"

George replied, "Some good things [have happened], some bad things." He added, "You must know about John being assassinated."

Maharishi replied, "I was very sorry to hear about it."

After some time, George said, "I came to apologize."

"For what?" Maharishi asked.

"You know for what," replied George.

"Tell Deepak the real story," Maharishi said.

George replied, "I don't know about it 100 percent, but here's what I know transpired." George told Deepak that Maharishi asked the Beatles to leave Rishikesh because they were using drugs during the meditation course. But Maharishi refused to come out publicly to humiliate the band members.

The topic turned to the Beatles' appearance on *The Ed Sullivan Show,* when it was reported there was no crime in the USA during that hour. Maharishi said, "When I heard this, I knew the Beatles were angels on earth. They created such beautiful music for the world. It doesn't matter what John said or did, I could never be upset with angels."

On hearing that, George broke down and wept. There was another long silence.

Then George told Maharishi, "I love you" and Maharishi responded, "I love you too." Later George phoned Deepak and told him, "A huge karmic baggage has been lifted from me, because I didn't want to lie."[206]

In 1968, when John and George returned early from Rishikesh, Paul asked what happened. John said Maharishi made a pass at the blonde American who looked like Mia Farrow. Paul asked, "Yes? What's wrong with that?"

Feeling duped, used, and angry as hell, John answered, "Well, you know, he's just a bloody old letch just like everybody else. What the fuck, we can't go following that!"

Paul said, "But he never said he was a god. In fact very much the opposite, he said, 'Don't treat me like a god, I'm just a meditation teacher.'"

Paul, who believed this was just John's excuse to leave the ashram, commented: "It's really funny, John's reaction to this sexual thing. It seemed a little prudish to me. It became public that we didn't like Maharishi but I never felt that way."[207]

Upon their return to London, the Beatles observed a policy of silence about what happened in India. They decided if they told the story, it would reflect poorly on them.[208] This seemed to lend credence to Deepak's claim. If his report was true, the Beatles wouldn't want to reveal that Maharishi asked them to leave.

Within a week after returning from Rishikesh to Kenwood, John resumed his daily long-standing addiction to alcohol, speed, barbiturates, and psychedelics, which he mixed with a mortar and pestle in his sunroom.

By May 1968, Yoko Ono had replaced Alexis as John's constant appendage. That month John and Yoko recorded "The Maharishi Song," which viciously attacked the guru for being silly and evasive, fabricating stories, misbehaving sexually, living high on the hog, and acting unholy. In a *Rolling Stone* interview, John referred to Maharishi as "a fucking idiot" due to the guru's remarks about Brian Epstein's death.[209]

When reporters asked Maharishi about the Beatles' allegations, he replied, "I think I would love them, whatever they say. When asked "Why do you think they made such a statement?" Maharishi replied, "I am unaware completely, why. I only extend my love to them."[210]

When John and Yoko moved into Ringo's old flat on Montegu Square in July 1968, they began taking heroin, "as a celebration of ourselves as artists," according to Yoko. The drug stupor continued through most of 1969.[211]

John and Yoko graced their album cover *Unfinished Music No. 1: Two Virgins* (released November 11, 1968) wearing only a smile, an amulet, a foreskin, some nipples, and lots of black fluffy pubic hair. A decade later John admitted "Norwegian Wood" "was about an affair I was having. I didn't want my wife, Cyn, to know. I'd always had some kind of affairs going."[212]

By the time the Two Virgins album dropped, John had calmed down about India. He told *Rolling Stone*, "I had some great experiences, meditating eight hours a day—some amazing things, some amazing trips—it was great. And I still meditate off and on. George is doing it regularly. I believe implicitly in the whole bit. It's just that it's difficult to continue it. I lost the rosy glasses."[213]

In 1978 John characterized meditation as a way to slip out of the "straitjacket of the mind."[214] Maybe he should have sloughed off that straitjacket a decade earlier. His denouncement of Maharishi seemed like "pot, kettle, black" to me. Three months before John's death, he finally conceded, "At first I was bitter about Maharishi being human. Well, I'm not bitter anymore. [He's] human and I'm only thinking what a dummy I was, you know. Although I meditate and I cry."[215]

In 1978 Cynthia Lennon wrote, " I believe that Maharishi is a very wise and beautiful being. No matter what anyone says, he has always worked for the betterment of mankind. And if one man can even partially succeed in a single lifetime, then he is worthy of praise, not degradation or insult."[216]

George Harrison never really believed Alexis. He accused the Greek of slandering Maharishi to cajole John away from him. In 1970 George said, "It's probably in the history books that Maharishi 'tried to attack Mia Farrow'—but it's total bullshit. There were a lot of flakes there; the whole place was full of flaky people. Some of them were us."[217]

⁓⁓⁓⁓⁓⁓⁓⁓⁓⁓⁓⁓⁓⁓

In 1992 George held a concert in London with Ringo and Eric Clapton to benefit Maharishi's ill-fated "Natural Law" political party (another quixotic Maharishi scheme). Then George phoned Paul from LA, giggling: "Maharishi would like you, me and Ringo to stand as Members of Parliament for Liverpool. We'll win!"

Paul's response: "A week before the election! You've gotta be kidding!"[218]

In 1999, the *Boston Globe* reported Paul still practiced TM daily. During a four-hour visit in Vlodrop, Holland, his daughter Stella video-recorded Maharishi saying: "Enjoy!" which Paul declared "the same message from 30 years ago that he wrote in my book. And you know what? That is actually awfully good advice."[219] "Now I say to my own kids, 'Go and get a mantra, because then if you ever want to meditate, you'll know how to do it.'"[220]

On April 4, 2009, Paul, Ringo, Mike Love, Paul Horn, and Donovan performed at the "Change Begins Within" benefit for the David Lynch Foundation for Consciousness-Based Education and World Peace. Advocated by many celebrities, it offers TM to veterans, abused women, HIV victims, PTSD victims, prisoners, the homeless, schoolchildren, and more. Paul said, "In moments of madness, [TM] has helped me find moments of serenity." "I would like to think that it would help provide them a quiet haven in a not-so-quiet world."[221]

"Change Begins Within" benefit: l. to r.:
Paul McCartney, David Lynch, Ringo Starr.
Gregorio Binuya/ABACAUSA.COM/Newscom

In 2011, George said, "I still practice Transcendental Meditation and I think it's great. Maharishi only ever did good for us, and although I have not been with him physically, I never left him."[222] George bequeathed a large scholarship fund for Maharishi University.[223]

Prudence, Mia, and John Farrow were among seven children of film star Maureen O'Sullivan ("Jane" in Tarzan movies) and Academy Award–winning screenwriter-director John Farrow. An undisciplined, defiant teenager, Prudence suffered reckless, self-destructive years of decadence and near insanity, induced by alcoholism and drug abuse.

January 23, 1968, Cambridge, Massachusetts:
Maharishi meets Mia Farrow at Sheraton
Hotel the day before they leave for India.
Associated Press

Prudence learned TM in 1966, believing it would answer all her problems. A psychiatrist warned if she didn't stop this damaging meditation practice, more dangerous than LSD, she'd become a zombie. She voluntarily entered a mental institution, but continued meditating and declined medication. Mia extricated her from the institution.

After Mia married Frank Sinatra in 1966, Prudence felt Mia's fame usurped Prudence's identity and stole her life. Rude people would remark, "Why aren't you successful like Mia?"[224]

Prudence applied for TM Teacher Training in January 1967, but was too young. When older sister Mia wanted to study in Rishikesh (she knew the Beatles would be there in 1968), Maharishi invited her, though she hadn't learned TM. This fueled Prudence's jealousy.

Prudence met Maharishi in Boston to be evaluated for course acceptance. She found the emanation of peace surrounding him greater than any other spiritual teacher she'd met. After she poured out her heart to him, Maharishi extended his arm, made a fist, and declared, "You are mine!"[225]

Prudence felt overshadowed by her sister's fame, so Mia was a touchy subject. To get under Prudence's skin, Maharishi asked her in Rishikesh, "Do you know your sister is a great person?"

Startled, Prudence replied, "No, I don't think she's a great person."

Maharishi laughed and asked, "Doesn't she want to do good?"

"Yes," Prudence said.

Maharishi said, "Tell me all about what good she wants to do."

"What kind of guru are you?" Prudence yelled. "Why don't you just go to Hollywood, where you can meet lots of stars and ask them these questions yourself?"

Maharishi replied, "Now go and rest."[226]

Prudence had presence of mind to understand Maharishi's method. His praise of Mia unmasked Prudence's repressed negative feelings about living in the shadow of her sister's fame. Prudence realized the "potency and danger" of those emotions: "Lacking confidence in myself had exacerbated the situation, increasing repressed feelings of anger and inadequacy."[227]

Prudence's happy ending was she overcame self-destructive tendencies and became a successful author, Sanskrit scholar, and meditation and yoga teacher.

Her brother John Farrow's story was less fortunate. A Yale neurobiologist, he taught TM, spoke at Maharishi's science symposiums, and helped create the MIU catalog. But in 2013 in Maryland, he was sentenced to twenty-five years in prison for child abuse and molestation.

Arriving at London's Heathrow Airport from Rishikesh on March 8, 1968, Mia Farrow wore a flowing caftan crafted by the ashram tailor out of embroidered cashmere shawls, and carried what she identified to a reporter as "a secret box given to me in India." When asked "by whom?" she answered, "If I said, it would no longer be a secret box."

Regarding her stay at the ashram, she reported, "It's been the most rewarding experience of my life." She explained, meditation "helps your general well-being because you go right to the source of thought, the source of creativity, the source of happiness." When asked by a reporter if she was "absolutely happy in your own mind that you're not being conned," she nodded and replied, "Yes."[228]

March 8, 1968: Mia Farrow arrives at Heathrow Airport from India. *Anthony Wallace/ Daily Mail/REX/Shutterstock.*

Mia's memoir, published thirty years later, reported that after she and Maharishi meditated in his cave on her birthday in 1968, they stood up, facing each other. "I was blinking at his beard when suddenly I became aware of two surprisingly male, hairy arms going around me." Mia panicked and bolted up the stairs, apologizing. She sprinted to Prudence, who explained, "It's an honor to be touched by a holy man after meditation, a tradition." But Mia dashed out the ashram gates, fearful when Maharishi's brahmacharyas followed her (she returned a few hours later but left the following day for Goa). In the 1970s Mia told former skin-boy Ned Wynn (son of actor Keenan Wynn and grandson of comedian Ed Wynn) it was clear Maharishi wanted her to lie down with him and have sex.

Mia's story changed from hair-stroking (1968) to hairy arms (1997). In her memoir she admitted, "At my level of consciousness, if Jesus Christ Himself had embraced me, I would have misinterpreted it."[229]

Prudence returned to Rishikesh to attend my Teacher Training Course in 1970. She was excited to tell Maharishi that her sister Mia had given birth on February 26. With detachment, Maharishi answered, "Send a telegram."

Then Prudence said, "She had twins."

Maharishi replied in a cold, humorless manner, "Send two telegrams."

Superstar Donovan Leitch first met Maharishi in Los Angeles onstage after a lecture in 1967. The guru invited him to visit him where he was staying in Beverly Hills. Donovan expressed being dumbstruck by him but irritated at Maharishi's aides hovering and fawning over their guru.

Donovan described his Initiation: "I'd had a little joint just before I got out of the limo, so I was feeling kind of mellow. All along one wall of this not great large house were seven hairy guys, like a rock band. I didn't recognize them. Anyway, in I went.

"It was dark. It was moody, and there was Maharishi. And Maharishi looked at me in the half-light. And he gave me the mantra. And he said, 'Do this, relax, repeat it silently, inside.' And then suddenly, something extraordinary happened. Which is what I wanted. I started falling down, down, down, down, down, down, down, down, down. And as I fell, I felt relief, relief, relief, relax, relax. After a time, which I couldn't measure, I heard him say, 'Now open your eyes.'

"And then an aide came in and said, Maharishi, it's time for the next initiation. And Maharishi said, 'And who is that?' And the aide said, 'They are called the Grateful Dead.' And I laughed, and Maharishi laughed, and he said, 'They should not call themselves the Grateful Dead. They should call themselves The Grateful Living.'"[230]

In autumn 1967, Mike Love first heard about TM and attended Jerry Jarvis's lecture at the Santa Monica Convention Center. Mike tried to learn TM, but the SIMS center in Westwood sent him away because it was for students only.

The Beach Boys appeared at a UNICEF Variety Gala in Paris on December 15, 1967. On their way to Paris, the Beach Boys stayed at the London Hilton, where John Lennon and George Harrison surprised Al Jardine by knocking on his door for the sole purpose of introducing them to TM. At the UNICEF rehearsal, attended by Maharishi, John, and George, the Beach Boys first met Maharishi, who was scheduled to appear but was cut from the lineup.

December 15, 1967, Paris: Maharishi with John and George, watch the UNICEF Gala rehearsal. Charlie Lutes, president of SRM, smiling in background. © *KEYSTONE Pictures USA*

Dennis Wilson described, "All of a sudden, I felt this weirdness, this presence this guy had. Like out of left field. First thing he ever said to me was 'Live your life to the fullest.'"[231] Dennis arranged a private lecture with Maharishi at Hotel de Crillon for the Beach Boys and wives. That's where, on December 16, 1967, Dennis Wilson, Carl Wilson, Al Jardine, and Mike Love learned TM. In 1968 Brian Wilson met Maharishi in the USA and also learned TM.

Maharishi with the Beach Boys: l. to r.: Dennis Wilson, Al Jardine, Mike Love, Maharishi, Bruce Johnston, Brian Wilson. *Mirrorpix/Newscom*

Mike described, "I wasn't dreaming. But the state itself was deeper than the deepest sleep. It was neither dark nor light." "I had found a place of infinite peace, of profound rest." He expressed, "This is so easy that anyone could do it, and if everyone did it, it would be an entirely different world."[232]

In January 1968 Mike attended Maharishi's lectures at the Plaza in New York and Harvard Law Forum in Cambridge, where Mia Farrow sat nearby. When Mike phoned Maharishi's hotel, the guru unexpectedly answered the phone himself and invited the Beach Boys to Rishikesh.

1970: Mike Love.
© *Ed Thrasher/mptvimages.com*

Comedian, TV star, and twice Golden Globe nominated actor Andy Kaufman learned TM in 1968, which helped him relax onstage. He said, "I knew I had the potential to entertain, but I was too shy. TM really brought the shyness out of me."[233]

An eccentric, politically incorrect comedian, Andy behaved unpredictably, leaving audiences and hosts bewildered. Andy's "Foreign Man" act led sitcom *Taxi* producers to invent a harebrained auto mechanic, Latka Gravas, with high-pitched voice and unidentifiable accent: "Tenk you veddy much."

In July 1970 Andy attended Maharishi's one-month course for twelve hundred meditators at Poland Spring Resort, Maine, where he plied Maharishi with questions about comedy. He took TM Teacher Training in Mallorca, February to June 1971. However, considered peculiar and unstable, he wasn't made a TM teacher.

Later Andy met Maharishi, convinced him of his sincerity, and was made an Initiator. He taught TM and volunteered at the Cambridge, Massachusetts, TM Center. Andy and Bob Zmuda, his comedy-writing partner, took the La Antilla course in 1973. Andy took advanced courses in Interlaken and Vittel, France, December 1973 to January 1974.

1984: Andy Kaufman meditating at home. © *Gunther/mptvimages.com*

At a course in Livingston Manor, New York, three hundred men gathered. A guy with crazy deer-in-headlights eyes, rumpled clothing, and black bushy hair explained in a bizarre foreign accent that he would lead the meeting. He acted out the Mighty Mouse theme song. Then beat savagely on a bongo with fierce facial expressions. Next he turned his back, combed his hair repeatedly, donned a leather jacket, turned around, sneered, and lip-synched "Love Me Tender." The audience howled with laughter. The entertainer was Andy Kaufman.

Though Elvis Presley considered Andy his favorite impersonator, his unconventional personae didn't live up to the extreme degree of constipation evidently required to qualify for TM advanced courses. Prune-faced TM-Sidhi Administrators invariably rejected Andy's applications. But a phone call to higher-ups would always secure his acceptance.

In 1983, that didn't happen.

Andy, suffering from chronic cough, had taken a turn for the worse. He'd been supporting the Movement financially, and sent another donation for $500 before applying for a course in December. But Andy's wrestling-with-women antics weren't a knockout with the new female TM-Sidhi Administrator. Apparently Andy was too hilarious to qualify for the course.

Jerry Jarvis, who said Andy "had a more profound understanding of Maharishi's teachings than many people I had ever come in contact with," assured him the misunderstanding would clear up.[234] But it didn't. It never did. Andy was never accepted to another TM course.

Bill Zehme, biographer, described: "He felt hurt, and the hurt touched his spirit, which had always been sustained by meditation. He felt betrayed inside his secret soul. 'Who are they to tell me how to run my career?' he said over and over. He was angry and then very sad, but he didn't stop meditating."[235]

Soon Andy contracted a rare lung cancer, which he treated with both allopathic and natural medicine. His last resort was psychic surgery in the Philippines in March 1984. Tragically, he died two months later at age thirty-five. Andy's life was depicted in the biopic *Man on the Moon*. To prepare for that part, Jim Carrey learned TM. He won a Golden Globe.

∞∞∞∞∞∞∞∞∞∞∞∞∞∞∞∞∞∞∞∞∞∞∞

From the late 1970s to early 1980s, Doug Henning appeared in three Broadway shows and eight television specials. A sparkling, bubbly genius with shoulder-length dark shaggy hair, droopy hippy mustache, and gopher grin, Doug's bigger-than-life personality exuded warmth, magnetism, and joy. He wore jeans, glitzy Elvis-like jumpsuits, and tie-dyed T-shirts.

Doug staged a stunning magic show before Maharishi on a Teacher Training course in Europe in the 1970s, aided by his assistant, TM teacher Barbara DeAngelis. They married in 1977 and divorced in 1981. Doug was her second husband. Barbara's third husband, John Gray, was Maharishi's skin-boy in La Antilla in 1973. Unlike skin-boys who lied incessantly and hoarded Maharishi jealously as though he were Tolkien's "precious" One Ring of Mordor, Johnny actually *let us into the room*.

Barbara DeAngelis and John Gray taught seminars titled "Making Love Work"— perhaps the most ironic double-entendre ever. They got blacklisted from the TM Movement for teaching something—anything other than TM. After divorcing, they made love work elsewhere. Barbara is now married to her fifth husband and John, to

August 11, 1998: John Gray at American Heart
Association benefit. © *Globe Photos/*
ZUMAPRESS.com.

his second wife. They both became the biggest
best-selling relationship authors. John, author of
Men Are from Mars, Women Are from Venus, sold
about 50 million books and counting.

After John Gray donated $50,000 to the Nat-
ural Law Party, he was invited to Vlodrop to visit
Maharishi. However, an argument ensued. One
TM leader warned Maharishi about John's "inappropriate books." Another claimed
John's books helped people. John ended up speaking with Maharishi, who attempted
to recruit him for various projects. John declined, saying he was happy with his life and
just wanted to visit.

It was love at first sight when Doug Henning met MIU student Debby Douillard. They
engaged within one week and wed on December 6, 1981, during the lavish women's
dome inauguration, attended by two thousand Fairfieldians. The couple built a spectacular mansion near campus.

Debby and Doug Henning wedding at the Golden Dome, where the magician
conjures a dove from a book used in the ceremony. *Associated Press*

At his height of stardom, Doug hung up his magic wand to trade up for real magic—levitation and other supernormal powers. "The moment I saw Maharishi, I knew that he knew the truth of life," he said. So in 1986, off Doug and Debby flew to Switzerland to live with Maharishi.

As Doug sank slowly into Maharishi-Land, then Never-Never Land, and Never-to-Surface-Again-Land, magic fans asked, "Whatever happened to Doug Henning?" The charismatic magician and his brilliant career vanished in Maharishi smoke. Poof.

Maharishi and Doug's brainstorm was a theme park, Veda Land, set against a Himalayan backdrop, where a building would levitate over water, a winged chariot would dive into the atomic structure of a rose, riders would visit seven states of consciousness, and flying robots would perform magic tricks.

In 1992 Doug announced plans for the $1.5 billion park on 1499 acres, two miles from Niagara Falls, Ontario. But Maharishi scrapped it due to the existence of a gambling casino in the same town. Property was acquired near Disney World Resort in Florida, but that scheme vanished into thin air.

Then abracadabra! Doug reappeared as stalwart TM drone, spouting the party line in robotic monotone, donning the TM uniform: business suit, white shirt, gold tie. Doug's adorable personality evaporated as he sold off illusions to David Copperfield. In 1993 Doug ran as unlikely candidate in Canada for Maharishi's "Natural Law Party."

Shortly after receiving a liver cancer diagnosis in 1999, Doug was sent to Canada, where he tragically died in 2000 at age fifty-two.

<hr />

Though Deepak Chopra was born in Delhi, he took his medical training in the USA and served as endocrinologist and Chief of Staff at New England Memorial. He learned TM in 1980. Within a week he stopped drinking. Two weeks later he stopped smoking. He declared TM "Real Meditation," and described, "I was feeling healthier physically. I was more productive, I was more creative, and I was at peace."[236]

Deepak and wife Rita met Maharishi in 1985 in Washington, DC, at an Ayurveda conference. They stole out of the lecture hall early to catch a plane. Suddenly everyone else spilled out of the hall and Maharishi made a beeline toward them, handed them roses, and persuaded them to meet him upstairs.

During their two-hour meeting, Maharishi told Deepak to study Ayurvedic medicine: "Sickness is interrupted intelligence, but we can bring it back into line. That's all we do from our side. Nature takes care of it."[237]

When the couple finally arrived at the airport, they found all planes on the Eastern seaboard delayed. Such happy "coincidences" were staple in Maharishi's magical world.

Deepak left New England Memorial to become founding president of the American Association of Ayurvedic Medicine and medical director of Maharishi Ayurveda Health Center in Lancaster, Massachusetts.

The MD from India with movie-star looks, silky voice, and magnetic personality became the perfect TM and Ayurveda spokesperson. Under Maharishi's direct guidance and support, Deepak, his "golden boy," traveled worldwide as his emissary.

Maharishi's message à la Deepak proved advantageous. Westerners who feared Indian gurus weren't afraid of the relatable Deepak. He didn't wear robes or sit cross-legged on deerskins. His hair was short; he was clean-shaven; his accent didn't invoke blank, perplexed stares. A gifted, articulate speaker, he brought his unique charm to the timeless message of *Sanatana Dharma*.

Deepak was lauded a genius—original and innovative. The public assumed his Indian birthright had bestowed his profound grasp of Vedic wisdom. Yet before meeting Maharishi, Deepak knew practically nothing about Vedic anything. Under Maharishi's training, employing his guru's phrases, delivery method, and expressions, Deepak became a hip, slick, Westernized Maharishi clone (no offense intended—au contraire, considering how powerful Maharishi was, this is a great recognition of Deepak's talent).

March 29, 1988, The Hague. Deepak Chopra speaks about "The Physiology of Peace" at International Law and Peace Conference. *Associated Press photo/Albert Overbeek*

Maharishi assigned two Purusha course men to ghostwrite Deepak's books. When asked how he authored eighty-five books, Deepak claimed he wrote them on plane flights. In 2017 in *The Atlantic,* Deepak's new response to that same question: "I have eternity. I don't believe in the concept of time"[238] (evidently those "plane flights").

Before *Perfect Health* came out in 1990, PR professionals from Purusha arranged millions of TM meditators to preorder the first printing, making it a *New York Times* bestseller. This pattern continued for his first three books. In this way Maharishi propelled Deepak to stardom.

Deepak, who considered himself just a "regular guy," [239] suddenly found himself in the position of being an official TM spokesperson. His patients at the Ayurvedic clinic included Elizabeth Taylor, Michael Jackson, and Donna Karan. He said the pomp and ceremony that TM meditators accorded him wherever he traveled made him uncomfortable because it bordered on veneration: "I wondered why Maharishi, the first 'modern' guru, allowed and encouraged it. It seemed inconsistent with Vedanta's central theme that the material world is illusion, not to mention the freedom from materialism that is expected of one who is enlightened."[240]

After a while Deepak began to feel he was being used: "You know how the Movement is. They were always taking my credentials and putting them in front. I did feel exploited. I did feel used. But I was uncomfortable articulating that. Particularly in Maharishi's presence."[241] Then in 1991 Deepak got stuck in the crossfire of conflict-of-interest controversies over an article about Ayurveda published in *JAMA*.

That same year, Deepak Chopra's father, a cardiologist in Delhi, saved Maharishi's life when he collapsed with acute pancreatitis, kidney failure, septicemia, and heart attack. Poison orange juice from a "foreign disciple" was suspected. Maharishi flew to England for kidney dialysis. Upon arrival he suffered cardiac arrest, on life support with a pacemaker, then miraculously revived. Deepak nursed Maharishi back to health for a year, while followers believed he was "in silence." After recovering, Maharishi flew to Vlodrop, Holland, where he remained until his death.

Deepak noticed other TM leaders competing with him for Maharishi's attention and leadership in the Movement. Maharishi told Deepak to pay no mind to jealous disciples who treated him rudely, but Deepak was sensing some spiritual popularity contest. "I started to be uncomfortable with what I sensed was a cultish atmosphere around Maharishi."[242] "I was never upset with Maharishi. But the people around him. I never had real anger—although I never understood all their gimmicks."[243] What Deepak disliked most was "the self-righteous attitude. That we are the best. What we know no one else knows. It wasn't true."[244]

In July 1993, Maharishi confronted him: "People are telling me that you are competing with me." He asked Deepak to stop traveling, stop writing books, and move into the ashram. Maharishi gave him twenty-four hours to decide. Deepak perceived him acting like "an irascible, jealous old man whose pride had been hurt."[245]

With family responsibilities, economic concerns, children in school, and a wife who wouldn't live in an ashram, Deepak declared he didn't need twenty-four hours and would leave immediately. He told Maharishi he had no ambitions to be a guru, the idea appalled him, and he was dismayed Maharishi would believe rumors. Deepak took his wife Rita's hand and walked out.

When Deepak returned to Boston, Maharishi offered to put him in charge of the whole Movement; he could be a great spiritual leader and everyone would follow him. Deepak replied, "I don't want to be a spiritual leader. I am a very regular guy—with a wife and kids. I just have the gift of the gab."[246]

Maharishi's comment to his close disciples: "Apparently the absolute is not big enough for Deepak." TM spinmeisters then got to work. On July 16, 1993, the "Maharishi National Council of the Age of Enlightenment" officially announced Deepak was "no longer affiliated with the TM Movement." All meditators were told to "ignore Deepak," not contact him, or promote his courses, speaking engagements, tapes, or books. "This is extremely important for the purity of the teaching."[247]

Deepak's response: "I am not really sure what is meant when people ask me if I've left the Movement." "I still practice TM and the Sidhis, and will continue to recommend them and refer people to the Centers and Clinics."[248]

In 1993 Deepak became director at Sharp Institute for Human Potential and Center for Mind/Body Medicine in Del Mar, California, and in 1995 founded the Chopra Center in La Jolla. At some point, Maharishi asked Deepak to send a portion of his proceeds to the TM Movement. He refused.

"In some people's eyes I dropped Maharishi in order to launch myself," Deepak said. "This perception has led to recriminations in the TM Movement. One is faced with the sad spectacle of people striving to gain enlightenment while at the same [time] vilifying anyone who dares to stray from the fold."[249]

In Vlodrop in 1994, Deepak told Maharishi he was leaving permanently. He expressed immeasurable gratitude and said he would love Maharishi forever. "Whatever you do will be the right decision for you," Maharishi replied. "I will love you, but I will also be indifferent to you from now on."[250]

Deepak described this remark as "hurtful." Certainly it was—deliberately. A master at both praise and hurt delivered it. Like any guru worth his salt, Maharishi shook his disciples with his cosmic saltshaker. He routinely sent them into a tailspin and brought them to impossible impasses. To what end? I surmise, to remove the veils of ignorance.

Deepak said he saw an "unfair, jealous, biased, and ultimately manipulative" man. I believe whatever Maharishi said or did was another step in the process of annihilating the false ego, while awakening higher consciousness.

Deepak himself said, "The role of a disciple isn't to question a guru, but the exact opposite: Whatever the guru says, however strange, capricious, or unfair, is taken to be truth. The disciple's role is to accommodate to the truth, and if it takes struggle and 'ego death' to do that, the spiritual fruits of obedience are well worth it. In essence the guru is like a superhuman parent who guides our steps until we can walk on our own."[251]

Since Deepak understood this "struggle and ego death" process, I don't think he could have missed that Maharishi mirrored his own reflection. Just as Krishna broke down Arjuna with a few words in the *Bhagavad Gita,* so Maharishi, the master psychologist, broke down his disciples with his healing words.

In a 1997 interview, Deepak declared, "I hold no personal animosity towards anyone in the TM movement and, despite my differences with Maharishi, I have gratitude for his having started me on my journey exploring the field of awareness."[252]

∞∞∞∞∞∞∞∞∞∞∞∞∞∞∞∞∞∞∞

Maharishi's life was blessed with so many wonders and miracles, they became commonplace. Like Maharishi's first meeting with Deepak, he often detained disciples past their scheduled departure time, yet they found their plane or train coincidentally and conveniently delayed. Even the train carrying the Beatles to Wales in 1967 was handily suspended for six minutes past its scheduled departure until the three late-arriving Beatles boarded the train.

∞∞∞∞∞∞∞∞∞∞∞∞∞∞∞∞∞∞∞

Charlie Lutes was frantically speeding Maharishi to a ferry to Vancouver Island for a lecture. Maharishi told Charlie not to worry but just keep driving fast—over a hundred miles an hour. When they arrived late, the purser said it was their lucky day. The captain, never failing to sail on time in eighteen years, hadn't cast off yet because he was "standing on the bridge like he was in a trance."[253]

∞∞∞∞∞∞∞∞∞∞∞∞∞∞∞∞∞∞∞

When fog prevented Maharishi's plane landing in Calgary, an amazing corridor of clear air suddenly appeared. This tunnel led straight to the landing strip. The pilot never saw such a bizarre weather phenomenon.

∞∞∞∞∞∞∞∞∞∞∞∞∞∞∞∞∞∞∞

On a humid day at a four-week course in the Austrian Alps in the early 1960s, an ancient Sanskrit text was read to Maharishi: "If it is true that this is a yogi, a very happy man, then the heavens will give you a sign." Suddenly a fierce wind tore at the students' clothing and hair. Yet strangely, not a hair on Maharishi's head stirred. Then a heavy downpour fell with lightning and thunder. But the two hundred course participants sitting on the hilltop remained bone dry with Maharishi as he lectured. Right above them, blue sky peeked through a small round hole in the clouds. As soon as Maharishi finished and all were safely in their cars, the sky tore open and flooded the entire area.[254]

∞∞∞∞∞∞∞∞∞∞∞∞∞∞∞∞∞∞∞

On a Teacher Training Course in Europe in the early 1970s, Maharishi sat on his dais, holding a droopy flower on its last legs, sad and wilted. As he likened the sap permeating the flower to the infinite consciousness permeating creation, that flower started perking up, as though seeking sunlight. Within a couple of minutes, the flower totally revived and stood up like a little soldier. Hundreds of people witnessed it.

∞∞∞∞∞∞∞∞∞∞∞∞∞∞∞∞∞∞∞

A man received special instructions from Maharishi after a hernia operation. Upon waking from anesthesia, he repeated the words "body and mind are one," while focusing on his wound. A powerful current of energy flowed through him. His soreness disappeared. Next day his doctor was stupefied to find the incision completely closed, miraculously.

∞∞∞∞∞∞∞∞∞∞∞∞∞∞∞∞∞∞∞

One course participant in Europe wanted to return to the USA. Maharishi told her not to leave, but she was insistent. Soon after her arrival in the States, she suffered a terrible car accident that rendered her physically and mentally impaired. It took years for her to recover. Taking Maharishi's advice might have prevented this.

∞∞∞∞∞∞∞∞∞∞∞∞∞∞∞∞∞∞∞

When Deepak Chopra phoned Maharishi to say he was flying to India to visit his ailing mother, Maharishi urged him to meet the president, vice president, prime minister, and Speaker of the House, and tell them about Ayurveda.

Maharishi kept Deepak on the phone so long, he missed his flight. Plus his seat on his connecting flight was taken. The stewardess seated him in the only spot available—first class. An Indian seated next to Deepak drank cognacs continually, all the way from New York to London.

When he asked Deepak why he wasn't drinking cognac, he replied, "I'm making my own," and shared his experiences of meditation and Ayurveda, all the way from London to Kuwait. When they finally arrived in Delhi, the man asked Deepak whether he would like to meet the president, vice president, prime minister, and Speaker of the House.

Deepak, in shock, asked, "Who are you? Who sent you?"

The man said he was bringing a three-million-dollar relief check to India for a gas leak disaster in Bhopal (nearly 4000 deaths and over 550,000 injuries). At a loss for what to say to these government officials, now he knew. He wanted Deepak to tell them about meditation and Ayurveda.

Afterward, when Deepak tried to tell Maharishi about the meeting with the government officials, Maharishi waved him off. As usual, he wasn't interested.[255]

∞∞∞∞∞∞∞∞∞∞∞∞∞∞∞∞∞∞∞

Millie Hoops, a TM meditator dying of breast cancer, told her friend Nancy Cooke, "Maharishi promised he would be with me when I die, to guide me across to the other side where Guru Dev would be waiting."[256] Maharishi had made an audiotape for Millie, to help her prepare for death.

A month later, a small group of devotees, including Efrem Zimbalist Jr., Charlie Lutes, and Nancy Cooke, gathered around Maharishi at Helena and Roland Olson's home. Shortly before 2:00 a.m., amidst an animated conversation, Maharishi stopped abruptly and left the room. Hiking up his robes, he ran upstairs to his bedroom. A few minutes later he returned to the group and continued until 3:00 a.m.

Next day Nancy discovered Millie Hoops had died at 2:00 a.m. Nurses in attendance reported a bearded man in white robes came down the corridor out of the darkness, carrying a bunch of red roses. His arrival was noted on the nurses' register.

Smiling at the nurses, he headed straight for Millie's room, without asking directions. One nurse, peering through the open door, saw him gesture over Millie's head. Soon after he left, Millie died. Maharishi was upstairs in the Olsons' home and, at the same time, in the hospital twenty miles away, fulfilling his promise to Millie. In India it's called "bilocation."

PART VII

RIDICULOUS TO SUBLIME

You are the master of all the laws of nature if you
know the transcendental field.
—Maharishi Mahesh Yogi

23

FROM TEAR-FILLED TO FEAR-FIELD

1981 TO 1985

We are not born to be the slave of circumstances. We are born to be the master
of creation. I want to be the master of masters, not the master of slaves.

—MAHARISHI MAHESH YOGI

A few weeks after I started working at the Sidha Dress showroom, in October 1981,
Maharishi announced a ladies' "Thousand-Headed Mother Divine" course and men's
"Thousand-Headed Purusha" course—a "24-hours bliss program to be held in Switzer-
land with Maharishi." I resolved to join it.

Since Mother Divine was a lifetime commitment, I decided to visit my mother
(Father had already passed on) for two weeks. Then I would feel free to dedicate my life
as a Mother Divine hermit.

However (with Maharishi there was always a "however"), after my maternal visit I
was mortified to find I wasn't accepted for the course! Out of hundreds in South Fallsburg, three were rejected: "Susan the Great," an octogenarian, and me.

Maharishi's message for us three: "Go to Fairfield. We need 2000 flyers to create
coherence." *What the blip! Maharishi considers me just one of the mob!* Worse yet, by
visiting my mother, I lost my quasi-ersatz "job" at the Sidha Dress showroom.

The "Thousand-Headed" courses, hyped as "with Maharishi in Switzerland," got
shipped elsewhere, far from Maharishi, shortly after they began, and subsequently
relocated repeatedly. All Purush-niacs and Mother Divine-iacs were required to raise
$1000 per month for room and board. Much of their time was spent soliciting well-
heeled meditators for sponsorships.

Mother Divine-ers were told the best thing for their "evolution" was a celibate
marriage with a Purusha male. Not sure how that would transpire, since communicating with anyone (other than their sponsors and banks, I guess) was forbidden. Thank

God Maharishi excluded me. Begging for sponsors and enticing some Purusha to marry me? Tenk you veddy much, but no tenks!

∞∞∞∞∞∞∞∞∞∞∞∞∞∞∞∞∞∞∞∞

Though bidden to join two thousand warm bodies as a speck in Maharishi's mob, "creating coherence" in Fairfield, I contrived to dodge the fragrant perfume of Iowa hogs and enchanting frozen Iowa tundra.

While the idea of approaching Mindy Lebowitz nauseated me, I muffled my gag reflex and phoned her in Switzerland. She asked Maharishi to let me move to his latest acquisition, "College of Natural Law," a dilapidated wino hotel five blocks from the White House in Washington. By getting "special permission," from Maharishi, I could feel "privileged" rather than just a lowly kernel in his cornfield.

Did I say I was a manipulative little brat, or that my mind was just slightly warped? Either way, I don't think I'd win the title of Miss Best Disciple 1981.

Off I went to Washington, DC, in January 1982.

Maharishi's latest idealistic scheme: create coherence in the federal government and transform the nation. TM national headquarters would move to DC, "Creating Coherence Courses" would be held, and families would relocate there and "fly" together.

With drywall and paint, the rundown hotel morphed into a passable meditation center, decorated in typical Maharishi-esque style—cream-colored walls, red carpets, white trim, gold curtains, gold velour upholstery, furniture trimmed with metallic gold paint, crystal chandeliers, and world flags.

The "Mother Divine" attendees moved into the building, and I hopped around on foam with them daily. One named Natalie knew I still carried a torch for Robert Schumacher. Yet she appeared at my door, flaunting her new, sexy lavender suit with matching wild fingernails (wild for the 1980s, anyway)—her calculated attire for landing a job as Robert's secretary in New Jersey. Natalie brazenly declared her plot to marry Robert—a scheme that succeeded swiftly.

One year later, after many visits to the White House, Capitol, and Smithsonian, and after getting mugged at knifepoint at a movie theater, I received an unexpected call from Seelisberg. Mindy Leibowitz informed me, "When Maharishi heard you were in Washington, he said you should move to Fairfield." Then the kicker: "He needs 2000 flyers there."

My strategy for evading Iowa's delightful ambiance was foiled, and my delusion about being "special" was shattered. Boohoo! In May 1983 I reluctantly left the posh but apparently perilous Washington, DC, for the hokey but seemingly safe Iowa cornfields. *Just one of the mob.*

Nearly a decade later, in 1991, Maharishi advised his sidhas in DC to "save yourself from the criminal atmosphere."[257] His coherence-creating group of flyers put their homes on the market and relocated to Fairfield.

∞∞∞∞∞∞∞∞∞∞∞∞∞∞∞∞∞∞∞

Fairfield's climate was groovy for growing corn—not so nifty for human habitation. Temperatures rose and dipped to unimaginable extremes while humidity persisted relentlessly. Due to the punishing climate and absence of gainful employment, attracting and keeping "yogic flyers" became nearly impossible. Maharishi used radical coercive tactics—threatening no less than the end of the world.

Saving the world or not, meditators reveled in the unmistakable spiritual atmosphere of two thousand like-minded seekers meditating together. But the majority struggled in subpoverty. Many came, tried, failed, and bailed. It seemed Fairfield's only redeeming feature was remoteness. Far from any rat race, its location inspired meditation.

Hardly anyone in Fairfield had spent time in Maharishi's direct presence. I'd spent seven years. Strangely isolated by my intimate association with him, I didn't fit into the social milieu. There was no advantage to befriending me. I was just another slob hopping around on foam mattresses with a thousand other women.

My jewelry design business prospered. I hired women to ink in my designs. They were grateful for any work in Fairfield's dismal economy. I bought a charming two-bedroom house, circa 1900, near the town square. The bright and cheerful but drafty thirteen-hundred-square-foot dwelling on a small corner lot had ten-foot ceilings and tall windows. Its oak floors inclined slightly, especially on the second floor, due to a less-than-solid foundation. I guess my own foundation was a bit rocky, too.

An Amish contractor made renovations, while I planted gold drop potentilla shrubs and evergreens. I unearthed a huge rose quartz crystal partially buried, mysteriously, in the backyard. My home filled with ferns, banyan trees, Chinese scheffleras, and other tropical plants, standing and hanging. Soon they became trees, touching the ceiling. I parked my white Buick Lesabre in my rickety, unattached, one-car garage.

∞∞∞∞∞∞∞∞∞∞∞∞∞∞∞∞∞∞∞

In 1959 Maharishi predicted a fraction of the world practicing TM would create coherent positive energy and significantly improve quality of life globally. Over fifty scientific studies proved his theory. TM researcher David Orme-Johnson defined the "Maharishi Effect": "A phase transition to a more orderly and harmonious state of life, as measured by decreased crime, violence, accidents, and illness, and improvements in economic conditions and other social indicators."[258]

"Phase transition" refers to the particle coherence required for a quantum mechanical phase transition, creating a Bose-Einstein condensate, as in superfluidity, superconductivity, laser light, and absolute zero kelvin (glad we got that straightened out . . . in case you can follow any of it).

For the Maharishi Effect to manifest would require 1 percent of a population practicing TM, or square root of 1 percent practicing group TM-Sidhi Program. To this end, from December 17, 1983 to January 26, 1984, in subzero ice and snow, about five thousand sidhas crowded into teeny Fairfield, joining two thousand already in residence, for the "Taste of Utopia Course." Two extra dorms sprouted on campus, and two hundred mobile homes became "Utopia Park." Several friends from my International Staff days stayed or dined with me. I received an oversized certificate for my efforts. Whoop-de-doo.

Course attendees met with Maharishi in a gigantic, hastily constructed metal building called "The Shed." Due to disgruntled meditators' lawsuits accusing Maharishi of various things they whined about, he traveled with armed bodyguards and sometimes dodged process servers by exiting through the back door. However, in Fairfield the sheriff managed to serve him a subpoena anyway.

From far-off Australia, Leslie Marshall and new husband Peter stayed in my home. I always admired Leslie and her friend Harriet. They were so utterly devoted to Maharishi, who entrusted them with greatest responsibility on Staff.

"Where's your best friend, Harriet? Is she coming?" I asked.

"Australia, working for the TM Movement," Leslie said.

"How about you?" I asked.

"Not working for the Movement, that's what. Got our own business now," Leslie said. "Publishing."

"You're kidding. You were always so devoted to Maharishi."

"Got burnt out on the Movement. So hypocritical."

"I'd never believe that if I didn't hear it from your lips," I said.

Leslie said, "You were always the true believer. I remember so vividly, Susan. No one was as attached to Maharishi as you."

"No. You're kidding. But we all were."

"Not so, Susan. You were definitely the most desperately devoted of any disciple I ever saw. Way off the top of the scale."

"But it can't be," I protested. "You were just as devoted."

"No way, Susan. Everyone used to talk about you. So hopelessly attached to Maharishi."

"Everyone?" I asked, dumbfounded.

"Yes. I remember one incident vividly, in Hertenstein," Leslie replied. "You were standing next to Maharishi's car. Staring at him intensely like a teenager with an impossible crush. He was about to drive off to Engleberg for a few days. Your plead-ing, desolate eyes longed despairingly for him to invite you to 'Come, come in the car.' When he looked at you, you lit up like a lightbulb. When he drove off, every ounce of your energy drove off with him. I never saw anyone look so utterly empty. Like he was the Sun and you were the Moon, with absolutely no light of your own. Every ray of light was reflected."

Picking up my jaw from my lap, I said, "Oh my God! It's hard to believe what I'm hearing, Leslie. But I have to trust you. Like Robert Burns says, 'to see ourselves as others see us.' Wow!"

After Leslie's stunning revelation, I began to question myself. Was I a devoted dis-ciple, or groveling groupie? Was I pursuing enlightenment, or seeking approval?

I considered myself a sincere spiritual student. But why this seeming unhealthy at-tachment to Maharishi? Why did he keep me around so long, yet sent nearly everyone else away? He did say, "You are too dependent on me as a person. I won't always be here."

Leslie's disclosure raised lots of questions, but no answers.

⁕⁕⁕⁕⁕⁕⁕⁕⁕⁕⁕⁕⁕⁕⁕

I always loved meditation. I loved hopping around on foam with hundreds of women, immersed in the vast ocean of inner silence. I would be perfectly content meditating all day, every day. Crazy as it sounds, I began to wonder whether I was addicted to TM.

If I didn't meditate in the morning, I craved the TM fix all day. If I waited too late for evening meditation, I became irritable. Others shared similar feelings. Beach Boy Mike Love said, "My addiction, if it's an addiction, is to meditation."[259] But why would meditation be addictive? What made us so dependent on TM?

After two decades of meditation, I questioned my spiritual attainment. In 1967, Ma-harishi claimed five to eight years to Cosmic Consciousness. He dangled the carrot of ultimate possibilities. He promised the sun. Yet our allotment seemed to be moon rays.

Attempting to reach Maharishi's unachievable standards, I tried to be unwavering-ly devoted and tow the TM line. *Someday I'll be enlightened,* I thought. But, after all this meditation, how "evolved" was I? I was immeasurably happier than before starting my TM journey. But when was graduation day? No one ever seemed to graduate.

While on International Staff, I was frequently fearful of losing my position. Was I spiritual, or self-absorbed? Had I become more humble, compassionate, generous, kind, patient, nonjudgmental, loving, accepting? Or a "b" with an "itch"? Or "itch" with a "b"?

⁕⁕⁕⁕⁕⁕⁕⁕⁕⁕⁕⁕⁕⁕⁕

Maharishi used to say if we meditated twenty minutes twice daily, it didn't matter what we did the remainder of our time. TM was touted as a mechanical technique anyone could do without giving up anything—no rules or regulations. *Whatever happened to that?*

Maharishi often said for TM to last generations, we must maintain "purity of the teaching." This made sense and was simple enough, namely: Teach TM exactly as Maharishi told us, and practice TM exactly as we learned it.

But gradually the "purity of the teaching" proviso inflated into a leviathan. No longer did it encompass just the hours devoted to meditation. Now we were expected to dedicate every other hour to "purity." Following a strict routine of asanas, pranayama, meditation, early bedtime, pure diet, pure thinking, and ideal lifestyle equated with "on the program." Any deviation was "off the program."

Our "evolution was enhanced" by vegetarian diet, Ayurvedic treatments and herbal remedies, fasting, enemas, pulse taking, scripture reading, Vedic astrology, exorbitantly priced *yagnas* (Vedic rituals), celibacy, dressing modestly in pastel colors, and Indian ragas played at prescribed hours. *Vastu* (Indian *Feng Shui*) defined our homes' architecture, with east entrances and other complications. We took cold showers, slathered our bodies and hair with warm sesame oil, slept heading east or south, faced east for morning meditation and north for evening, and avoided pets. Optimum meditation time was *Brahma Muhurta,* ninety-six minutes before sunrise.

Teachings, philosophies, and practices other than TM were forbidden. As restrictions escalated, the list of prohibitions lengthened: psychics, mediums, tarot, astrology, prayer, religion, classes on *any subject* not TM-sanctioned, visiting spiritual masters, and even traveling to India for a vacation!

The tyrannical Board of Governors made its mission to ferret out anyone "off the program." A menacing cloud hung over our heads, the horror of getting blacklisted—expelled from the golden domes and future courses, spurned from the elect clique of eventually-to-be-enlightened, our only chance for spiritual evolution obliterated.

For TM teachers, writing books that weren't TM advertisements or teaching/leading/guiding *anything* other than official TM courses was grounds for banishment. First on the chopping block were authors like John Gray and Barbara DeAngelis, who taught harmless relationship classes—nothing at all threatening TM's proprietary methods.

Depression, addiction, or instability was labeled "unstressing"—handy blanket denial for the mentally ill, who never got help, since counseling, psychiatry, psychology, and AA weren't recommended. Unstressing also became a nifty excuse for abusive, obnoxious, and even criminal behavior.

It seemed ideal "on the program" behavior included burying negative emotions, telling lies on TM course applications to avoid rejection, speaking TM platitudes, and generally acting like hypnotized automatons.

Maharishi's paranoia about "purity of the teaching" perhaps began in the 1970s in Switzerland, when several "golden boys" unexpectedly abandoned Maharishi. Some left due to Maharishi's increasing tendency to justify sketchy means to reach his goal of saving the world. Others left due to Maharishi's trysts with his girlfriends (yes, skin-boys called them "girlfriends").

At Maharishi's bidding, skin-boys ordered "thirty of the finest saris" from India for a certain shapely blond, Jocelyn. Late at night, after all others had been dismissed, she would be summoned, dressed in a sari and makeup. After "reading the mail" or "reciting poetry" to Maharishi, she would emerge from his chamber rumpled, mussed, and smeared. One skin-boy cracked open Maharishi's door to ask permission to enter. Maharishi, half-undressed and bare chested, pushed hard on the door to stop the intrusion. Jocelyn was inside his room.

Weary of her yearlong ordeal, Jocelyn wanted to escape. Trying to persuade her to remain, Maharishi asked Jerry Jarvis to deliver to her an envelope stuffed with pesetas. But she fled to Switzerland and stayed with Leslie and Harriet, with help from her best friend Alice (who also claimed to have had Close Encounters of the Erotic Kind with Maharishi). Alice was promptly sent back to the USA. Maharishi phoned Jocelyn repeatedly, imploring her to return to Mallorca, even shouting—to no avail.

During our time in Seelisberg, sometimes girlfriends mistakenly rang the call buzzer. One skin-boy walked in on Maharishi lying on his bed, the girlfriend nearby, and a feeling of "whoops" in the air. During the 1968 Rishikesh course with the Beatles, a German fashion model claimed Maharishi fondled her repeatedly. In Lake Tahoe, 1972, skin-boy Gregory tried to open Maharishi's bedroom door to announce an urgent overseas phone call. But the door was uncharacteristically bolted from inside and Maharishi unexpectedly didn't respond. A dozen people waiting in his anteroom witnessed his female nightly visitor finally answer the door. Around the same time, her husband became angry and suspicious and refused to return to the estate.

Several skin-boys and "girlfriends" reported similar incidents.

It was unthinkable to imagine Maharishi as a sexual being. I'd believed his title Bal Brahmachari (lifelong celibate). Yet several women personally confessed to me they had sexual intercourse with him, or were bidden to. In every case, I found their testimonies credible. One liaison with a Canadian woman spanned more than eighteen months: 1972 to 1974. Two "girlfriends" were with me in Rishikesh, where skin-boys spotted them tiptoeing in and out of Maharishi's bungalow. I had wondered about Maharishi's fascination and fawning over Vivian. Now I knew why. (She was one of us six that traveled to Bangalore with Maharishi in 1970, and her affair with Maharishi lasted more than one year.)

Those who suspected Maharishi's dalliances reacted first with disbelief, denial, then condemnation. Staunch devotees discarded the rumors as lies, dreams, or fantasies.

The TM Movement's official position was Maharishi was a life celibate. Women who claimed to be Maharishi's paramours were branded "psychotic."

Remarkably, some devotees believed Maharishi's many lovers proved he was "The Messiah," since Lord Krishna had hundreds of concubines called *gopis*. That's quite a stretch. But hey, nearly every other famous guru's disciples claim him/her to be an *avatar* (God incarnate). So why not join the club of ludicrous claims?

A long list of Indian yogis, after hitting the West, seemed to contract amnesia concerning their brahmacharya vows. Scantily clad women in miniskirts batting eyelashes at powerful male virgins raised in a culture where it was scandalous for women to show their ankles—it was like living in a porn movie. Maharishi seemed yet another guru caught with his dhoti down.

As of today, I don't care what Maharishi did in his private bedroom. He never made a pass at me. If he had, I would have run far, fast, and final. Since he seemed to pursue petite, curvaceous "girlfriends," at nearly a foot taller than him and a beanpole at 5'9" and 110 pounds, I probably wasn't his type. Thank God!

One time in Switzerland Maharishi said to a small group of us in his private meeting room, "I thought I had to be a monk and live the lonely life. But I was wrong." October 14, 1969 on BBC, Maharishi declared to reporter Leslie Smith, "I had the idea that I must renounce the world in order to be really a spiritual man, a *yogi*. But, what I found out is that this spiritual life is not dependent on the renunciation of the world. It's only solely dependent on morning and evening practice of meditation."[260] He repeatedly refused to be any kind of role model, and often told us, "Do as I say, not as I do."

<hr />

In India it's believed enlightened masters know they're not the "doers" of action. They don't identify with ego as the doer, because they've realized their higher self is God, and God's activity is done through them.

People in ignorance believe "I am the doer" and thereby incur karmic consequences. In *Bhagavad Gita,* Lord Krishna says all action and reaction are the play of *gunas*—modes of operation *(sattva:* purity and creativity, *rajas:* desire and action, and *tamas:* ignorance and destruction).

When we realize our true nature, we rise above these *gunas.* Our higher self is then silent witness to *gunas* acting upon each other: "I AM not the doer." Actions of the enlightened are always life supporting and free from karmic consequences.

So the question is whether Maharishi's female encounters were based on ignorance (with karmic results) or enlightenment (free from karmic results). While writing this book, I called upon Maharishi in spirit and asked him why he had sexual relations with women. He answered, "Very necessary. It was necessary for their soul growth and evolutionary path."

You might disagree with Maharishi's explanation—or question the validity of the message's source. Or you might reject the entire concept of Maharishi having a sex life. But Maharishi's spirit did ask me to include his answer in this book.

If Maharishi had publicly denied being a monk, would disciples have forgiven or condemned him? Knowing how insanely twisted people are about sex (especially related to spirituality), I believe his confession would have destroyed the good he was doing by teaching meditation to millions. Still, it's surprising he successfully kept his secret until his death.

∞∞∞∞∞∞∞∞∞∞∞∞∞∞∞∞∞

Since Maharishi professed to be a monk and never denied it, several golden boys branded him a hypocrite. They were especially angry (and still are), since they were requested to maintain celibacy while, as they put it, "Mahesh was getting all the action."

It was a shock when some of the brightest of Maharishi's flock walked out. He said, "I'm in a lot of pain. It's too hard to lose these people. I'm going to put a lot of restrictions now on who can come on courses."

Maharishi reacted by stripping nearly all semblance of freedom from the Movement, and imposing unbearably strict policies recalling George Orwell's dystopian *1984* "Thought Police." Maharishi's frequent rants reviled everything unless its name was "TM." He became wary of turncoats, warning TM teachers in an official statement: "Don't talk to your friends, because your friend might be a spy of the destructive forces." In Courchevel he went so far as ordering skin-boys to read course participants' private mail before it went out.

Maharishi controlled us through fear and intimidation. If we didn't "fly" regularly in the dome, we'd be responsible for nuclear holocaust or the end of the world. Every telephone-broadcast from Maharishi in the domes terrorized us. His coercive brainwashing methods were extremely effective motivators.

Maharishi used highly successful bait—susceptibility to flattery. He convinced us of our superiority over the Great Unwashed. We were highly evolved Sidhas, Governors, and Citizens of the Age of Enlightenment—or whatever outlandish title he bestowed that week (Title-of-the-Week Club, or rather, Title-of-the-Weak Club). Our vanity hooked us into his artificially devised hierarchy.

We lived in *Fear-Filled*, not Fairfield. Sincere, guileless TM devotees lived under extreme fear of the Board of GovernNazis policing the Movement. No one wanted to chance banishment from the presumptive heavenly paradise of the TM umbrella.

But isn't an umbrella a rather small place to make your home?

In the 1960s, everything had been simple. In the 1980s, I still loved TM and Maharishi's knowledge, but I hated his pitiless policies. Meditators blamed administrators for the unbending rules, but I knew who maintained control, micromanaged every detail, and delegated authority only to those who never deviated one millimeter.

Maharishi could promise anything with impunity. Later, an underling would snatch it away. So many bad cops encircled the good cop, protecting him from wrath—quite convenient. In the Swiss Alps in the 1970s, I didn't know how unsuitable I was to be one of Maharishi's cops. I really believed I could be that person—loyal to his Movement forever. Uh . . . Not so much. My temperament wasn't compatible with rigid conformity.

In the 1980s in Fairfield, the ungodly repression became increasingly overbearing. MIU library purged "negative" books and spiritual non-TM books. Books by Ramana Maharishi, Vivekananda, Shivananda, Yogananda, and other God-realized souls were banned. Books on yoga, meditation, and New Age teachings disappeared.

At MIU and MSAE (Maharishi School for the Age of Enlightenment), teachers reprimanded students for original opinions. Debate was discouraged. Kids who drew "negative" images, such as monsters, were taken to task. If Edgar Allan Poe had attended MIU, "The Pit and the Pendulum" would have received low marks. "Entertaining negativity" was "off the program."

When fifty-two hostages were held in the American Embassy in Tehran, the MIU dean called a student who'd missed a flying session to his office and blamed him for the incident. Such insufferable narrow-mindedness intensified youngsters' rebelliousness, driving them to sex, drugs, cigarettes, and alcohol.

All the joy of yogic flying vanished when making noise during the program became prohibited. We used to squeal, shout, and laugh our way across the foam. Now we had to curb our enthusiasm like good little silent TM robots.

Maharishi said TM brought "support of nature," meaning good fortune, effortless opportunities, and happy coincidences. Some meditators misinterpreted this to mean an ideal life should always run smoothly and perfectly. Therefore problems weren't faced and solved with maturity. Instead they were deemed bad omens "without nature support." Such twisting of Maharishi's words became an excuse to shirk tough responsibilities, and to denounce anyone whose life didn't match a "nature support" utopian fantasy.

When Maharishi said to enjoy 200 percent of life, 100 percent absolute and 100 percent relative, Fairfieldians misinterpreted this to mean spiritual plus material success equals "more highly evolved." This widened the divide between haves and have-nots. Trust-fund meditators, deemed more enlightened, were treated like royalty.

TM administrators began to assume a robotic, stilted demeanor, pretentious affectation, and peculiar singsong inflection. The "r" in Maharishi disappeared: "Mahaawshi said this, Mahaawshi said that." After witnessing such artifices repeatedly, ad nauseam, I felt like stuffing a sock in their mouths and sealing it with duct tape.

Fairfield residents donated tens of thousands to compete in Maharishi's artificial, illusory pecking order of snobs. Overextended parents, paying tuition to MSAE plus endless TM programs, were implored to raise additional money for teachers' salaries. Under great personal sacrifice, they managed to eek out the funds. But all that money mysteriously disappeared. Most teachers were laid off.

Money raised from Fairfieldians for campus upkeep never found its way to campus. MIU was in shambles. The beleaguered MIU President, straining to keep the university afloat, was forced to solicit money from donors, take flack from haters, keep Maharishi's wrath at bay, battle his own demons, and maintain a persona of calm optimism.

One guy worked on MIU staff full-time for fifteen years and subsisted on a pathetic stipend. The moment he was diagnosed with cancer, he was fired and evicted from his dorm. A middle-aged MIU professor who'd served since 1973 was banned from campus after contracting cancer. He went home to California, trying to recover so he could return to the privileged position of working at MIU for room and board, a tiny stipend, and no health insurance.

In 1995, when MIU morphed into MUM (Maharishi University of Management), several professors and staff, who'd survived twenty-plus years on their stipend, were dismissed without fanfare or pension. These highly educated devotees had founded MIU, written its curriculum, and garnered great respect and high status. Now they were reduced to hanging TM posters on health food store bulletin boards. In 2001, when the rate for TM initiation rose from $575 to $1500, they could no longer make a living.

Skin-boy Mark Landau said, "Repeatedly I would see [Maharishi] use people and then just kick them out. Oftentimes he would discard them when they ran out of money. He would use people and then brush them off like flies."[261]

Like many spiritual or monastic groups led by a charismatic leader, the TM Movement could be categorized a "cult." A cult can be healthy, if it cult-ivates enlightenment. But I began to think Maharishi had robbed loyal followers of money, dignity, and self-esteem. I'd spent over two decades in a dictatorial, repressive organization, largely motivated by fear. So had everyone around me.

I recalled the warning from the man I met at the Guggenheim, twenty years previously. Was he trying to save me from this organization's manacles?

My bliss bubble was tearing at the seams. It was ready to burst.

24

INTO THE HEART OF GOD

1985 TO 1986

One's happiness is under one's own control. One's misery is under someone else's control. Do not follow me, follow your own Self.

—MAHARISHI MAHESH YOGI

Instead of following the TM Movement wearing blinders, my ever-curious mind began exploring other areas. Healers, spiritual teachers, psychics, channelers, shamans, hypnotists, astrologers, palmists, and gurus—all found Fairfield ripe territory for augmenting their coffers. Here lived two thousand impressionable meditators, seeking the next big spiritual thing. *Ka-ching!* I joined other mavericks indulging in "off the program" New Age classes.

Rich Bell was quite a character. A six-foot-tall, corpulent, brown-eyed, Black-Irish phenotype with a winning smile, rich melodic voice, deep gut laugh, and captivating aura, he filled any space with electrifying magnetic presence. He exuded a certain unjustifiable self-confidence, considering he was a mighty odd duck.

An incessant storyteller, always quick to make a joke (usually about the most inappropriate thing), he loved hearing himself talk. Loud and bombastic, missing basic social skills, he could always be counted on to embarrass everyone, especially in restaurants, where he besieged every waitperson with insufferable demands.

In 1986 my next-door neighbor introduced me to Rich. He was visiting from San Diego. Immediately I regretted meeting him, because he subsequently hounded me relentlessly about teaching a spiritual practice different from TM (horror of horrors). He kept repeating the same annoying mantra: "You should learn this technique I'm teaching. You need it."

Need it? Me? Ha. I know all there is to know about meditation.

I was arrogant as ever about TM's superiority. I presumed Rich was another shyster fleecing gullible meditators, despite his previously attending MIU. Whatever the hell he was selling, I wasn't buying. With a flip of my wrist, I flicked him away like a fly.

Such a haughty attitude was common in Fairfield. The TM creed had been hammered into our brains—TM was the only path to enlightenment. All other practices were useless. We inhabited a rarified, "more evolved" plane, vastly superior to ignorant hoi polloi squatting outside the lofty gates of insulated TM grace.

"Townies" (local residents) ridiculed "ru's" (a demeaning epithet for TM meditators) as obnoxious pricks and prickettes from California who invaded Fairfield like stuck-up know-it-alls. Ru's overpaid for houses, drove up real estate values, and made property ownership for locals impossible. Still, the town's economy improved, so townies swallowed their pride and stomached our unendurable hauteur.

Within a decade, four hundred new businesses sprang up. Retail sales rose 227% from 1976 to 1988. Income rose 55% from 1980 to 1984. There were twenty-two millionaires in a population of nine thousand. *Wired* magazine called Fairfield "Silicorn Valley of America" in 1997.[262]

<hr/>

In 1986 New Age classes reached such fever pitch it caused uproar. Announcements in the domes banned all extracurricular activities not officially condoned. The New Age was officially forbidden. Unfazed, I arranged a mini-psychic fair/expo at the local VFW Hall.

I was horrified to get a call from a TM-Sidhi Administrator, asking about the fair. I denied knowing anything; otherwise I risked everything. Panic-stricken, I phoned vendors, psychics, and potential attendees and canceled the event. It's hard to convey the magnitude of our collective state of fear. I dreaded the worst possible punishment: My dome entry badge confiscated, and therefore (I believed) all hope of spiritual advancement dashed.

The following week, a TM Executive Board member phoned. "Susan, The Board wants you to meet us on Wednesday at 3:00. We want to discuss your activities." I struggled to gasp my next breath. My heart hammered in my chest and adrenaline ripped through my bones.

The ominous Board of tyrants could expel anyone deemed "off the program." "Discuss your activities" was a euphemism for "threaten, intimidate, and terrorize." Would they slap my hands, or chop them off? Which option was anyone's guess. I envisioned one timid young woman facing six bullies, dragged through a torturous wringer.

I don't know what possessed me to phone that peculiar creature Rich Bell. Perhaps I was seized with a terror of drowning so immediate, I grappled for the nearest flotation device.

Rich seemed to know exactly what to do. He asked me to grab a pen and dictated something called "Self-Authority Affirmation." He advised me to repeat it audibly for fifteen minutes right before the Board meeting. I'd never used affirmations before, but was willing to try anything.

"I AM in control. I AM the only authority in my life. I am divinely protected by the light of my being. I close off my aura and body of light to all but my own God Self. Thank you, God, and SO IT IS."

I was so frightened, I repeated the affirmation for thirty minutes straight. Amazingly, each repetition filled me with increasing inner strength. By the appointed hour, I was brimming with energy and solid as steel.

I entered the office, expecting six glowering men to pounce on me. Instead I encountered four puppy dogs with no intention of slapping or chopping any hands. The meeting turned to my advantage when I wouldn't admit any "wrongdoing." Oddly polite, they apologized for any inconvenience and sent me on my merry way. I floated out of the office, high on my own energy. The entire crisis vanished.

I was so impressed with the power of Rich Bell's affirmation that I asked him to teach me his new practice (not so new, but new to me). Rich laughed. "Guess you just needed a little proof. Miracles can start now."

"I'm gonna leap before I look," I replied.

I underwent a great personal transformation through this method, originated by Dr. Peter and Ann Meyer in San Diego. Their background of intensive spiritual studies included Mind Science, Religious Science (now called Centers for Spiritual Living, and *never* in any way associated with Scientology), medium Adele Gerard Tinning, and Self-Realization Fellowship, where they discovered Babaji (the "Yogi-Christ" from Yogananda's *Autobiography of a Yogi*).

Coauthors of *Being a Christ*, Peter and Ann received revelations and visitations from Babaji, Jesus, and other divine beings, beginning in 1962. Their "Teaching of the Inner Christ" was one of many spiritual teachings inspired by

Picture of Babaji drawn by Paramahansa Yogananda's brother Sananda Lal Ghosh.
Photo courtesy of Wikimedia Commons

Babaji. Others included Self-Realization Fellowship, Kriya Yoga, Ananda, Rebirthing, and more.

In India thousands of spiritual masters and millions of dads are called "Babaji," meaning "respected father." However, one "Babaji" is the famed ascended master believed to be immortal by spiritual practitioners worldwide. When called upon, Babaji can appear in physical or nonphysical form to boost our spiritual evolution. A beloved light being and teacher of teachers, his personality radiates wisdom, love, joy, and humor.

When Ann and Peter Meyer separated, Peter founded "Teaching of Intuitional Metaphysics." Years of meditation and silence prepared me for this teaching, which Peter later renamed Divine Revelation®. It appeared at my time of opening to new discoveries, and helped me hear the Voice of God, which I'd sought since childhood. That's why meeting Rich Bell, Ann and Peter's student, changed my life so suddenly and dramatically.

<hr />

Rich facilitated my initial "breakthrough" experience. He first explained the four goals for the session:

"Inner contact" with divinity would be a loving feeling of deep relaxation, inner peace, comfort, divine love, joy, strength, freedom, confidence, energy, contentment, wholeness, and oneness.

"Inner name" meant identifying a divine being, deity, ascended master, or inner teacher, such as Holy Spirit, Jesus, Saint Germaine, Mother Mary, Buddha, Krishna, Hashem, Muhammad, or another.

"Inner signal" was a sign to recognize which divine being was present, like a unique identity badge. It would come in one of six ways: subtle sight, sound, smell, taste, touch, or involuntary body movement.

"Inner message" was a meaningful communiqué from a divine being through visual (clairvoyance), auditory (clairaudience), or kinesthetic (clairsentience) perception.

After the explanation, Rich led me into another world, the realm of Spirit. I passed through the portal softly and serenely, as though it were a wisp of air, then floated through downy clouds of exquisite lightness. As I moved through the mist, a magnificent light from afar drew near.

Then a tremendous burst of blinding light, incomparable in its splendor, radiating warmth and delight, exploded in my forehead, its rays rushing through my bloodstream, permeating every cell. My body shivered with the brilliance of its glory.

A resplendent light, white, then a shimmering pale blue, encircled my head and spiraled down my body. I trembled with ecstasy. This gentle, enchanting light encompassed my body and filled my field of vision, bringing an indescribable sense of peace.

Rich asked, "What are you experiencing?"

"The light," I replied. "It's so beautiful."

"Holy Spirit," Rich said, "Please give Susan your signal."

My upper body shook. A fair white dove of such radiance soared above me, spreading immense wings, alighting in my inner vision. Glistening, iridescent, and lustrous, this magnificent dove of pure light shone like a million suns, just above my forehead, to my left.

"I see a great dove," I said. "Indescribable."

"And your body is shaking," Rich added.

"I am in ecstasy," I said.

Rich said, "Your body shaking, along with the vision of the dove, is your signal for Holy Spirit. You'll receive that same sign whenever you contact her. Signals are tests that help us identify specific inner teachers."

"So each inner name has a signal that goes with it?"

"Yes, Susan," Rich said.

"Does everyone get the same signal for Holy Spirit?"

"No," Rich said. "You get your own signal."

"Now you'll get a message. Take a few deep breaths. Holy Spirit, please give Susan your message."

My mind melted into a subterranean pool of serenity. I sank to the depths of a fathomless ocean, where nothing existed but profound silence. No sound. No stirring. Wave upon wave of deep rapture drew me in to a singular point of nothingness.

From the depth of that silent, still point, whose center was nowhere and circumference was everywhere, a faint stir arose in my heart. It whispered with such love and gentleness that my eyes filled with emotion and body trembled with elation.

I love you, my child, the Voice said.

Rich said, "Say what it's telling you. Say it audibly."

"It's saying, "I love you, my child." I burst out in tears. "I love you, my child."

"What else does it say?" Rich asked.

"I am always here. I shall never leave you. You are my little child. Trust in me. My radiant light and divine love are always with you. Call upon me at any moment and I will appear."

"Good, good," Rich said. "Very good."

I entered a new state of awareness never traversed in previous visits to inner space. The feeling of happiness was inexpressible. I wept with joy when I met my "I AM Self," which spoke words of comfort from my heart. This divine Voice was a loving, tender, "still small Voice" of peace and wisdom.

At last, I now hear the Voice of God that I've sought since childhood.

The words that poured from my mouth amazed me. *Such a blessing! This direct revelation from Spirit, this oracle is the key that unlocks all mysteries and answers all questions.*

I was home at last, home to the hearth I'd sought for lifetimes, to the haven of solace I could turn to anytime. The prodigal daughter returned to partake of the fatted calf. For I was dead but now live again. I was lost but now found.

Never will I be alone again.

I met divine beings of radiant light, the Brotherhood of ascended masters and deities. Those beings of glory that dwelled in the magnificent tabernacle of the most high, the Holy of holies—they became my new companions and teachers. From then on, anytime day or night, I could, at will, tear back the veil that shades the resplendent Ark and drink my fill from the Holy Grail, the cup that runneth over with glistening golden liquid—the immortal nectar of unfailing wisdom.

∞∞∞∞∞∞∞∞∞∞∞∞∞∞∞∞∞∞∞∞∞∞

After this life-changing breakthrough, I meditated with Rich daily. My experiences deepened. I felt I'd received something very precious. Although, without decades of Maharishi's training, I would not have responded so powerfully.

Before Rich returned to San Diego, I asked him to record an audiotape so I could practice Divine Revelation daily. I didn't give up TM and TM-Sidhi Program. But I added this method to my daily practice.

TM, a highly effective meditation technique, helped me experience the imperishable absolute, *satchitananda*—the goal of yoga. However, I was missing the direct mystical contact with my higher self and beautiful, celestial light beings that are available whenever we call upon them. Just by asking, now I could receive cascades of divine love, divine light, divine wisdom, divine inspiration, divine healing, and ecstatic divine union. This was a way to see God, feel God, and know God within, as inner divinity, as my own higher self.

∞∞∞∞∞∞∞∞∞∞∞∞∞∞∞∞∞∞∞∞∞∞

Brad Wagner, an exceedingly scrawny, youthful-looking man with wire-rim glasses, dark hair, thin face, close-set eyes, prominent aquiline nose, tiny mouth, jaw, and chin, and intangible beard growth that barely needed a razor, was a TM teacher I'd met in Switzerland. We became best friends in Fairfield. One night in 1986, we stared at the fire in his cozy house, chatting away, as usual.

"I just learned this amazing practice from Rich Bell," I said. "I think it's what I've been looking for all my life—a way to hear God's Voice. Isn't it incredible?"

"Pshaw. I don't believe that nutcase Rich is capable of giving you any kind of experience like that. Yes it *is* incredible, as in, 'not credible.'"

"No, no, Brad. It's true. You can't judge a person from appearances. How can you tell what's inside?" I pointed at my heart.

"Don't be ridiculous. Hearing the Voice of God? You mean like Moses, Abraham, or Elijah? The burning bush?"

"Yes, Brad. Yes. I always knew it was possible. Ever since I was a child. Now I know it is. I've done it myself!"

"You? Hrumph. No one can. No one in this day and age, at least."

"Really? You seem to think God is only known by a few prophets who lived thousands of years ago in some faraway land, and wrote that one book. Do you think God only spoke to those men, and since then, God has gone mute?"

Brad laughed and said, "But those were great prophets, holy men, emissaries of Spirit visiting earth temporarily—not us mere mortals. God can't be known directly. Everyone knows that. No one can talk with God. No one, that is, except Jesus, Buddha, Guru Dev, and other saintly beings—maybe Maharishi, but I doubt it."

I answered, "You obviously think Spirit is far away and unattainable, Brad. You pray to God, yet you think God doesn't hear your prayers. You assume you'll never see God until you're dead. Perhaps not even then."

Brad said, "Well it says in the *Bhagavad Gita* that Arjuna saw a vision of Lord Krishna, but Arjuna was a legendary soul. He wasn't like us."

I replied, "I don't think Spirit is reserved for a select clique of saints and prophets. God isn't the property of religious institutions. Those great souls haven't signed an exclusive contract with God. Ordinary people can hear the divine Voice. I think people like you or me can see God, feel God, and hear God right here, right now."

Brad said, "Are you nuts, Susan? People who say they hear God get carted off in straitjackets."

"That might be true, but somewhere within every soul is a deep longing to know and realize God. How do you know whether some of these so-called crazy people aren't actually hearing a divine Voice?"

Brad replied, "That doesn't mean it will ever happen to me. I've been meditating for nearly twenty years. It hasn't happened yet."

"That's because we never ask for it. We're so busy thinking mantras and sutras that we never take time to ask God to appear. The Voice of Spirit is there. All we have to do is ask. Arjuna got the vision because he asked. Actually, he begged for it."

"Well you've got a point there, Susan. I guess I've never asked God to come."

"This is real, Brad. I've proven it to myself. The 'still small Voice' within, the intuitive Voice, is the Voice of God. Rich helped me awaken that."

"I don't know, Susan. If what you're saying is real, I would be careful. The *Yoga Sutras* says it's dangerous to accept invitations from celestial beings and presiding deities."

"Yes, it does. Patanjali says powers and pride from associating with celestial beings are distractions to the goal, which is God realization. But how can we attain God realization without experiencing God? Was the vision of Krishna a 'distraction' for Arjuna? I really think Patanjali was referring to lower astral beings, which distract people from God realization—faker spirits and other beguiling entities. In my first meditation with Rich, I saw the blue light of Lord Krishna. It couldn't compare to Arjuna's vision, but I believe it was real."

Brad objected, "But any duality prevents you from the supreme goal of Vedanta, which is *advaita,* the nondual absolute."

"That's true, Brad. But if you recall, great saints like Ramakrishna Paramahansa, after walking every path and religion, discovered that to attain full realization he had to experience both absolute bliss consciousness and devotion to the Divine Mother. As Maharishi says, there are two aspects of God—the impersonal and personal. TM meditation brings us satchitananda—the impersonal, unmanifest absolute. But it doesn't bring us the personal God."

I paused for a few seconds, and then continued, "I think there is one thing missing from the absolute, Brad."

"What's that, Susan?"

"Don't you know what it is?"

"How could anything be missing from perfect peace, perfect contentment, oneness, wholeness, and completeness?"

"There is one thing missing, Brad." I paused and then said, "It's divine love."

"Hmmm. You have a point there. Did you experience divine love in this meditation with Rich?"

"Yes, I'm experiencing it every day since I learned this new method."

"Well, Susan, I'm still skeptical. What does 'God' say to you now, if you're so enlightened?"

"God says, Spirit says . . . Let me get quiet and take some deep breaths." I closed my eyes and breathed deeply. A faint inner Voice grew and took shape. I felt compelled to speak what was given to me.

25

LETTING GO OF THE DREAM

1986 TO 1989

Do not base your life on the likings and dislikings or whims of others. What you are in life, whether you enjoy or suffer, it is your own responsibility.

—MAHARISHI MAHESH YOGI

When Brad asked me for a divine message, I spoke these words:

"God says, 'Brad, you are loved. There is so much love around you. Though your heart cries out in loneliness, though you feel your heartfelt dreams have slipped away and will never come to pass—do not despair. You are not a wretched creature. You have not been abandoned. You are worthy to be loved. You deserve love. Trust that you will find the love you seek. You are not alone. For I am with you now and always. I love you with immeasurable love. You are filled with my unfathomable love. I love you always. Be at peace.'"

Brad suddenly broke down crying.

My eyes popped open. "Brad, what's wrong?"

Brad didn't answer. He wept.

In tears, Brad said, "I've been flashing on some past-life experiences, painful memories." He sniffed, removed his glasses, and dried his eyes with his handkerchief. "Whenever I love a woman, she always leaves me."

"It's okay, Brad. I'm here," I said.

He crawled onto my lap like a baby. I crouched over him, stroked his head, and held him in my arms. Then I returned to a deep meditative state.

Suddenly a wave of loving compassion overcame me, along with a strong desire to help Brad. In a flash, light burst forth in my inner eye. A multicolored, multidimensional vision of Babaji's form appeared in a ball of radiant light. It shone with the splendor of the Milky Way on a high-desert moonless night.

I imbibed Babaji's energy, as though I were a conduit or vessel. No longer was I acting or thinking as Susan. Now Babaji was within me, acting through me. My breathing became deep, short, and regular. Mighty healing energies poured through me.

I saw a vision of the subtle area of Brad's heart. It was cracked in many places. Babaji's healing energies began to flow through me into Brad's heart. As I witnessed this stunning phenomenon, Brad's heart was knit together and made whole. After it was mended, I imagined smoothing it over softly and gently like coddling a baby. As this healing occurred, I experienced profound bliss. Energy poured through me as the essence of unconditional love, harmony, and rapturous delight.

What's most astounding is that, when it was over, Brad described what he experienced—the same vision of Babaji, of Brad's cracked heart and its healing, exactly as I saw in my inner vision!

Not long afterward, Brad met the love of his life and married her. He became a direct-response television-advertising infomercials mogul.

<hr/>

I found Spirit gives us the simplest phrases, but these pregnant words carry tremendous potency at that time for that person. Divinely inspired words lift a person or situation in ways we don't realize. The power of the inner Voice lies in its simplicity, uncanny spot-on insight, ageless wisdom, humor, and incalculable love.

The only concern of our inner guru is our spiritual development. Anytime we ask, it guides and heals us, answers any question, solves problems, makes wise decisions, and imparts inspiration, insights, and creative ideas. The inner guru acts like a human guru, with one exception—it has no human failings. Eventually we realize both the human guru and inner guru are manifestations of our own higher self.

The saint Anandamayi Ma, who never had a physical guru, said, "While some aspirants may depend on outer teaching, why shouldn't others be able to receive guidance from within, without the aid of the spoken word? Why shouldn't this be possible, since even the dense veil of human ignorance can be destroyed? In such cases the guru's teaching has done its work from within."[263]

<hr/>

My experiences with the Divine Revelation methods deepened quickly. Never before had such extraordinary inner visions and wisdom poured from deep within. Many divine teachers, deities, and masters became my inner friends and loving guardians.

Although I'd spent decades dwelling in the silence of consciousness, I now delved into a joyful realm that added richer tapestry to my experience. I always loved meditation. Divine Revelation just embellished what was already a deeply spiritual life. Now it was time to savor many spheres of spiritual awareness I'd missed on previous journeys to inner space.

The more I practiced Divine Revelation, the more I wanted to share it. I invited Rich Bell to return to Fairfield and teach classes in my home. A prayer circle formed. Our numbers grew by word of mouth. I purchased more and more folding chairs to squeeze into my house for gatherings.

Despite concern that attendees might get into trouble with the TM Executive Board of Governors, we continued the twice-weekly meetings. We knew how profoundly Divine Revelation had transformed us. It was a way to take back our integrity from what we perceived an oppressive organization. We embraced self-empowerment—many of us for the first time.

As my awareness expanded, I was motivated to practice Divine Revelation daily. Each meditation was supposed to have a theme. For the first year, mine was always "deepening my inner contact." Thus I developed a profound inner connection. After a year, I began asking questions—rarely. It took time to cultivate the habit of asking and receiving inner guidance.

I invited Peter Meyer and other ministers from Teaching of Intuitional Metaphysics to teach in Iowa. A being of great humility, Peter spoke sweet, profound messages from Spirit. He reminded me of the Nazarene, expressing simple words, rich with deep meaning. I called Peter "a saint in disguise," due to his unassuming, gentle personality.

I was so thrilled with the escalation of positive changes in my life that I was inspired to teach others. I studied with Rich Bell and Peter Meyer for several years and then became Peter's assistant. My training was mainly by osmosis as we facilitated breakthrough sessions. I observed and learned as we helped people connect with Spirit and receive divine messages.

<hr />

I arranged for Peter Meyer to teach a one-month Divine Revelation Teacher Training class in San Diego. Paramahansa Yogananda's seaside ashram in Encinitas was nearby. Once day fellow student Michael Dennard and I visited the hermitage. Yogananda's book, *Autobiography of a Yogi,* had been my introduction to the yogis of the East—and to my inner teacher Babaji.

What a delightful setting on a high cliff overlooking the Pacific, with immaculate gardens, lotus and coy ponds, swans, palms, succulents, and meditation alcoves. The gentle sun glistened on ocean waves while birds chanted the glories of Yogananda, who personified God in flesh, who defied death, whose corporeal form remained sweet and fresh, weeks after his demise.

In this enchanting refuge of sublime serenity, Michael and I attended the chapel service. Led by an ochre-robed monk, it oddly resembled a Christian church service. After the sermon, the monk said, "Now we will meditate. When you close your eyes, picture the guru in your third eye. Try to get a vision and message from him."

I closed my eyes. Immediately Paramahansa Yogananda appeared. A powerful surge of bliss overtook my body. My spine arched and eyes rolled back. My breath became shallow and quick as I entered an altered state.

Suddenly I felt a tap on my arm. My eyes popped open. An usher leaned toward me with index finger pressed against his lips. He frowned with scorn. "Shush," he said.

I ignored the interruption and went back into meditation. Yogananda reappeared in a radiant burst of light. He said, *I welcome you. I love you with immeasurable love. I am so happy you are bringing many to God. Beloved child of God, Babaji and I have been guiding you since you took your first breath. I am with you now and will be with you always.*

Tears filled my eyes. Once again my breathing quickened as *kundalini* energy rushed up my spine. Yogananda continued, *Remember when Babaji appeared to you near your apartment? Then you found my book and began your spiritual journey.* I remembered the strange man who appeared so many years ago. That was Babaji!

Yogananda said, *Remember when I visited you at the Guggenheim Museum in New York years ago?*

That was a visitation from Yogananda!

Why did you tell me to cancel my trip to Maharishi's ashram? I asked.

Yogananda replied, *That was a test of your commitment. At that time it was necessary for you to study with a spiritual master in the flesh. Maharishi was available and you passed that test. Then you could come to Babaji.*

My body trembled. My breathing became quick and shallow as I became a conduit for divine electric currents, infusing me with energy. My back arched, neck bent backward, and eyes rolled back in my head. I realized this was my inner signal for Yogananda.

Someone was shaking my arm. My eyes popped open abruptly. Now two ushers were glaring at me. One whispered, "If you continue to make a spectacle of yourself, we will throw you out of here."

I disregarded them and returned to meditation. Yogananda appeared again, laughing.

After the service was over, I said to Michael, "Isn't it ironic? I followed the monk's instructions exactly. I received the precise experience he told us to ask for. Yet I was scolded for succeeding!"

"So what else is new?" Michael said. "Welcome to every spiritual organization. They talk about spiritual experiences, but don't want anyone to actually have one. It's okay for some great saint or yogi of ages past, but not ordinary people today."

"You're so right," I agreed. "The only people deemed worthy to realize God are holy men like Jesus or Yogananda. But not us. That's how religious leaders control us, Michael. Swami Vivekananda, who relied solely on direct experience, said, 'If there is a God, we must see Him, if there is a soul we must perceive it; otherwise it is better not to believe. It is better to be an outspoken atheist than a hypocrite.'"[264]

Eventually I became a minister of Teaching of Intuitional Metaphysics, Peter's New Thought organization, similar in philosophy to Unity Church and Centers for Spiritual Living.

1989, Iowa City, Iowa: Peter Meyer presents a ministerial license to me.

One night during a long walk on the MIU campus, I suddenly felt the urge to speak-through an audible message from Spirit. As I did this, my consciousness lifted. Tremendous bliss, expansion, and inner radiance filled my aura. This taught me I could contact Spirit anytime—not just with eyes closed during meditation.

In time, I gained greater proficiency at asking questions and receiving clear messages, whether meditating, walking, driving my car, or giving a lecture. But I was not using the teaching to its full capacity. That came gradually.

Soon I began traveling throughout North America, teaching Divine Revelation and facilitating breakthrough sessions.

Meanwhile in Fairfield, the TM administration's iron screws tightened. TM spies tracked all suspicious public meetings and docketed license numbers of cars parked near forbidden events. Guilty parties were hauled before the Board of Gover-Nazis for "interviews" and got their dome badges revoked.

The Board didn't look too kindly on spiritual practices other than TM. Divine Revelation, in particular, was a way to become self-directed, self-reliant, self-empowered, self-responsible, and no longer dependent on the TM Movement.

I became quite unpopular with TM administrators. The Board called me to several meetings attended by the TM lawyer, Arnold Silverman. They asked me to stop my activities, which I did not. They asked me to leave Fairfield, which I would not. Finally, I brought my own lawyer to a meeting. The Board never called me again.

※※※※※※※※※※※※※※※

One night in autumn 1989, a gathering took place in the dome. About a thousand meditators sat or reclined on white, cotton-encased foam mattresses that covered the vast floor space.

The head TM-Sidhi Administrator, who seemed badly in need of a laxative, got on the mike, speaking with an irritating, pretentious, singsong inflection: "We have been advised there are certain sidhas channeling in the dome. Mahaaaawshi says anyone who channels in the dome will get their dome badge revoked. You'll be sent home and barred from all Capitals of the Age of Enlightenment everywhere in the world."

This announcement obviously pointed directly at my group, since the Sidhi Administrators wrongly accused me of "channeling." While channeling is generally defined as being a channel for astral entities and spirits, in contrast, Divine Revelation is being a channel for God.

"Channeling" is a term that often refers to a form of mediumship where an astral entity, earthbound spirit, faker spirit, or ghost uses the medium's body. The medium enters a trance while a creepy, eerie voice gives bad advice through him or her. This drains mediums' energy, causes weakness, dims consciousness, and shortens life.

Unlike channeling, Divine Revelation helps us experience and communicate with God. Contacting deities, ascended masters, angelic beings, and light beings in the spiritual plane increases strength and life energy and awakens higher awareness. Since Divine Revelation is diametrically opposed to channeling, to be unjustly blamed before a thousand TM practitioners made my blood boil.

Though I felt afraid, upon hearing this prima-dingbat slander my group and me, I mustered every ounce of courage, stood up, and headed toward the audience mike. The head GovernNazi, Brett Matthewson, spotted me. He'd been Maharishi's most cold-hearted, arrogant skin-boy in Switzerland. "Turn the audience mike off! Turn it off!" Brett cried. Clearly agitated, he tried to prevent me from speaking.

As Brett did this, the crowd chanted in unison, "Let her speak! Let her speak! Let her speak!"

Sweating, with legs buckling, I managed to say, in a shaky voice, but with conviction, "I abhor the insinuations and accusations that have been made here today towards my prayer group."

Brett said, "We weren't pointing towards any particular group, Susan."

"That's total bullshit, and you know it, Brett." The crowd cheered. I continued, "I came up to this mike to let everyone know—I am *not* teaching channeling. And no one in my prayer group is practicing anything in the dome other than TM and TM-Sidhi Program. I am a minister of a church in a country that has freedom of religion. The TM Movement is persecuting my prayer group and me for praying to God as we wish."

Shaken and trembling, I returned to my seat. The crowd cheered. But it was a hollow victory—totally meaningless. I was done in Fairfield. It was over.

∞∞∞∞∞∞∞∞∞∞∞∞∞∞∞∞∞∞∞∞∞∞∞∞∞

Most people in my Divine Revelation group denied participating in the group and thereby kept their dome badges. The most outspoken lost their badges. They groveled like worms on their bellies to the Board, begging for mercy. They were granted conditional dispensation: Volunteer for years at a TM Center. Then you might be allowed back into the dome—that is, if you behave like good little androids.

No surprise when the phone call came from Brett Matthewson. "You will no longer be granted the privilege of flying in the dome. Your badge will not be renewed."

Click. The phone hung up.

My God, I choked. *What have I done?* Even then, I felt my heart tug. In the back of my mind, I wondered whether I'd blown my only chance at spiritual enlightenment. *What if this has all been a test, and I just failed?*

Yes, it probably was a test. Did I fail? ... Or did I pass?

∞∞∞∞∞∞∞∞∞∞∞∞∞∞∞∞∞∞∞∞∞∞

Repeated public announcements in the dome pointed the finger of wrath at my tiny Divine Revelation group. As I walked down the street, suspicious eyes glared from passing cars. In the health food store, meditators averted their gaze or scowled in contempt. Terror ripped through Fear-Field. I was scorned, shunned, and demonized.

What amazed me was how the few dozen people who learned Divine Revelation could wreak so much havoc. *It's such a minuscule group*, I kept thinking. *How could this powerful organization, with millions of meditators, be threatened by our trifling little prayer circle?*

I strained to keep my house while also traveling and teaching Divine Revelation. No one would rent a room from the evil, black, sinister Fairfield witch, whom everyone avoided like the plague because her satanic "off-the-program" communicable disease might infect them. Meditators were petrified to associate with the ghastly demonic Soooooosssaaan. It was bad luck to even whisper her name, especially as a black cat crossed your path. Eek!

2 6

NOW MIRACLES COULD BEGIN

1989 TO PRESENT

It is our joy to be considered impossible, and it is our greater joy to make the impossible a living reality.

—MAHARISHI MAHESH YOGI

Quite a melodrama I created—sabotaging myself and getting myself thrown out of the dome. How else could I break away after twenty-two years of dedication? Evidently I had to write and star in my own Shakespearean tragedy. This drama and resultant financial losses forced me to sell the house. I bought a Ford pickup and Airstream travel trailer and began traveling throughout North America, teaching Divine Revelation.

Peter Meyer was scheduled to teach a Teacher Training Class in New York City. At the last minute, he canceled and substituted me. Since I had no lesson plan, right before each session began, I asked Spirit what to teach, and received one or two words of cryptic direction. Even with no curriculum, this simple guidance resulted in mind-blowing spiritual insights and experiences during every session.

After this profound teaching experience, entirely led by Spirit, I realized if such miracles could take place in one week, why not make miracles all the time? If I would endow enough faith in my inner Voice, it could guide me daily.

As I resolved to be led by Spirit, my life took on new depth and meaning. At first I would forget to ask for inner guidance. But with time, I asked more frequently. Soon life became an exciting adventure. I never knew what my next thrilling assignment would be. My limited viewpoint began to expand to universal vision. I gained faith to continually jump off cliffs (metaphorically), as Spirit inspired me to accomplish daunting tasks I previously never had the nerve to do.

I was guided to live in a travel trailer with no home base, tour around the world, and teach Divine Revelation with no money or safety net. I was guided to write a book—a seemingly impossible prospect, since I knew nothing about publishing.

Following the inner Voice wasn't easy. I encountered internal struggle and confronted fears and limitations. It took courage, especially when inner guidance conflicted with previously held cherished ideas and societal beliefs. The inner guru much resembled a human guru. My ego envelope was stretched well beyond its comfort zone.

With greater faith, miraculous experiences became commonplace. God's grace expanded within me. Years of restriction crumbled as I broke through habits, patterns, and conditions that had bound me to the past. The simplest everyday happenings took on mystical flavor. Though the instances seemed mundane, in my eyes they were vastly meaningful, as my fledgling attempts at following divine guidance bore fruit.

Sufi master Radha Mohan Lal said, "The Goal of every Path of Yoga is to lead a Guided life. Guided by that which is Eternal. To be able to listen to this Guidance is the whole purpose of the Spiritual Training."[265]

During every step of writing and publishing my first book, *Divine Revelation*, I followed divine guidance with faith. The book wrote itself, guided by Spirit. After I finished, my inner Voice said, "Now go to the library and find yourself a literary agent." Perusing the list of agents, I got a gut feeling about one—Jeff Herman, though it made no sense. He represented business books.

I didn't have quite enough faith to send my proposal solely to Jeff. I sent it to thirty agents. But, Jeff, first to respond, phoned two days after receiving my proposal. I signed with him. He sent my manuscript to several publishers but received only rejections. Months later, I received a letter from Jeff Herman Literary Agency: "We are very sorry, but we have had a staff shortage in our agency, and we can no longer represent you."

I was devastated. Why had Spirit led me to this agent?

I went into meditation to ask for guidance, and received a strange message: "No, Jeff Herman is still your agent. Don't sign with another agent, and don't try to sell the book yourself."

This message made no sense. I could have signed with one of twelve agents who wanted to represent me, or submitted my book to a small publisher. Yet I knew this strange message was clear and true.

I wrote to Jeff: "My intuition says you would be the best agent to represent me." You can imagine how that went over with this business book agent.

I heard nothing—for months.

Finally I received a reply. I was so excited to open the envelope—until I did. It said, "We really appreciate your faith in us. But we still cannot represent you."

I went back into meditation. Unbelievably, I received the identical message: "Jeff Herman is still your agent. Don't sign with another agent, and don't try to sell the book yourself."

Though I thought, *I must be out of my mind,* I followed guidance with faith and sent Jeff a second letter: "My intuition still says you would be the best agent for me."

What happened? Nothing.

Months rolled by. No response.

By this time, it was too late to revisit the other agents. It's hard to express how challenging this was. I've never been good at sitting around doing nothing when I want to get something done. Yet I was guided to wait with faith, meanwhile thinking, *I must be nuts for following this inner Voice.*

Unexpectedly, Jeff Herman telephoned out of the blue: "We're very impressed with your perseverance. We've decided to represent you. Come to my office and meet my partner. We're going to handle your book."

I went to his office in downtown Manhattan. Business books were stacked along the walls. Needless to say, I felt out of place. Jeff's partner arrived—a beautiful woman with long, black, curly hair. I sensed an immediate heartfelt affinity with her. It turned out Deborah, who worked in this business book agency, was a psychic. And she gave me a reading! Perhaps that's why Spirit guided me to this agency.

<hr />

Jeff Herman told me to get endorsement blurbs from famous authors for the book cover. I didn't know these authors, yet I prepared twenty letters with faith—like a fool. *I have to figure I'll get these endorsements,* I thought. *I don't know any better. I just trust God.*

I sealed my letters and drove to the post office. A one-legged man hopping on crutches entered the building ahead of me. I thought, *This must be a bad omen.* At that moment my inner Voice said clearly, You have no leg to stand on.

I realized, *It's true. I don't know these authors. I really have no leg to stand on.* Deflated and demoralized, I dropped my letters into the mail slot and left the post office in a slump. Laboring toward my truck, I eyed the one-legged man getting into his car and driving off. Suddenly my inner Voice exclaimed, You may have no leg to stand on, but you will be successful anyway, just as this man can drive and get around, even with his challenge.

Spirit was right. To my utter delight, I received fifteen endorsements from famous authors—too many to fit on the cover of *Divine Revelation.*

It turned out pretty well. Several months later, Jeff phoned to say he sold the book to Simon & Schuster! I nearly went into cardiac arrest! Anyone who knows about publishing would recognize it's a total miracle for a first-time, unknown New Age author to get published by one of the biggest publishers in the world. My book came out in the same catalog as Hillary Rodham Clinton's *It Takes a Village*, for God's sake!

What?

Even more remarkable, I knew nothing about writing. I attended art school. Yet my editor said it was the best-written book she'd ever edited at Simon & Schuster. More than two decades later, the book is still in print, plus thirteen other titles of mine.

How did this miracle happen? By trusting inner guidance and following it with faith, even when it's challenging. It's easy to listen to our inner Voice. Anyone can learn how by reading my books *Divine Revelation* and *Awaken Your Divine Intuition*. It's easy to distinguish between the true divine Voice and other voices in our mind, by studying my ten-test system in these books.

Then what's the hard part?

Doing what we're guided to do.

Spirit wants us to expand beyond our ego box. So we're given demanding challenges that dismantle previous boundaries. As we take leaps of faith, we realize either God will catch us . . . or we have to learn how to fly—really fast! The leap becomes easier every time, and we're lifted higher. By listening to our "still small Voice," trusting its guidance, and following it with faith, miracles become commonplace.

∞∞∞∞∞∞∞∞∞∞∞∞∞∞∞∞∞∞∞∞∞∞∞

My publisher was having problems—cutbacks in staff and budget. Advertising and promotion planned for *Divine Revelation* were canceled. There was only one solution. I had to promote the book myself. As the book neared publication, I was recovering from a serious leg injury. I felt more than a little anxiety and apprehension. I wanted to travel to promote my book, but didn't have confidence or courage.

Another small detail—I was broke.

Spirit guided me to plan an extensive book tour—bookstore signings, conference lectures, expo booths, and media interviews. This tour would cost tens of thousands of dollars.

I sold my trailer and pickup, bought a used Ford cargo van with borrowed money, and set out on the road, where I found uncanny support and assistance everywhere. Little miracles occurred daily. Synchronous coincidences that weren't really coincidental placed me in the right place at the right time doing the right thing when the right people showed up.

Whenever I asked Spirit for guidance, I received messages to invest in more promotional endeavors. I told Spirit, "Okay, God. I don't know how to make this happen. If you really want it, then please Show Me The Money!"

This simple prayer worked.

I started with no money. Yet I traveled worldwide and taught thousands of people, just by trusting and following inner guidance. Whenever I needed money, the right amount appeared through following Spirit's suggestions—even seemingly crazy ones, such as holding spiritual retreats that I didn't know would succeed. I was blessed and supported more than I could have imagined. I felt such gratitude to God for blessings I received.

1990, New York City: I am teaching Divine Revelation and demonstrating "Brain Gym" at The Learning Annex.

Madly dashing about the country to lecture several times a week was both exhausting and thrilling. Whenever I arrived at my destination, I closed my eyes, took deep breaths, and spoke a healing prayer. I asked Spirit to fill me with divine love and light, which lifted all stress and depletion. Light filled my body and love vibrated through my mind. Waves of peace and relaxation coursed through me. Within five minutes, I was entirely refreshed and invigorated, simply by opening my heart to Spirit.

That's the magic of prayer. That's the miracle of Divine Revelation.

I attempted to present a well-dressed, professional persona, like I was staying in hotels and jet-setting in airplanes. But I slept in a van, showered at truck stops, strained to use a small mirror while applying makeup, and contorted into a medley of pretzel positions to change clothes. The gypsy-free-spirit-wandering-on-the-road prophet was occasionally invited to stay in someone's home. That was always a relief.

When I arrived in south Florida, I drove to the only truck stop near Miami—the worst I'd ever encountered, in a rundown neighborhood. The filthy showers trickled streams of lukewarm water. I wasn't looking forward to sleeping there after my appearance at a Borders bookstore in Aventura.

As I was signing books after my lecture, an unexpected friend appeared. "Please sign a book for me." It was the jewelry manufacturer Sam Ziefer, my former jewelry design client.

"Where did you hear about my lecture?" I asked.

"I didn't," Sam replied.

"Do you come to this Borders bookstore often?"

"Never. I've never been here before!" he said.

"But how—"

"I was at home," he said. "Suddenly I got an irresistible urge to buy a particular CD for my daughter for Hanukkah. I went to the mall to buy the CD, but the store was already closed. So I decided to stop by Borders and buy the CD here."

"That's amazing. What a coincidence," I said.

"Where are you staying?" Sam asked.

"At the truck stop. I sleep in my van."

"No, you won't. You'll come and stay with my family. This seems to be more than synchronicity. It's miraculous," Sam said.

"Miracles, miracles. Everyday miracles," I said. "God provides. Thank you!"

I ended up staying in Sam's luxurious gated home on a beautiful pond with his lovely wife and children.

∞∞∞∞∞∞∞∞∞∞∞∞∞∞∞∞∞∞∞∞∞∞∞∞∞

Since 1969, when I first set foot in India, I dreamed about Maha Kumbh Mela ("great festival of the pot of immortal nectar"), a Hindu religious festival in Allahabad that recurs every twelve years. At the holiest bathing spot in India, where the Ganges, Yamuna, and mythical Saraswati rivers meet, adepts and aspirants, saints and seekers, holy men and women, seers, sages, and swamis assemble for ritual bathing at the auspicious moment.

But this one was special. A powerful planetary alignment would occur in January 2001—a nexus of cosmic energy converging every 144 years, bringing dramatic changes to human destiny. Spirit guided me to bring a tour group to the fair. Yet how? I knew nothing about arranging overseas tours, let alone to India.

With blind faith, following inner guidance, I found an Indian travel partner on the Internet. My inner Voice said I could trust Amit Sharma, he would not steal my money, and everything would go splendidly. I advertised the tour, booked participants, and sent bank wire transfers for thousands of dollars to a stranger on the other side of the world.

A staggering 100 million people attended the 2001 Kumbh—the "greatest recorded number of human beings assembled with a common purpose," according to *Guinness Book of Records*. In a profound act of faith, pilgrims converged from every corner of India. The mélange of pilgrims, holy people, half-beggars, half-bandits, and ash-smeared dreadlocked naked sadhus exhibited an exotic display, unique in the world.

We sampled a spiritual smorgasbord, wandering among thirty square miles of giant tents sponsored by religious organizations, topped with colorful flags and cloth towers. At night tents lit up like carnival rides, while competing drones of Sanskrit chants and religious musicals blared from thousands of loudspeakers. A dreamlike, surrealistic quality imbued the atmosphere.

Incredibly, when I met Amit, I discovered he'd arranged several group tours for a TM meditator/ Vedic astrologer I knew. What were the odds? Plus, ever the saint magnet, during the event I gained unusually close access to great saints that never granted audiences to anyone from the West.

Since this first tour to Kumbh Mela, Spirit has guided me to a joyous livelihood as a tour organizer to sacred destinations, spiritual retreats, and conferences on land and cruise ships. My travel website is www.divinetravels.com.

Thank you, wonderful God!

<hr>

These miraculous incidents are just samples of thousands I've enjoyed since starting to trust and follow the inner Voice of Spirit decades ago. Indeed, I live a charmed life. I'm grateful for every precious moment and every spiritual blessing. Always and ever, God is here whenever I call. The essence of Divine Revelation is summarized in one statement: "Ask, and it shall be given you."[266]

HOW TO SPOT AN ENLIGHTENED MASTER

When a calf approaches its mother, the milk begins to flow from her udder, ready for the calf to drink without effort. Such is the glory of devotion and faith in a disciple. He surrenders at the feet of the Master and cuts short the long path of evolution.

—MAHARISHI MAHESH YOGI

A man searched the world for his perfect guru. But he only found selfish, mean, deceiving fools and madmen. After years of seeking, he found one who fulfilled all his expectations. A friend asked, "What made you decide he was perfect?"

He replied, "After talking to him, I came to that conclusion."

"What did he say?" his friend asked.

"Well, he told me I was the most perfect, highly evolved disciple in the world!"

Kabir was a famed Indian fifteenth-century poet and saint. His devotees asked him who was a true disciple. Kabir called his son and foremost disciple, Kamal, and said, "I have dropped my spindle while weaving. Bring me a lamp so I can find it." Though it was broad daylight, Kamal brought the lamp without hesitation.

Kabir said, "Kamal, today many devotees will be coming for lunch. Please prepare some sweets and add a handful of salt to them." Kamal complied unwaveringly.

Then Kabir turned to his devotees and said, "Don't you think Kamal knew my commands were ridiculous? But the moment you obey the guru's commands without question, that moment meditation comes to you spontaneously and the Lord grants His darshan."

The great female saint Anandamayi Ma said, "Follow the guru's instructions with-out arguing. As long as the reason of the individual is in power, how can the knots be undone?"[267] "Carry out conscientiously the guru's orders, which vary according to the temperament and predisposition of the aspirant. The average person can have no knowledge of the factors necessary to bring to completion the hitherto neglected facets of his being. Try to follow closely the path indicated by the guru, and see how everything just happens spontaneously."[268]

In 1990, David and Earl Kaplan founded the most profitable business in Fairfield, Books Are Fun, then sold it to *Readers Digest* for $380 million, and finally bought it back for $17.5 million in 2009. TM devotees for twenty-five years, the twin brothers donated over $150 million to the TM Movement.

In 1993, the Kaplans purchased and developed "Heavenly Mountain" in Boone, North Carolina to house the "Spiritual Center of America" and Maharishi's 350 Pu-rusha and three hundred Mother Divine course participants. They spent $40 million erecting roads and buildings on 1261 acres. On the adjacent fifty-six hundred acres they founded a TM community. Many families moved there.

David Kaplan had joined the Purusha course, so he lived on the property. In January and February 1999 he became ill and nearly died. Maharishi announced in April that anyone not "one-pointed" should leave Purusha. David claimed he quit Purusha because he'd been in love with Linda for a year, and when he got married, he was "kicked-out of the movement."[269] Though it was widely believed David was blacklisted for impregnating Linda while on Purusha, she claimed she got pregnant right after David left Purusha. They were married that September and divorced six years later.[270]

David's ousting (plus the TM Movement's failure to make mortgage payments and pay property taxes) prompted the brothers to investigate Maharishi.

The twins traveled to India and dug up rankling Swamis and Shankaracharyas who, since 1953, repeatedly fought bitter lawsuits in their bid to seize the coveted title Shankaracharya of Jyotir Math (Guru Dev's office). Those Swamis recycled the same fantastic accusations churning for decades: Maharishi poisoning Guru Dev and steal-ing his *shri yantra,* a ruby-studded wealth-bestowing religious object.

And hiding it . . . where? In his loincloth?

In 2004, Earl Kaplan wrote: "Due to our findings I can no longer support or be associated with Maharishi Mahesh Yogi, his ideas, his knowledge, or any of his organ-izations."[271] In 2005, the Kaplans evicted Purusha and Mother Divine from Heavenly Mountain. Homeowners filed lawsuits against the brothers for reneging on the prom-ised TM community.

In 2011, Heavenly Mountain's west campus of 381 acres was auctioned off, with a reserve price of $2.48 million, to the highest bidder—Sri Sri Ravi Shankar, founder of Art of Living Foundation. Coincidentally, in the 1980s, Ravi had served on Maharishi's Staff as *Sama Veda* pundit, chanting Sanskrit verses in the ancient oral tradition.

Ravi made some stunning claims: that he was Maharishi's favorite disciple, that Maharishi predicted he would generate the new millennium's spiritual revolution, that Maharishi wanted him to be a Shankaracharya, that all TM meditators will join his Art of Living organization, and that Ravi is none other than (drumroll) the reincarnation of Guru Dev!

Ravi hijacked the Holy Tradition painting I designed and Frances Knight completed. Ravi substituted himself for Maharishi's image and hung it in his Art of Living centers. Stunning! See www.divinerevelation.org/HolyTradition.html.

Ravi ascribed himself "His Holiness Sri Sri" and claimed to hold an advanced science degree. Reality is he learned TM in Melkote, Karnataka, and attended an advanced course in Rishikesh. When Maharishi invited Ravi to Switzerland, he dropped out of school at age seventeen.

Ravi helped Maharishi build his ashram in Noida, near Delhi, and in 1980 organized a celebration with six thousand pundits. But Ravi became ill, and his father brought him home to Bangalore (now Bengaluru). In 1985, Maharishi asked Ravi to gather students and teach Vedic chanting. Ravi's father recruited 150 boys. When Maharishi asked Ravi to transfer the students to Noida, he refused. Maharishi never spoke with him again.

Ravi claimed to be a "close disciple of Maharishi," yet never became a TM teacher. He appeared at Maharishi's cremation and placed himself prominently before the cameras on the global Internet feed.

Maharishi's comment about Ravi: "He is dangerous. Sugar-coated poison."[272]

⚬⚬⚬⚬⚬⚬⚬⚬⚬⚬⚬⚬⚬⚬⚬⚬⚬⚬⚬⚬

After investigating Maharishi, the Kaplans hurled vicious verbal attacks. The ego will attack anything seeking to destroy it. Destroying the ego so the higher self can surface is what spiritual masters do. It's Point 1 on their resume. Point 2 is driving disciples "out of their minds" so God can enter and truth can dawn.

Amritananda Mayi (Ammachi), the female "hugging saint," once said to a close disciple, "You have to get mad at me. I'm the ego-killer."

The night before Paramahansa Yogananda was initiated into Kriya Yoga, his guru Swami Yukteswar asked, "Will you love me unconditionally no matter what I do?" Yogananda replied, "Sir, what if I should ever find you less than a Christ-like master? Could I still love you the same way?" Yukteswar glared at him sternly and said, "I don't want your love. It stinks."[273]

"Sri Yukteswar's training cannot be described as other than drastic," Yogananda wrote.[274] He described his guru as a hypercritical perfectionist with no tolerance for shallowness or inconsistency. Though his blunt, sharp "flattening-to-the-ego treatment" was rough, Yogananda resolved to endure "the weight of his disciplinary hammer."[275]

Yukteswar said, "If you don't like my words, you are at liberty to leave at any time." "I want nothing from you but your own improvement." "I am hard on those who come for my training. That is my way. Take it or leave it; I never compromise." "I try to purify only in the fires of severity, searing beyond the average toleration."[276]

Maharishi was never this forthcoming about his methods, but he treated those of us who needed his cure with no less callousness. Still, many of Maharishi's close devotees received no harsh treatment whatsoever.

Yoganananda wrote of his guru, "I am immeasurably grateful for the humbling blows he dealt my vanity. The hard core of egotism is difficult to dislodge except rudely. With its departure, the Divine finds at last an unobstructed channel."[277]

One day, upon entering Ramakrishna Paramahansa's room, his disciple Narendra (who later became Swami Vivekananda) was ignored. Subsequent visits received the same icy treatment—for an entire month. When Ramakrishna declared, "I have not exchanged a single word with you all this time, and still you come," Narendra replied, "I come to Dakshineswar because I love you and want to see you. I do not come here to hear your words." Ramakrishna embraced his disciple and admitted he was testing him to see if he would stay, despite the outward indifference."[278]

Irina Tweedie, author of *Chasm of Fire,* said her teacher forced her to face the darkness within herself, "by using violent reproof, even aggression." Her mind was kept in a state of continual confusion, unable to function. "I was beaten down in every sense," she said.[279] Her guru Radha Mohan Lal declared, "My harsh words help you, my sweetness never will."[280]

Bhagawan Nityananda of Ganeshpuri said, "There are various tests to which a devotee is subjected: they could be of the mind or the intellect, of the body, and so on. In fact, God is conducting tests all the time; every occurrence in life is a test."[281]

I believe a spiritual master is a precious treasure. When we're lucky to discover one, it's wise to make the most of it. Without enlightened beings lifting humanity to higher consciousness, souls would be lost in suffering forever. That's why in India gurus are revered as God.

To perceive a true spiritual master, we must rise above our conditioning and see through eyes of unconditional love. Once we establish a link of divine love with faith and open heart, we don't need convincing the guru is real. The flow of energy from guru to disciple begins, and we see reality through the master's eyes.

The Western ego, highly fearful and skeptical, dismisses spiritual masters as charlatans. We believe we shouldn't give away our "power." But unless we give away our so-called "power," we'll never become empowered. We hold on tightly to "power," until we realize our life isn't working. Then we're ready to surrender to *real* power—a higher power. A guru's job is to bring us to that point.

Our purpose on earth is to realize the Godhead, our inner divinity. A genuine spiritual master will break down our ego structure to unearth our cosmic identity. This is a huge accomplishment. Labor pains of this birth continue for lifetimes.

We appreciate the necessity of mentors to master any skill. So why do we abhor gurus? Maybe it's because "ego death" isn't something we'd readily order off the lunch menu. Few of us want spiritual enlightenment—even while we claim to. We generally run far and fast from gurus and from God.

<hr />

When their egos were threatened, the Kaplans accused Maharishi of a long list of sins, including being a "very dark and evil being" and pulling off "the biggest spiritual scam in modern history."[282]

If a doctor performs an operation, the patient might curse the doctor. But the doctor does his job anyway. For his nature is to heal the patient. A guru is like a physician who cures his disciples of ignorance.

Ammachi said, "People who see the blacksmith pounding a hot piece of iron with his hammer may think that he is a cruel person. The iron piece may also think that there cannot be another brute as mean as him. But while dealing each blow, the blacksmith thinks only of the new form which will emerge. Children, the real Guru is also like this."[283]

After five decades considering it, in my opinion the worst Maharishi could be accused of was smother-mothering his flock with best intentions to maintain "purity of the teaching." As a Hindu guru, his job description was to lift people from suffering and raise their consciousness. That's all I ever saw him do.

At the same time, Maharishi never claimed to be anything. People fabricated their own myths about his level of consciousness, infallibility, supernatural faculties, or intentions for good or evil. No wonder devotees became disenchanted when they expected him to match their private version of an extraordinary fairytale.

I was one of them.

How to recognize an enlightened master? The definitive authority is the ancient scripture, *Bhagavad Gita*. There the student Arjuna asks his guru Krishna (who is God incarnated):

"O, Krishna, what is the mark of a God-realized soul, stable of mind and established in samadhi? How does the man of stable mind speak, how does he sit, how does he walk?"[284]

In answering this question, Lord Krishna ignores outer signs, such as how we sit or walk, because nothing on the surface reveals our inner awareness:

"Arjuna, when one thoroughly abandons all cravings of the mind, and is satisfied in the self through the self, then he is called stable of mind," Krishna says. "The sage, whose mind remains undisturbed in sorrows and pains and indifferent amidst pleasures, and who is free from passion, fear and anger, is called stable of mind. He who is unattached to everything, and meeting with good and evil, neither rejoices nor recoils, who neither likes nor dislikes, his realization is stable."[285]

How can we judge anyone's level of consciousness? Only the individual can measure him/herself against Krishna's scale. A guru might have millions of followers, but not be "stable of mind." Yet someone living an unassuming, conventional life might be fully realized.

~~~~~~~~~~~~~~~~~~~~~~~~~~~~~~~~

We tend to judge others based on personal bias, filtered by clouded ego projections. With gurus, our projections are extreme—skewed by notions of how holy people are "supposed" to behave.

Paramahansa Yogananda said disciples "seek a guru made in their own image." When people complained they didn't understand his guru, Yogananda retorted, "Neither do you comprehend God! When a saint is clear to you, you will be one!"[286]

We fantasize enlightened people are omniscient, omnipotent, and possess no emotions or failings. They mustn't have sex, make money, or make mistakes. They must be self-effacing, austere, chaste, pious (whatever that means), and, above all—poor.

What we don't realize is enlightened beings are human beings. Absurd expectations of anyone, enlightened or otherwise, surely bring disillusionment. Lama Anagarika Govinda said, "Always remember, your guru will be in a mortal body and only be a certain percent divine; so forgive his weakness and keep your eye on the divine."[287]

One of Maharishi's devotees, Geoffrey Baker, said, "As soon as you begin to doubt him, everything starts to come apart. But it's all in you. If you start to question it, to think, 'Ah, he's just an old man who doesn't know what he's doing,' then that's exactly what he will become. And all of this will come to naught."[288]

Chögyan Trungpa Rimpoche (1939-1987), founder of Naropa Institute, was eleventh in the line of Trungpa tulkus, teachers of Kagyü lineage—one of four main Tibetan Buddhist schools. After his rigorous monastic education, he headed the Surmang monasteries in eastern Tibet. When Chinese Communists took control in 1959, at age twenty he escaped to India.

In Scotland in 1967, he founded the first Tibetan Buddhist practice center in the West. After a car accident left him partially paralyzed, he relinquished monastic vows and became a lay teacher. In 1970 he moved to the USA, wrote fourteen books, established hundreds of Shambhala Training centers, and made Buddhist wisdom understandable to Western minds.

Renouncing his monk robes, Chögyan Trungpa became a "disgrace to Tibet." Notorious for sexual liaisons with students, he seduced a teenage virgin, Diana Judith Pybus (married name Mukpo), during their first private meeting. They married when she was sixteen and he was thirty-three. A smoker and rampant alcoholic, he died of liver disease.

Yet after his death, his body remained in samadhi five days and didn't decay. His heart remained warm. Atmospheric phenomena indicating the "Rainbow Body" in Tibetan Buddhism appeared at his cremation, May 26, 1987. These included rainbows, circling eagles, and *Ashe*-shaped clouds (Tibetan letter representing primordial life essence).

Dalai Lama described Chögyan Trungpa: "Exceptional as one of the first Tibetan lamas to become fully assimilated into Western culture, he made a powerful contribution to revealing the Tibetan approach to inner peace in the West."[289]

The purpose of Lord Krishna's birth was to restore good in an evil world. He protected and gave victory to the virtuous, destroyed evil, and established dharma (righteousness). Krishna resorted to any means, including deception, trickery, and manipulation, to overcome the enemy. In the ancient Indian scripture *Mahabharata,* he said committing a "sin" for the purpose of dharma was not a sin at all.

Like Krishna, many revered spiritual masters have been known to act outrageously. I witnessed Maharishi make severely shocking statements deliberately—to shake us, burn off our karma, purify us, and quicken our evolution.

When Maharishi lectured at the Paris Hilton in December 1967, an attendee asked what his TM Movement intended to do about the problem of world hunger. Maharishi replied, "The hungry man who learns to meditate will soon become a happy hungry man." Nearly the entire audience stood up, chanted, "Charlatan, charlatan, charlatan," demanded their money back, or walked out.[290] Yet Maharishi sat there in bliss, undisturbed, despite hurls of insults. Perhaps his hyper–politically incorrect statement was his way of separating wheat from chaff.

Albert Vogel, a journalist in Vietnam, traveled with his wife by motorcycle all the way to Rishikesh. An anti-war and anti-USA-involvement socialist, he told Maharishi the

Vietnamese had the right to their own country without USA interference. At that time, 400,000 American troops were in Vietnam.

Maharishi said to Albert, "No, no, no, the US should win the war."

Albert protested, "Maharishi, the young people of America don't want to fight that war."

Maharishi then said, "Yes, you are right. Young people of America should not have to fight that war. They are the flowers of the ages. They should go to Africa and get the Africans and make them go fight the war."

Albert said, "But Maharishi, what are you saying? The Africans shouldn't have to go fight the Vietnam War."

Maharishi became even more inflammatory, "Yes, yes, you get them and you put them on boats and give them guns and make them fight. It will be good for them."

Talk about politically incorrect—yikes!

Albert was shaken to his core. How could Maharishi make such flagrant remarks? Pale and stunned, Albert stumbled from Maharishi's house looking as if a bus just sideswiped his motorcycle. A course participant tried to explain to Albert that Maharishi was just pressing his buttons and messing with his head. Albert stared back blankly, entirely clueless.

We could never entirely fathom why Maharishi said senseless, absurd things to people. I trust it was for their spiritual growth. As the Sufi master Radha Mohan Lal said, "Sometimes Saints have to do things people will misjudge, and which from the worldly point of view could be condemned. Because the world judges from appearances. A Saint is beyond good and evil."[291]

⊙⊙⊙⊙⊙⊙⊙⊙⊙⊙⊙⊙⊙⊙⊙⊙⊙⊙⊙⊙

One of my friends, Regina Hughes, was perhaps the only other woman besides me that Maharishi berated in front of others, though not in front of four hundred others as he did to me. But he treated her worse—accusing her of having "dry rot on the brain," being "a demon," "harboring spies," "making her fame and fortune" by publishing a TM book, and many other choice phrases. It wasn't all crime and punishment, however. He also gave her love and attention. However, decades later, she's still traumatized by Maharishi's harsh treatment.

⊙⊙⊙⊙⊙⊙⊙⊙⊙⊙⊙⊙⊙⊙⊙⊙⊙⊙⊙⊙

My friend Brad Wagner was standing on line in La Antilla to give Maharishi a flower. As he took the flower from Brad, Maharishi frowned and said, "You are contacting spirits! My Initiators are not mediums for spirits."

What's Maharishi talking about? I thought. *Brad isn't a medium.* I asked Brad, "Why did he say that to you?"

The flustered Brad, clearly disturbed, said, "I have no idea." This statement haunted Brad for years. He could never ascertain the reason for such a ludicrous accusation.

∞∞∞∞∞∞∞∞∞∞∞∞∞∞∞∞∞∞∞∞

A young American, Nathaniel, was taking Teacher Training with Maharishi in Rishikesh. He'd contracted hepatitis in India months earlier, which left him in a state of perpetual lethargy. Maharishi gave him small tasks to focus on, such as looking after a key. One day Maharishi yelled at him, "Look at how you look. It's awful. I can't bear to look at you. Go away. Get out of my sight." Nathaniel, utterly shaken and deflated, fled to his room. There he had his first clear meditation in months. Maharishi's shouting gave him the energy needed to cut through his fog.[292]

∞∞∞∞∞∞∞∞∞∞∞∞∞∞∞∞∞∞∞∞

Another misconception about spiritual masters is that only "good" things happen to them. They could never break a leg, smash their car, get bronchitis, contract cancer, become paralyzed, get robbed or raped, or undergo anything unfortunate. People would ask, "Maharishi, if you're enlightened, why do you get sick?"

From Socrates to Jesus, Ramakrishna Paramahansa to Ramana Maharishi, Ammachi, and Maharishi Mahesh Yogi, "bad" things happened to spiritual masters—and to everyone else. No one escapes karmic consequences. Yet we expect spiritual masters to be whatever ridiculous pipedream we've invented in our heads.

Why do we persist in magical thinking? Because we hold out hope that spiritual enlightenment means *our own* life will be problem-free in some fantastic Neverland. We want escape. We want this misery to stop. However, that's just our projection of illusory, materialistic imagining.

∞∞∞∞∞∞∞∞∞∞∞∞∞∞∞∞∞∞∞∞

What I recognized in Maharishi, and other spiritual masters I've been lucky to meet, was a holy vibration of serenity, grace, and blessedness, which inspired those with eyes to see. I believe he was a spiritual master—and a human being. Even though I felt his brilliance, I was just as disenchanted and resentful as other followers when my bliss bubble burst in Fairfield in the 1980s.

Mark Landau, former skin-boy, said, "It was like this divine air would come down from heaven and we would be breathing it. And I got addicted to that. Maharishi could be very harsh, believe me. So for a while I had trouble putting the paradox together. How could he be so awful and so wonderful at the same time? But he was."[293]

Maharishi didn't act as people's fantasy of how true saintly beings "should" act. And I didn't (and still don't) act as people's expectations of how true disciples or spiritual seekers "should" act.

Though I could easily join ranks with cynical detractors who believe, as one reporter said, "Lennon was right. The giggling guru was a shameless old fraud," I won't. There is too much contrary evidence. For God's sake, Maharishi transformed the world by introducing and popularizing meditation into Western culture!

A hundred years from now, who will be remembered? The visionary who gave hope to humanity? Or scoffers who projected their own fears and hang-ups on him? Yet the stigma of those such as John Lennon and Alexis Mardas lives on. Maharishi often said, "The knowledge from an enlightened person breaks on the hard rocks of ignorance." He also predicted, "I have no pockets, but when I'm gone, they'll say it was all about the money."

The Sufi master Radha Mohan Lal said that bad teachers try to mold their behavior to their followers' expectations. If they seek name, fame, and money, they will "always be kind, benevolent, compassionate, uttering at all times wise, profound sentences." But good teachers obey "a law of which the world knows nothing. As it is the nature of the fire to burn or consume, or the wind to blow, so it is with the Sat Guru; he just *is.*"²⁹⁴

Master Lal also said people can't understand the motives or actions of good teachers and therefore condemn them: "Love does not conform to conventional ideas; Love can appear in the shape of great cruelty, great injustice, even calamity. In this respect the Sat Guru is similar to God. He cannot be judged or measured."²⁹⁵

In 1989 in Fairfield, letting go of the TM Movement was a real struggle. Since I was psychically attached for over two decades, many convoluted emotions churned inside. My ego was tied to TM status symbols. By embracing Divine Revelation, not only did I lose respect from peers. I also lost layers of absolutes comprising sets and subsets of BS (belief systems). To break away required tremendous inner resolve and strength.

My main problem was healing my relationship with Maharishi. My personal involvement with him made letting go incredibly challenging.

Until one day in meditation . . .

Upstairs in the puja room in my house in Fairfield, amongst *murthis, shaligrams, rudraksha* beads, *Shiva lingas,* and paintings of deities, I sat below a framed, crinkled, yellowed drawing precious to me, scribbled by Maharishi with a blue felt-tip pen one day in Switzerland—a day when he wanted to remind me of what was important.

There in my little Hindu temple I had an unexpected revelation, profoundly moving and deeply transformational.

Maharishi suddenly appeared before my inner eye in blazing color. His radiant glowing face and blissful smile filled my visual field with delight, the familiar feeling that he bestowed upon his disciples with his glance—that sudden swell of energy, like a soft, gentle wave lapping onto white crystalline sands on a sun-laden beach.

That wave of grace flowed over me, filling my mind with crystal clarity and profound understanding, washing pure love around and through me, cleansing my soul. The joyous love vibration from his heart touched my heart with rapture.

I asked him, "Why? Why did I have to leave? Why couldn't I stay with you?"

With great compassion and gentleness, the tender, loving, melodious voice of Maharishi said, *"Come come, my dear child. I love you so much. Do not doubt it for an instant. Come to me now and do not fear. I am always with you. You are my little child, Susan the Artist. I will love you always."*

Tears came to my eyes.

His voice continued, *"I always knew that you would not stay. That was never the plan for you. I trained you especially for this purpose, to take your own path and bring people to higher consciousness in your own way. I bless Divine Revelation and all those who come to it. You will bring many to God. That is your mission. Remember what I said to you so long ago? 'Don't look to anyone. When you don't look to anyone, then everyone will look to you.'"*

My heart was touched with deep emotion. I wept with immeasurable joy.

He handed me a glowing light sword and continued, *"Now is time for you to stand and take this sword of truth. Cut through the ignorance around you. Walk into the light of divine love. You are a beloved child of God. Your direction is clear. I have been a lighthouse to guide you. Now is your time to become a beacon for others. Trust in God's infinite love and live in the radiance of God's eternal flame. I give you my love and my blessings. Live in peace and enjoy."*

∞∞∞∞∞∞∞∞∞∞∞∞∞∞∞∞∞∞∞∞

I was profoundly moved. Absorbed in deep silence, I realized how Maharishi's influence touched people everywhere. He did what he came to do—transformed this planet from ignorance to enlightenment. The most powerful people of his generation sat at his feet—people who significantly impacted moving our culture into higher consciousness.

In 1959, when Maharishi came to America, few people outside India ever heard of any spiritual practice. Now a significant number meditated. Eastern philosophy was commonplace. Millions touched by TM took little pieces of Maharishi and then went off, scurrying about the planet—all of them deeply transformed by simply closing their eyes and experiencing inner peace.

But it wasn't the man. It wasn't Maharishi. It was the power of the unseen hand of God, moving the trends of time in a new direction. A spiritual revival was dawning, and we were all part of it.

My journey brought me into close contact with this unparalleled spiritual master, who, through his personal and spiritual power, transformed individuals and changed the world. I walked with the most influential guru of the twentieth century. But now it was time to walk my own path. I realized when Maharishi said, "don't look to anyone," he was referring to *everyone*—including himself.

My fears and doubts ceased. I knew I had taken the correct fork in the road. Now all that was left was to fulfill my destiny.

∞∞∞∞∞∞∞∞∞∞∞∞∞∞∞∞∞∞

Before long, all of us who participated in the spiritual revolution of the 1960s will be gone. But children and grandchildren of today and future generations will continue to carry that torch lit in the hearts of humanity by Maharishi. His influence will continue to reverberate from the timeless Ganges in Rishikesh to all the hearts he touched throughout the world.

EPILOGUE AND EPITAPH

We only leave this world with two things: the vibration we've achieved in our life and the love we've given to others. The two are really one and the same.
—MAHARISHI MAHESH YOGI

Until his death at age ninety, Maharishi lived in Vlodrop, Holland. Working day and night, he was still trying to establish world peace. "Maharishi Peace Palaces" were theoretically being built in one hundred US cities and three thousand cities worldwide. The plan was pundits would vibrate world peace by chanting the Vedas around the clock in these palaces.

Starting in 2002, about 150 wealthy devotees took Maharishi's "Enlightenment Course," forking over a cool million dollars *per person* to fly to Vlodrop, watch Maharishi on a video feed, and donate to the alleged permanent establishment of ten thousand pundit boys in India chanting day and night for world peace. Course graduates were bestowed golden medals and crowns and dubbed *"Raja"*(the Sanskrit word for "king"). They rode around in ostentatious royal white chariots drawn by white steeds, driven by formal coachmen in red uniforms and top hats, accompanied by marching bagpipers and flagbearers heralding their arrival—even when no one was there to greet them.

Hollywood director David Lynch was a graduate, though he didn't accept the title or crown. He has continued to be a spokesperson for TM worldwide. The David Lynch Foundation has gained quite a foothold among the Hollywood elite supporting its meditation programs.

Near his death, Maharishi was in the public eye again. He conducted an aggressive worldwide publicity campaign and building project. Large ads appeared in the *New York Times,* newspaper articles about TM abounded, and "Maharishi Ayurveda Health Spas" cropped up everywhere. Sadly, nearly all closed a few years later.

Maharishi died February 5, 2008. On the same day, for the first time ever, NASA beamed a song, the Beatles' "Across the Universe" directly into deep space toward

February 10, 2008, Allahabad, India: Crowned Rajas led by Lebanese neuroscientist
Tony Nader, whom Maharishi titled "Maharaja Adhiraj Rajaraam, First Sovereign Ruler
of Global Country of World Peace." He was named Maharishi's official successor on
October 12, 2000. *Associated Press/Rajesh Kumar Singh*

Polaris, the North Star. Recorded exactly forty years previously, this song, written by
John Lennon, quoted Maharishi's oft-repeated Sanskrit phrase honoring his guru: Jai
Guru Deva. As part of the celebration, people around the world simultaneously played
the song at the same time it was transmitted by NASA.

"The Global Consciousness Project" of Princeton University's Engineering
Anomalies Research Lab, which tracks meaningful correlations in random data, has
found whenever great events synchronize feelings of millions of people, their network
of seventy random number generators exhibits nonrandom patterns. On February 11,
2008, a striking U-shaped pattern occurred in morning and early afternoon hours, during Maharishi's cremation in Allahabad, India.

In 1968, when filmmaker Alan Waite asked Maharishi what he would like to be
remembered for, his answer was "Nothing." [296] But my hope is he will be remembered
as a great spiritual master who played a leading role in an unparalleled revolution of
consciousness. Right now the enigmatic guru might still be up to his old tricks—even
from the beyond.

WHO'S WHO IN TM

Here's a surprising list of just a few celebrities who learned TM:

50 Cent (singer)
Paula Abdul (singer)
Sam Allardyce (England football manager)
Ron Altbach (musician, *Beach Boys*)
Jennifer Aniston (actress)
Judd Apatow (film producer)
Arthur Ashe (tennis player)
Jane Asher (actress)
Janet Attwood (author)
Michael Balzary (musician, *Red Hot Chili Peppers*)
Ed Beckley (infomercial king)
Beth Behrs (actress)
Kristen Bell (actress)
Itzhak Bentov (inventor, author)
Gabrielle Bernstein (speaker)
Leonard Bernstein (composer)
Richard Beymer (actor)
Buddy Biancalana (baseball)
Cilla Black (singer)
Harold Bloomfield (author)
Bronk Bond (baseball)
Matt Bomer (actor)
Larry Bowa (baseball)
Jenny Boyd (model)

Pattie Boyd (model)
Tom Brady (football)
Russell Brand (comedian)
Jeff Bridges (actor)
Jerry Brown (Governor of California)
Gisele Bündchen (fashion model)
Mark Bunn (Australian football)
Kersi S. Cambata (transportation magnate)
Steve Carlton (baseball)
Wes Carr (singer)
Jim Carrey (actor)
Deepak Chopra (author)
Ellen Corby (actress)
Sheryl Crow (singer)
Rivers Cuomo (singer, *Weezer*)
John Cusack (actor)
Ray Dalio (hedge fund manager)
Blythe Danner (actress)
Hunter Davies (*Beatles* biographer)
Barbara De Angelis (author)
Ellen DeGeneres (TV host)
Kat Dennings (actress)
John Denver (singer)
Laura Dern (actress)
Cameron Diaz (actress)

Novak Djokovic (tennis player)

Donovan (musician)

Doris Duke (tobacco heiress)

Lena Dunham (actress)

Clint Eastwood (film director)

Graeme Edge (musician, *Moody Blues*)

Mal Evans (*Beatles* road manager)

John Fahey (musician)

Marianne Faithfull (singer)

Colin Farrell (actor)

Mia Farrow (actress)

Prudence Farrow (film producer)

Marilyn Ferguson (author)

Timothy Ferriss (author)

Jane Fonda (actress)

Ben Foster (actor)

Michael J. Fox (actor)

Squire Fridell (actor)

Buckminster Fuller (inventor)

Greta Garbo (actress)

Jeff Garlin (comedian)

Adam Gaynor (musician, *Matchbox 20*)

Aileen Getty (heiress)

Billy Gibbons (musician, *ZZ Top*)

Philip Goldberg (author)

Jeff Goldblum (actor)

Heather Graham (actress)

John Gray (author)

Leroy F. Greene (California legislator)

Judy Greer (actress)

Merv Griffin (TV host)

John Hagelin (physicist)

George Hamilton (actor)

Tom Hanks (actor)

Ben Harper (musician)

Bob "The Bear" Hite (musician, *Canned Heat*)

George Harrison (musician)

Olivia Harrison (film producer)

Yukio Hatoyama (Prime Minister Japan)

Goldie Hawn (actress)

Louise Hay (publisher)

Justin Hayward (musician, *Moody Blues*)

Mariel Hemingway (actress)

Doug Henning (magician)

Jim Henson (puppeteer)

Bill Hicks (comedian)

Claire Hoffman (journalist)

Paul Horn (musician)

Steve Howe (musician)

Kate Hudson (actress)

Arianna Huffington (editor)

Hugh Jackman (actor)

Michael Jackson (singer)

Mick Jagger (singer)

Jewel (singer)

Jim James (musician, *My Morning Jacket*)

Al Jardine (musician, *Beach Boys*)

Brian Josephson (Nobel laureate)

Andy Kaufman (comedian)

Caroline Kennedy (Ambassador to Japan)

Miranda Kerr (model)

Kesha (singer)

Nicole Kidman (actress)

Larry King (TV host)

Lenny Kravitz (singer)

Robby Krieger (musician, *The Doors*)

Stanley Kubrick (film director)

Jared Kushner (presidential advisor)

Peggy Lee (singer)

John Lennon (musician)

Cynthia Lennon (author)

Sean Taro Ono Lennon (musician)

David Letterman (TV host)

Tinker Lindsay (screenwriter)

Charles Lloyd (musician, *Beach Boys*)

Lindsay Lohan (actress)

Shelley Long (actress)

Jennifer Lopez (singer)
Mike Love (musician, *Beach Boys*)
Daisy Lowe (model)
George Lucas (film producer)
Steve Lukather (musician, *Toto*)
David Lynch (film director)
Kyle MacLachlan (actor)
Shirley MacLaine (actress)
Madonna (singer)
Ray Manzarek (musician, *The Doors*)
Pete Maravich (NBA player)
Cheech Marin (comedian)
Jim Marshall (NFL player)
Mary Martin (actress)
James McCartney (musician)
Paul McCartney (musician, *Beatles*)
Stella McCartney (fashion designer)
Willie McCovey (baseball)
Cynthia McFadden (TV journalist)
Marshall McLuhan (philosopher)
Peter McWilliams (author)
Eva Mendes (actress)
Alyssa Miller (model)
Moby (musician)
Mary Tyler Moore (actress)
Rupert Murdoch (media mogul)
Joe Namath (football player)
Martina Navratilova (tennis player)
Olivia Newton John (singer)
B.J. Novak (actor)
Denis O'Dell (film producer)
Rosie O'Donnell (actress)
Mike Oldfield (musician)
Maureen O'Sullivan (actress)
Mehmet Oz (TV host)
Gwyneth Paltrow (actress)
Mary-Louise Parker (actress)
Chuck Percy (US Senator)
Katy Perry (singer)

Tom Petty (musician)
Mike Pinder (musician, *Moody Blues*)
Gary Player (golfer)
Debra Poneman (author)
Priscilla Presley (actress)
John C. Reilly (actor)
Burt Reynolds (actor)
Emil Richards (percussionist)
Paul Rodgers (singer)
Robin Roberts (TV broadcaster)
Bill Robinson (baseball)
Smokey Robinson (singer)
Rick Rubin (record producer)
Peter Russell (author)
Tim Ryan (US congressman)
Paul Saltzman (producer)
Juan Manuel Santos (President of
    Colombia, Nobel laureate)
Susan Sarandon (actress)
Vidal Sassoon (hairdresser)
Amy Schumer (comedian)
Arnold Schwarzenegger (actor, politician)
Rusty Schweickart (Apollo 9 astronaut)
Martin Scorsese (film director)
Bill Scranton III (Lieutenant Governor of
    Pennsylvania)
Steven Seagal (actor)
Jerry Seinfeld (comedian)
Sri Sri Ravi Shankar (guru)
Rupert Sheldrake (scientist)
George Shapiro (talent manager)
Marci Shimoff (author)
Russell Simmons (entrepreneur)
Nikki Sixx (musician, *Mötley Crüe*)
Jeffrey M. Smith (activist)
Willie Stargell (baseball)
Ringo Starr (musician, *Beatles*)
John Steinbeck IV (journalist)
George Stephanopoulos (TV journalist)

Howard Stern (radio host)
Ali Stephens (model)
Cat Stevens (singer)
Patrick Stewart (actor)
Sting (musician)
Maya Stojan (actress)
Patrick Swayze (actor)
Elizabeth Taylor (actress)
Ray Thomas (musician, *Moody Blues*)
Eric Trump (businessman)
Ivanka Trump (businesswoman)
Liv Tyler (actress)
Usher (singer)
Steve Vai (musician)
Elizabeth Vargas (TV journalist)
Eddie Vedder (musician, *Pearl Jam*)
Kurt Vonnegut (author)
Bill Walton (basketball player)
Alice Walker (Pulitzer Prize winner)
Barbara Walters (TV journalist)
Naomi Watts (actress)
Florence Welch (singer, *Florence and the
      Machine*)
Marianne Williamson (author)
Bill Wilson (cofounder of AA)
Brian Wilson (musician, *Beach Boys*)
Carl Wilson (musician, *Beach Boys*)
Dennis Wilson (musician, *Beach Boys*)
Oprah Winfrey (TV mogul)
Stevie Wonder (singer)
C. V. Wood (developer, Disneyland)
Jim Wright (US Speaker of the House)
Ned Wynn (screenwriter)
Efrem Zimbalist Jr. (actor)
Raquel Zimmermann (model)
Barry Zito (baseball player)

BIBLIOGRAPHY

BOOKS

Badman, Keith. *Beatles, off the Record.* London: Omnibus Press, 2002.

Batchelder, Ram Das, *Rising in Love.* Philadelphia, PA: John Hunt Publishing, 2014.

Beatles, The. *The Beatles Anthology.* San Francisco: Chronicle Books, 2000.

Blakely, Richard. *The Secret of the Mantras.* Providence, RI: CreateSpace Independent Publishing Platform, 2013. Kindle Edition.

Bourque, Judith. *Robes of Silk Feet of Clay: The True Story of a Love Affair with Maharishi Mahesh Yogi, the TM guru followed by the Beatles, Deepak Chopra, David Lynch, and millions more.* Judith Bourque, 2010.

Boyd, Pattie. *Wonderful Tonight: George Harrison, Eric Clapton, and Me.* Crown Archetype, 2008.

Brown, Peter. *The Love You Make: An Insider's Story of The Beatles.* Berkley, 2002.

Bruns, Prudence Farrow. *Dear Prudence: The Story Behind the Song.* North Charleston, SC: Amazon Digital Services LLC, 2015. Kindle Edition.

Buskin, Richard. *Days in the Life: The Lost Beatles Archives.* San Rafael, CA: Star Publishing, 1999.

Cooke de Herrera, Nancy. *All You Need Is Love: An Eyewitness Account of When Spirituality Spread from East to West.* New York: Open Road, 2005. Google Play.

Cooke de Herrera, Nancy. *Beyond Gurus.* Grass Valley, CA: Blue Dolphin Publishing, 1992.

Coleman, Ray. *Lennon.* New York: McGraw Hill, 1984.

Cross, Craig. *Beatles-Discography.com: Day-By-Day Song-By-Song Record-By-Record.* Bloomington, Indiana: iUniverse, Inc., 2005.

Dragemark, Elsa. *The Way to Maharishi's Himalayas.* Oslo, Norway: Forenede Trykkerier AS, 1972.

Farrow, Mia. *What Falls Away.* New York: Bantam, 1997.

Forsthoefel, Thomas A. and Cynthia Ann Humes. *Gurus in America.* Albany: State University of New York Press, 2005.

Giuliano, Geoffrey. *Revolver: The Secret History of the Beatles.* London: John Blake, 2005.

Hayward, Jeremy. *Warrior-King of Shambhala: Remembering Chögyam Trungpa*. Somerville, MA: Wisdom Publications, 2008.

Hoffman, Claire. *Greetings from Utopia Park: Surviving a Transcendent Childhood*. New York: Harper, 2016.

Holy Bible, The. Iowa Falls, Iowa: World Bible Publishers, no date.

Inauguration of the Dawn of the Age of Enlightenment. Seelisberg, Switzerland: MIU Press, 1975.

International Symposium on the Science of Creative Intelligence. Seelisberg, Switzerland: MIU Press, 1971.

Kane, Larry. *Lennon Revealed*. Philadelphia: Running Press, 2007.

Kane, Larry. *Ticket to Ride*. Hawthorne, CA: Dynamic Images, Inc., 2010. Kindle Edition.

Leitch, Donovan. *The Autobiography of Donovan: The Hurdy Gurdy Man*. New York: St. Martin's Press, 2005. Google Play.

Lennon, Cynthia. *A Twist of Lennon*. New York: Avon Books, 1978. Google Play.

Love, Mike with James S. Hirsch. *Good Vibrations: My Life as A Beach Boy*. New York: Blue Rider Press, 2016.

Mahesh Yogi, Maharishi. *Bhagavad Gita, a New Translation and Commentary with Sanskrit Text*. Harmondsworth, Middlesex, England: Penguin Books Ltd., 1969.

Mason, Paul. *The Maharishi: The Biography of the Man Who Gave Transcendental Meditation to the World*. Shaftsbury, Dorset: Element Books Ltd., 1994.

Mason, Paul. *The Beatles, Drugs, Mysticism & India*. Premanand, 2017.

Midal, Fabrice. *Recalling Chögyam Trungpa*, Boulder, CO: Shambhala, 2005.

Miller, Jon Michael. *Maharishi, TM, Mallory, & Me: Memoir of a Once TM Superstar*, North Charleston, SC: CreateSpace Independent Publishing Platform, 2011. Kindle Edition.

Norman, Philip. *Shout! The Beatles in Their Generation*. New York: Fireside, 2005.

Olson, Theresa. *Maharishi Mahesh Yogi: A Living Saint for the New Millennium*. Fairfield, IA: 1st World Library, 2004.

Orme-Johnson, Rhoda. *Inside Maharishi's Ashram: A Personal Story*. North Charleston, SC: CreateSpace Independent Publishing Platform, 2017. Kindle Edition.

Saltzman, Paul. *The Beatles in Rishikesh*. New York: Viking Studio, 2000.

Sheff, David. *All We Are Saying: The Last Major Interview with John Lennon and Yoko Ono*. New York: St. Martin's Griffin, 2010. Google Play.

Shotton, Pete and Nicolas Schaffner. *John Lennon: In My Life*. New York: Stein & Day, 1983.

Tillery, Gail. *The Cynical Idealist: A Spiritual Biography of John Lennon*. Wheaton, IL: Quest Books, 2009. Google Play.

Turner, Steve. *A Hard Day's Write: The Stories Behind Every Beatles Song*. New York: It Books, 2005.

Tweedie, Irina. *The Chasm of Fire: A Woman's Experience of Liberation through the Teaching of a Sufi Master.* Longmead, UK: Element, 1979.

Wenner, Jann S. *Lennon Remembers.* London: Verso, 2000.

Yogananda, Paramahansa. *Autobiography of a Yogi.* Yogoda Satsanga Society of India, Kolkata: 2001.

Zehme, Bill. *Lost in the Funhouse: The Life and Mind of Andy Kaufman.* Crystal Lake, IL: Delta, 2009. Google Play.

ARTICLES

Hedgepeth, William. "The Non-Drug Turn-On Hits Campus." *Look.* Feb. 6, 1968: 64-66.

Horn, Paul. "A Visit with India's High-Powered New Prophet." *Look,* Feb. 6, 1968: 68-78.

Howard, Jane. "Year of the Guru." *Life.* Feb. 9, 1968: 52-56.

Lapham, Lewis H. "There Once Was a Guru from Rishikesh, Part I." *The Saturday Evening Post.* May 4, 1968: 23-29.

Lapham, Lewis H. "There Once Was a Guru from Rishikesh, Part II." *The Saturday Evening Post.* May 18, 1968: 28-33.

Lefferts, Barney. "Chief Guru of the Western World." *New York Times Magazine.* Dec. 17, 1967: 44-58.

"Mystics: Soothsayer for Everyman." *Time.* Oct. 20, 1967: 86.

Naughton, Jim. "Head for the Hills, Disciples! TM's Maharishi Holds Out No Hope for D.C." *The Washington Post.* December 16, 1991: a.01.

"On the Newsfronts of the World: The Beatles with their Guru," *Life.* Sept. 8, 1967: 26

Ramanujam, R. "The Guru," *Newsweek.* Dec. 18, 1967: 67.

Wainwright, Louden. "Invitation to Instant Bliss," *Life.* Nov. 10, 1967: 26.

INTERNET ARTICLES

Atmananada. "Words of Sri Anandamayi Ma." http://www.anandamayi.org/books/atmnda.htm.

"Beatles are angels on earth, said Maharishi." *The Times of India.* February 15, 2006. http://articles.timesofindia.indiatimes.com/2006-02-15/india/27803944_1_maharishi-mahesh-yogi-vlodrop-beatles#ixzz2WigMzH6e.

"The Beatles in India." The Beatles White Album. http://www.thewhitealbumproject.com/india.

"Beatles Rarity of the Week—'Spiritual Regeneration'" Beatles Rarity. October 20, 2014. http://www.thebeatlesrarity.com/2014/10/20/beatles-rarity-of-the-week-spiritual-regeneration-impromptu-performance-in-india-1968.

Boyce, Barry. "Ocean of Dharma." Lion's Roar. April 4, 2017. https://www.lionsroar.com/ocean-of-dharma-january-2012.

Calio, Jim. "Yoko Ono's Ex-Husband, Tony Cox, Reveals His Strange Life Since Fleeing with Their Daugher 14 Years Ago." *People*. February 3, 1986. http://people.com/archive/yoko-onos-ex-husband-tony-cox-reveals-his-strange-life-since-fleeing-with-their-daughter-14-years-ago-vol-25-no-5.

Chiu, David. "The Real 'Dear Prudence' on Meeting Beatles in India." *RollingStone*. http://www.rollingstone.com/music/news/the-real-dear-prudence-on-meeting-beatles-in-india-20150904.

"Chogyam Trungpa." Shambhala. https://shambhala.org/teachers/chogyam-trungpa.

Chopra, Deepak. "First Meeting Maharishi." Beliefnet. http://www.beliefnet.com/columnists/intentchopra/2008/02/first-meeting-maharishi-by-dee.html.

Chopra, Deepak. "The Maharishi Years - The Untold Story: Recollections of a Former Disciple." February 2, 2008. http://www.huffingtonpost.com/deepak-chopra/the-maharishi-years-the-u_b_86412.html.

Cott, Jonathan. "John Lennon: The *Rolling Stone* Interview." *Rolling Stone*. http://www.rollingstone.com/music/news/john-lennon-the-rolling-stone-interview-19681123?page=6.

Dawson, Jeff. "Mia Farrow: A Life Less Ordinary." October 4, 2013. http://jeffdawsonblog.blogspot.com/2013/10/mia-farrow.html.

Dolan, Mike. "Midnight in the Oasis." Trancenet. http://minet.org/www.trancenet.net/personal/dolan/midnight.shtml.

Duke, Alan. "Surviving Beatles Unite to Promote Meditation." Paul Horn. December 10, 2010. http://paulhornmusic.com/2010/12/mccartney-and-lynch-benefit-concert.

E.L.E. "John Lennon & Yoko Ono: Arrested in Mallorca." Palma Daily. October 25, 2016. http://www.inpalma.com/en/blogs/palma-daily/john-lennon-and-yoko-ono-arrested-in-mallorca.

"Ex-Beatle remembers his spiritual guru Maharishi Mahesh Yogi." Outlook. February 7, 2008. http://www.outlookindia.com/newswire/story/ex-beatle-remembers-his-spiritual-guru-maharishi-mahesh-yogi/543012.

"The Fan Club." Trancenet. http://minet.org/www.trancenet.net/news/weekly/tfan.shtml.

Fiske, David. "Stalking Personal Power and Peace." http://www.esotericarts.org/SPP&P.pdf.

"From Linda Kaplan." Fairfield Life, Yahoo Groups. https://groups.yahoo.com/neo/groups/FairfieldLife/conversations/messages/26836.

Hamblin, James. "The Seduction of 'Wellness Real Estate.'" Feb. 27, 2017. https://www.theatlantic.com/health/archive/2017/02/wellness-real-estate/517560.

Hedegaard, Erik. "The Ballad of Mike Love." *Rolling Stone*. February 17, 2016. http://www.rollingstone.com/music/features/the-ballad-of-mike-love-20160217.

Hoffman, Claire. "David Lynch Is Back . . . as a Guru of Transcendental Meditation." Feb. 22, 2013. http://www.nytimes.com/2013/02/24/magazine/david-lynch-transcendental -meditation.html.

Hudson, Alexandra. "Beatles' guru Mahesh Yogi dies." Reuters. February 6, 2008. http:// www.reuters.com/article/idINIndia-31787520080206.

Kang, Bhavdeep. "How Ravi Shankar broke with Maharishi Mahesh Yogi and became Sri Sri." Mar 21, 2016. http://scroll.in/a/805429.

Kipp, Rachel. "2. Dear Prudence." The Beatles White Album. http://www.thewhitealbumproject.com/songs/side-one.

Knapp, John M. "Deepak Chopra Interview." "Exclusive interview of Deepak Chopra on spirituality, free speech, the Maharishi, leaving TM, and much more." Trancenet. August 1, 1996. http://web.archive.org/web/20040606082458/http://trancenet.org.

Knapp, John M. "Earl Kaplan's Letter." *TM-Free Blog.* April 2, 2008. http://tmfree.blogspot.com/2008/04/earl-kaplans-letter.html.

Knapp, John M. "Letter from David Kaplan." *TM-Free Blog.* April 2, 2008. http://tmfree.blogspot.com/2008/04/letter-from-david-kaplan.html.

Lutes, Charles F. "Memoirs of Charlie Lutes: Chapter 4: Making Teachers, Shagging Yogurt." http://www.maharishiphotos.com/mem4a.html.

Lutes, Charles F. "Memoirs of Charlie Lutes: Chapter 2: Holy Man from the Himalayas." http://www.maharishiphotos.com/mem2a.html.

"Maharishi, Maharishi Not." Leaving the Art of Living. December 14, 2009. http://artoflivingfree.blogspot.com/2009/12/maharishi-maharishi-not.html.

Mason, Paul. "Introduction to Lifestory and Teachings of Guru Dev Shankaracharya Swami Brahmananda Saraswati. http://www.paulmason.info/gurudev/introduction.htm.

Miles, Barry. *Paul McCartney: Many Years From Now.* New York: Henry Holt and Company, 1997, Chapter 9. http://www.wingspan.ru/bookseng/myfn/bmiles09.html.

Miles, Barry. *Paul McCartney: Many Years From Now.* New York: Henry Holt and Company, 1997, Chapter 10. http://www.wingspan.ru/bookseng/myfn/bmiles10.html.

Lennon, John. "The Maharishi Song." Genius. https://genius.com/John-lennon-the-maharishi-song-lyrics.

Maass, Peter. "Welcome to Silicorn Valley." *Wired.* September 1, 1997. https://www.wired.com/1997/09/callback.

"Maharishi Talks of His First Sight of Gurudev Transcript." http://www.alkpurusha.net/maharishi-talks-of-his-first-sight-of-guru-dev-transcript.

Mardas, Alex. Statement to *New York Times.* March 4, 2010. http://www.nytimes.com/2008/02/07/arts/music/07yogi.html, with Editor's note appended. Link to: http://graphics8.nytimes.com/packages/pdf/arts/Mardas.pdf.

Mason, Paul. "Introduction to Lifestory and Teachings of Gurudev Shankaracharya Swami Brahmananda Saraswati." http://www.paulmason.info/gurudev/introduction.htm.

McCartney, Paul. "Paul Pays Tribute to Maharishi Mahesh Yogi." February 7, 2008. https://www.paulmccartney.com/news-blogs/news/paul-pays-tribute-to-maharishi -mahesh-yogi.

McKinley, Jesse. "Doug Henning, a Superstar Of Illusion, Is Dead at 52." *New York Times.* February 9, 2000. http://www.nytimes.com/2000/02/09/arts/doug-henning-a -superstar-of-illusion-is-dead-at-52.html.

Mendes, Evencio. "Guru Bhati in the Ninth Bhava." https://www.scribd.com/document/ 82054532/Guru-Bhakti-in-the-Ninth-Bhava.

Miles, Jeremy. *Dancing Ledge.* https://dancingledge.wordpress.com/tag/jenny-boyd/

Mitra, S. "Maharishi Mahesh Yogi: Successful Meditation." *India Today.* http://indiatoday.intoday.in/story/maharishi-mahesh-yogi-visits-new-delhi-to -attend-vedic-conference/1/410282.html.

Morse, Steve. "McCartney Breaks His Silence with a Rock 'N' Roll Album." *Boston Globe.* October 3, 1999. www.billsartbox.com/id185.html.

"Multi-million pound ending to Yoko Ono family feud which started in Majorca with Lennon." *Majorca Daily Bulletin.* January 19, 2001. https://majorcadailybulletin. com/news/local/2001/01/19/2177/multi-million-pound-ending-yoko-ono-family -feud-which-started-majorca-with-lennon.html.

"NASA Beams Beatles' 'Across the Universe' Into Space." https://www.nasa.gov/topics/ universe/features/across_universe.html.

Nikhilananda, Swami. *Vivekananda A Biography.* Chapter 4: Training of the Disciple. http://www.ramakrishnavivekananda.info/vivekananda_biography/04_training.htm.

"Nityananda." Sages, Saints, and Avatars. http://www.cosmicharmony.com/Av/ Nityanan/Nityanan.htm.

"Om Namo Narayani Om Hari Durga Ma." Sri Ananadamayi Ma. http://www.anandamayi.org/bhavas.

Orme-Johnson, David, PhD, "Societal Effects." Truth About TM. http://www.truthabouttm.org/truth/SocietalEffects/Rationale-Research/index.cfm.

"Paul McCartney and Ringo Starr Live Webcast Today." Uncut. April 3, 2009. http://www.uncut.co.uk/news/paul-mccartney-and-ringo-starr-live-webcast-today -april-3-56504.

Pillai, Ajith, and Pushpinder Singh. "Remains of Yesterday." *Frontline.* http://www.frontline.in/arts-and-culture/remains-of-yesterday/article5085673.ece.

Reuters. "Reader's Digest to Buy a Book Discounter." *New York Times.* August 31, 1999. http://www.nytimes.com/1999/08/31/business/reader-s-digest-to-buy-a-book -discounter.html.

"Rgvedasamhita, Mandala 9," http://www.theasis.net/RgV/rv9_2.html.

"Ringo Starr Leaves India." March 1, 1968. The Beatles Bible. https://www.beatlesbible. com/1968/03/01/ringo-starr-leaves-india.

Rooney, Ben. "Maharishi Mahesh Yogi, guru to Beatles, dies." *The Telegraph*. February 6, 2008. http://www.telegraph.co.uk/news/worldnews/1577866/Maharishi-Mahesh -Yogi-guru-to-Beatles-dies.html.

Shankar, Jay. "Maharishi Mahesh Yogi, guru to pop celebrities, dies at 91." *Vancouver Sun*. February 6, 2008. https://www.pressreader.com/canada/vancouver-sun/20080206/ 281801394649389.

"Stories about Maharishi." http://mmy.klemke.de/M1000000.htm.

Sudarshan. "A brief account of Sri Sri Ravishankar and Maharishi Mahesh Yogi." October 9, 2010. https://aolfree.wordpress.com/2010/10/09/a-brief-account-of-sri-sri-ravishankar -and-maharishi-mahesh-yogi-by%C2%A0sudarshan.

"Swami Kriyananda: In Memoriam." May 1, 2013. https://www.ananda.org/news/2013/ swami-kriyananda-in-memoriam.

Thompson, George. "Celebrities Who Meditate." *The Telegraph*. June 28, 2011. http:// www.telegraph.co.uk/health/healthnews/8602265/Celebrities-who-meditate.html.

Tomkins, Mike. "The Growth of Maharishi's Movement." http://pages.citebite.com/ i6t7e2l8cyov.

Vivekananda, Swami. *Raja-Yoga*. Chapter 1: Introductory. 1893. http://www. ramakrishnavivekananda.info/vivekananda/volume_1/raja-yoga/introductory.htm.

Wenner, Jann S. "John Lennon: The *Rolling Stone* Interview, Part One." January 21, 1971. http://www.rollingstone.com/music/features/the-rolling-stone-interview-john -lennon-19710121.

"When Maharishi Threw Beatles Out." *The Times of India*. February 15, 2006. http://timesofindia.indiatimes.com/india/When-Maharishi-threw-Beatles-out/ articleshow/1415230.cms.

Whistleblower. "His Holiness Titles & Lineage." June 2, 2010. http://aolfree.wordpress. com/2010/06/02/his-holiness-titles-lineage.

"William Blake Quotes." Brainy Quote. https://www.brainyquote.com/quotes/ quotes/w/williambla396783.html.

Wofford, Ben. "His Holiness Sri Sri Ravi Shankar to Inaugurate World Class International Center for Peace and Well-Being." http://www.hcpress.com/news/his-holiness-sri -sri-ravi-shankar-to-inaugurate-world-class-international-center-for-peace-and-well -being.html.

Zehme, Bill. "Lost in the Funhouse." http://andykaufman.jvlnet.com/aktime.htm.

MOVIES AND INTERNET MOVIES

"Maharishi Mahesh Yogi – The Seven States of Consciousness – Part 1 (1967) Vinyl." You Tube. https://www.youtube.com/watch?v=ScwYJ7GHixw&t=21s.

"Maharishi Mahesh Yogi - Transcendental Meditation - Biography." Vimeo. History
    Channel International, 2007. https://vimeo.com/120745864.

"Maharishi on History Channel eng heb." You Tube. https://www.youtube.com/
    watch?v=xcaErBuD9-E.

"Maharishi's First Sight of Gurudev." http://vimeo.com/23247596.

"The most embarrassing thing I've ever been on" - John Lennon and Paul McCartney
    Beatles Interview. You Tube. https://www.youtube.com/watch?v=J-fprFK62dY.

Parker, Alan G. *It Was Fifty Years Ago Today: Sgt Pepper & Beyond.* 2017.

"Paul McCarney & John Lennon 1968 Full Interview." You Tube. https://www.youtube.
    com/watch?v=Qp0i90n0BP8.

Richardson, Gary. "Maharishi Mahesh Yogi - Beatles Urban Legend." You Tube.
    History Channel International. July 31, 2009. https://www.youtube.com/
    watch?v=Je5-Bs_3iHU.

Sieveking, David. *David Wants to Fly,* GoodMovies, 2010. http://www.alluc.ee/l/
    David-Wants-to-Fly-2010/y8xe7d2g.

ENDNOTES

CHAPTER 1

1. Tweedie, *The Chasm of Fire*, 47-48.

CHAPTER 2

2. Yogananda, *Autobiography of a Yogi*, 92.
3. Yogananda, *Autobiography of a Yogi*, 93.
4. Tweedie, *Chasm of Fire*, 41.
5. "Maharishi Mahesh Yogi – The Seven States of Consciousness."
6. Susan Shumsky's handwritten lecture notes.
7. License: https://creativecommons.org/licenses/by-sa/3.0/legalcode

CHAPTER 4

8. Mason, *The Beatles, Drugs, Mysticism & India*, 38.
9. Ramanujam, "The Guru," 67.
10. Brown, *The Love You Make*, 231.
11. Mason, Paul. *The Beatles, Drugs, Mysticism & India*, 57.
12. Coleman, *Lennon*, 339-340.
13. Blakely, *The Secret of the Mantras*, 184.
14. Parker, *It Was Fifty Years Ago Today*.
15. Mason, *The Beatles, Drugs, Mysticism & India*, 79.
16. Shotten, *John Lennon In My Life*, 139.
17. "On the Newsfronts of the World," 26.
18. Wainwright, "Invitation to Instant Bliss," 26.
19. Howard, "Year of the Guru," 52.
20. "Mystics: Soothsayer for Everyman," *Time*, 86.
21. Lefferts, "Chief Guru of the Western World," 44-58.
22. Ramanujam, "The Guru," 67.
23. Hedgepeth, "The Non-Drug Turn-On Hits Campus," 68-78.
24. Horn, "A Visit with India's High-Powered New Prophet," 66.
25. Horn, "A Visit with India's High-Powered New Prophet," 66.
26. Mason, *The Beatles, Drugs, Mysticism & India*, 114.

27. Badman, *Beatles, off the Record,* 342.

28. Lapham, "There Once Was a Guru from Rishikesh, Part 1," 28.

29. Paul McCartney & John Lennon 1968 Full Interview

30. "The most embarrassing thing I've ever been on."

31. Norman, *Shout!,* 324.

32. Beatles, *The Beatles Anthology,* 286.

33. Lapham, "There Once Was a Guru from Rishikesh, Part 1," 25.

34. "William Blake Quotes." Brainy Quote.

35. Mason, *The Beatles, Drugs, Mysticism & India,* 58.

36. Susan Shumsky's handwritten lecture notes.

37. Susan Shumsky's handwritten lecture notes.

38. Susan Shumsky's handwritten lecture notes.

39. Orme-Johnson, *Inside Maharishi's Ashram,* Location 2694.

40. *Tat Wale Baba-Rishi of the Himalayas,* Copyrighted: Free Use.

41. Creative Commons: Attribution-NonCommercial 3.0 Unported (CC BY-NC 3.0).

CHAPTER 6

42. Susan Shumsky's handwritten lecture notes.

43. Susan Shumsky's handwritten lecture notes.

44. Batchelder, Ram Das, *Rising in Love,* 27.

CHAPTER 7

45. Tweedie, *The Chasm of Fire,* 105.

46. *International Symposium,* 21.

CHAPTER 8

47. Calio, "Yoko Ono's Ex-Husband, Tony Cox, Reveals His Strange Life."

48. "Multi-million pound ending to Yoko Ono family feud."

49. E.L.E. "John Lennon & Yoko Ono: Arrested in Mallorca."

50. Susan Shumsky's handwritten lecture notes.

51. Susan Shumsky's handwritten lecture notes.

52. Susan Shumsky's handwritten lecture notes.

CHAPTER 12

53. Susan Shumsky's handwritten lecture notes.

54. *Inauguration of the Dawn of the Age of Enlightenment,* 24.

55. *Inauguration of the Dawn of the Age of Enlightenment,* 24.

56. *Inauguration of the Dawn of the Age of Enlightenment,* 2.

CHAPTER 13

57. Mason, "Introduction to Lifestory and Teachings."
58. Mason, "Introduction to Lifestory and Teachings."
59. "Maharishi Talks of His First Sight of Guru Dev Transcript."
60. "Maharishi on History Channel eng heb."
61. "Maharishi's First Sight of Guru Dev."
62. Mason, "Introduction to Lifestory and Teachings."
63. Susan Shumsky's handwritten lecture notes.
64. Susan Shumsky's handwritten lecture notes.
65. Susan Shumsky's handwritten lecture notes.
66. Susan Shumsky's handwritten lecture notes.
67. Cooke de Herrera, *All You Need Is Love,* 59.
68. Susan Shumsky's handwritten lecture notes.
69. "Maharishi's First Sight of Guru Dev."
70. Mason, "Introduction to Lifestory and Teachings of Guru Dev."
71. Tomkins, "The Growth of Maharishi's Movement."
72. Tomkins, "The Growth of Maharishi's Movement."
73. Lutes, "Memoirs of Charlie Lutes: Chapter 4."
74. Lutes, "Memoirs of Charlie Lutes: Chapter 2."
75. Mason, *The Maharishi,* 37.

CHAPTER 14

76. Wainwright, "Invitation to Instant Bliss," 26.
77. Tweedie, *The Chasm of Fire,* 82.
78. Orme-Johnson, *Inside Maharishi's Ashram,* Location 2151.
79. Orme-Johnson, *Inside Maharishi's Ashram,* Location 2151.
80. Batchelder, Ram Das, *Rising in Love,* 142.
81. Yogananda, *Autobiography of a Yogi,* 119-120.
82. Tweedie, *The Chasm of Fire,* 94.

CHAPTER 15

83. Mendes, "Guru Bhati in the Ninth Bhava."
84. Susan Shumsky's handwritten lecture notes.

CHAPTER 16

85. Farrow, *What Falls Away,* 122.
86. Cooke de Herrera, *All You Need Is Love,* 167.
87. Cross, *Beatles-Discography.com,* 173.
88. Blakely, *The Secret of the Mantras,* 146.

89. Cooke de Herrera, *All You Need Is Love,* 168.

90. Cooke de Herrera, *All You Need Is Love,* 171.

91. Cooke de Herrera, *All You Need Is Love,* 171.

92. Cooke de Herrera, *All You Need Is Love,* 171.

93. Cooke de Herrera, *All You Need Is Love,* 172.

94. Bruns, *Dear Prudence,* 201-202.

95. Mason, *The Beatles, Drugs, Mysticism & India,* 149.

96. Farrow, *What Falls Away,* 125.

97. "Maharishi on History Channel eng heb."

98. Badman, *Beatles, off the Record,* 340.

99. Miles, *Paul McCartney,* Chapter 10.

100. Miles, Dancing Ledge.

101. Lennon, *A Twist of Lennon,* 169-170.

102. Cross, *Beatles-Discography.com,* 175.

103. Mason, *The Beatles, Drugs, Mysticism & India,* 178.

104. Kane, *Ticket to Ride,* 122.

105. Saltzman, *The Beatles in Rishikesh.*

106. Beatles, *Beatles Anthology,* 281.

107. Beatles, *Beatles Anthology,* 284.

108. "Ringo Starr Leaves India."

109. Beatles, *Beatles Anthology,* 281.

110. Badman, *Beatles, off the Record,* 343.

111. Giuliano, *Revolver,* 118-119.

112. Blakely, *The Secret of the Mantras,* 192.

CHAPTER 17

113. Love, *Good Vibrations,* 188.

114. Mason, *The Beatles, Drugs, Mysticism & India,* 193.

115. Love, *Good Vibrations,* 189-190.

116. Love, *Good Vibrations,* 238.

117. Dragemark, *The Way to Maharishi's Himalayas,* 178.

118. Badman, *Beatles, off the Record,* 340.

119. Badman, *Beatles, off the Record,* 340.

120. Blakely, *The Secret of the Mantras,* 177-179.

121. Mason, *The Beatles, Drugs, Mysticism & India,* 222.

122. Badman, *Beatles, off the Record,* 340.

123. Buskin, *Days in the Life,* 160-161.

124. Norman, *Shout!,* 323.

125. Mason, *The Beatles, Drugs, Mysticism & India,* 198.

126. Bruns, *Dear Prudence*, 213-214.

127. Cooke de Herrera, *All You Need Is Love*, 214.

128. Boyd, *Wonderful Tonight*, 117.

129. Lennon, *A Twist of Lennon*, 171.

130. Coleman, *Lennon*, 339-340.

131. Turner, *A Hard Day's Write*, 163.

132. Cooke de Herrera, *All You Need Is Love*, 207.

133. Miles, *Paul McCartney: Many Years From Now*, Chapter 10.

134. Turner, *A Hard Day's Write*, 151.

135. Pillai, "Remains of Yesterday."

136. Turner, *A Hard Day's Write*, 152.

137. Sheff, *All We Are Saying*, 199.

138. Kipp, "2. Dear Prudence."

139. Blakely, *The Secret of the Mantras*, 217-218.

140. Turner, *A Hard Day's Write*, 159.

141. Beatles, *Beatles Anthology*, 283.

142. Badman, *Beatles, off the Record*, 281.

143. Sheff, *All We Are Saying*, 190.

144. "The Beatles in India."

145. Beatles, *Beatles Anthology*, 282-283.

146. Mason, *The Beatles, Drugs, Mysticism & India*, 208.

147. Turner, *A Hard Day's Write*, 155.

148. Mason, *The Beatles, Drugs, Mysticism & India*, 208.

149. Sheff, *All We Are Saying*, 199.

150. Miles, *Paul McCartney*, Chapter 9.

151. Turner, *A Hard Day's Write*, 149.

CHAPTER 18

152. Norman, *Shout!*, 323.

153. Cooke de Herrera, *All You Need Is Love*, 208.

154. Miles, *Paul McCartney*, Chapter 10.

155. Cooke de Herrera, *All You Need Is Love*, 211.

156. Mason, *The Beatles, Drugs, Mysticism & India*, 258.

157. Kane, *Lennon Revealed*, 60-61.

158. Mason, *The Beatles, Drugs, Mysticism & India*, 219.

159. Brown, *The Love You Make*, 188.

160. Miles, *Paul McCartney*, Chapter 10.

161. Brown, *The Love You Make*, 247.

162. Cross, *Beatles-Discography.com*, 176.

163. Dolan, "Midnight in the Oasis."

164. Blakely, *The Secret of the Mantras,* 242.

165. Miles, *Paul McCartney,* Chapter 10.

166. Dolan, "Midnight in the Oasis."

167. Mardas, Statement to *New York Times.*

168. Mardas, Statement to *New York Times.*

169. Turner, *A Hard Day's Write,* 167.

170. Brown, *The Love You Make,* 288.

171. Lennon, A Twist of Lennon, 174.

172. Wenner, "John Lennon: The *Rolling Stone* Interview."

173. Lennon, *A Twist of Lennon,* 174.

174. Beatles, *Beatles Anthology,* 286.

175. Cross, *Beatles-Discography.com,* 177.

176. Beatles, *Beatles Anthology,* 285.

177. Beatles, *Beatles Anthology,* 286.

178. Wenner, *Lennon Remembers,* 28.

179. Wenner, *Lennon Remembers,* 28.

180. Lennon, *A Twist of Lennon,* 176.

181. Lennon, *A Twist of Lennon,* 176.

182. Lennon, *A Twist of Lennon,* 176-177.

183. Miles, *Paul McCartney,* Chapter 10.

184. Mason, *The Beatles, Drugs, Mysticism & India,* 237-238.

185. Shotton, *John Lennon: In My Life,* 162.

186. https://www.beatlesbible.com/songs/sexy-sadie

187. https://www.beatlesbible.com/songs/sexy-sadie

188. Beatles, *Beatles Anthology,* 286.

189. Beatles, *Beatles Anthology,* 263.

190. Miles, Dancing Ledge.

191. Wenner, "John Lennon: The *Rolling Stone* Interview."

CHAPTER 19

192. Miller, *Maharishi, TM, Mallory & Me,* Chapter 49.

193. Mahesh Yogi, *Bhagavad Gita,* 2:45, 126.

194. Mahesh Yogi, *Bhagavad Gita,* 2:48, 135.

CHAPTER 20

195. Susan Shumsky's handwritten lecture notes.

196. "Rgvedasamhita, Mandala 9."

197. Susan Shumsky's handwritten lecture notes.

198. Susan Shumsky's handwritten lecture notes.

199. "Stories about Maharishi."

200. Mitra, "Maharishi Mahesh Yogi: Successful Meditation."

201. Susan Shumsky's handwritten lecture notes.

CHAPTER 21

202. Susan Shumsky's handwritten lecture notes.

203. Mahesh Yogi, Bhagavad Gita, 2:47, 133.

CHAPTER 22

204. "When Maharishi Threw Beatles Out."

205. Rooney, "Maharishi Mahesh Yogi, guru to Beatles, dies."

206. "Beatles are angels on earth, said Maharishi."

207. Miles, *Paul McCartney,* Chapter 10.

208. Brown, *The Love You Make,* 250.

209. Wenner, *Lennon Remembers,* 24.

210. Richardson, "Maharishi Mahesh Yogi - Beatles Urban Legend."

211. Brown, *The Love You Make,* 260.

212. Sheff, *All We Are Saying,* 204.

213. Cott, "John Lennon: The *Rolling Stone* Interview."

214. Tillery, *The Cynical Idealist,* 83.

215. Tillery, *The Cynical Idealist,* 80.

216. Lennon, *A Twist of Lennon,* 171.

217. Beatles, *Beatles Anthology,* 285.

218. Miles, *Paul McCartney,* Chapter 10.

219. Morse, "McCartney Breaks His Silence with a Rock 'N' Roll Album."

220. Miles, *Paul McCartney,* Chapter 10.

221. Duke, "Surviving Beatles Unite to Promote Meditation."

222. Thompson, "Celebrities Who Meditate."

223. Shankar, "Maharishi Mahesh Yogi, guru to pop celebrities, dies at 91."

224. Bruns, *Dear Prudence,* 172.

225. Bruns, *Dear Prudence,* 189.

226. Bruns, *Dear Prudence,* 203-205.

227. Bruns, *Dear Prudence,* 209-210.

228. Mason, *The Beatles, Drugs, Mysticism & India,* 181-182.

229. Farrow, *What Falls Away,* 128-129.

230. "Maharishi Mahesh Yogi - Transcendental Meditation - Biography."

231. Mason, *The Beatles, Drugs, Mysticism & India,* 91-92.

232. Love, *Good Vibrations,* Chapter 10, 179.

233. Zehme, "Lost in the Funhouse" website.

234. Zehme, *Lost in the Funhouse,* Chapter 12, 394.

235. Zehme, *Lost in the Funhouse,* Chapter 12, 394.

236. "Maharishi Mahesh Yogi - Transcendental Meditation - Biography."

237. Chopra, "First Meeting Maharishi."

238. Hamblin, "The Seduction of 'Wellness Real Estate.'"

239. Knapp, "Deepak Chopra Interview."

240. Chopra, "The Maharishi Years - The Untold Story."

241. Knapp, "Deepak Chopra Interview."

242. Hoffman, "David Lynch Is Back."

243. Knapp, "Deepak Chopra Interview."

244. Knapp, "Deepak Chopra Interview."

245. Chopra, "The Maharishi Years - The Untold Story."

246. Knapp, "Deepak Chopra Interview."

247. Forsthoefel and Hume, *Gurus in America,* 54.

248. Forsthoefel and Hume, *Gurus in America,* 54.

249. Chopra, "The Maharishi Years - The Untold Story."

250. Chopra, "The Maharishi Years - The Untold Story."

251. Chopra, "The Maharishi Years - The Untold Story."

252. Knapp, "Deepak Chopra Interview."

253. Lutes, "Memoirs of Charlie Lutes," Chapter 4.

254. "Stories about Maharishi."

255. Susan Shumsky's handwritten lecture notes.

256. Cooke de Herrera, *All You Need Is Love,* 100-101.

CHAPTER 23

257. Naughton, "Head for the Hills, Disciples!"

258. Orme-Johnson, "Societal Effects."

259. Hedegaard, "The Ballad of Mike Love."

260. Mason, *The Beatles, Drugs, Mysticism & India*, 269.

261. Sieveking, *David Wants to Fly.*

CHAPTER 24

262. Maass, "Welcome to Silicorn Valley."

CHAPTER 25

263. Atmananada, "Words of Sri Anandamayi Ma."

264. Vivekananda, *Raja-Yoga,* Introductory.

CHAPTER 26

265. Tweedie, *The Chasm of Fire*, 65-66.

266. *Holy Bible*, Matthew 7:7.

CHAPTER 27

267. "Om Namo Narayani Om Hari Durga Ma."

268. Atmananada, "Words of Sri Anandamayi Ma."

269. Knapp, "Letter from David Kaplan."

270. "From Linda Kaplan," Fairfield Life.

271. Knapp, "Earl Kaplan's Letter."

272. "Maharishi, Maharishi Not," Leaving the Art of Living.

273. "Swami Kriyananda: In Memoriam."

274. Yogananda, *Autobiography of a Yogi*, 118.

275. Yogananda, *Autobiography of a Yogi*, 119.

276. Yogananda, *Autobiography of a Yogi*, 119.

277. Yogananda, *Autobiography of a Yogi*, 119.

278. Nikhilananda, *Vivekananda A Biography*.

279. Tweedie, *Chasm of Fire*, 7.

280. Tweedie, *Chasm of Fire*, 105.

281. "Nityananda," Sages, Saints, and Avatars.

282. Knapp, "Earl Kaplan's Letter."

283. Batchelder, Ram Das, *Rising in Love*, 7.

284. Mahesh Yogi, *Bhagavad Gita*, 2:54, 106.

285. Mahesh Yogi, *Bhagavad Gita*, 2:55-57, 107-113.

286. Yogananda, *Autobiography of a Yogi*, 121.

287. Cooke de Herrera, *All You Need Is Love*, 18.

288. Blakely, *The Secret of the Mantras*, 180.

289. Midal, *Recalling Chögyam Trungpa*, x.

290. Blakely, *The Secret of the Mantras*, 3.

291. Tweedie, *Chasm of Fire*, 78.

292. Fiske, "Stalking Personal Power and Peace."

293. Sieveking, *David Wants to Fly*.

294. Tweedie, *Chasm of Fire*, 169.

295. Tweedie, *Chasm of Fire*, 169.

EPILOGUE AND EPITAPH

296. "Maharishi Mahesh Yogi - Transcendental Meditation - Biography."

ACKNOWLEDGMENTS

I am grateful to supporters who contributed their love and energy to this book: Curt DeGroat, Jared Stoltz, Fred Den Ouden, Casey Coleman, Rob Gordon-McCutchan, Billy Clayton, Mark Landau, Pamela Reeve, Judith Bourque, Susan Seifert, Connie Fisher, Carl Roles, and Robert Quicksilver. Thank you to the staff at Skyhorse Publishing, especially Mike Lewis, Julie Ganz, Rain Saukas, Jessica L. Moss, and Margaret Grumeretz. Thank you, Julie, for clarifying the manuscript with your illuminating suggestions, and for your calm, steady patience when faced with many delays and obstacles.

For your patience and generosity in granting photo licenses, thank you to Victor Daczynski, Paul Mason, Paul Saltzman, Ronald Pledge: Contact Press Images, Lisa Roper: Alamy, Matthew Lutts: Associated Press, Verity Manning: BBC, Shannon Marano: Getty Images, Andrew Howick: MPTV, Cameron Warnick: Newscom, Tom McShane: RexFeatures, Peter: Ringier AG, Paul Keene: Avico, Frank Seltier: Photo Office, Marvin Lichtner and Cris Piquinela: *Saturday Evening Post.*

Foremost, I am grateful to Jeff and Deborah Herman and Paul De Angelis, without whom this book would never have gotten published. Thank you Jeff, my anchor, for believing in this project for the past twenty years, and for your constant and continual friendship and support. Thank you, Paul, for being an awesome mentor in the writing process.

ABOUT THE AUTHOR

Susan Shumsky, DD has dedicated her life to helping people take command of their lives in highly effective, powerful, positive ways. She is the bestselling, award-winning author of thirteen books, published by Simon & Schuster, Random House, New Page, and Skyhorse Publishing.

A pioneer in the human potential field, she has spent fifty years teaching thousands of people meditation, prayer, affirmation, and intuition. Her book titles include *Divine Revelation, Miracle Prayer, Exploring Meditation, Exploring Auras, Exploring Chakras, How to Hear the Voice of God, Ascension, Instant Healing, The Power of Auras, The Power of Chakras, Awaken Your Third Eye, Awaken Your Divine Intuition,* and *Color Your Chakras.*

Shumsky is a highly respected spiritual teacher and founder of Divine Revelation®—a unique field-proven technology for contacting the divine presence, hearing and testing the inner voice, and receiving clear divine guidance. For twenty-two years, her mentor was Maharishi Mahesh Yogi, guru of the Beatles and guru of Deepak Chopra. Shumsky served on Maharishi's personal staff for six years.

Her websites are www.drsusan.org and www.divinetravels.com.